ADAM CAMPBELL FAMILY HISTORY

Scotch-Irish Ancestry and 19th Century American Migration

Including Descendant Families:

Ball	Felts	Mize	Reid
Bolin	Hayes	Morgan	Somers
Campbell	Harvell	Parks	Trowbridge
Coleman	Huie	Puckett	Vanhoy
Combs	Jennings	Rash	Williams
Cooper	Johnson	Redman	Wood
Dobbins			

GARRY E. MOORE, PHD

First published in 2025

Published in the United States by Garry E. Moore
garry.e.moore.author@gmail.com

ISBN: 979-8-9991125-2-1 (paperback)
ISBN: 979-8-9991125-0-7 (hard cover)
ISBN: 979-8-9991125-1-4 (ebook)

Cover and interior design: Rachel Royer
Copyediting: Sydney Spencer
Typesetting: Lori Weidert
Proofreading: Keri Hales

To our Campbell family historians who have helped preserve our heritage and to other family members who have accommodated our obsession.

To our departed family members who have shared their stories, especially Emory L. Coleman, H. P. Vanhoy, John Webster Vanhoy, Dorothy Mae Bain, B. W. Campbell, Wayne Campbell, Rex Ellis, Thomas Jay Campbell, and Donald R. Raney Sr.

Congratulations!

You've just completed an incredible transformation, diving deep into self-awareness and growth. Each exercise, question, and moment of reflection has helped you build a clearer, healthier mindset. Through this workbook, you've confronted your fears, identified your beliefs, and gained insights into how your thoughts shape your reality. You've embraced practices that will help you manifest the life you desire, making it your own.

Even if you didn't complete every activity, each step you took has brought you to a higher level of awareness. Remember, self-discovery is an ongoing journey, and every small effort plays a role in your growth. Simply reflecting on the questions and pondering them is a valuable part of this process, one that raises your consciousness.

As you continue forward, keep this workbook close as a tool for self-therapy. It's there to help you reconnect with yourself, reflect, or take your growth to new heights whenever needed. Whether it's the start of a new year, the launch of a new career, the beginning of a fresh chapter in your life, or the excitement of a new relationship— or even as a birthday gift to yourself— this workbook can be your trusted companion through all your new beginnings.

Continue to grow, explore, and embrace your transformation, always knowing that you are becoming the best version of yourself.

Best wishes on your continued journey,
The Authors

Amani Aseel & Sona Seraj

CONTENTS

CHAPTER 6   JOHN CAMPBELL   79

CHAPTER 7   MARY "POLLY" (CAMPBELL) COLEMAN   85

CHAPTER 8   SARAH "SALLY" (CAMPBELL) BALL   95

CHAPTER 9   PERCIPHULL CAMPBELL SR.   107

PREFACE

It has been my great fortune to be a member of this Campbell family line on my mother's side. There have been many avid genealogists and family storytellers who have been working on this story for over 100 years. The first known recorded history was written for the August 1925 Campbell Family Reunion at the Methodist Church grounds in Union Grove, North Carolina. This history, titled *History of the Campbell Family*, by H. P. Vanhoy, contains details of this Campbell family line in North Carolina from family members and records available in Iredell County at the time. I attended several of the Campbell family reunions that were still being held in Union Grove in the 1980s. Together with aunts and uncles and other cousins, we have been improving on the depth and completeness of this Campbell family story over time. I have made connections with numerous family members in North Carolina, as well as distant cousins researching the same Adam Campbell family line in Arkansas, Texas, and many other states. In 2024, I finally decided that after 100 years, it was time to put the accumulated history with photographs and stories into a book to share with current and future family members.

Adam Campbell, referred to as Pierce Campbell in the 1925 history, was one of the first settlers in what is now Union Grove Township in northern Iredell County, North Carolina. He died before the first U.S. Federal Census in 1790, and there is no cemetery headstone marking his presence. However, I have pieced together his life in Culpeper County, colonial Virginia, and move to Rowan County, North Carolina, before the American Revolution, from thorough analysis of early North Carolina land grants, tax records, and the Revolutionary War Pension applications of two of his sons. A new Y-DNA analysis of male descendants of Adam Campbell has also proven, for the first time, his Scotch-Irish ancestry and connections to his children's families that migrated to the south and west during the early 1800s.

Records show that Adam Campbell's children depended on slaves in the 1800s to run their farms and mills in North Carolina and Mississippi. Analysis of genealogical records and Y-DNA results has provided new insight into the lives of some of these slaves and their African American descendants.

My background in military intelligence writing has influenced the style of writing in this book, which contains important facts and analysis about family relations and events with conclusions supported by multiple sources of information that are documented in extensive references. Documented accounts of military service, family migration, public office, significant neighbors of Adam Campbell, burial locations, newsworthy events, and new scientific Y-DNA genealogical analysis are included in this book.

To make this book more manageable, the emphasis is on the first four generations of Adam Campbell's family, which includes over 700 family descendants from Campbell, Ball,

Coleman, and Hayes ancestors. Additional family members in this book are included from the 1925 reunion history, neighbors of Adam Campbell, and known slaves and their descendants, for a total of over 1,400 people. Documented accounts of military service, family migration, public office, significant neighbors, burial locations, and newsworthy events are included.

While full references can be found in my Moore Family Tree on Ancestry.com, references for the first four generations and significant new references are included in each section of this book to support narratives. Some genealogical dates and connections are speculative, which is indicated by qualifiers "abt." (about) or "bef." (before). Speculative relations are indicated as "possible," "probable," or "may" when references are insufficient or direct connections cannot be made from available sources. Early marriage dates are the marriage bond dates, which may be before the actual date of the marriages. In some cases, marriage dates are estimates based on the birth of the first child and given only as a year.

I would like to acknowledge the contributions of past family genealogists and historians: DAR member Dorothy Mae Bain (1922–1998), artist Elizabeth (Gaither) Campbell (1924–2012), Oliver Campbell (1925–1992), Thomas Jay Campbell (1937–2004), Wayne Campbell (1937–2004), Wilford Campbell (1922–1999), Emory L. Coleman (1932–2014), Rex Ellis (1947–2013), Donald R. Raney (1933–2020), Union Grove history teacher Homer M. Keever (1905–1979), and former Iredell Genealogical Society president and researcher Mildred M. Miller (1932–2011). The family stories, pictures, and Y-DNA test takers from the following living cousins are appreciated: Justin Anderson, Brenda Baker, Theresa Blatchford, Kermit Breed, Ruth Bryant, Jennifer Coffman Byrum, Bobby Campbell, Bradley Campbell, Glenn Campbell, Harold Campbell, Harry Campbell, Johnnie Campbell, Jonathan Campbell, Kevin Harold Campbell, Meredith Campbell, Donna Carlson, Teresa Cleghorn, John W. Coffey, Joann Green-Coleman, Cheryl Ann Curry, Ronald Davis, Dennis Ellenburg, Glenn Steven Ellis, Scott Alan Fletcher, Jarod Gatson, Roger Harvell, Dwayne D. Hayes, Randy Henderson, Pen Jackson, Esther Art Jacobs, Trenna Warren-Kistler, Elsie Knight, Kathy Snyder-Knight, Mike Martin, Rebecca Matlick, Rani Clayton Moss, Herman Major, John Miller, Karen Montana, Doug Nelson, Kathlyn Neumann, Rhonda Norton, Maggie Parks, Amy Pena, Shari Sell-Premer, Heidi Prochnau, Linda Rector, Amanda Clugston, Emily Stokes Rowe, Cheryl Smith, Dan Smith, Preston Somers, B. Stone, De Shann Stroud, Mamie Taylor, Christy Thomas, Carrie Vanhoy, and Elaine White.

The following organizations provided access to research services, reviews, and material used in the preparation of this book: Ancestry.com, FamilySearch, FamilyTreeDNA.com, Kevin Guy Campbell of the Clan Campbell Society of North America, North Carolina Historical Records Online, J. D. Lewis's "The American Revolution in North Carolina" database, and the Moravian Music Foundation.

Garry E. Moore
Rosemount, Minnesota
garry.e.moore.author@gmail.com

ADAM CAMPBELL AND HIS CHILDREN

ADAM CAMPBELL

Adam Campbell was the first known Campbell ancestor in this Campbell family line to live in North Carolina. Prior to coming to North Carolina, Adam married Elizabeth Morgan, probably in Culpeper County, Colony of Virginia. Elizabeth is believed to be the sister of Adam's neighbor Theophilus Morgan Sr. and his wife Catherine. The Morgans also moved from Virginia to the same area of North Carolina where Adam and Elizabeth were living. While sources for the date of Adam's and Elizabeth's births have not been found, it is estimated that they were born in about 1735.

Adam and Elizabeth were living in Culpeper County when their first six children were born between 1755 and 1767. Adam arrived with his family in Rowan County, North Carolina, by 1774, and was one of the first pioneers in this northern part of Rowan County. On Aug 31, 1778, he applied for a North Carolina land grant of 300 acres located north and south of Hunting Creek in Rowan County, where he had been residing for several years.[1] This land became part of Iredell County when it was formed from Rowan County on Nov 3, 1788. Adam had begun improving the land and was assessed taxes on his land and improvements, as listed in the 1778 Rowan County Tax List.[2] Adam and Elizabeth had another son and possibly a daughter after moving to Rowan County.

The Revolutionary War delayed the issuing of almost all North Carolina land grants until 1783. By this time, Adam had died. An analysis of surveys of his and other adjoining land reveals that Adam died between May 25 and Oct 10, 1779, and that his wife and sons were issued the land grants for which he had applied.[3] Elizabeth Campbell was listed in the 1790 Census of Iredell County, along with sons Perciphull, William, and John, as well as her son-in-law, William Ball.[4] Elizabeth died sometime between May 15, 1798, when she sold 200 acres of her land to her son Perciphull Campbell,[5] and the 1800 Census, in which she did not appear. While there are no known headstones for Adam and Elizabeth, their remains

FIGURE 1.1 Campbell Family Cemetery, Union Grove Township, 1985.

may be located in or near the Campbell Family Cemetery in Iredell County, which is within Adam's original land grant (Figure 1.1). His sixth child, Perciphull Campbell, and Perciphull's wife are buried at this cemetery.

Adam is referred to in H. P. Vanhoy's *History of the Campbell Family*, written in 1925, as *Pierce Campbell, the first*. His wife is referred to as *Betty Morgan* in this history. In North Carolina land grants and deeds, their names appear only as *Adam Campbell, Elizabeth Campbell*, or *Widow Campbell*.[6] The Vanhoy Campbell Family History was researched by John Webster Vanhoy Sr., a lawyer and brother of H. P. Vanhoy. They used locally available sources in the county seat in Statesville, family traditions, and communications with relatives living in Arkansas to write this history. While recent genealogical analyses show that most of what was reported was accurate, there are some missing pieces about descendants who moved out of Iredell County after the American Revolution and in the early 1800s. This book includes new information from years of genealogical research and recent DNA analysis to give a more complete story of Adam Campbell's descendants. Vanhoy's historical document states that the Campbells were of "Scotch-Irish" (or "Scots-Irish") descent.[6, 7] (See Chapter 3 for additional details on Adam's ancestry derived from DNA analysis.)

Colony of Virginia

The Revolutionary War pension applications of Adam's two oldest sons and one census record confirm that Adam's first six children were born in Culpeper County. The Revolutionary War pension application for Adam's son, William Campbell, states that William was born in Culpeper County on Aug 1, 1756.[8] The pension application for Adam's second-oldest son, John Campbell, was filed by John's widow, Cora Campbell, and Adam's youngest son, Perciphull Campbell. This application confirms that John was born in Culpeper County, Virginia, in 1759.[9] Adam's son Perciphull was the only child known to live long enough to be listed in the 1850 U.S. Federal Census, in which Perciphull was listed in Iredell County, North Carolina, as P. Campbell, a farmer, age 81 and born in Virginia.[10]

Culpeper County, Virginia, was established in 1749 with territory portioned from Orange County. In May 1749, the first Culpeper Court was convened near the present location of the town of Culpeper. In Jul 1749, George Washington, at age 17, was commissioned as the first county surveyor.[11]

There are court records for an Adam that was probably our Adam Campbell appearing in two court cases in Culpeper County, Virgina, on Apr 22, 1763, i.e., David Johnson versus Adam Campbell, and William Turner versus Adam Campbell. Nothing more is known about these cases.[12]

North Carolina

Adam traveled from Culpeper County to North Carolina along what was called the Great Wagon Road or Philadelphia Wagon Road, which began at the port of Philadelphia, where many immigrants entered the colonies. A contemporary map drawn in 1751 (Figure 1.2) shows the area from Culpeper County in Colonial Virginia to Anson County in the Colony of North Carolina.[13] The route of this road south of Staunton, Virginia, was not passable by wagons until after 1751. The map depicts the Brushy Mountains, the Yadkin River, and an area called Mulberry Fields (bottom of Figure 1.2). Mulberry Fields was a name given to this area by European settlers in the 1750s. By the late 1770s, the lands surrounding Mulberry Fields were renamed Wilkes, after John Wilkes, a member of the British Parliament who was thought to be sympathetic to American independence. Adam Campbell and his family settled in the area just south of Mulberry Fields that became Rowan County when it was formed from Anson County in 1753 and later Wilkes and Iredell Counties in 1778 and 1788, respectively.[14]

While there are no known cemetery headstones or death certificates for Adam or Elizabeth Campbell, their first presence in North Carolina and the dates of their deaths can be deduced from tax lists, North Carolina land grants issued to Adam and his neighbors, and

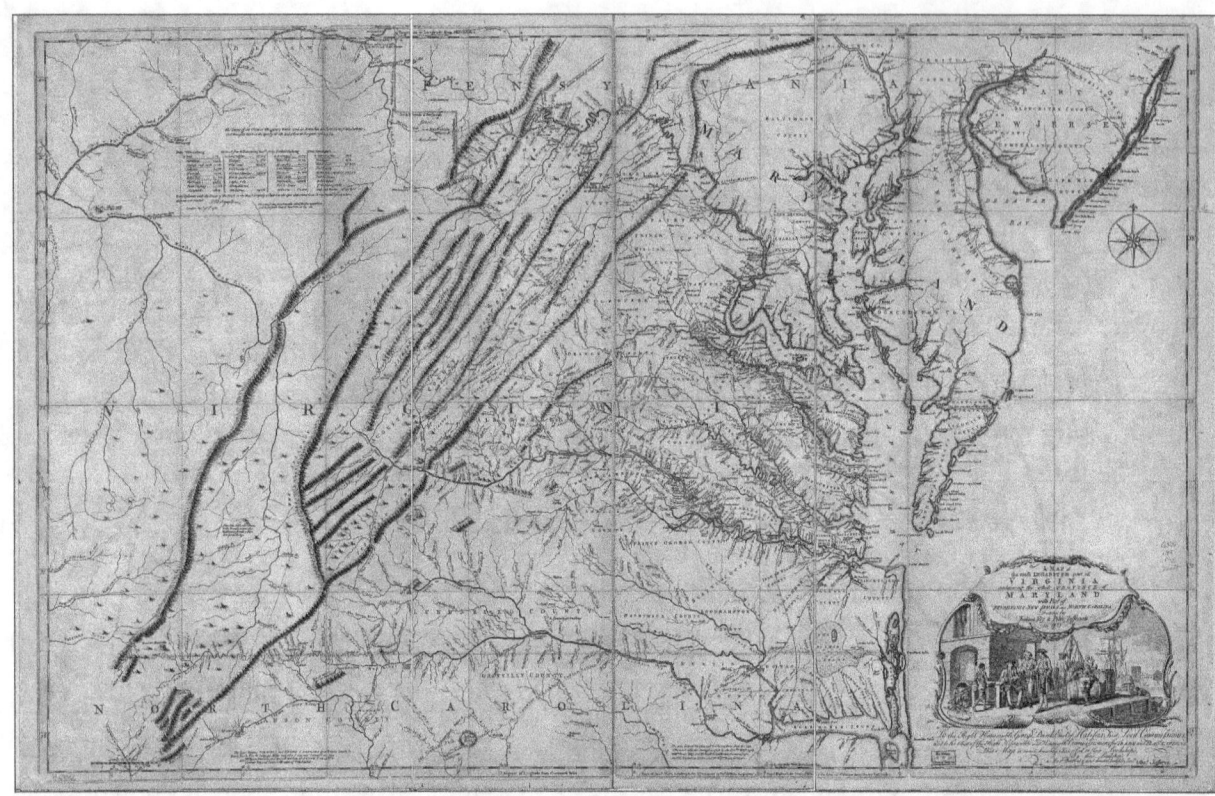

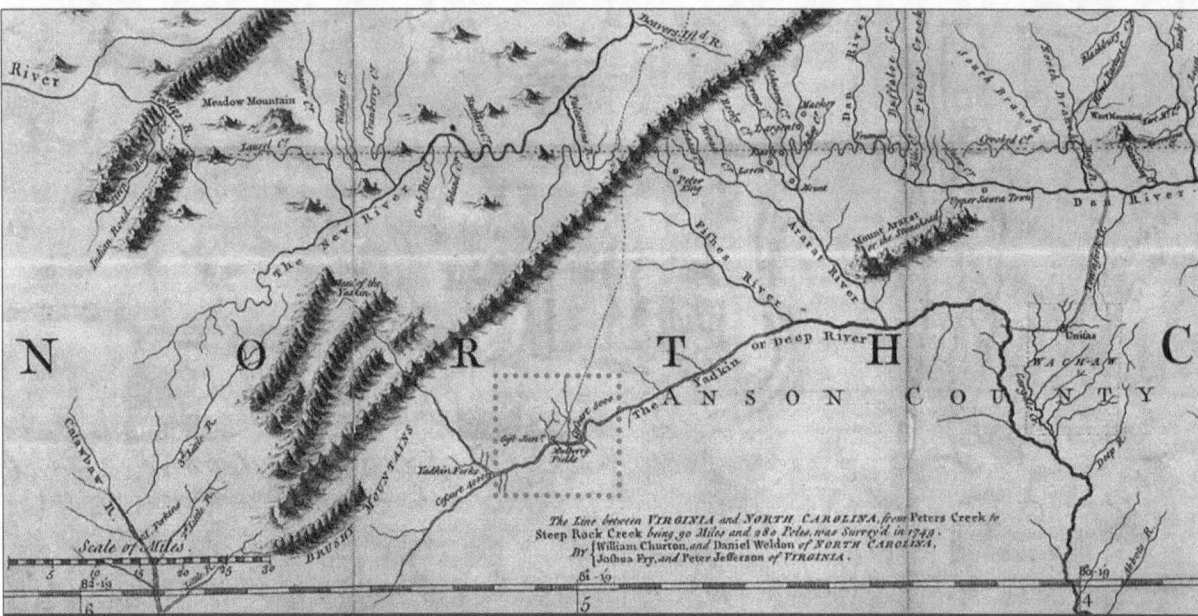

FIGURE 1.2 *(Top)* Map of Maryland with part of Pennsylvania, New Jersey, and North Carolina, Joshua Fry and Peter Jefferson, 1751; *(Bottom)* Close up view of the Mulberry Fields area (as highlighted).

records of their children. The evidence below places Adam Campbell in North Carolina by Jun 1774 and his death date between May 25 and Oct 10, 1779.

Tax Lists

Adam probably did not move to North Carolina or had not established property in North Carolina prior to 1768, since the surviving tax lists for colonial Rowan County, North Carolina, in 1758/1759, 1761, and 1768 did not include Adam Campbell or any of the ancestors of the descendants of his maternal relations. However, the 1778/1779 Tax List for Rowan County, State of North Carolina, did include Adam Campbell, his son William Campbell, and several ancestors of his descendants' maternal relations. This is an important document because this was the same time period during which there was an influx of settlers in the northern section of Rowan County that later became Iredell County.[2]

In 1778, Rowan County included what would become Iredell County, Alexander County, and Davidson County. The area did not include Surry, Yadkin, or Wilkes Counties. Surry County was formed from Rowan County in 1771. Wilkes County was formed from portions of Surry County in 1778. Yadkin County would not be formed until 1850 from portions of Surry County. So, the Rowan County Tax List of 1778 did not include Wilkes or Surry County residents, but it did include the areas that would become Iredell, Davidson, and Rowan Counties. Separately, there are surviving North Carolina State Census records for Wilkes County in 1784–1787 and 1793 and Surry County in 1784–1787 that have been searched for Campbell ancestors and descendants.

To understand how the taxes were assessed, it is important to understand the legal basis for the taxes, which were imposed by the newly organized state of North Carolina after colonial rule. After independence, the new state of North Carolina raised taxes on citizens to support the state and county governments, as well as national efforts in preparation for war with Great Britain through acts passed on Nov 15, 1777, and Apr 17, 1780.[15]

This tax was used to defray the quota of the expense of the war and the credit of money committed by Congress and the state. This was a proportional tax on freemen. Justices divided each county into districts in Apr 1780. Taxpayers were to provide an account of their taxable property on oath. Assessors valued the property. "Property" included lands, lots, houses, slaves under 60 years of age, money, money at interest, and stock in trade, horses, and cattle. Freemen (except continental and state soldiers) not possessing an estate of 400 pounds were to pay a poll tax equal to that of an estate of 400 pounds. Married men with estates of 100 pounds were to pay a poll tax equal to that of an estate of 100 pounds. Moravians, Quakers, "Menonists," Dunkards, and all others refusing to take the oath of allegiance were to pay triple tax. Those failing to return an inventory of taxable property were charged quadruple tax.[15]

In April 1780, courts established districts in each county. Three men were appointed in each district to value taxable property. Taxpayers were to pay their taxes by Feb 1 each year. Counties were to pay the collected taxes to the state by Mar 1 each year. This method applied to subsequent taxes for which the purpose may be specified in that act. The first tax levied was a qualifying tax, i.e., it included lands, lots, houses, slaves, money, money at interest, and stock in trade, horses, and neat cattle (horned oxen) as taxable property. Freemen, except continental and state soldiers, not possessing an estate of 100 pounds were to pay a poll tax equal to that of an estate of 100 pounds.[15]

Adlai Osborne (1744–1814), clerk of the court in Rowan County, compiled a "List of Taxable Property in the County of Rowan, North Carolina, Anno 1778."[2,16] It is fortunate that this list by Adlai Osborne has survived and was transcribed and published. This list contains the names of individual heads of households and the valuation of their properties. The total tax collected in Rowan County was 13,683 pounds, 16 shillings, and 9 pence, some of which went to the county, the poor, and the Rowan County Courthouse in Salisbury. There were at least 2,500 residents listed in Rowan County, which would amount to an average tax of about 5.5 pounds.

Each district in Rowan County was assigned to a militia captain, who evidently resided in the region defined by the district. The northern region of a map of early Iredell County settlers compiled by the Iredell County Genealogical Society is shown in Figure 1.3 with highlights on individuals included in the 1778 Tax List by each captain's district.[17]

Adam Campbell and his son, William Campbell, were included in the 115 households of Capt. Nichols's District in 1778.[2] Adam's property was assessed at a value of 529 pounds. William's property did not meet the 100-pound threshold, so he was listed as poles only. Adam's son, John Campbell, was not included in the 1778 Tax List but was listed in Capt. Gordan's District in Wilkes County in 1784.[18] In order to accrue this property assessment, Adam Campbell must have been in Rowan County several years before 1778.

Early Records of Adam Campbell's Children

The Revolutionary War records of Adam Campbell's two oldest sons and his oldest daughter's marriage and census records provide some additional insight into the earliest date that Adam and Elizabeth Campbell were in North Carolina. Specifically, the following chronology of events helps to narrow down the earliest date that he was in North Carolina.

❖ Apr 13, 1767–Culpeper County, Colony of Virginia: Adam's youngest son was born in Virginia.[10]

❖ 1774–North Carolina: Adam's oldest child, Keziah, was married on about Jun 1774 in Surry County, North Carolina, which was one year before her first son, Jonathan Hayes, was born in Surry County. [19, 20, 21]

❖ 1775–North Carolina: Adam Campbell's oldest son, William Campbell, enlisted in the Surry County Regiment of the North Carolina Militia in 1775.[8]

❖ 1775–North Carolina: Keziah Campbell's oldest son, Jonathan Hayes, was born in North Carolina in about 1775. He married Rachel Mitchel in Wilkes County on Oct 30, 1798.[22]

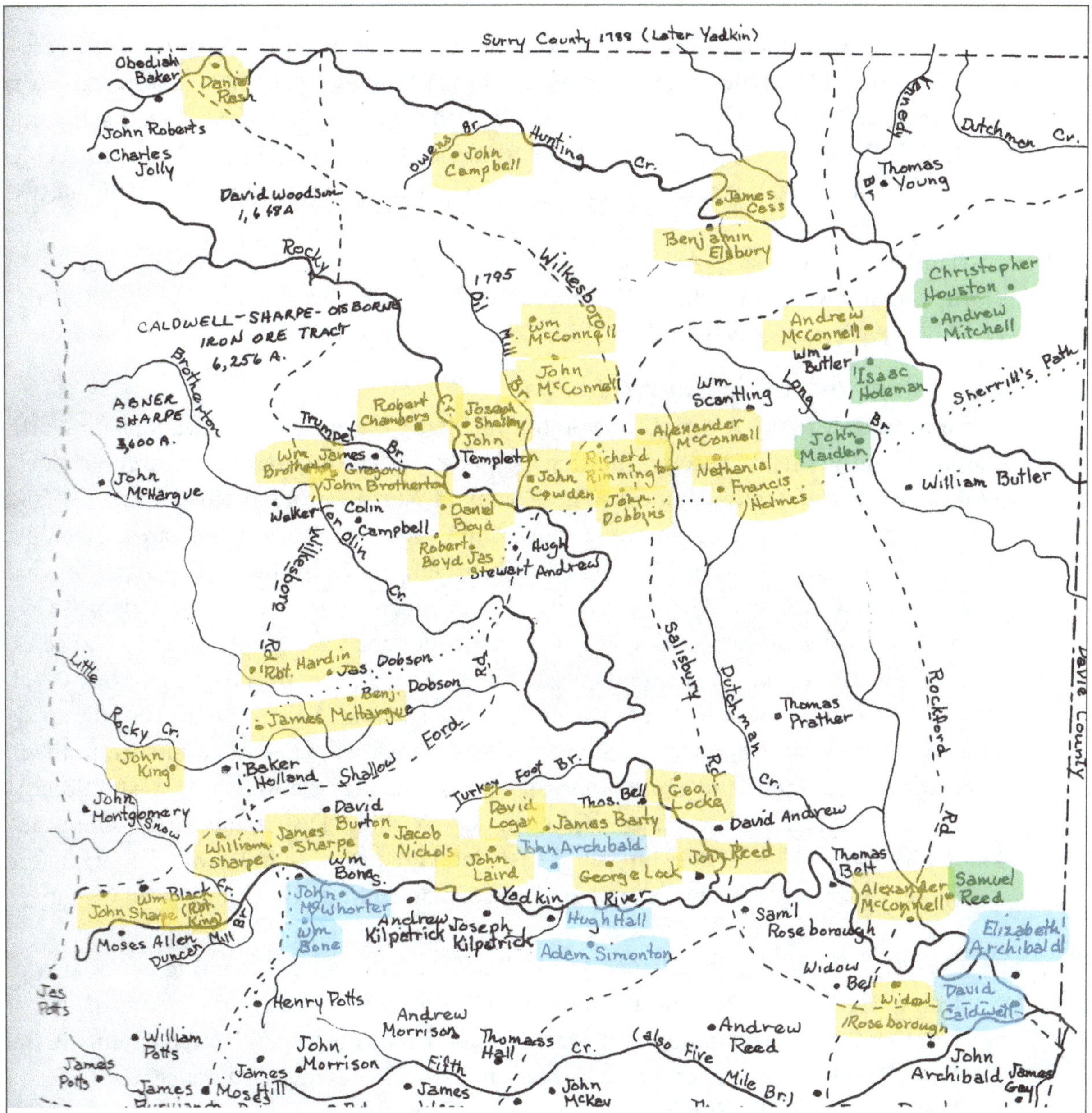

Yellow: Listed in Captain Nichols's District Green: Listed in Captain Reed's District Blue: Listed in Captain Caldwell's District

FIGURE 1.3 Map of early Rowan County residents north of the Yadkin River, highlighting names by each captain's district appearing in the 1778 Tax List. Adam Campbell lived where John Campbell is indicated.

He was listed in the 1800 Census as head of household in Wilkes County, North Carolina, with a female aged between 16 and 25 and one household member under 16. His father, Henry Hays, was also listed next to him in this census.[23]

- 1777–North Carolina: Perciphull Campbell's wife, Sarah (Cook) Campbell, reported in John Campbell's pension application that she had been a neighbor of John Campbell for

65 years in 1843, e.g., since 1777. Perciphull and Sarah Campbell's land, which Perciphull bought from Elizabeth Campbell in 1795 (100 acres) [24] and 1798 (200 acres), [25] was located at the point of rocks on Hunting Creek in the part of Rowan County that became Iredell County in 1788. Sarah Campbell stated that John and Cora had two small children before she and Perciphull Campbell were married (about 1788 in Wilkes County). [9]

This chronology places Adam Campbell (about age 39) and Elizabeth (about age 39) in North Carolina sometime after 1767 and before Jun 1774 when his youngest child, Perciphull, was 8 years old and his oldest child, Keziah, was 19 years old.

Land Grant Records in North Carolina

Around the time of the American Revolution, settlers were entering applications for North Carolina land grants to become the first property owners in what are currently Iredell, Wilkes, Surry, and Yadkin counties. The Colony of North Carolina issued Granville land grants from 1748 to 1763, primarily in the Third Creek and Fourth Creek areas below Ft. Dobbs. The Colony of North Carolina issued very few grants in the northern end of what was then Rowan County. After the Declaration of Independence, the State of North Carolina established state land grants. Married men could apply for grants of up to 640 acres. The applications for these land grants peaked in 1778, with 55 entries in the Hunting Creek region in Rowan County where Adam Campbell was residing. Adam, like many of the applicants, lived and made improvements on the land before it was entered and issued to them. However, most of these land grants were not issued until after the American Revolution. [3]

Adam Campbell lived on Hunting Creek in Capt. Nichols's District, above the South Yadkin River to the Wilkes County line. Of the 630 land grants issued in Rowan County before 1778, there were only 6 Granville land grants issued on Hunting Creek in Rowan County. [3]

❖ Dec 21, 1753: The colony issued the earliest land grant in the Hunting Creek area of Rowan County for 630 acres to "John Boon," beginning at an oak on the north side of Hunting Creek. [3] A John Boone appears in Capt. Reed's District of Rowan County in the 1778 Tax List with property assessed at 1 pound, 690 shillings, 10 pence. Capt. Reed's District included the Hunting Creek area near Houstonville. [2] Squire Boone (1696–1765), father of Daniel Boone, obtained a land grant for 640 acres on the south side of Grants Creek near Salisbury on Apr 30, 1753. John Boone (1727–1803) was the nephew of Squire Boone. [3] His wife was Rebecca Bryan (abt. 1735–1820). Their nine children were born there. Most of this family migrated to Tennessee, though some of their descendants lived at this Hunting Creek site until the 1850s, and some distant relatives still live in Davie County. [26]

❖ Jan 30, 1755: The colony issued James Carter and Jonathan Boon a grant for 776 acres on the east side of Hunting Creek on the northwest side of the south fork of the Yadkin River. [3] A Jonathan Boon appears in Capt. Willson's District in the 1778 Tax list with property assessed at 944 shillings. [2]

❖ Jun 10, 1758: The colony issued William Robinson a grant for 66 acres on "both sides of Hunting Creek on the fork of Richland Creek, waters of Reed Fork of Haw River."[3] A William Robinson appears in Capt. Morrison's District in Rowan County with property assessed at 116 pence and Capt. Willson's District with property assessed at 499 pence in 1778. Capt. Morrison's District included the area that would later become Davidson County.[2]

❖ May 1, 1761: The colony issued Richard Vigers a grant for 350 acres "on both sides of Hunting Creek fork of Richland Creek waters of the Reed Fork of Haw River."[3] He was not listed in the 1778 Rowan County Tax List.

❖ Dec 21, 1761: The colony issued Isaac Willcockson a grant for 320 acres on both sides of Hunting Creek and both sides of a branch known by the name of Long Branch.[3] He appears in Capt. Johnston's District in Rowan County in 1778 with property assessed at two pounds and 17 shillings. Capt. Johnston's District was below the South Yadkin River.[2]

❖ Mar 16, 1762: The colony issued William Churton a grant for 350 acres "on both sides of Hunting Creek, a fork of Richland Creek waters of Reedy fork of Haw River."[3] He did not appear in the 1778 Rowan County Tax List.

The colony issued 630 Granville land grants in Rowan County between 1751 and 1764. Most of these grants were located along the South Yadkin River, Fourth Creek, Second Creek, and near Salisbury in what is now Rowan County. The Regulator Movement in North Carolina between 1766 and 1771 contributed to a lack of colonial land grants. It was not until after 1777 that the entering of grants returned, albeit as land grants of the State of North Carolina. However, most grant applications entered between 1778 and the end of the American Revolution were not issued for several years. Some grants entered in 1778 from Rowan County were issued in the newly formed Iredell County.[3]

On Aug 31, 1778, Adam entered into the record of Rowan County a vacant land grant, no. 1462, for 300 acres on both sides of Hunting Creek. This land was "adjoining Theophilus Morgan's conditional line between Adam and Peter Good and James Woodburn at the point of rocks on Hunting Creek, including his own improvement." He must have been on this land for some unknown time and presumably had been making improvements that would lead to the 529-pound property assessment. However, the state did not issue the land to Adam. He died before the land could be surveyed and issued. The state conveyed the 300 acres of land to his widow, Elizabeth Campbell, and his son, William Campbell.[1, 3]

There are mentions of Adam Campbell in the land grant documents of his neighbors, which provide a clue about when he might have died. Below are listed, in chronological order, the land grant records for Adam; those of his neighbors who mentioned him; and the land grant records of Elizabeth Campbell (his wife), John Campbell (second oldest son), and William Campbell (his oldest son). References to Campbells are in italics. The last entry for Adam Campbell is May 20, 1779. Thereafter, *Elizabeth Campbell* or *Widow Campbell* appears, which implies that he died between May 25 and Oct 10, 1779, and this would also be consistent with his appearance on the 1778 Tax List in Capt. Nichols's District.

❖ Apr 1, 1778: *John Campbell's* land grant entry for 250 acres of land in Rowan County lying on the east side of the road from Robert Chamber's to Hunting Creek, on the head of Owen's and Doyles Branches waters of Hunting Creek and on the south side of said creek, including vacancy for quantity, signed by James Brandon.[27]

❖ Aug 16, 1778: John Henderson's land grant entry for 200 acres of land lying on the side of Hunting Creek, joining said creek, *Adam Campbell's* claim to the south all the rest vacant lands, letter signed by James Brandon.[28]

❖ Aug 31, 1778: *Adam Campbell's* land grant entry for 300 acres of land on both sides of Hunting Creek, adjoining Adam Campbell's and Theophilus Morgan's conditional line between him and Peter Good and James Woodburn at the point of rocks including his own improvement.[1]

❖ Sep 4, 1778: *William Campbell's* land grant entry for 200 acres of land on the north side of Hunting Creek joining the Surry County line and Theophilus Morgan and Simonton's land, letter signed by James Brandon.[29]

❖ Dec 30, 1778: Adam Simonton's (assignee of James Woodburn) land grant entry for 300 acres of land on the south fork of Hunting Creek, adjoining *Adam Campbell* at a place called point of rocks, joining Nathaniel Mimsy at the first hollow below the mouth of the Buck Shoal, including improvements where he now lives, letter signed by James Brandon.[30]

❖ May 25, 1779: Martin Morgan's land grant entry for 100 acres of land on the fork of Rocky Branch and Hunting Creek, adjoining *Adam Campbell*. A letter from Rowan County to Surveyor of Iredell County in Feb 1804 contained the original survey request that was dated May 20, 1779 (Figure 1.4).[31]

❖ Oct 10, 1779: *Elizabeth Campbell's* land grant entry for 200 acres on the south side of Hunting Creek joining the lines of John Henderson and John Hughes, including the improvement whereon she now lives, letter signed by James Brandon (Figure 1.5).[32]

❖ Nov 15, 1779: John Hughes's land grant entry, 400 acres of land on the south side of Hunting Creek, adjoining *Widow Campbell*, letter signed by James Brandon.[33]

❖ Dec 25, 1779: Vacant land grant entry no. 2381, Rowan County; a researcher, Emory L. Coleman, reported that James Woodburn filed for 400 acres on the waters of Hunting Creek and adjoining Adam Campbell and his own land. This record is not online, and the date cannot be verified.[34]

❖ Dec 10, 1782: Adam Simonton's (assignee of James Woodburn) land grant entry, 290 acres of land on the north side of the south fork of Hunting Creek, adjoining *William Campbell's* corner, letter signed by Griffith Rutherford, surveyor.[35]

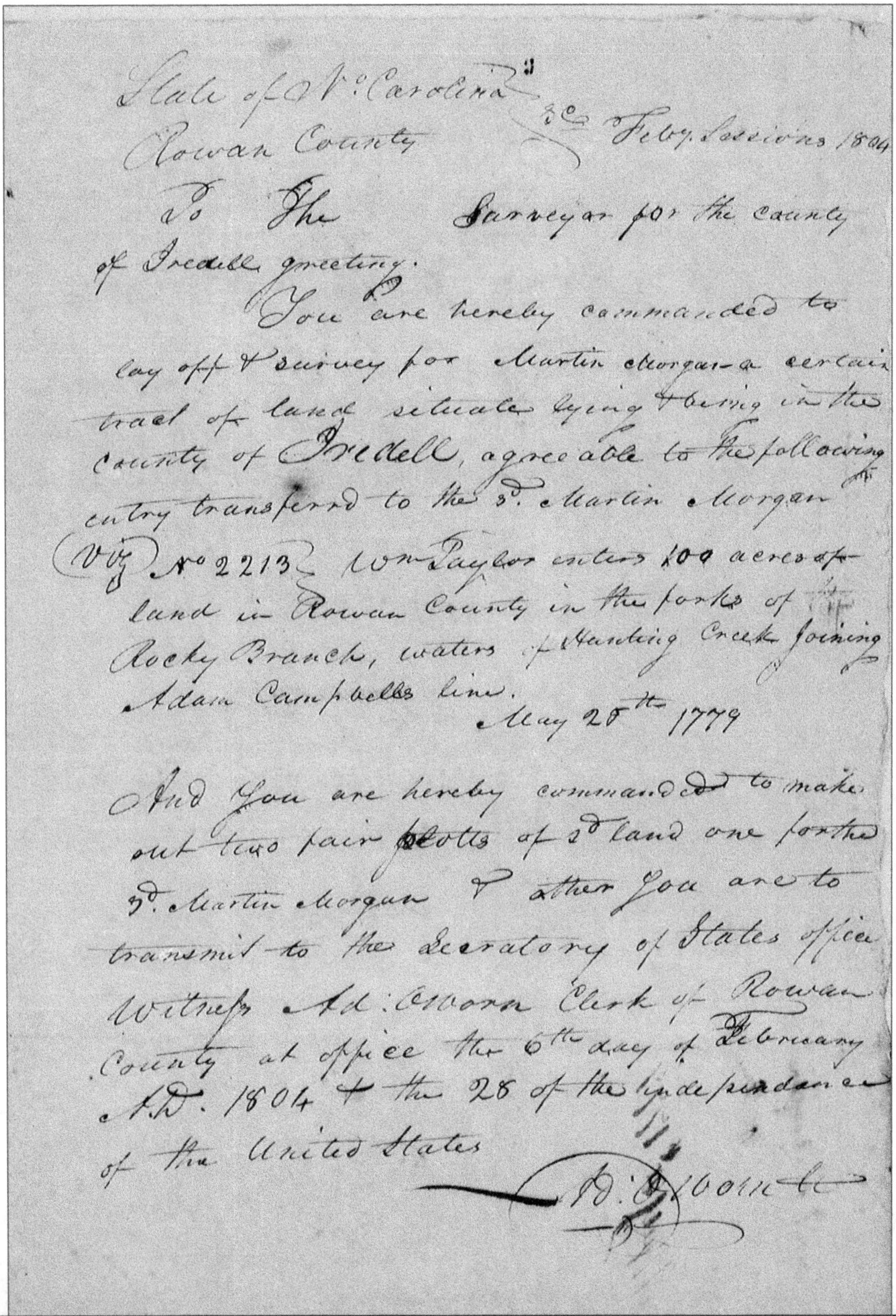

State of No. Carolina }
Rowan County } Feby. Sessions 1804

To The Surveyor for the County
of Iredell greeting.
You are hereby commanded to
lay off & survey for Martin Morgan a certain
tract of land situate lying & being in the
County of Iredell, agreeable to the following
entry transferred to the sd. Martin Morgan
(Viz) No. 2213 Wm Taylor enters 100 acres of
land in Rowan County in the forks of
Rocky Branch, waters of Hunting Creek joining
Adam Campbells line.
May 25th 1779

And You are hereby commanded to make
out two fair plotts of sd land one for the
sd. Martin Morgan & other You are to
transmit to the Secratory of States office
Witness Ad: Osborn Clerk of Rowan
County at office the 6th day of February
A.D. 1804 & the 28 of the Independance
of the United States
Ad: Osborn C

FIGURE 1.4 May 25, 1779, Martin Morgan's land grant entry for 100 acres of land on the fork of Rock Branch and Hunting Creek, adjoining Adam Campbell. A letter from Rowan County to Surveyor of Iredell County in Feb 1804 containing the original survey request that was dated May 25, 1779. This is the last record to mention Adam Campbell by name. He must have been alive on May 25, 1779.

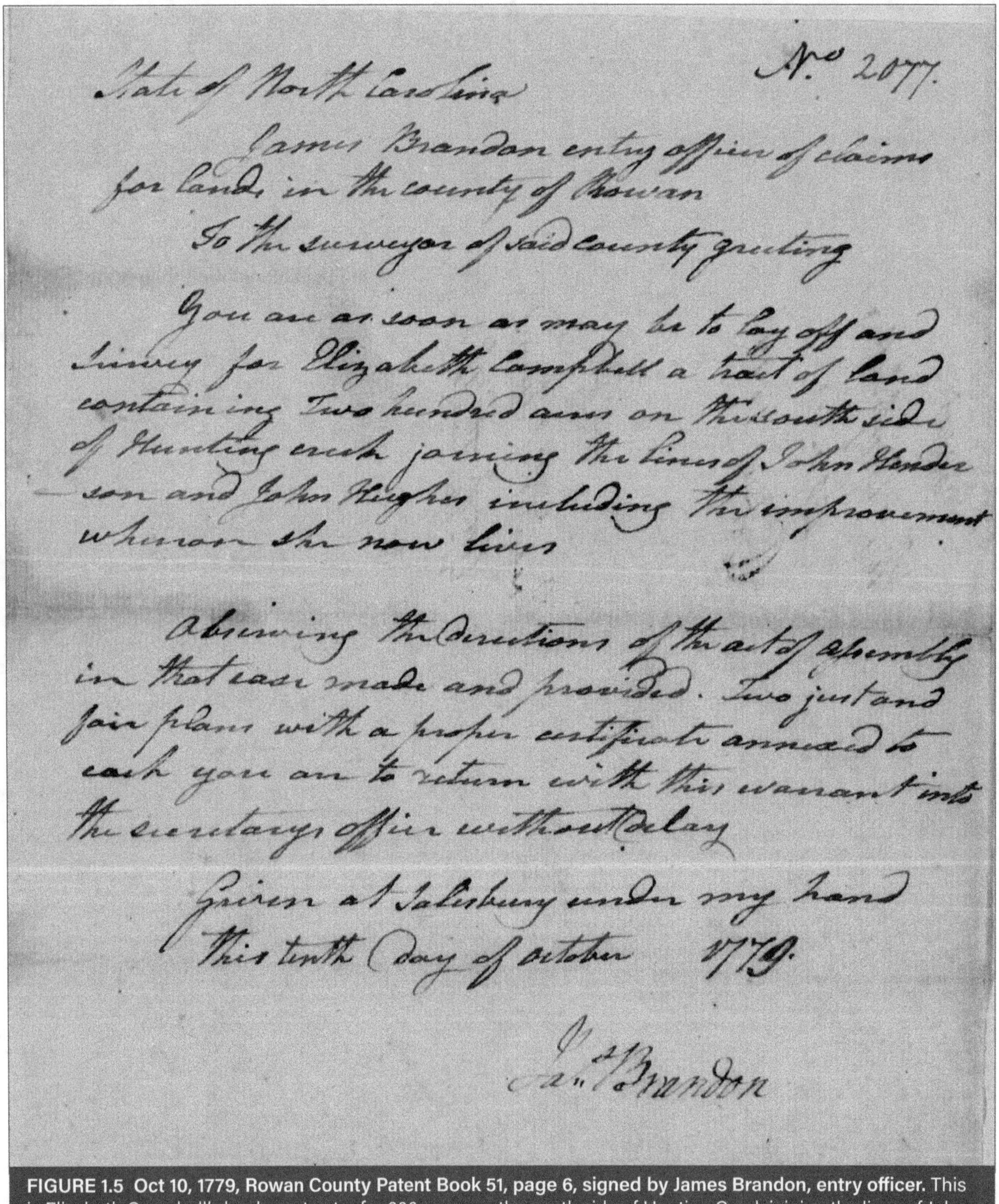

State of North Carolina No. 2077.

James Brandon entry officer of claims for lands in the county of Rowan

To the surveyor of said county greeting

You are as soon as may be to lay off and survey for Elizabeth Campbell a tract of land containing Two hundred acres on the south side of Hunting creek joining the lines of John Henderson and John Hughes including the improvement whereon she now lives

Observing the directions of the act of assembly in that case made and provided. Two just and fair plans with a proper certificate annexed to each you are to return with this warrant into the secretarys office without delay

Given at Salisbury under my hand this tenth day of october 1779.

Jas. Brandon

FIGURE 1.5 Oct 10, 1779, Rowan County Patent Book 51, page 6, signed by James Brandon, entry officer. This is Elizabeth Campbell's land grant entry for 200 acres on the south side of Hunting Creek joining the lines of John Henderson and John Hughes. There is no mention of Adam Campbell. Hereafter, Elizabeth is also referred to as Widow Campbell.

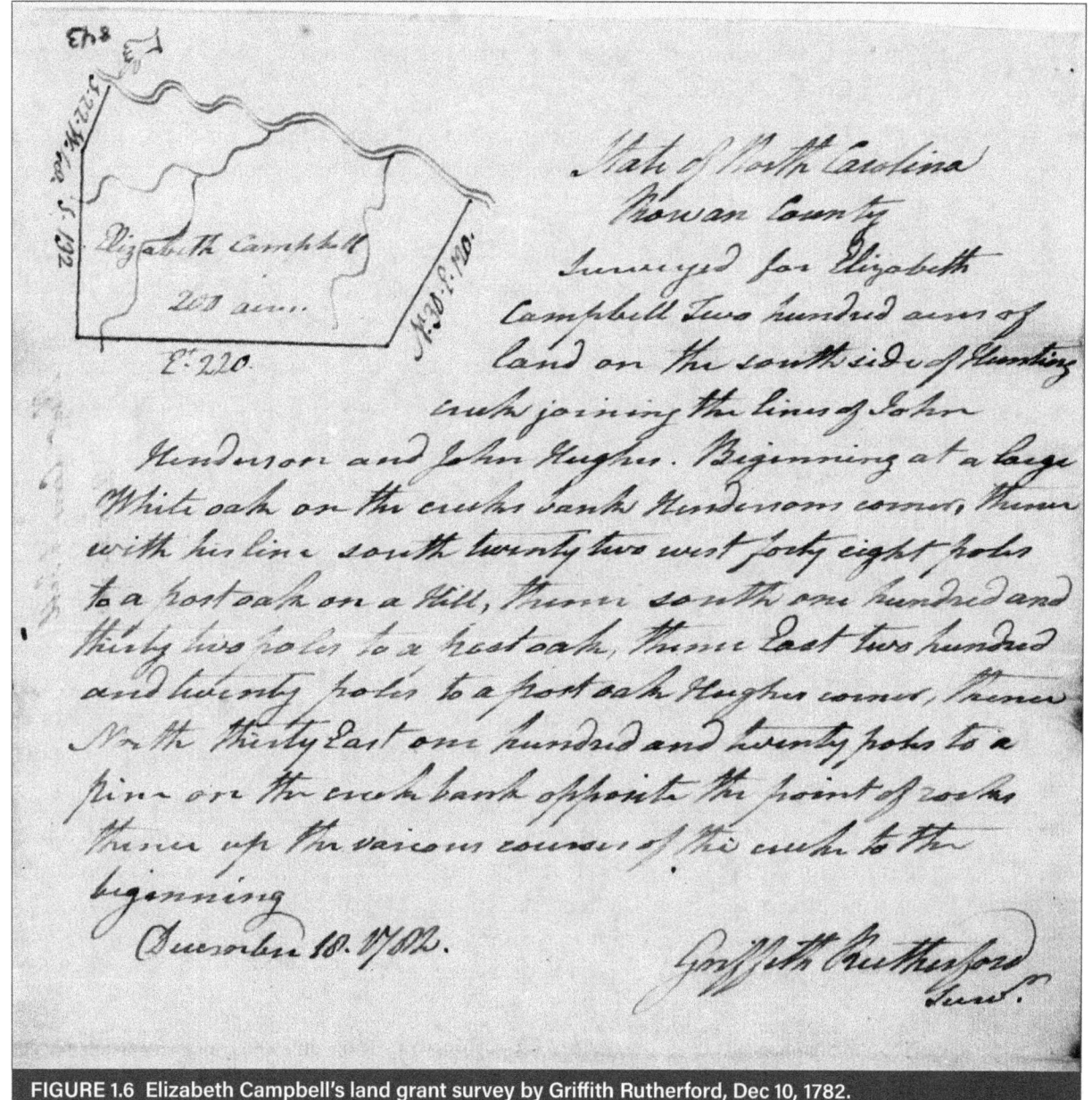

FIGURE 1.6 Elizabeth Campbell's land grant survey by Griffith Rutherford, Dec 10, 1782.

❖ Dec 10, 1782: *Elizabeth Campbell's* land grant entry, 200 acres of land on the south side of Hunting Creek joining the lines of John Henderson and John Hughes, letter signed by Griffith Rutherford (Figure 1.6).[36]

❖ Dec 10, 1782: John Hughes's land grant entry for 400 acres of land on the south side of Hunting Creek, adjoining *Elizabeth Campbell's* lower line, letter signed by Griffith Rutherford.[37]

- ❖ Dec 10, 1782: *William Campbell*'s land grant entry for 175 acres of land on the north side of Hunting Creek, joining the lines of Adam Simonton and Theophilus Morgan, letter signed by Griffith Rutherford.[38]

- ❖ Dec 17, 1782: John Henderson's land grant for 200 acres of land on the south side of Hunting Creek, joining *Widow Campbell's* upper line, letter signed by Griffith Rutherford.[39]

- ❖ Oct 10,1783: Adam Simonton's (assignee of James Woodburn) land grant entry for 290 acres of land on the north side of Hunting Creek at point of rocks, adjoining *William Campbell*, letter signed by Alex Martin.[40]

- ❖ Oct 10, 1783: *Elizabeth Campbell*'s land grant entry for 200 acres of land on the south side of Hunting Creek, joining the lines of John Henderson and John Hughes, letter signed by Alex Martin.[41]

- ❖ Oct 10, 1783: John Henderson's land grant for 200 acres of land on the south side of Hunting Creek, joining *Widow Campbell's* upper line, letter signed by Alex Martin.[42]

- ❖ Dec 12, 1786: Martin Morgan's land grant for 300 acres of land on the Straight Creek waters of Hunting Creek, on Henderson's line, *Campbell's* corner, letter signed by Griffith Rutherford.[43]

- ❖ May 12, 1790, *John Campbell's* land grant for 200/250 acres of land in Iredell County, lying on Doyles Branch and Owens Branch waters of Hunting Creek, Survey by Abner Sharpe, Deputy for William Sharpe, Chief Justice, letter signed by Abner Sharpe, Deputy for William Sharpe, Chief Justice.[44]

- ❖ Sep 6, 1804, Martin Morgan's land grant entry for 100 acres of land in Iredell County lying in the forks of the Rocky Branch waters of Hunting Creek, on Nimrod Lonsford's line (no mention of Campbell), letter signed by David Beal, Iredell County Surveyor. The survey request was sent from Rowan County to the Surveyor for Iredell County in Feb 1804. The state issued the land on Dec 15, 1804.[45]

It is interesting to note that the surveyor for the land grants in Rowan County before the formation of Iredell County in 1788 was Griffith Rutheford, who was the commander of the Rowan County Regiment in which Adam's sons served during the American Revolution.

CHILDREN

Adam and Elizabeth Campbell had at least three sons and three daughters. The H. P. Vanhoy history mentioned only one son (Perciphull or Pierce), and three daughters (Polly, Sally, and Kizzie), perhaps because other families had moved out of North Carolina or current family members in Iredell County were no longer in touch with other descendants. Early land grants, colonial era records, and American Revolution pensions applications were not readily available in 1925, and the researchers did not search the Rowan County records in Salisbury.[6]

Recent DNA evidence and the discovery of a family history written by descendants that moved to Mississippi and Texas have helped to identify an additional son, Theophilus Marion Campbell, born in North Carolina.[46, 47]

One additional daughter (Malinda [Campbell] Wood) may have existed. Her family line is well documented, but there is a lack of definitive evidence to link her family directly with Adam Campbell.[48]

All eight known and possible children are listed below. Expanded information on these families is included in separate chapters of this book for each child. Names that are either listed in the H.P. Vanhoy *History of the Campbell Family* or a history of his son Theophilus Marion Campbell's family written in 2013 by the late Don Ran,[47] appear in **bold** throughout this book and the index. The d'Aboville System Numbers for family members, their spouses, and children appear with the names of descendants throughout this book, starting with Adam and Elizabeth as number *1.0*, his children as *1.X*, his grandchildren as *1.X.X*, etc.

1.1 **Keziah "Kizzie" Campbell** (1755–1845) appears in the Vanhoy history as marrying a Hayes, which we now know was **Henry Hayes Sr.** (abt. 1750–bef. Feb 1805).[6] She married in about 1774 in Surry or Wilkes County.[72] Although many of her children remained in Wilkes County after Henry's death, it is believed that Kizzie moved, after 1830, to Hancock County, Indiana, where she died and was buried at the Hayes Cemetery in Hancock County.[6, 8,49, 50, 51, 52, 53, 54]

1.2 William R. Campbell (Aug 1, 1756–Jan 19, 1840) does not appear in the Vanhoy history. He married Nancy Ann Hendren (1750–1849) in Rowan County on Apr 3, 1792. He may have had another wife before Nancy. In about 1796, William and Nancy left North Carolina for Madison and Clay County, Kentucky; then Crawford County, Indiana, by 1820; and in 1836, they moved to Bureau County, Illinois, where they both died.[4, 8, 55, 56, 57, 58, 59, 60, 61]

1.3 John Campbell (1759–Mar 23, 1834) does not appear in the Vanhoy history. John married Carah or Cora Mullis (1760–1850) in 1784 or 1785 in Wilkes County. John and Carah Campbell lived near John's brother Perciphull Campbell in Iredell County. Cora was born in Virginia. John and Corah are believed to have died in Iredell County, but their burial location is not known. While John's descendants continued to live in North Carolina for several generations, the Campbell families in Iredell County did not know about John and his descendants because they did not have access to his Revolutionary War pension records in 1925.[9, 62, 63, 64, 65, 66]

1.4 **Mary "Polly" Campbell** (1760–aft. Sep 11, 1834) appears in the Vanhoy history.[6] She married Charles Coleman (1756–May 23, 1826) in Wilkes County in about 1780. Mary and Charles died in Wilkes County.[67, 68, 69, 70, 71]

1.5 **Sarah "Sally" Campbell** (Sep 9, 1763–Mar 23, 1844) appears in the Vanhoy history.[6] She married **William Ball** (Jul 9, 1766–Apr 25, 1844) in about 1788 in Iredell County.[72] William

Ball also appears in the Vanhoy history.[6] Sally and William lived near Ford's Branch and Hunting Creek in Iredell County, near Perciphull Campbell and Thomas Rash.[73] Sally and William died in Wilkes County.[4, 74, 75, 76, 77, 78, 79]

1.6   **Perciphull Campbell Sr**. (Apr 13, 1767–Jun 6, 1853) appears in the Vanhoy history as *Pierce Campbell, the second*. [6] He settled on what was called, in 1925, the J. P. Bolin place on Hunting Creek, adjoining the land of his father, Adam Campbell.[6] He married **Sarah "Sally" Elizabeth Cook** (Jun 2, 1767--Feb 28 1848) in Wilkes County in about 1788. Perciphull and Sally died in Iredell County and were buried at the Campbell Family Cemetery in Union Grove Township, Iredell County, North Carolina. Their descendants were prominent in the Vanhoy History.[4, 62, 63, 64, 80, 81, 82, 83, 84]

1.7   Malinda Campbell (1776–1838) did not appear in the Vanhoy history. Definitive evidence for a connection to Adam Campbell or North Carolina is missing. However, there was a Malinda Campbell that was born in North Carolina and married Miller A. Wood (Nov 11, 1769–Nov 29, 1838). They lived in Logan County, Kentucky, until 1832, when they moved to Illinois. They had a son, Miller Chapman Wood, who moved to Minnesota in 1864.[48]

1.8   **Theophilus Marion Campbell** (1777–1855) did not appear in the Vanhoy history, but he is included in a chapter of the Raney book written in 2013. DNA evidence from one of Theophilus's descendants and the Raney history provides a linkage to Adam Campbell. Theophilus was born in North Carolina and moved south where he fought in a Mississippi unit in the War of 1812 and later lived in Madison County, Alabama.[46, 47] (Note: This person should not be confused with Theophilus M. Campbell (1797–1855), who was a son of Perciphull Campbell Sr.)

Some of Adam Campbell's descendants remain, to this day, in the same area of North Carolina where Adam first settled before the American Revolution. The story of his children shows how many of the succeeding generations moved west and south in the 1800s. Figures 1.7 and 1.8 show the new states where the first descendants of each successive generation of Adam Campbell were born and died, thus showing the migration of his family in the 19th century. The first generation included Adam and Elizabeth, born in either Scotland or Virginia. The second generation included the eight children and their spouses, born in the Colony of Virginia, North Carolina, and Massachusetts. The third generation included 123 children and their spouses, with 94 people born in North Carolina and 29 people born in other states. The fourth generation included 586 children and their spouses, with 297 born in North Carolina and 22 other states (including 72 in Alabama, 51 in Kentucky, 51 in Indiana, and 42 in Tennessee). The fifth generation included 500 known children and their spouses, with 208 born in North Carolina and 17 other states (including 160 in Arkansas, 37 in Tennessee, 27 in Mississippi, 12 in Texas, and 11 in Georgia). Figure 1.8 shows that the first five generations of Adam Campbell's descendants died in 30 different states. The largest

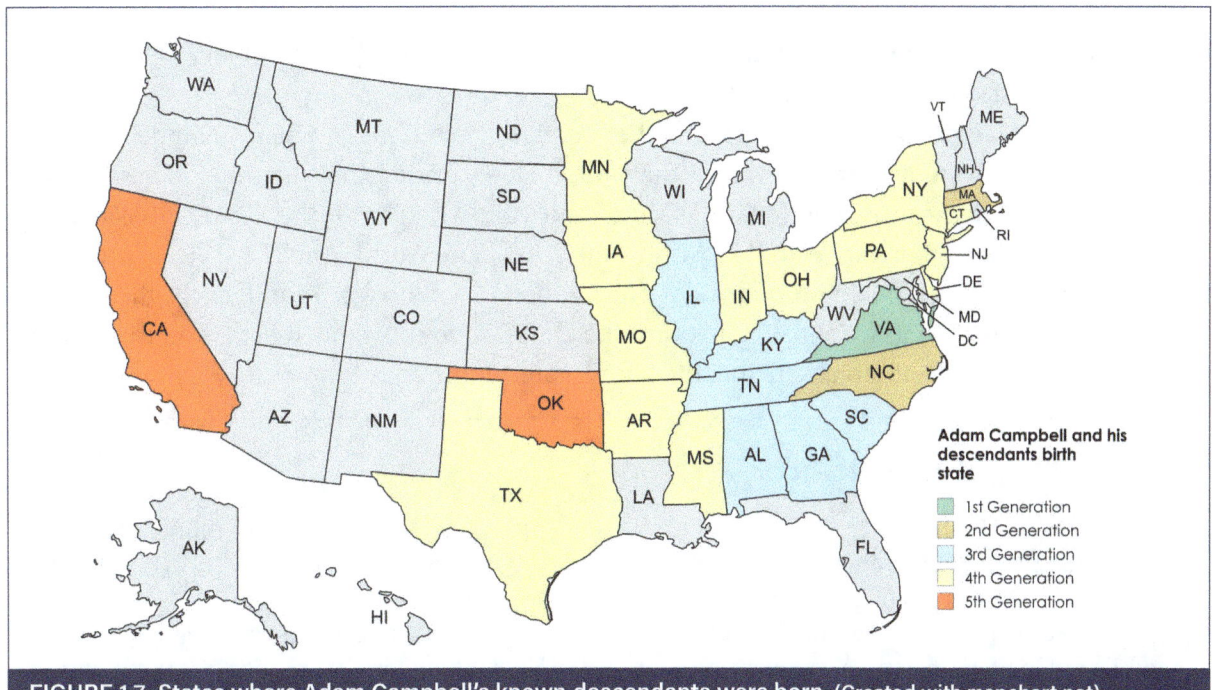

FIGURE 1.7 States where Adam Campbell's known descendants were born. (Created with mapchart.net)

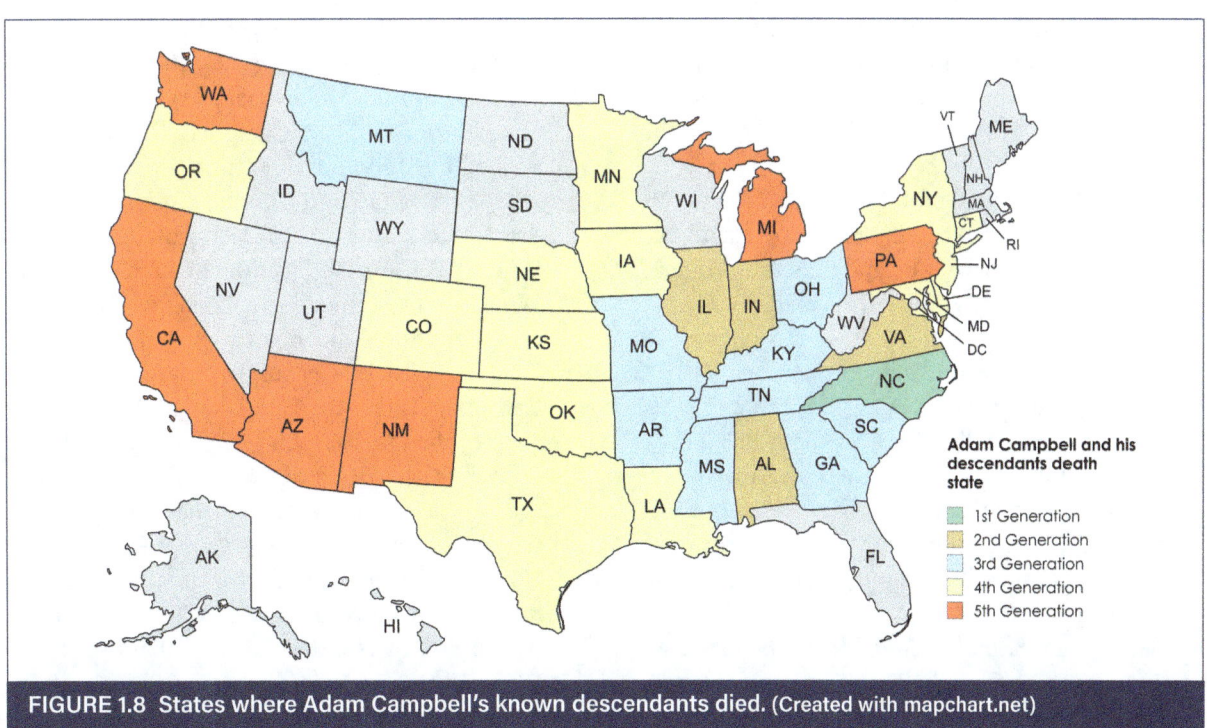

FIGURE 1.8 States where Adam Campbell's known descendants died. (Created with mapchart.net)

number died in North Carolina (383), followed by Arkansas (182), Indiana (89), Alabama (78), Tennessee (78), and Texas (37).

At least one family member in the first five generations of Adam Campbell's descendants fought in every major war in the United States during their lifetimes. These include the U.S. American Revolutionary War (2), the War of 1812 (3), the U.S. Civil War (101), the Spanish–American War (1), World War I (6), and World War II (8). Descendants of Adam Campbell fought on both sides during the U.S. Civil War; 71 fought for the Confederate States of America and 30 fought for the Union Army. Expanded details on these family members' military service are included in Chapters 4 through 11.

CHAPTER 1 REFERENCES

1. Aug 31, 1778, "North Carolina Land Grant," Vacant Land Entry no. 1462; on both sides of Hunting Creek; for Adam Campbell, adjoining Theophilus Morgan's conditional line between him and Peter Good and James Woodburn; at point of rocks in Rowan County, including his own improvement. (Note: This record is not online. It is quoted by Emory L. Coleman in 1994, who has seen the original or an index of vacant land grant entires.)

2. 1778, "List of Taxable Property in the County of Rowan, North Carolina, Anno 1778," transcribed from several lists returned by August Term anno domini 1778, by Adlai Osborne, clerk of court, indexed by Annie Walker Burns, Washington, D.C.

3. 2014, "NC Land Grant Images and Data," NC historical records online, created by David McCorkle, https://www.nclandgrants.com/query/, access date various times in 2023 and 2024.

4. 1790, U.S. Federal Census, Iredell County, North Carolina, page 396, Elizabeth Campbell X12XX, Penniful Campbell 11XXX, John Camp 143XX, William Campbell 111XX, William Ball 111XX (Format for 1790 Census: Free white males of 16 years and upwards, including heads of families; free white males under 16; free white females including heads of families; all other people; slaves; X is blank).

5. May 15, 1798, *Iredell County Deed Book C*, page 118, Elizabeth Campbell sold 200 acres of land in Iredell County to Perciphull Campbell, located opposite Point of Rocks on a creek; witnessed by Theophelus Campbell, John Morgan, and Nimrod Lunceford; filed on Sep 12, 1797, signed May 15, 1798.

6. Aug 1925, "Descendants of Pierce Campbell Holds Reunion," *Statesville Morning Register*, Aug 1925, as well as a handout given at the reunion, *History of the Campbell Family*, compiled by H. P. Vanhoy, a descendant of Sarah Campbell, daughter of John R. Campbell, who married William A. Vanhoy.

7. 2023, "Scotch-Irish Americans," Wikipedia, https://en.wikipedia.org/wiki/Scotch-Irish_Americans, access date Dec 29, 2023.

8. Oct 13, 1822, "Revolutionary War Pension Application for William Campbell, S32162," transcribed by Will Graves, https://revwarapps.org/s32162.pdf, Crawford County, Indiana.

9. Apr 9, 1833, Aug 23, 1843 "Revolutionary War Widows Pension Application for John Campbell, W-6616," transcribed by C. Leon Harris, https://revwarapps.org/w6616.pdf.

10. 1850, U.S. Federal Census, Iredell County, North Carolina, page 440, Family 544: P. Campbell, age 81, born in Va; John P. Parks, age 22; Theos C. Parks, age 15; Family 542: Milon Campbell, age 24; Clementine Campbell, age 23; Leolen D. Campbell, age 3; Preston C. Campbell, age 1.

11. 2025, "Culpeper County, Virginia," Wikipedia, https://en.wikipedia.org/wiki/Culpeper_County,_Virginia, access date Feb 24, 2025.

12. 1763, *Abstracts from County Court Minute Book of Culpeper County, Virginia, 1763–1764*, by A. M. Pritchard, Joseph K. Reubush Company, pub-

lished in 1930, Dayton, Virginia, page 312, April 22, 1763, William Turner versus Adam Campbell dismissed agreed; page 360, David Johnson versus Adam Campbell; page 356; https://search.lib.virginia.edu/sources/uva_library/items/u490928, access date Dec 29, 2023.

13. 1751, "A Map of the most Inhabited part of Virginia, containing the whole Province of Maryland with Part of Pennsylvania, New Jersey and North Carolina," drawn by Joshua Fry & Peter Jefferson in 1751, http://hdl.loc.gov/loc.gmd/g3880.ct000370, access date: Feb 28, 2025.

14. Jun 9, 2023, "Welcome to Mulberry Fields," *The Wilkes Record*, by Lane Dyer, columnist, https://thewilkesrecord.com/welcome-to-mulberry-fields-p6403-149.htm, access date: Feb 28, 2025.

15. Apr 30, 2013, "North Carolina Tax Laws in Force During the American Revolution," Subcommittee of revolutionary Taxes, Genealogy Committee, National Society Sons of the American Revolution, John D. Sinks and Harold Ford, https://members.sar.org/media/uploads/pages/228/GWAzx1n4wgyQ.pdf.

16. "Adlai Osborne," Wikipedia, https://en.wikipedia.org/wiki/Adlai_Osborne, access date Jan 16, 2024.

17. 1988, "Iredell County Early Landowners," adapted by Garry E. Moore from original map by Mildred J. Miller, Iredell County Genealogical Society.

18. 1784–1787 North Carolina State Census, Wilkes County, Capt. Gordon's District, Isham Harvell, John Campbell, Abraham Cook.

19. 1850, U.S. Federal Census, District 2, Letcher County, Kentucky, Jonathan Hayes, aged 75, born in North Carolina.

20. 1790, U.S. Federal Census, Wilkes County, North Carolina, page 154–155, Henry Hays, 1 male over 16, 3 males under 16, 4 females, 8 total household members; Isom Harvell, 5th Company, 132; Martha Mise, 5th Company, 002.

21. 1800, U.S. Federal Census, Morgan District, Wilkes County, North Carolina, page 473, Henry Hays, 2112111629; Jonathan Hays, 11113.

22. Oct 30, 1798, "North Carolina Index to Marriage Bonds, 1741–1868," John Hays and Rachael Mitchel, Wilkes County, North Carolina, bond 000165628, record 01114, bondsman Henry Hays, witness Wm B Lenoir, CL.

23. 1800, U.S. Federal Census, Morgan District, Wilkes County, North Carolina, page 43, Jonathan Hays1x1xxxx13x; Henry Hays 21x1x2111x.

24. 1795, *Iredell County Deed Book B*, page 314, Elizabeth Campbell sold 100 acres of land in Iredell County for 20 pounds to Perciphull Campbell; located on a creek in Iredell County; witnessed by Miller Wood, Miller Wood Sr., Nimrod Lunceford, Jurat; filed on Jun 15, 1795, signed on Nov 11, 1795.

25. 1798, *Iredell County Deed Book C*, page 118, Elizabeth Campbell sold 200 acres of land in Iredell County to Perciphull Campbell; located opposite Point of Rocks on a Creek; witnessed by Theophilus Campbell, John Morgan, and Nimrod Lunceford; filed on Sep 12, 1797, signed on May 15, 1798.

26. Jul 7, 2016, "Find a Grave," Joppa Cemetery, Mocksville, Davie County, North Carolina, Memorial ID: 39781779, story for John Wilcoxson Sr. by Mike Wilcox.

27. Apr 1, 1778; *North Carolina Land Grant Book 82*, page 284, John Campbell, Patent entered Apr 1, 1778, Plat entered Jul 7, 1794, for John Campbell, signed by James Brandon.

28. Aug 16, 1778, *North Carolina Land Grant*, Book 51, John Henderson, page 7, patent issued Oct 10, 1783, plat entered Aug 16, 1778, no. 702, for John Henderson, signed by James Brandon, entry officer of claims for lands in the County of Rowan, Aug 16, 1778.

29. Sep 4, 1778, *North Carolina Land Grant Book 51* Rowan County Patent, William Campbell, page 5, plat entered Sep 4, 1778, patent issued Oct 10, 1783, for William Campbell, entry signed by James Brandon, Sep 4, 1778.

30. Dec 30, 1778, *North Carolina Land Grant Book 51*, Rowan County Patent, Adam Simonton, page 43, Patent issued Oct 10, 1783, Plat Entered Dec 30, 1778, Plat Entered Dec 30, 1778, no. 1611, for Adam Simonton, signed by James Brandon, Dec 30, 1778.

31. May 25, 1779, *North Carolina Land Grant Patent Book 120*, Rowan County , Martin Morgan, page 138, patent issued Dec 15, 1804, plat entered May 25, 1779, no. 2213, File no. 545, for Martin Mor-

gan, letter from Rowan County to surveyor for Iredell County, dated Feb 1804 and containing the original survey request from May 20, 1779 (see appendix).

32. Oct 10, 1779, *North Carolina Land Grant, Patent Book 51* Rowan County, Elizabeth Campbell, page 6, plat entered Oct 10, 1779, patent issued Oct 10, 1783, no. 2077, signed by James Brandon entry officer, Oct 10, 1779 (see appendix).

33. Nov 15, 1779, *North Carolina Land Grant Patent Book 51* Rowan County, John Hughes, page 164, plat entered Nov 15, 1779, patent issued Oct 10, 1783, no. 2102, signed by James Brandon.

34. Dec 20, 1994, "Addition to the Campbell Family History," research notes by Emory L. Coleman, Winston-Salem, North Carolina; lists land grants for Campbell Family.

35. Dec 10, 1782, *North Carolina Land Grant Patent Book 51*, Rowan County, Adam Simonton, page 43, patent issued Oct 10, 1783, plat entered Dec 30, 1778, survey signed by Griffith Rutherford, Surveyor, Dec 10, 1782.

36. Dec 10, 1782, *North Carolina Land Grant Patent Book 51*, Rowan County, Elizabeth Campbell, page 6, plat entered Oct 10, 1779, patent issued Oct 10, 1783, survey plat signed by Griffith Rutherford on Dec 10, 1782.

37. Dec 10, 1782, *North Carolina Land Grant Patent Book 51*, Rowan County, John Hughes, pages 42–43, plat entered Nov 15, 1779, patent issued Oct 10, 1783, signed by Griffith Rutherford, surveyor, Dec 10, 1782.

38. Dec 10, 1782, *North Carolina Land Grant Patent Book 51*, Rowan County, William Campbell, page 5, plat entered Sep 4, 1778, patent issued Oct 10, 1783, for William Campbell, signed by Griffith Rutherford, surveyor, Dec 10, 1782.

39. Dec 17, 1782, *North Carolina Land Grant Patent Book 51*, Rowan County, John Henderson, page 7, patent issued Oct 10, 1783, plat entered Aug 16, 1778, plat survey signed by Griffith Rutherford, Dec 17, 1782.

40. Oct 10, 1783, *North Carolina Land Grant Patent Book 51*, Rowan County, Adam Simonton, page 43, patent issued Oct 10, 1783, plat Entered Dec 30, 1778, for William Campbell, signed by Alex Martin, Oct 10, 1783.

41. Oct 10, 1783, *North Carolina Land Grant Patent Book 51*, Rowan County, Elizabeth Campbell, page 6, plat entered Oct 10, 1779, patent issued Oct 10, 1783, file no. 843, Alex Martin signed on Oct 10, 1783.

42. Oct 10, 1783, *North Carolina Land Grant Patent Book 51*, Rowan County, John Henderson, page 7, patent issued Oct 10, 1783, plat entered Aug 16, 1778, file no. 846, signed by Alex Martin, Oct 10, 1783.

43. Dec 12, 1786, *North Carolina Land Grant Patent Book 64*, Rowan County 64, Martin Morgan, page 392, patent issued Jul 11, 1788, plat entered May 18, 1778, plat survey signed by Griffith Rutherford, surveyor.

44. May 12, 1790, *North Carolina Land Grant Patent Book 82*, Iredell County, John Campbell, page 284, patent entered Apr 1, 1778, plat entered Jul 7, 1794, signed by Abner Sharpe, deputy for William Sharpe, chief justice.

45. Sep 6, 1804, *North Carolina Land Grant Patent Book 120*, Iredell County, Martin Morgan, page 138, patent issued Dec 15, 1804, plat entered May 25, 1779, signed by David Beal, Iredell County Surveyor.

46. Clan Campbell Society of North America DNA Project, Subgroup R1b1-group79, https://www.familytreedna.com/groups/campbell/dna-results, access date Feb 23, 2025.

47. 2013, *Raney Family History*, by Don Raney (1933–2020), Garland, Texas, Chapter 26, Theophilus Marion Campbell, available at Family Search, http://www.familysearch.org/library/books/idurl/1/55897, access date Feb 21, 2025.

48. 1888, *Album of History and Biography of Meeker County, Minnesota*/Chicago, Alden Ogle & Company, page 454, biography of Miller Chapman Wood, son of Miller and Melinda (Campbell) Wood, https://tile.loc.gov/storage-services/public/gdcmassbookdig/albumofhistorybi00alde/albumofhistorybi00alde.pdf, access date Dec 27, 2023.

49. 1790, U.S. Federal Census, Wilkes County, North Carolina, page 154x155, Henry Hays, 1 male over 16, 3 males under 16, 4 females, 8 total household members; Isom Harvell, 5th Company, 132; Martha Mise, 5th Company, 002.

50. 1800, U.S. Federal Census, Morgan District, Wilkes County, North Carolina, page 473, Henry Hays, 2112111629; Jonathan Hays, 11113.

51. 1810, U.S. Federal Census, Wilkesborough, Wilkes County, North Carolina, page 862, Kipiah Hays, 2121316.

52. Aug 7, 1820, U.S. Federal Census, Wilkes County, North Carolina, page 523, Keziah Hays, 11111133.

53. 1830, U.S. Federal Census, Wilkes County, North Carolina, page 391, 2112144.

54. Feb 1895, "Inventory of estate of Henry Hays, deceased, Wilkes County, North Carolina," *Will Book 2*, page 145, 147, 148; sale acct. Mar 5, 1805; administrator, Keziah Hays, one still mentioned in will.

55. Apr 3, 1792, "North Carolina Marriage Records, 1762-1883," Rowan County , William Campbell and Ann Hendren, bondsman John Hendren, witness Brice W. James.

56. 1810, U.S. Federal Census, Clay County, Kentucky, Will Campbell.

57. 1800, Kentucky, Tax List, Garrard County, William Campbell.

58. 1820, U.S. Federal Census, Crawford County, Indiana, Wm. Campbell.

59. 1830, U.S. Federal Census, Crawford County, Indiana, Wm Campbell.

60. Feb 2, 1847, Gallatin County, Illinois Wills and Probate Records, William Campbell, probate began on Dec 28, 1846, Johnston Brown administrator.

61. 1835, U.S. Pension Roll, Crawford County, Indiana, William Campbell, age 79, N.C. State Troops, annual pension $40.00, received $120, placed on pension roll on Nov 29, 1833; pension commenced Mar 4, 1831.

62. 1800, U.S. Federal Census, Iredell County, North Carolina, page 149, Piercephul Campbell, 21x11xxx1xxx1; John Campbell, x1x1x5xxx1xxx; Daniel Ball, 2112x31x11xx.

63. Aug 6, 1810, U.S. Federal Census, Iredell County, North Carolina, page 206, John Campbell, xx2xxx41xxxx; page 176, Purciphull Campbell, 1111x3x11xxx4.

64. Aug 7, 1820, U.S. Federal Census, Iredell County, North Carolina, page 234, Sampson Ball, John Campbell, Purciphul Campbell, Esq, Adam Campbell, Pierciphull Campbell Sr., John Campbell, Reuben Fletcher, Mary Fletcher, James Fletcher, Reuben Morgan.

65. 1784–1787, North Carolina State Census, Capt. Trible's District, John Campbell.

66. 1850, U.S. Federal Census, Iredell County, North Carolina, page 898, Family 536: Cary Campbell, age 91; Nancy Campbell, age 58; Syrien I Campbell, age 22; Family 537: John M. Campbell, aged 49; Catharine, aged 40; Theus., aged 25; Carolus, aged 24; William, aged 18; Mary, aged 15; F. M., aged 12.

67. Sep 11, 1834, "North Carolina Wills and Probate Records, 1665-1998," Wilkes County, North Carolina, Will of Mary Coleman, probated Aug 1835.

68. 1830, U.S. Federal Census, Wilkes County, North Carolina, page 382, Mary Coleman.

69. Aug 6 1810, U.S. Federal Census, Wilkesborough, Wilkes County, North Carolina, page 876, Charles Coleman.

70. 1820, U.S. Federal Census, Wilkes County, North Carolina, page 497, Charles Coleman.

71. May 23, 1826, Wilkes County, North Carolina Estate Records; Charles Coleman, deceased, died on Osborn Creek; widow Mary Coleman; estate of 524 acres on Osborn Creek, plantation, and mill.

72. Marriage date is an estimate based on birth of first child and census records when available. Marriage bonds or licenses have not been found.

73. "North Carolina Land Grant File, 1693-1960," Ancestry, William Ball: for 300 acres in Rowan County, Book 71, page 117, issued May 18, 1789; for 100 acres in Iredell County, Book 115, page 404, issued Sep 23, 1801; for 50 acres in Iredell County, Book 115, page 404, issued on Sep 23, 1802; for 250 acres in Iredell County, Book 136, page 140, issued Jan 5, 1825.

74. 1800, U.S. Federal Census, Iredell County, North Carolina, William Ball, 31211338.

75. 1810, U.S. Federal Census, Wilkes County, North Carolina, William Ball, 1121211429.

76. 1820, U.S. Federal Census, Wilkes County, North Carolina, page 542, William Ball, 11121122266.

77. 1830, U.S. Federal Census, Wilkes County, North Carolina, page 377, William Ball, 111133.

78. 1840, U.S. Federal Census, Becknals District, Wilkes County, North Carolina, page 22, William Ball.

79. Jan 30, 1844, "North Carolina Wills and Probate Records, 1665-1998", Wilkes County, North Carolina, Sampson Ball and Iredell Privette bound with $200 as administrators of the estate of William Ball, deceased.

80. 1830, U.S. Federal Census, Iredell County, North Carolina, page 28/30, Percival Campbell Sr., Percival Campbell Jr., John Campbell Sr., Biram Ball, Sampson Ball.

81. 1840, U.S. Federal Census, Iredell County, North Carolina, no. 4, Pierciful Campbell (26 people, including 19 slaves), Hannah Campbell, Wm Campbell, Hannah Campbell, Wm Campbell, Wm Hays, Charles Hays.

82. 1850, U.S. Federal Census, Iredell County, North Carolina, page 440, Family 544: P. Campbell, age 81, born in Va; John P. Parks, age 22; Theos C. Parks, age 15; Family 542: Milon Campbell, age 24; Clementine Campbell, age 23; Leolen D. Campbell, age 3; Preston C. Campbell, age 1.

83. 1850, U.S. Federal Census Slave Schedules, Iredell County, North Carolina, P. Campbell: 10 slaves; John R. Campbell: 1 slave; Williamson Campbell: 1 slave; B. Morgan: 2 slaves.

84. Headstones at Campbell Family Cemetery, Union Grove Township, Iredell County, North Carolina, showing birth and death dates on headstones, photographed by Garry E. Moore in 1982, also available on Find a Grave.

CHAPTER 2
NEIGHBORS OF ADAM CAMPBELL

A short biography of the neighbors of Adam Campbell helps to illustrate connections to other nearby families that Adam and his children knew through marriage, military service, and politics. These biographies include references to available historical records, including the Rowan County Tax List of 1778;[1, 2] information from land grants in Rowan, Iredell, and Wilkes Counties;[3] names from a map that William Sharp made in 1773 showing where the members of the Fourth Creek Congregation lived;[4] Revolutionary War service records;[5] the 1790 U.S. Census records in Iredell,[6] Wilkes, and Surry Counties;[7] and family histories from other family genealogies.

FAMILY RELATIONS

William Ball

William Ball Jr.[8] (Jul 9, 1766–bef. Jan 30, 1844) married Adam Campbell's fifth child, Sarah "Sally" Campbell, on Sep 9, 1788, in Rowan County. William's parents were William Ball Sr. (Oct 30, 1745–1806) and Elizabeth Ann Osborne (1742–Oct 24, 1794). Sarah and William lived on Ford's Branch of Hunting Creek in Iredell County near her brother, Perciphull Campbell, and Thomas Rash. The original land grant for the 300 acres next to Adam Campbell was most likely William Ball Sr. In 1812, William Ball Jr. and Sarah moved to the area of Osborne's Creek in Wilkes County.[3] See Figure 2.1 for the location of his land and Chapter 8 for additional details about this family.

Cass Family

James Cass/Cast (1738–Jul 15, 1816) was in the Capt. Nichols's District in 1778 and had property assessed at 513 pounds.[1] His land holdings included 500 acres on Ford's Branch of Hunting Creek, 200 acres on the south fork of Hunting Creek including his mill shoal

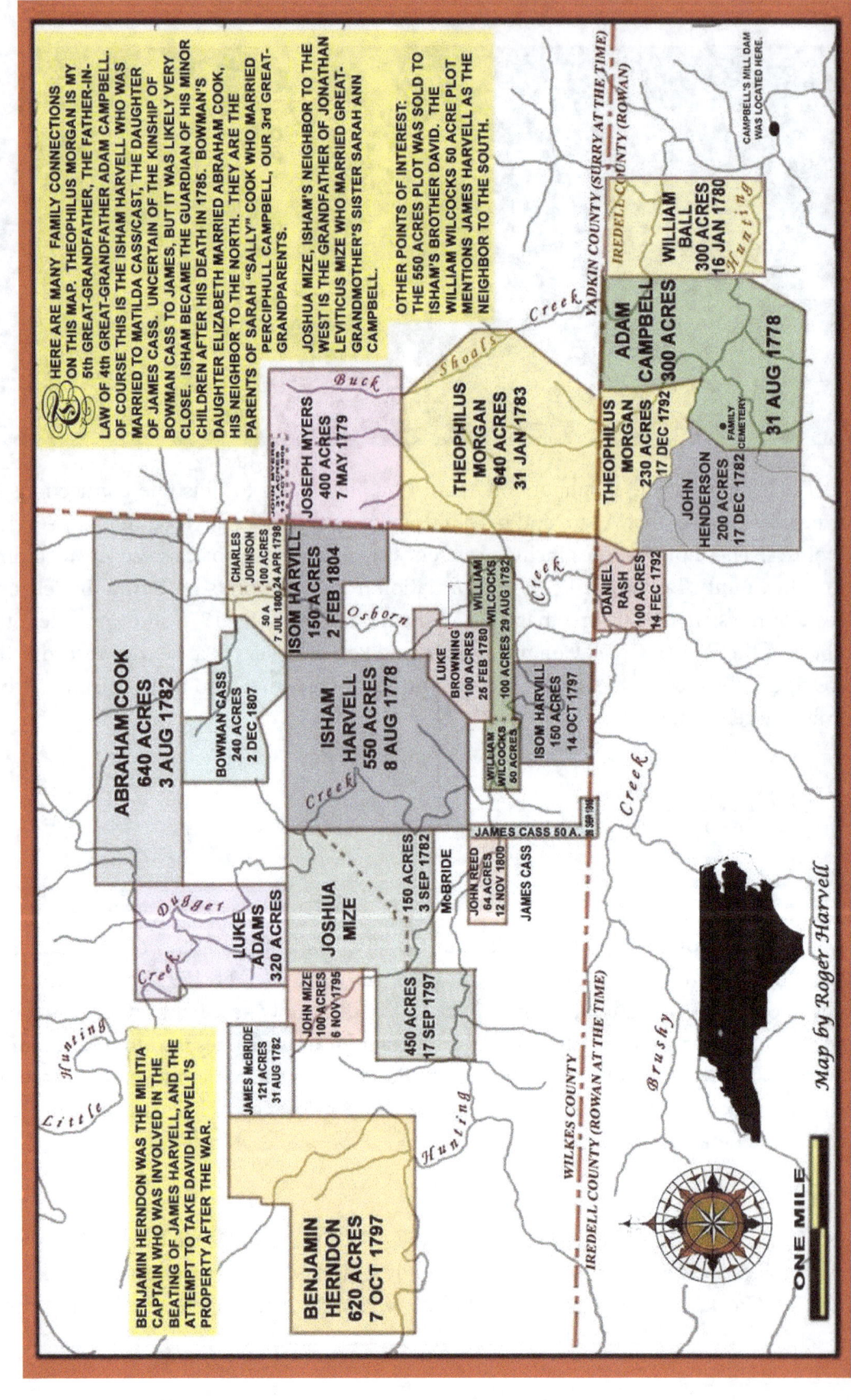

FIGURE 2.1 Map of Rowan County, North Carolina, land grants of neighbors of Adam Campbell within current Iredell, Wilkes, and Yadkin Counties, by Roger Harvell, Izard County, Arkansas.

24

in Rowan County, and 100 acres on Hunting Creek in Wilkes County that he was issued in 1783, 1783 (respectively), and 1799.[3] The surname Cass/Cast does not appear in the 1787 State Census or the 1790 U.S. Federal Census for Wilkes County. James Cast and Elijah Cast appear in the 1790 U.S. Census for Iredell County.[6] James Cass's daughter, Matilda Harriet Cass (1762–Mar 15, 1815), married Isham John Harvell Sr. (1756–1813).[7] See Figures 2.1 and 2.2 for the location of his land, and Chapter 9 for more details about this family.

Bowman Cass (also spelled Cast) (1740–possibly1785) lived in Surry County and Wilkes County. He appeared on a list of taxables taken by Benjamin Cleveland in Surry County in 1774 with one pole. In 1775, Bowman appeared on John Hudspeth's list of taxables in Surry County. On Jan 16, 1785, Ezekial Cast was bound to Isham Harvill to learn the shoemaker trade. Samuel Cast was also bound to Isham Harvell to learn the occupation of a farmer, and Winnefred Cast was bound to Isham Harvill to learn the occupation of a spinster. On Jan 28, 1785, the court stated that the request for the three children of Bowman Cass being bound to Isham Harvill was done through misinformation, and the bond was withdrawn. Bowman's land holdings included 232 acres on both sides of the middle fork of Hunting Creek that he entered in 1778 and was issued in 1807 in Wilkes County.[3] Bowman's daughter, Elizabeth Cass (1760–Mar 15, 1815) married Abraham Cook (1721–Aug 11, 1801), who was his neighbor to his north in Wilkes County.[7]

Abraham Cook

Abraham Cook (1721–Aug 11, 1801) was not living in Rowan County in 1778, but he was living in Capt. Gordan's District in Wilkes County in 1784.[10] His land holdings on Hunting Creek in Wilkes County included 400, 500, 500, 100, and 640 acres, issued in 1784.[3] Abraham and his wife Elizabeth Cass, daughter of Bowman Cass, may have been the parents of Sara Elizabeth Cook (1767–1848), wife of Perciphull Campbell (1767–1853). See Figure 2.1 for the location of his land and Chapter 9 for more details about this family.

John Moore Dobbins

John Moore Dobbins Sr. (Oct 17, 1712–Jan 1800) was in the Capt. Nichols's District and had property assessed at 3,403 pounds in 1778.[1] His land holdings included 350 acres on the south side of the Yadkin River and both sides of Walnut Branch, 636 acres on Rocky Creek, and 200 acres on Moors Creek in Surry County.[3] John was a slave owner and lived on Dutchman's Creek.[9] He died in Iredell County. He was a First Major in the Rowan County Regiment.[5] His son, John Dobbins Jr. (1763–Sep 27, 1820), was in Capt. Cowin's District and was assessed "Poles Only" in 1778. John Dobbins Jr. married Margaret Reid (1772–Jan 24, 1851), and they were both buried at Bethany Presbyterian Church cemetery. One of the six children of John Dobbins Jr., Milas Dobbins (1800–1862), married Frances "Fanny" Campbell (1809–1846), daughter of Perciphull Campbell Sr., as mentioned in the Vanhoy history. Milas and Frances were buried at the Bethany Presbyterian Church cemetery.[10] See Figure 2.2 for the location of his land and Chapter 9 for more details about this family.

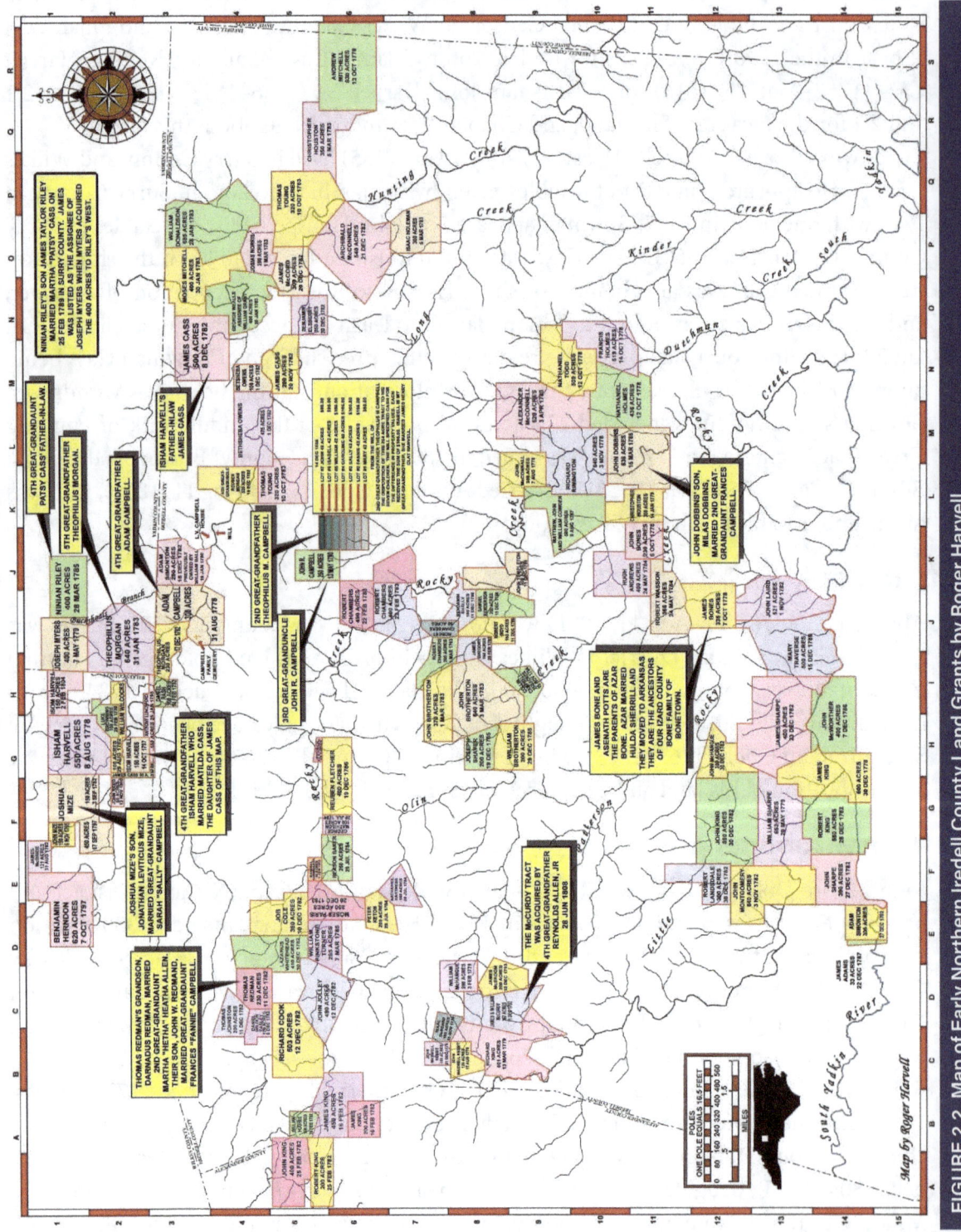

FIGURE 2.2 Map of Early Northern Iredell County Land Grants by Roger Harvell.
Note: John R. Campbell should be John Campbell, Adam Campbell's son.

26

Benjamin Dobson

Benjamin Dobson (abt. 1740–1810) was in the Capt. Nichols's District and had property valued at 555 pounds. His land holdings included 300 acres on the north side of South Rocky Creek.[3] Benjamin was the great-great-great grandfather of Joseph Franklin Dobson Jr. (1886–1942), who married Tabitha Ann Campbell (1888–1949), daughter of Theophilus Campbell (1839–1906). See Chapter 9 for more details about this family.

Isham John Harvell

Isham John Harvell Sr. (1756–1813) lived in Wilkes County, so he did not appear in the Rowan County Tax List of 1778. His land holdings included 550 acres on both sides of the little fork of Hunting Creek that he was issued in 1784 and 150 acres on the Iredell–Wilkes line on Hunting Creek that he entered for in 1797.[3] He was in the North Carolina Militia, probably in the Wilkes County Regiment. He appears in Wilkes County in the North Carolina State Census of 1784–1787.[11] He died in Hardin County, Tennessee.[12] His great-great-grandson, James Henry Clay Harvell (1844–1918), married Isabella M. Campbell (1850–1926), daughter of Theophilus Marion Campbell (1797–1855). See Figure 2.1 for the location of his land and Chapter 9 for more details about this family.

Mize Family

Joshua Mize (Mar 10, 1726–Mar 16, 1790) lived in Wilkes County. His land holdings included 150 acres on Hunting Creek in Wilkes County and 400 acres on the north fork of Hunting Creek in Surry County. He appears in Capt. Gordon's District in Wilkes County in 1787.[10] His wife's first name was Martha, who appears in the Wilkes County Census in 1790.[13] His son, John Mize (abt. 1750–Nov 18444), owned land in Wilkes County on Hunting Creek that he obtained through land grants, beginning in 1794.[3] His great-grandson, Hartwell Hayes Sr. (Feb 28, 1787–Dec 4, 1859) was the son of Keziah Campbell (Aug 1, 1755–Jun 1, 1845).[3] See Figure 2.1 for the location of his land and Chapter 4 for more details about this family.

Benjamin Mize (1755–1820) appears in Capt. Nichols's District in Rowan County in 1778 with a property value of 108 pounds.[1] Benjamin was the son of Joshua Mize. He later moved to Kentucky. His great-grandson, Jonathan Leviticus Mize (1833–1891), married Sarah Ann Lodema Campbell (1836–1874). See Chapter 9 for more details about this family.

Morgan Family

Theophilus Morgan Sr. (1720–bef. Feb 13, 1807) was a neighbor and close friend of Adam Campbell. He appears in Capt. Nichols's District in 1778 with a property value of 684 pounds.[1, 14] His land holdings included 230 acres on Straight Creek waters of Hunting Creek next to Campbell and Henderson obtained in a Rowan County land grant issued in 1783, 640 acres in Iredell County on the Surry and Wilkes County lines obtained in a Rowan County land grant issued in 1783, and 640 acres in Surry County in the southwest corner on the Wilkes County line. His land was in what is now Yadkin County.[3] Theophilus's second wife was Catherine "Unknown Last Name" (1720–1820), who may have also been married previously.[15] Elizabeth Morgan (1735–1798), who married Adam Campbell (1735–1799), was probably Theophilus Morgan Sr.'s sister. See Figure 2.1 for the location of Theophilus Morgan Sr.'s land.

Theophilus Morgan Jr. (1755–Aug 1, 1843), son of Theophilus Morgan Sr., married Ruth Owens (1760–1812), daughter of Basil Owens, on Aug 6, 1784.[16] Theophilus Morgan Jr. served in the Mecklenburg County Regiment during the American Revolution.[17] After 1810, Theophilus Morgan Jr. and his family moved to Robertson County, Tennessee.

Reuben Morgan (1756–Jan 10, 1823), son of Theophilus Morgan Sr., appears in Capt. Nichols's District in 1778 with a property value of 292 pounds.[1] His land holdings included 300 acres on Hunting Creek obtained in a land grant from Rowan County issued in 1783, and 100 acres in the fork of Rocky Branch issued in 1804.[3] Reuben served in the First and Third North Carolina Regiments during the American Revolution.[18]

Martin Morgan (1758–1830), son of Theophilus Morgan, did not appear in the 1778 Rowan County Tax List. His land holdings included 300 acres of land on Straight Creek waters of Hunting Creek next to Campbell and Henderson issued in Rowan County in 1788; and 100 acres lying in the forks of Rocky Branch, Nimrod Lunceford's line, adjoining Adam Campbell's corner, originally filed by William Taylor in 1778 and issued in 1804 in Iredell County.[3] Martin's son, Bartlett Morgan (1790–aft. Aug 31, 1870), married Sarah Sallie Campbell (1805–1870), daughter of Perciphull Campbell Sr. (Apr 13, 1767–Jun 6, 1853). See Chapter 9 for more details about this family.

Basil Owens

Basil or Bazelle Owens (1735–1781) appears in Capt. Nichols's District in 1778, with property assessed at 1,700 pounds.[1] His land holdings included 475 acres on Hunting Creek, including Anthony's Shoals, and 100 acres on Hunting Creek above Anthony's Shoals that he entered in 1778 but was issued to his widow after his death.[3] According to a high-ranking North Carolina loyalist, Col. Samuel Bryan, Basil Owens and his son, William Owens (abt. 1762– aft. Oct 25,1786), fought under his command in the North Carolina Volunteers against the American Army in the American Revolution.[19] Col. Bryan was in Capt. Johnston's District in 1778. William was wounded at the Battle of Hanging Rock, South Carolina. Basil died on Jan 15, 1781, possibly at the Battle of Cowpens, South Carolina. Basel was survived by his wife, Bethsheba (Claybrooke) Owens (1740–bef. 1820), to whom the state issued Basil's land on Hunting Creek in 1783. She lived there until at least 1810.[20] Owens Branch on Hunting Creek may be named for Basil Owens. Basil's daughter, Ruth Owens (1760–1812), married Theophilus Morgan Jr. (1755–1843) on Aug 6, 1784, in Rowan County.

Daniel Andrew Rash

Daniel Andrew Rash (abt. 1733–Nov 11, 1839) appears in Capt. Nichols's District in 1778 with property assessed at 430 pounds.[1] Daniel was born in Motherkill, Kent County, Delaware, and had Welsh ancestors. He moved to North Carolina in the 1770s. His land holdings included 100 acres on Hunting Creek adjoining the Wilkes County line issued in 1783 in Rowan County; 200 acres on Brush Creek; 50 acres on the south fork of Hunting Creek; 119 acres on Long Branch waters of Hunting Creek; and 100 acres on Hunting Creek in Wilkes County issued in 1815, 1784, and 1799 respectively.[3] Daniel served in the North Carolina Militia during the American Revolution. He was wounded in battle in 1780.[21] He was a neighbor of Theophilus Morgan. Daniel's daughter, Mary Elizabeth Rash (1785–1860) married Robert Henry Coleman Sr. (1785–1846), son of Mary Polly Campbell (1760–1834), daughter of Adam Campbell. See Figure 2.1 for the location of his land and Chapter 7 for more details about this family.

Thomas Erastus Redman

Thomas Erastus Redman[22] (1745–1836) did not appear in the 1778 Tax List. He was a private in Capt. James Johnson's 6th Virginia Regiment in the American Revolution. His unit crossed the Delaware with George Washington and fought in the battles at Trenton and Princeton, New Jersey.[23] His land holdings included 239 acres on Dropping Off Branch of Rock Creek issued in 1783 in Rowan County, and 31 acres on the south side of the mountain dividing Rocky Creek and Hunting Creek issued in Iredell County in 1809.[3] There was a Redman Mill on Drop Off Branch.[24] Thomas was buried at the Redman Family Cemetery near New Hope in Iredell County. His great-grandson, John Wanta Redman (Apr 14, 1836–Apr 18, 1883), married Frances Elizabeth Campbell (May 20, 1839–Jan 20, 1922), daughter of Theophilus Marion Campbell (1797–1855). See Chapter 9 for more details about this family.

John Reid

John Reid (1738–Nov 16, 1816) appeared in Capt. Nichols's District in 1778 with property assessed at 1,760 pounds.[1] His land holdings included 100 acres on Dutchman's Creek, 400 acres on the South Yadkin River, 191 acres on the south side of the Yadkin River, 188 acres on the west side of the Yadkin River, 195 acres on Flat Creek, 62 acres on Flat Creek in Rowan County issued in 1780 and 1784, as well as 50 acres on Beaver Creek (a branch of the south fork of New River), 64 acres on Hunting Creek, and 50 acres on Beaver Creek issued in Wilkes County.[3] John Reid was a member of the 4th Creek Congregation and lived along Snow Creek. He died in Houstonville, where his son, Capt. Samuel Reid (1761–1805), was living before he moved to Blount County, Tennessee, after the American Revolution. John Reid was buried at Bethany Presbyterian Church. His grandson, Milas Dobbins (Dec 27, 1800–Nov 24, 1862), married Frances Campbell (May 2, 1809–Feb 23, 1846), daughter of Perciphull Campbell Sr. (1767–1853). See Chapter 9 for more details about this family.

Collin Campbell

Collin Campbell (Jan 27, 1749–bef. Sep 2, 1808) did not appear in the 1778 Tax List. There is no known relation between Collin Campbell and Adam Campbell. Collin was born in

Scotland. His land holdings included land issued in Iredell County: 15 acres on Buffalo Shoals Creek issued in 1802, 400 acres at Island Ford of the Catawba River issued in 1794, 250 acres on the middle for of Rocky Creek issued in 1795, 200 acres on the Catawba River issued in 1801, 200 acres near Robert McLeod issued in 1801, and 100 acres on the Catawba River issued in Rowan County in 1790.[3] His home was on Brotherton or Olin Creek.

REVOLUTIONARY WAR VETERANS

Col. James Cathey Brandon Jr.

Col. James Cathey Brandon Jr. (abt. 1734–aft. Jun 17, 1790) was the entry officer for Land Grant Claims in Rowan County and appeared on several of the Campbell land grant entries. James's father, James Brandon Sr., obtained a land grant for 640 acres on Dec 8, 1753, on the south side of the Yadkin River in Rowan County.[3] James Brandon Jr. lived in Capt. Armstrong's District of Rowan County in 1778.[1] During the American Revolution, he was an officer in the Rowan County Regiment of Militia, obtaining the rank of colonel in 1782.[25] He was buried at the Thyatira Presbyterian Church near Mill Bridge in Rowan County.[26]

Col. Benjamin Herndon

Col. Benjamin Herndon (Dec 10, 1749–Dec 30, 1819) appeared in Capt. Gordon's District in Wilkes County in 1784. He was living with his wife, Sarah Pines, in Culpeper County, Virginia, in 1773. After 1775, Benjamin and his family moved to the Morgan District in Wilkes County. They resided on their plantation called "Horseshoe" on the Yadkin River in Wilkes County, near the present town of Ronda, for 15 years.[27] Benjamin was a member of the Wilkes County Regiment of the North Carolina Militia, under the command of his neighbor, Col. Benjamin Cleveland. He held the ranks of captain, major, and lieutenant colonel. John Campbell served under his command in 1780. In the Battle of Kings Mountain, Lt. Col. Herndon commanded a company of 60 men and fought so bravely that he was awarded a pair of silver spurs for his action. At one time he was captured by "Bloody Bill" Cunningham and was about to be executed when he was rescued by a group of his own men. It is said that Lt. Col. Herndon was held in the highest esteem by the men he commanded, and more than once, he spoke on behalf of an accused man and saved him from lashings or worse. He was twice a member of the North Carolina State Senate, seated Nov 20, 1786, and twice a member of the House of Commons, seated Apr 23, 1783. He was also one of the first justices of Wilkes County, and entry taker of that county[28, 29, 30] See Figure 2.1 for the location of his land.

Benjamin received many land grants for his Revolutionary service. These grants were in North Carolina, Tennessee, and South Carolina. The grants in North Carolina were all in Wilkes County and were for 250,300 and 320 acres.[3] In 1788, he received a 4,000-acre land grant in the Middle District of Tennessee. In 1793, he received an 840-acre land grant in Davidson County, Tennessee. He later received a 1,000-acre land grant in the Ninety-Six District, Newberry County, South Carolina.[26]

By 1790, the Herndon family was quite large, and they were preparing for the marriage of the oldest child, Mary Boswell Herndon, to James Martin Lewis of Surry County. At the "Horseshoe" plantation, at this time, there were nine children, including three who had been born in Virginia and six more who had been born at "Horseshoe." These were Frances, Elizabeth, Benjamin Jr., Sarah Pines, Barbara Asbury, and Nancy Coke. At the time of the 1790 Census in North Carolina, Benjamin Herndon owned 22 slaves.[26]

Shortly after 1790, the Herndon family left Wilkes County and traveled to the banks of the Enoree River in South Carolina to their 1,000 acres in the Ninety-Six District, Newberry County. There, Benjamin Herndon built his home, called "Mollihon." This home was built with slave labor and was still standing in 1957 and occupied by tenant farmers. It was later owned by Marvin Abrams of Whitmire, South Carolina, a member of the state senate of South Carolina. Benjamin was buried at the Herndon Family Cemetery at Mollihon.[26]

Capt. Christopher Houston

Capt. Christopher Houston (Feb 18, 1744–May 17, 1837) appears in Capt. Reed's District, just to the east of Capt. Nichols's District, with property assessed at 899 pounds in 1778.[1] His land holdings included 350 acres on Hunting Creek, 320 acres on the north side of Hunting Creek, 640 acres on Hunting Creek, and 300 acres on Rocky Creek (as assignee of Charles Lovelace) that he was issued in 1787, 1783, 1783, and 1787 respectively.[3] His home was on Hunting Creek, just east of the Campbells. There was a "Christ" (short for Christopher) Houston living on the Catawba River in the 1773 Map of the Fourth Creek Congregation. He was a slave owner. During the American Revolution, he was a captain in the North Carolina Rangers from 1776–1782. He was at the Battle of Ramseur's Mill, where his cousin James Houston was injured.[5]

Christopher was instrumental in establishing Iredell County in 1788 and the county seat in Statesville in 1789. He recognized the need for a town in the northern end of the county on Hunting Creek, so he founded Houstonville in 1789, where he was the first postmaster. He moved to Maury County, Tennessee, in 1815 and was buried at the Houston Family Cemetery in Marshall County, Tennessee. Christopher was a Presbyterian.[31, 32, 33, 34]

Nichols Family

Capt. Jacob Nichols (1740–Apr 20, 1797) appears in Capt. Jacob Nichols's District in the Tax List of 1778 with property assessed at 1,656 pounds.[1] Jacob lived just north of the South Yadkin River but had extensive land holdings in Iredell County, including 400 acres on Beaver Dam Branch of Hunting Creek, 640 acres on Little Dutchman's Creek, 640 acres on the big branch of Hunting Creek, 150 acres on the south side of the South Yadkin River, 400 acres on Hunting and Rocky Creek, 133 acres on the south side of the South Yadkin River, 640 acres on the South Yadkin River, another 420 acres on the South Yadkin River, and 150 acres on the south side of the South Yadkin River issued between 1784 and 1789.[3] There was a Nicholson Mill on Little Hunting Creek.

During the American Revolution, Jacob was a captain under Col. Griffith Rutherford in the Rowan County Regiment from 1776 to 1781. He was engaged in several battles, including Great Cane Brake in South Carolina, Snow Campaign in South Carolina, Cherokee Expedition in 1776, Brier Creek in Georgia, Ramseur's Mill, Camden in South Carolina, Shallow Ford, Cowan's Ford, and Tarrant's Tavern.[5] Jacob was killed by one of his slaves in 1797. He was an elder of the Bethany Presbyterian Church and is believed to be buried at the Old Fourth Creek Cemetery, although no headstone has been identified.[35]

Captain Joshua Nichols (Jul 10, 1758–Sep 7, 1841) was the son of Jacob Nichols. Joshua appears in Capt. Nichols's District in the 1778 Tax List with property assessed at 214 pounds.[1] Joshua served as a captain in the Rowan County Regiment under his father, Jacob Nichols.[5] In 1780, he served in the Mecklenburg County Regiment. In Sep 1780, he served as a private in the North Carolina State Cavalry, Western District. He also served as a captain in a South Carolina unit. He acquired a land grant in Tennessee and moved west after 1810 and died near French Lick in Orange County, Indiana.[36]

Joshua Nichols Sr. (abt. 1710–Sep 30, 1793) appears in Capt. Nichols's District in the Tax List in 1778 with property assessed at 783 pounds.[1] He was born in England and was the father of Capt. Jacob Nichols. He moved to Rowan County in about 1751.[9]

General Griffith Loch Rutherford

General Griffith Loch Rutherford (1721–Aug 10, 1805) was born in Ireland, and his family was originally from Scotland. His parents died in 1739 on the voyage to America or shortly thereafter. His relatives raised him in Pennsylvania, where he learned how to survey land before he came to Rowan County in 1753. In 1756, he bought 960 acres of land in Rowan County on the South Fork of Grants Creek, about 7 miles southwest of Salisbury.[3] He began his extensive military career in 1760 in the North Carolina Colonial Militia during the French and Indian War, where he obtained the rank of captain. He participated in the battle at Fort Dobbs in 1760. He embraced the cause against the rebels during the Regulator Movement and commanded a local militia that participated in the Battle of Alamance. During the American Revolution, he was commissioned as a colonel on Sep 9, 1775, over the Rowan County Regiment of Militia, then the 1st Salisbury District Minutemen. The State of North Carolina promoted him to brigadier general on May 4, 1776, as commander of the Salisbury District Brigade of Militia, which included 17 militia regiments. On Aug 16, 1780, the British captured him at the Battle of Camden. They exchanged him for British prisoners on Jun 14, 1781.[37, 38]

According to a biography by the North Carolina Revolutionary War scholar, J. D. Lewis, "Griffith Rutherford was a man of strong character, resolute and determined, and of unusual capacity, and early in life attained a position of prominence. He was a member of the Colonial Assembly as early as 1769, and about that time he was also sheriff of Rowan County. He was in the Colonial Assembly of 1770 and 1771, and at the same time was a captain of the militia. He continued to represent his county in the Assembly, and was a member of

Legislature of 1773 and 1774. In 1775 he was elected a member of the Provincial Congress, and was appointed a member of the Rowan County Committee of Safety and colonel of militia. He was in all the subsequent Provincial Congresses and assisted in forming the State Constitution. For years he was one of the most prominent men in North Carolina."[35]

In 1792, Griffith Rutherford moved to Sumner County, Tennessee, where he acquired nearly 13,000 acres of land in the Washington District, which is now Sumner County, Tennessee. Upon the organization of the territory of the United States south of the Ohio River, in 1794, President Washington appointed Griffith Rutherford as a member of the Legislative Council, and he was chosen as president of that body. He died in Sumner County, Tennessee, but the location of his burial site is not known. In 1946, a memorial to General Griffith Rutherford was erected in the Murfreesboro public square in Rutherford County, Tennessee.[36]

Griffith Rutherford was a surveyor in Rowan County and signed the North Carolina land grant surveys in Rowan County referenced in this book in the 1780s. The name Rutherford appears as a middle name in several Campbell descendants. Additionally, Rutherfordton and Rutherford County, North Carolina, and Rutherford County, Tennessee, were so named after Griffith Rutherford.

Capt. William Sharp

Capt. William Sharp (Dec 13, 1742–Jul 6, 1818) appears in Capt. Nichols's District in 1778 with property assessed at 2,496 pounds.[2] William Sharp's home was just north of Snow Creek. His land holdings were extensive in Rowan County and Iredell County.[3] He was a member of the Rowan County Committee of Safety that met before the American Revolution to plan for independence. He was a lawyer, politician, and delegate to the Continental Congress from Rowan County. There was a Sharp mill on the South Yadkin River near his home. He served as a captain from 1780–1781 in the Rowan County Regiment. His brothers James Sharp (1751–1828) and John Sharp (1744–1812) appeared on Capt. Nichols's Tax List with property assessed at 1,738 and 942 pounds, respectively. Another brother, Joseph Sharp, was in Capt. Morrison's District with property assessed at 862 pounds. All four brothers served in the Rowan County Regiment and were all buried at the Snow Creek Methodist Church.[39] See Figure 2.2 for the location of his land.

Thomas Cadet Young

Thomas Cadet Young (1733–1829) moved to Hunting Creek in 1778. His land holdings included 900 acres on the south side of Hunting Creek at the forks issued in 1783, 320 acres on branches of Hunting Creek at the head of Rocky Branch and Owen's Branch, 720 acres on Long Branch of Hunting Creek issued in 1787, and 640 acres on the north side of Hunting Creek issued in 1783 as assignee of Josias Norris (all in Rowan County), as well as 248 acres on the south side of Hunting Creek issued in Iredell County in 1799.[3] Thomas's sons Francis and John May Young were known to John Campbell, son of Adam Campbell.[40] During the American Revolution, Thomas Young and eight of his neighbors formed an association to

FIGURE 2.3 Young Family Cemetery near Houstonville and Thomas Cadet Young's headstone.

manufacture gunpowder for home consumption. Young's great log home was said to have been a meeting place for Whigs, and he was hated intensely by the Tories, who conspired to kill the nine men in the powder-making enterprise. Thomas was buried in the Young Family Cemetery (Figure 2.3). Many of the family headstones are in a haphazard cemetery, just north of Houstonville in Iredell County. [41, 42]

CHAPTER 2 REFERENCES

1. 1778, "List of Taxable Property in the County of Rowan, North Carolina, Anno 1778," transcribed from several lists returned by August Term anno domini 1778, by Adlai Osborne, clerk of court, Indexed by Annie Walker Burns, Washington, D.C.

2. 2004, *Rowan County, North Carolina Tax Lists, 1758/1759, 1761, 1768, 1778, 1779*; compiled by John D. and E. Diane Stemmons, published by Census Publishing, LC, Sandy, Utah.

3. "NC Land Grant Images and Data," NC historical Records Online, created by David McCorkle in 2014, https://www.nclandgrants.com, access date various times in 2023 and 2024.

4. 1976, *Iredell Piedmont County*, by Homer M. Keever, published for the Iredell County Bicentennial Commission by Brady Printing Company; mills, pages 149, 113, 130, 154; Williamsburg, page 180.

5. "The American Revolution in North Carolina," online database, https://www.carolana.com/NC/Revolution/revolution_patriot_troops_nc.html, access date: Feb 25, 2025; "Rowan County Regiment of Militia," by J. D. Lewis, Wikipedia, https://en.wikipedia.org/wiki/Rowan_County_Regiment, access date: Feb 25, 2025.

6. 1790, U.S. Federal Census, Iredell County, North Carolina; page 396: Elizabeth Campbell, x12xxx; Penniful Campbell, 11xxx; William Campbell, 111xxx; Theophilus Morgan Jr., 123x1; Reubin Morgan, 123x2; Martin Morgan, 113xx; William Ball, 121xxx; page 397: John Dobbins, 2xxx6; James Cast, 135xx; Elijah Cast, 111xx.

7. 1989, *Some Pioneers from Wilkes County, N.C.*, compiled by Mrs. W. W. Absher, Southern Historical Press, ISBN 0–8308–644–4, page 137, Bowman Cast.

8. Some genealogists speculated that William Ball Jr. may have had a middle name of Silas, but no sourcing has been found.

9. 1790, U.S. Federal Census, Iredell County, North Carolina; page 396: Elizabeth Campbell, x12xxx; Penniful Campbell, 11xxx; William Campbell, 111xxx; Theophilus Morgan Jr., 123x1; Reubin Morgan, 123x2; Martin Morgan, 113xx; William Ball, 121xxx; page 397: John Dobbins, 2xxx6; James Cast, 135xx; Elijah Cast, 111xx.

10. "Find a Grave," Bethany Presbyterian Church Cemetery, headstones, Iredell County, North Carolina.

11. 1784–1787 North Carolina State Census, Wilkes County, Capt. Gordon's District, Isham Harvell, John Campbell, Abraham Cook, Joshua Mise.

12. "Find a Grave," Graham Cemetery; Walkertown, Hardin County, Tennessee; headstone, Memorial ID: 59836588, Isom Harrell.

13. 1790, U.S. Federal Census, Wilkes County, North Carolina; Martha Mise, 2 free white females.

14. 1768, "North Carolina, U.S., Compiled Census and Census Substitutes Index, 1790–1890," Rowan County, North Carolina, This appears to be an error in the ancestry database. Theophilus Morgan is not listed in the 1768 Tax List. See reference 2 for a more accurate list.

15. Feb 13, 1807, "North Carolina Wills and Probate Records, 1665–1998," Iredell County, page 912: Probate records of Theophilus Morgan, wife Catherine, son Reuben Morgan, witnessed by James Mehaffey and Perciphull Campbell, copy dated May 30, 1807.

16. Aug 6, 1784, "Rowan County, North Carolina Marriage Bonds," Theophilus Morgan Jr. and Ruth Owens, reel 21, page 1999, bond no. 000128014.

17. "The American Revolution in North Carolina," online database, by J.D. Lewis; Theophilus Morgan, Private in the Mecklenburg County Regiment in 1780 under Col. William Lee Davidson, lived in Rowan County.

18. "The American Revolution in North Carolina," online database, by J.D. Lewis, "Reuben Morgan" under Capt. Alexander Brevard, 1st and 3rd North Carolina Regiments.

19. "Loyalists in the Southern Campaign of the Revolutionary War," vols. 1 and 5, North Carolina Loyal-

ists, PRO T50, pages 362, 615, Ancestry.com, Basil Owens and his son, William Owens.

20. 1810, U.S. Federal Census, Iredell County, North Carolina, Bethsheba Owens; Pleasant Owens.

21. *Records of the Moravians in North Carolina*, vol. IV: 1780–1783, page 1675, Daniel Rash from Hunting Creek, wounded militiamen.

22. Usually spelled as "Redman," but "Redmond" occurs occasionally. Redman is used for consistency.

23. 1927, *The Old Free State: A Contribution to the History of Lunenburg County and Southside Virginia*, page 218, vol 1; by Landon Covington Bell; Richmond, Virginia, The William Byrd Press, Inc.

24. 1976, *Iredell Piedmont County*, by Homer M. Keever, published for the Iredell County Bicentennial Commission by Brady Printing Company; mills, pages 149, 113, 130, 154; Williamsburg, page 180.

25. "The American Revolution in North Carolina," online database, by J. D. Lewis, "James Brandon," https://www.carolana.com/NC/Revolution/patriot_leaders_nc_james_brandon.html, access date Jan 12, 2024.

26. "Find a Grave," Thyatira Presbyterian Church Cemetery, headstone, Mill Bridge, Rowan County, Memorial ID: 22487627, James Brandon.

27. Apr 8, 1794, *Wilkes County, North Carolina, Deed Book B-1*, Office of the Register of Deeds, page 444, Benjamin Herndon.

28. 1961, *The Herndon and Connor Families, Kith and Kin*, by Rita Jones Elliott, pages 9–12.

29. 2024, "Wilkes County Regiment, North Carolina Militia," by J. D. Lewis, https://www.carolana.com/NC/Revolution/nc_wilkes_county_regiment.html, access date Jan 2, 2024, Benjamin Herndon, Joseph Herndon, John Morgan.

30. 1902, *Historical Sketches of Wilkes County*, by John Crouch, Wilkesboro, North Carolina, https://tile.loc.gov/storage-services/public/gdcmassbookdig/historicalsketch01crou/historicalsketch01crou.pdf, access date Jan 1, 2024

31. 2024, "Houstonville, North Carolina," Wikipedia, https://en.wikipedia.org/wiki/Houstonville,_North_Carolina, access date Jan 2, 2024.

32. 2024, "Find a Grave," Houston Cemetery, Marshall County, Tennessee, Memorial ID: 6779539; Capt. Christopher Houston.

33. 1988, "Houston, Christopher," by Elaine Doerschuk, Revised by Jared Dease, Government and Heritage Library, Dec 2022, NCPedia, https://www.ncpedia.org/biography/houston-christopher.

34. 1820, U.S. Federal Census, Maury County, Tennessee; "Find a Grave," Houston Cemetery, Marshall County, Tennessee, Memorial ID: 6779539, headstone, Capt. Christopher Houston.

35. 1906, *Jacob Nichols Biography,* by Ephalet Nichols, descendant of Jacob Nichols, Genealogical Society of Iredell County.

36. 1841, "Find a Grave," Nichols Cemetery, Orange County, Indiana; Memorial ID: 215449288; headstone, Joshua Nichols.

37. "Griffith Rutherford" biography, by J. D. Lewis, https://www.carolana.com/NC/Revolution/patriot_leaders_nc_griffith_rutherford.html, access date Jan 12, 2024.

38. "Griffith Rutherford," Wikipedia, url: https://en.wikipedia.org/wiki/Griffith_Rutherford, access date Jan 12, 2024.

39. 1994, *William (Lawyer Billy) Sharpe*, by Jerry C. Cashion, 1994, revised by Jared Dease, Government and Heritage Library, Jan 2023, NCPedia, https://www.ncpedia.org/biography/sharpe-william-lawyer.

40. Apr 8, 1833, "Revolutionary War Widows Pension Application for John Campbell, W-6616," transcribed by C. Leon Harris, https://revwarapps.org/w6616.pdf, access date Apr 14, 2025.

41. 1985, "The Young Family of Bristol," by Walter Jorgensen Young, Library of Congress Photoduplication Service, Washington, D.C., published by Charles A. Carmichael, Fredericksburg, VA, Michael Cadet Young, https://www.seekingmyroots.com/members/files/G007680.pdf, access date Jun 17, 2025, pages 7–18.

42. Nov 20, 1947, *Statesville Daily Record*, Statesville, North Carolina, page 2, "Iredell Disputes Kentucky's Claim as Scout's Birthplace."

CHAPTER 3
ANCESTRY OF ADAM CAMPBELL

The oral family history incorporated into the 1925 Campbell Family Reunion *History of the Campbell Family* handout by H. P. Vanhoy states that Adam Campbell was Scotch-Irish.[1] *Scotch-Irish* is a term used primarily in the United States to refer to American descendants of Ulster Protestants who emigrated from Ulster (Ireland's northernmost province) to America during the 18th and 19th centuries. Their Scotch-Irish ancestors had originally migrated to Ulster mainly from the Scottish Lowlands and Northern England in the 17th century. Adam Campbell may have been one of the over 200,000 people who emigrated from Ulster to the original 13 American colonies from 1710 to 1775. The largest number of these emigrants landed in Pennsylvania. From that base, some went south into Virginia, the Carolinas, and across the South with a large concentration in the Appalachian region.[2]

Among the few surviving written records from the early 1700s in Scotland, there is one that shows a birth of an "Adam Campbell." This record lists Adam Campbell, son of Rogur (probably Roger) Campbell (birth and death dates unknown), born in rural Burnside of Balhaldie, just north of the medieval town of Dunblane, currently in the Stirling Council Area, Scotland, on Aug 30, 1735, and christened in the local parish on Aug 31, 1735.[3] Rogur Campbell also had a son Colin Campbell, born in 1742. Rogur did not leave a will that has been found. Currently, the record mentioned here is the only record that shows a birth date for an Adam Campbell that would be consistent with our Adam Campbell. However, no genealogical records have been found, to date, that would confirm a connection to the Adam Campbell who came to Rowan County, North Carolina, from Culpeper County, Virginia, in 1774.

Known Adam Campbell male descendants started a DNA research effort in 2024 to identify the ancestry of the Adam Campbell who came to North Carolina in 1774. The goal of this DNA research was to search for connections to Adam Campbell in early Campbells in colonial and post-colonial America, as well as Campbells in Scotland, Ireland, and England in ancient and modern times. FamilyTreeDNA performed testing and analysis of these DNA samples for both autosomal DNA (atDNA) and Y chromosome DNA (Y-DNA).[4]

AUTOSOMAL DNA RESULTS

Analysis of the atDNA from direct descendants of Adam Campbell reflects the DNA of both parents of the test taker, and therefore does not directly show Adam Campbell's ancestry. The atDNA test looks at chromosome pairs 1–22 and the X part of the 23rd chromosome. Many descendants of Adam Campbell, both male and female, have taken atDNA tests. The analysis of these tests shows a heritage that is similar to people who have taken atDNA tests and have a documented genealogy in the area of Scotland and surrounding countries. Figure 3.1 shows the origins from atDNA of one of Adam Campbell's descendants.[4]

These atDNA results can show relationships with other modern-day atDNA test takers. The atDNA analysis

FIGURE 3.1 Heritage of Adam Campbell's descendants based on atDNA, FamilyTreeDNA.com.

of Adam Campbell descendants revealed connections among close relations in modern times, i.e., first, second, and even third cousins, but it did not show relations for known fifth cousins. Identification of more distant and ancient ancestry requires Y-DNA from male descendants.

Y-DNA RESULTS

Scotland is not a unitary country in terms of ancient ethnicity. It is a multiethnic mosaic of at least five "ancient" lineages (original Pictish-Brythonic, Strathclyde Britons, Irish Gaels, Northumbrian Angles, and Norse). It is expected that the Y-DNA testing would help in identifying related Campbells or ruling out unrelated Campbell lines. Y-DNA analysis might also find matches to distant common ancestors of Adam Campbell, even before the Campbell surname was used or firmly established in male lines.[5]

The Y chromosome is one of 23 chromosomes found in the nucleus of cells. The Y chromosome is found exclusively in males and is transmitted in male individuals from one generation to the next almost without any change. Over time, however, the Y chromosome can accumulate one or more mutations that, while typically harmless and not affecting a man's health, can be determined by testing and can be useful for genealogical analysis. The two types of Y-DNA tests for genealogical analysis are Y-STR (short tandem repeat) and Y-SNP (single-nucleotide polymorphism) tests.[6]

The Y-STR tests the sequences between 12 and 111 (and sometimes even more) very short segments of Y-DNA at locations all along the Y chromosome. Certain sections of the DNA show a pattern of repeats in these markers, and the values for these markers indicate the number of repeating sequences. STRs mutate fairly frequently and are not permanent. Initially, a person's haplotype is inferred from atDNA and STR results compared to the results of other testers. Testers with similar haplotypes form a haplogroup. False matches can occur between two men with the same STR values by chance. The Y-SNP test helps to establish or confirm relationships and refine the haplogroup. A haplogroup is a name assigned to a singular parent at some point in time, beginning with the first humans. These haplogroups link back to previous haplotypes that trace back in time and eventually to the original human haplogroup.[6]

The Big Y-SNP test examines hundreds of thousands of single spots along the Y chromosome, allowing for a much higher resolution than STR tests. This test is used to provide additional information about more distant relationships between two individuals that expands on what is provided by atDNA and Y-STR tests. The Big Y-SNP test helps to confirm haplogroups within the time frame indicated by genealogical records. Unique permanent SNP mutations occur in every male line every 83 years on average.[6] In the course of the Adam Campbell Y-DNA project, a common haplotype was identified in the STR and SNP markers from four participants in the project with Big Y test results, which resulted in the new Haplogroup R-FTG6688.[4]

The Adam Campbell Y-DNA Project initiated in 2024 started with Y-DNA from four known male descendants of Adam Campbell using the genetic testing company Family-TreeDNA. The results are included in the Campbell Clan Society of North America DNA Project hosted by FamilyTreeDNA.com.[7] Comparisons to other male Y-DNA test takers using FamilyTreeDNA.com resulted in identifying additional previously unknown people related to Adam Campbell through unique Y-DNA signatures of known Adam Campbell descendants.[4]

The FamilyTreeDNA.com service provided matches of the STR and SNP results of known descendants of Adam Campbell to other test takers. Each test taker also provided genealogical research based on the earliest known ancestors (EKA), which are used to document connections to Adam Campbell. The resulting Y-DNA matches for nine test takers' Kits are included in the FamilyTreeDNA.com Clan Campbell Society of North America DNA Project and now form "Group R1b1-group79" of this project.

The results for 15 Y-DNA matches to Adam Campbell descendant test taker Kit 1 are shown in Table 3.1. The test taker of DNA Kit Number 1 in Table 3.1 has **Adam Campbell** (1.0) as the earliest known ancestor (EKA) and is a descendant of the **John D. Campbell** (1.6.4.2.3) branch of the Adam Campbell family. Kit numbers 1, 5, 6, and 10 established the new haplogroup, R-FTG6688, using SNP results. Other Kits that are also STR and/or SNP matches are also shown in Table 3.1. The Kits are in order of the most recent common ancestor (TMRCA) based on Kit 1's branch of the family. The first 10 Kits were all for an EKA that had the last name of Campbell and were within a genetic distance (GD) of five. The other six Kits had other EKA last names and were within a GD of between 8 and 10. In some cases,

TABLE 3.1 Results of Y-DNA Analysis of Adam Campbell Descendants and Matches

No., Kit, Relation	EKA	Test Type	Haplogroup	Branch of Family	GD STR Diff, SNP Variants	TMRCA (Actual A); (Predicted P)
1: 1019917, self	Adam Campbell (1.0)	Big Y	R-FTG6688	John D. Campbell, 1.6.4.2.3	0, self	1874–1940 A; Self
2: 1019912, 2nd cousin	Adam Campbell (1.0)	Y-111	R-Z253	John D. Campbell, 1.6.4.2.3	1, 0 of 111, NA	1874–1940, A; 1700–1900, P
3: 1019913, 2nd cousin	Adam Campbell (1.0)	Y-67	R-Z253	John D. Campbell, 1.6.4.2.3	1, 1 of 37, NA	1874–1940, A; 1600–1900, P
4: unk., 2nd cousin	Adam Campbell (1.0)	Y-37	R-M269	John D. Campbell, 1.6.4.2.3	1, 1 of 37, NA	1874–1940, A; 1600–1950, P
5: 1021127, 5th Cousin	Adam Campbell (1.0)	Big Y	R-FTG6688	William Franklin Campbell, 1.6.1.1.2	3, 2 of 111, 3	1767–1853, A; 1600–1900, P
6: 962242, TBD	David Campbell	Big Y	R-FTG6688	Grover Cleveland Campbell	3, 3 of 111, 3	1600–1900, P
7: 1020661, TBD	David Campbell	Y-111	R-M269	Grover Cleveland Campbell	4, 2 of 111, NA	1500–1850, P
8: 163152, 5th cousin, 1× removed	Theophilus Marion Campbell (1.8.0)	Y-37	R-M269	Guy Newton Campbell, 1.8.2.11.2	4, 4 of 37, NA	1735–1779, A; 650–1700, P
9: 743553, 5th cousin	Adam Campbell (1.0)	Y-67	R-Z253	William Rutherford Campbell,1.6.8	5, 5 of 67, NA	1767–1853, A; 900–1750, P
10: 971469, 5th cousin, 1× removed	Simon Campbell (1.8.2.X)	Big Y	R-FTG6688	John Otis Campbell, 1.8.2.X.10	5, 4 of 111, 6	1735–1779, A; 1450–1800, P
11: 427341, distant	William Clark, Scotland	Big Y	R-BY118534	John Sinclair Clarke, born in Scotland, died in USA; Distant Scottish ancestor	8, 7 of 111, 13	1450–1800, P
12: 906708, distant	Robert William Coates, Sr. (1600–1759), England	Y-111	R-M269	William Peter Couts, (1781–1865), Ohio Distant ancestor	8, 8 of 111, NA	1100–1700, P
13: 188952, 911161, distant	James W. Waddle/ Waddell (1842–1915). b. Tennessee d. Texas	Y-67 /Y-111	R-Z253	Distant ancestor	9, 15 of 67, NA	950–1650, P
14: 961774, distant	John Dew (1636–1678)	Y-111	R-M269	Distant ancestor	9, 7 of 111, NA	950–1650, P
15: 4151, distant	John Callum aka McGregor	Big Y	R-BY62134	Distant Scottish ancestor	10, 10 of 111, 13	377–912, P
16: 1013476, distant	Daniel Guynn, USA	Big Y	R-BY96356	Distant Scottish ancestor	14, 3 of 111, 28	622–1114, P

Kits that are matches have not yet been included in the Campbell Y-DNA project because the surname is not Campbell.[4, 7]

The information in columns one, two, three, and five comes directly from input from the test takers and traditional genealogy analysis.

❖ Column one shows the FamilyTreeDNA.com "Kit Number" (when known), and relationship to Tester 1 from genealogical sources (when known).

❖ Column two shows the EKA that was specified by the test taker.

❖ Column three shows the Y chromosome "Test Type" that was done for the test taker. The abbreviation indicates the number of Y-DNA STR markers that were analyzed, e.g., Y-111, 111 markers; Y-67, 67 markers; and Y-37, 37 markers. Big Y tests included 700 STR markers, as well as analysis of SNP. There are four Big Y test takers in this match list with the last name of Campbell.

❖ Column five shows the "Branch of Family" of Adam Campbell or other EKA that the test taker falls into when known from documented genealogies. The d'Aboville number in the Adam Campbell family line is indicated when known.

Columns four, six, and seven show the results of Y-DNA STR and SNP analysis of matches compared to test taker number 1.

❖ Column four shows the haplogroup calculated for the test taker's Kit, based on atDNA and/or Y-DNA SNP. Four of the seven Big Y testers, including Kit 1, resulted in a haplogroup of R-FTG-6688.

❖ Column six shows information compared to test taker number one: the predicted GD, the differences in the STR markers, and the number of non-matching SNP variants for Big Y test takers. The GD is based on the number of STR markers that were different from test taker number one for the first 111 STR markers. A GD is more precise when 111 STR markers are tested rather than only testing for 37 or 67 STR markers.

❖ Column seven shows the TMRCA from genealogical sources (actual) compared to test taker number 1 and from comparison to test taker number 1's Y-DNA STR results (calculated). The calculated date range is based on the number of STR markers tested and the GD with Kit 1. A GD of 8 or 9 is in the time frame of history when last names were not necessarily handed down from father to son, so some last names other than "Campbell" do appear. At a GD of 1 to 5, the last names are all "Campbell."

John D. Campbell

The test takers for Kits 1 to 4 all have the same great-grandfather, **John D. Campbell** (1874–1940) (1.6.4.2.3), who was a great-grandson of **Perciphull Campbell Sr.** (1767–1855) (1.6.0), i.e., they were second cousins of the test taker of Kit 1. The test taker for Kit 5 is a fifth cousin of the test taker for Kit 1 and he is descended from **Perciphull Campbell Sr.** (1.6.0). However, he was in a different branch of the family that moved to Arkansas before the U.S. Civil War. The SNP difference between Kits 1 and 5 is only 3 of 2,838 SNP markers (Z34141, FT259137, 5967996). Since SNP mutations occur once every 83 years on average, it is expected that there would be between two and three differences between the time that Adam Campbell was born in about 1735 and male descendants born in the 1940s and 1950s. See Chapter 9 for more details.

David Campbell

The results of the analyses for Kits 6 and 7 are significant because the relationship to Adam Campbell was not previously known. Both Kits have an EKA of David Campbell (abt. 1830–abt. 1880) and a TMRCA of Grover Cleveland Campbell (1892–1981). See Figure 3.2. The tester for Kit 6 is an uncle of the tester for Kit 7 and a third-generation descendant of David Campbell. Both Kits have a STR difference of 3 of 111 markers from Kit 1. Kit 6 has a Big Y test that resulted in only 3 SNP Variants (Z34141, BY29486, 6774976) from Kit 1. At a GD of 3 or 4, the predicted common ancestor for David Campbell and Adam Campbell existed sometime between 1650 and 1900 or 1500 and 1850 for Kits 6 and 7, respectively. The common ancestor was more likely than not living before 1767 and might have lived in North Carolina or Virginia.[8]

Grover Cleveland Campbell was one of 16 known children of Charles Edward Campbell Sr. (1866–1947) and Medora Belle "Dora" Cox (1870–1951). Charles and Dora were married on Jan 16, 1888, in Grayson County, Virginia, where all 16 children were born.[9] Charles's parents were David Campbell and Julia Snyder, according to Charles's death certificate.[10] Charles and both of his parents were born in North Carolina according to his death certificate, census records, and marriage registration. Charles had two siblings who were living at the time of his death, Emma (Snyder) Morris and Annie (Snyder) Boruff.[11] A search for

FIGURE 3.2
Grover Cleveland Campbell, abt. 1915, Halifax County, Virginia.

information about Charles before his marriage shows only a Charles E. Campbell, aged 13, working in a boarding house in Taylorsville Township, Alexander County, North Carolina, in June 1880.[12] Thus, Charles's father may have died before 1880 in North Carolina.

Theophilus Marion Campbell

The test taker for Kit 8 was a descendant of **Guy Newton Campbell** (1882–1916) (1.8.2.11.2), who was a great-grandson of **Theophilus Marion Campbell** (1777–abt. 1855) (1.8.0). Theophilus Marion Campbell was born in North Carolina in 1777 and moved to Madison County, Alabama, about the time of the War of 1812. Although this test was only a Y-37 Y-DNA test, it would be consistent with **Theophilus Marion Campbell** being a son or close relative of **Adam Campbell**. Unfortunately, this is an old test and cannot be enhanced to include more markers to confirm this relationship. The test taker was a Campbell and related to the Campbell spouse of an individual, Don Raney, who wrote a family history book that included a chapter on **Theophilus Marion Campbell's** family. Don Raney started the Y-DNA project for his Campbell family line on FamilyTreeDNA.com in the 1990s, but he died in 2020 before our Adam Campbell descendants were tested.[13] See Chapter 11 for more details about this family.

Simon Campbell

The test taker for Kit 10 is an African American Campbell descendant of John Otis Campbell (1886–1974) (1.8.X.10), who was a son of Simon Campbell (1840–1918) (1.8.2.X). His EKA, Simon Campbell, was born in 1840 in Mississippi and died in 1918 in Coffeeville, Yalobusha County, Mississippi. This Kit is only a GD of 5 from Kit 1 with a predicted common ancestor in the 1450–1800 time frame. The Y-DNA differences are only 4 of the first 111 STR markers, 1 of the next 6,161 STR markers, and 6 of 2,838 SNP markers (Z34141, Y6808, BY29486, 10129645, 19391151, 21315413). The most likely ancestor of Simon Campbell is **John Cook Campbell** (1802–aft. 1880) (1.8.2), who was the son of **Theophilus Marion Campbell** according to genealogical records. While there is some genealogical uncertainty, genealogical records and these Y-DNA results support the conclusion that Theophilus Marion Campbell was probably the youngest son of **Adam Campbell** and born in Rowan County after Adam Campbell moved to North Carolina in about 1774. Theophilus moved to Mississippi Territory (now Alabama) by 1810 and volunteered for the Mississippi Militia during the War of 1812. His son **John Cook Campbell**, born in North Carolina, moved with him to the Mississippi Territory. John Cook Campbell was a slave owner in Yalobusha County, Mississippi, and Simon Campbell was probably one of his slaves. The Big Y results for Simon Campbell most likely reflect his Y-DNA that he inherited from **Theophilus Marion Campbell's** descendants. See Chapter 11 for more details about this family.

William Clark

The test taker for Kit 11 is in the R-BY118534 Haplogroup and in the John Sinclair Clark (1887–1972) family line. John was born in Camelon (near Edinburgh), Scotland, on Aug 14, 1887. John migrated with his family from Scotland and arrived on the USS Columbus in New York on Jan 7, 1925. His father, William Clark (1855–1928), was born and died in Fifeshire, Scotland. William Clark's ancestors lived in Fifeshire, Scotland, since at least 1794. Adam Campbell and William Clark probably had a common ancestor sometime before 1735 in Scotland.[14] This Y-DNA analysis is the most definitive evidence to confirm Adam Campbell's ancient ancestral origins in Scotland.

HAPLOGROUP R-FTG6688

Haplogroup R-FTG6688 was formed when it branched off from the ancestor R-BY118534 and the rest of mankind around 1400. There are currently 4 Big Y-DNA testers (Testers 1, 5, 6, and 10) that fall into Haplogroup R-FTG6688. Figure 3.3 shows the probability of Haplogroup R-FTG6688's birth. The darker blue area indicates a 68% confidence interval (CI) that the R-FTG6688 ancestor lived between 1727 and 1877 with a mean of 1809, which is entirely consistent with the birth and death of Adam Campbell (1735–1779), as well as an ancestor of David Campbell.[7, 6]

Other Big Y test takers (Kits 11, 15, and 16) have a larger number of non-matching SNP variants (13, 13, and 28, respectively). Their common haplogroups are upstream of R-FTG6688 and existed in the Middle Ages, which is consistent with the different last surnames for people in this time period. These SNP results have helped to map out the Big Y Block Tree origins for Haplogroup R-FTG6688 and connect it in time with other haplogroups.

Figure 3.4 shows the Time Tree Path from Haplogroup R-BY62134 to the Big Y test takers in Table I. The test takers with other last names, John Callum McGregor (1735–1761), Daniel Guynn (1806–1887), and William Clark, have common ancestors prior to the modern age. Adam Campbell's line emerged in the modern age but may have connections to males in Scotland with different last names in the Middle Ages.

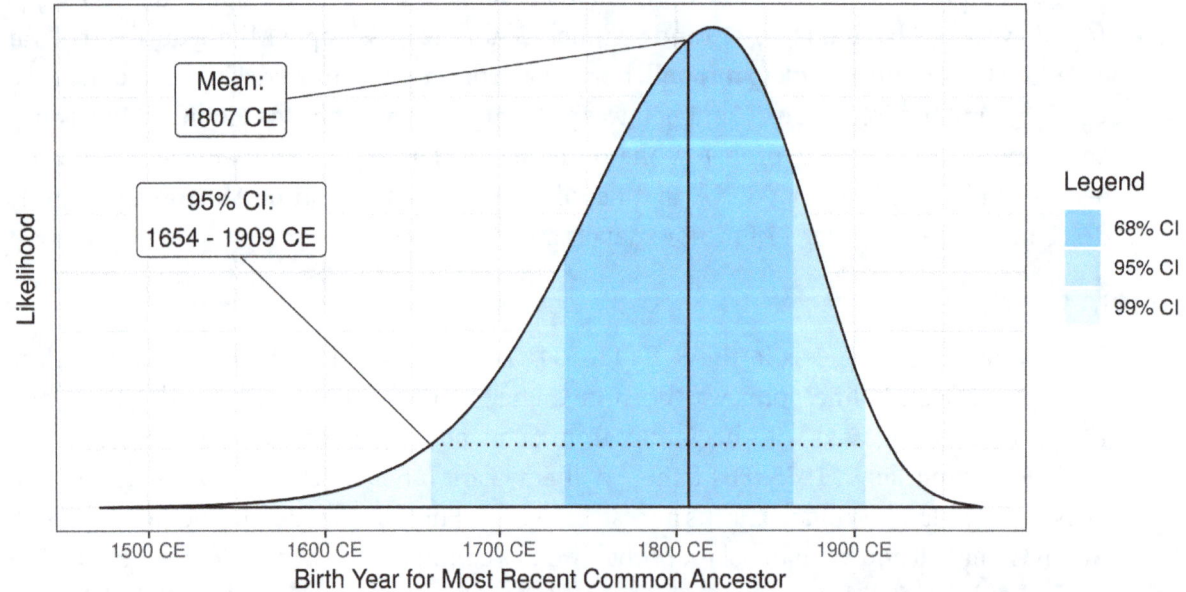

FIGURE 3.3 Haplogroup R-FTG6688 Probability of Birth Year.

TIME TREE PATH FROM R-BY62134 TO R-FTG6688
(Showing Kits 15, 16, 11, 1, 5, 6, and 10)

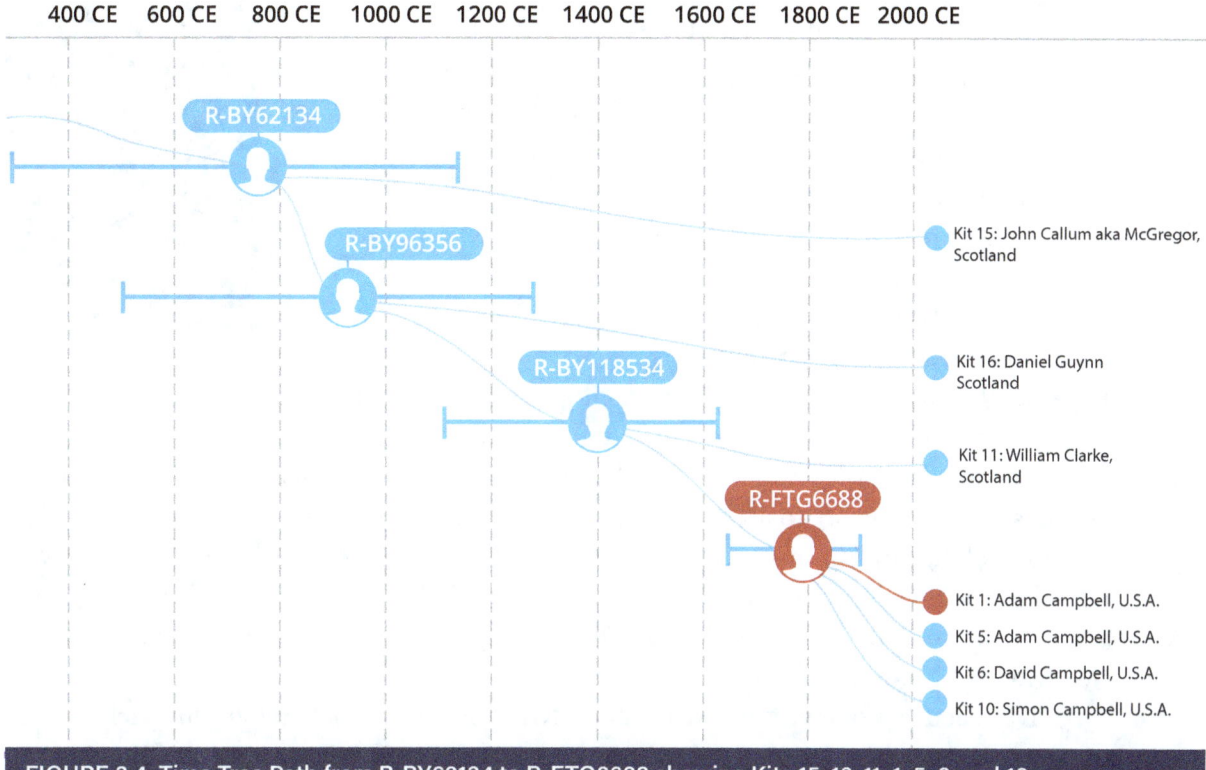

FIGURE 3.4 Time Tree Path from R-BY62134 to R-FTG6688 showing Kits 15, 16, 11, 1, 5, 6, and 10.

All human male lineages are traced back to a single common ancestor in Africa around 230,000 years ago, nicknamed Y-Adam. Mutations in the Y-DNA occurred over time with the migration path going through A, BT, CT, CF, F, GHIJK, HIJK, K, P, R and R-DF13 in the Metal Ages (about 2,500 BC) in the area of present-day England. From there, the haplogroup path goes to R-BY62134 in about year 700 in Scotland during the Middle Ages. The last 10 steps of the ancestral path of the R-FTG6688 Haplogroup shown in Table 3.2 forms a family tree of sorts.

The number of "Immediate Descendants" is the number of phylogenetic subclades, i.e., the number of known branches of the haplogroup formed by mutations of the Y-DNA. A large number indicates a rapid expansion event. The last column shows the number of tested modern descendants and ancient/archaeological samples that have been tested for the given-haplogroup. The people represented by the haplogroups in Steps 2 through 4 were living in Scotland in the Middle Ages.

The path of migration for Haplogroup R-DF13 and the location of ancient samples are shown in Figure 3.5. This Y-DNA SNP-based map tends to confirm the family history reported in the handout distributed at the Campbell Family Reunion in 1925 that Adam Campbell's ancestors were American Scotch-Irish. R-DF13 comprises over 99% of bearers of Haplogroup R-L21 or R1b1a2a1a2c, also known

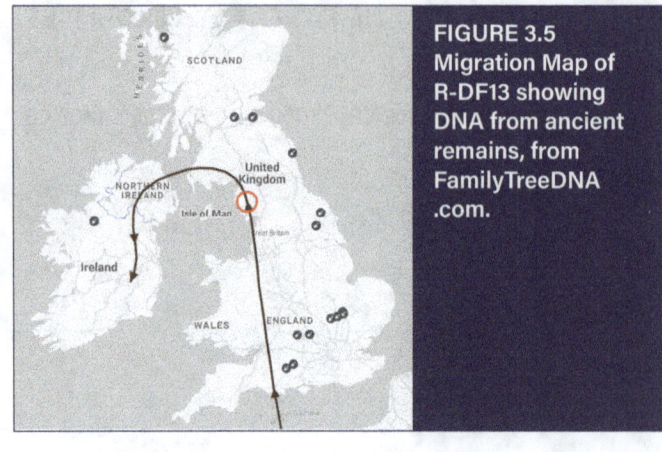

FIGURE 3.5
Migration Map of R-DF13 showing DNA from ancient remains, from FamilyTreeDNA .com.

as R-M529 or R-S145. R-DF13 is dominant among males in Ireland, Scotland, Wales, and Brittany, present in high frequencies in England and western France, and present also to a lesser extent in Iberia, Scandinavia, and the Low Countries. A subclade of R-DF13 (Z39589) includes "The House of Stuart," who ruled as kings of Scotland from 1371 and then, additionally, as kings of England and Ireland from 1603 until 1714. According to the Stewart DNA Project, they lie under the subclade R1b-L21 > DF13 > Z39589 > DF41/S524 > Z43690 > S775 > L746 > S781. This is as close as Adam Campbell's ancestors can get to being associated with royal Scottish heritage.[15]

Y-DNA analysis of modern and ancient DNA shows a path of haplogroups back to early man in the Stone Ages. Figure 3.6 shows the migration route for the ancestors of Haplogroup R-DF13, step 10, starting with Y-Adam (early Stone Age man), to step 45, in about 232,000 BCE.

TABLE 3.2 Ancestral Path of the F-FTG6688 Haplogroup

Steps	Haplogroup	Age Estimate	Immediate Descendants	Tested Modern, Ancient Descendants
1	R-FTG6688	1800 CE	3	3
2	R-BY118534	1400 CE	2	4
3	R-BY96356	900 CE	2	5
4	R-BY62134	700 CE	2	6
5	R-BY4303	1700 BCE	2	30
6	R-BY43439	2050 BCE	4	180
7	R-FGC3268	2300 BCE	5	912; 1
8	R-Z253	2400 BCE	12	11,787; 25
9	R-ZZ10_1	2500 BCE	7	16,349; 29
10	R-DF13	2500 BCE	12	75,898; 174

FIGURE 3.6 Migration Map for Haplogroup R-DF13, from FamilyTreeDNA.com.

CAMPBELL FAMILIES THAT WERE NOT RELATED TO ADAM CAMPBELL

Based on the haplogroups of the Y-DNA matches, several Campbell ancestors from Virginia and North Carolina are ruled out as having common ancestors within the past 500 years. The following are among the Campbell family lines that had very different haplogroups and lived near the same areas where Adam Campbell lived:

❖ Patrick Campbell (bef. 1700–bef. 1790), who owned 1,436 acres of land in the Beverly Manor in Augusta County, Virginia, in 1736, is not related in modern times to Adam Campbell.[16] Augusta was a large county in colonial Virginia, about 90 miles south of Culpeper County, Virginia. He is included in Campbell Y-DNA Project: R1b1-group30–050.[4]

❖ Other Campbells from Virginia in the 18th century, including both "Black" David and "White" David Campbell, were not related to Adam Campbell in modern times. They are included in two Campbell Y-DNA Projects: "R1b1-group30–050 FT66561," and "E-grp2 includes Black David Campbell of Augusta, Virginia and Campbells of Kishacoquillas Valley, Pennsylvania, Haplogroup E-CTS9320 and below."[4]

❖ Aeneas Campbell (1730–1812) of Montgomery County, Maryland, had a son Aeneas Campbell Jr. (1757–1828), who died in Iredell County and was buried at the New Hope Baptist Church in Iredell County. Their descendant's haplogroup is R-FTD38463. They are included in Campbell Y-DNA Project, Subgroup R1B1–30–011. The wife of one of their descendants, the late Esther Elizabeth (Gaither) Campbell, painted the picture of the Campbell Mill and bridge shown in Chapter 9.[4]

❖ There are other groups in the Campbell Y-DNA project that do not have common ancestors with Haplogroup R-FTG6688 after the beginning of the Middle Ages. This would include C, E, G, H, I, and J haplogroups.

CHAPTER 3 REFERENCES

1. Aug 1925, "Descendants of Pierce Campbell Hold Reunion," *Statesville Morning Register*, as well as a handout distributed at the reunion, *History of the Campbell Family*, compiled by H. P. Vanhoy, a descendant of Sarah Campbell, daughter of John R. Campbell, who married William A. Vanhoy.

2. 2023, "Scotch-Irish Americans," Wikipedia, https://en.wikipedia.org/wiki/Scotch-Irish_Americans, access date Dec 29, 2023.

3. 1735, Scotland Births and Baptisms, 156401950, Adam Campbell, born 30 Aug 1735, baptized 31 Aug 1735, Place: Dunblane, Perth Scotland, Household Members: Rogur Campbell, Adam Campbell, FHL Film No. 1040065, Publisher: Ancestry.com, Operations Inc., 2014.

4. FamilyTreeDNA.com, Family Finder, atDNA Origins, Y-DNA analysis, Kit numbers: 1019912, 1019913, 1019917, 1021127 in Clan Campbell Society of North America DNA Project, subgroup R1b1-group79; Kit numbers: 24159 and 982679 in subgroup R1b1-group30–011; Kit number: 11103 in R1b1-group30–50, https://discover.familytreedna.com/y-dna/R-FTG6688/story, access date Mar 2, 2025.

5. Nov 11, 2022, "Clans, Families and Kinship Structures in Scotland—An Essay," *Journal of Genealogy*, by Bruce Durie, https://www.mdpi.com/2313-5778/6/4/88, access date Mar 2, 2025.

6. 2016, *The Family Tree Guide to DNA Testing and Genetic Genealogy*, by Blaine T. Bettinger, Family Tree Books.

7. Campbell Clan Society of North America DNA Project, https://www.familytreedna.com/groups/campbell/about, access date Jan 22, 2025.

8. The EKA for Grover Cleveland Campbell was initially reported by descendants to be Alexander Campbell, who was born in 1767, either in Maryland or Virginia, and died between Mar 17 and Jun 5, 1845, in Highland County, Virginia. Recent genealogical analysis reveals that the EKA as David Campbell.

9. Jan 16, 1888, "Grayson County, Virginia Marriage Register," Charles Campbell (age 23, parents not given) and Frances D. Cox (age 21, parents Alex and Martha Cox), page 155, reg 2, page 58.

10. Mar 14, 1947, "Prince Edward County, Virginia, Death Records," Charles Edward Campbell (age 81), registration date: Mar 19, 1947, father David Campbell, mother Jula Snyder, spouse Dora Cox, certificate number 1947006989.

11. Mar 15, 1947, *Richmond Times-Dispatch*, page 7, obituary for C E Campbell with spouse Dora Cox Campbell.

12. June 1880, U.S. Federal Census, Taylorsville Township, Alexander County, North Carolina, page 26, dwelling 247, family 262, Milton Graham, head of household and boarding house

keeper; Barbary C. Graham, wife; Martha E. Graham, daughter, H Little, boarder and physician; Chas E. Campbell, bound, age 13, at work, born in North Carolina, both parents born in North Carolina.

13. 2013, *Raney Family History,* by Donald Raney, Garland, Texas, 2000, Chapter 27, "Descendents of Theophilus Marion Campbell," available through FamilySearch at https://www.family search.org/library/books/, identifier 2192061, access date Jan 22, 2025.

14. Jul 21, 1931, United States Petition for Citizenship no. 30168, John Clarke, Providence, Rhode Island, wife Annie, children Willaim, Annie S., and Margaret S.

15. "Haplogroup R-L21," Wikipedia, https://en.wikipedia.org/wiki/Haplogroup_R-L21, access date Mar 2, 2025.

16. 1954, "The Beverly Patent, 1736, including original grantees, 1738–1815 in Orange and Augusta Counties, Va.," compiled and drawn by J.R. Hildebrand, Patrick Campbell, D-8, https://www.usgenwebsites.org/vagenweb/augusta/Beverly Patent.html, access date Mar 2, 2025.

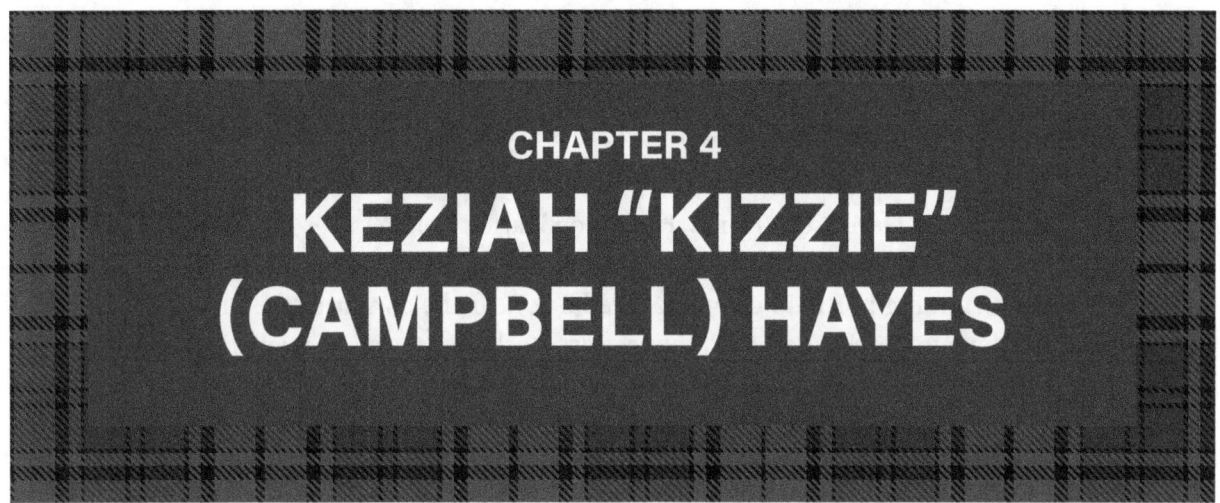

1.1 **Keziah "Kizzie (Campbell) Hayes** (Aug 1, 1755–Jun 1, 1845) was the oldest of the eight children of Adam Campbell (1735–1779) and **Elizabeth (Morgan) Campbell** (1735–1789) of Rowan and Iredell County, North Carolina. Keziah was born in Culpeper County, Virginia, and moved with her family to Rowan County in about 1775, where her first child was born.[1, 2] She married **Henry Hayes Sr.** (abt. 1750—bef. Feb 1805) in about Jun 1774 in Surry County. His last name is sometimes spelled as "Hays," but "Hayes" is most often used. Henry Hayes Sr. is sometimes referred to as *Henry Horne Hayes Sr.* It was uncommon to have a middle name in the 1700s. The references for Henry and his son Henry Hayes Jr. only state *Henry Hayes.* Horne could have been a nickname. It only appears on the tombstone of Henry Hayes Jr. at Liberty Baptist Church Cemetery in Wilkes County. This part of Surry County became Wilkes County in 1777. Kezia and Henry lived in Wilkes County near Osborn Creek, just north of the Rowan (later Iredell) County line (Figure 4.1). Only Kizzie Campbell and a husband named Hayes appeared in the notes from the 1925 *History of the Campbell Family* by H. P. Vanhoy.[3, 4, 5, 10, 12, 13]

Henry obtained and sold the following land in Wilkes County:[4, 5]

❖ Oct 14, 1779: NC Land Entry no. 1246, 100 acres lying on Osborn's Creek beginning at the county line (Wilkes and Iredell) and running down said creek.

❖ Mar 16, 1780: Land Entry no. 1718, 150 acres beginning at William Morgan's line on the south side of the little fork of Hunting Creek.

❖ Oct 21, 1797: Deed from Samuel Nickelson to Henry Hayes for 12 pounds, 100 acres on the west side of Osborn Creek beginning at a poplar at the mouth of a branch, running west 25 chains to a pine, north up the creek to the beginning, witnessed by William Mitchell, Charles Johnson.[6]

❖ Oct 27, 1797: Deed from Samuel Nickleson to Henry Hayes for 12 pounds, 100 acres on the west side of Osborn's Creek beginning at a white oak running south 6 chains to a red oak in Browning's line and Kell's line (adjacent to tract obtained on Oct 21, 1797).[7]

❖ Jan 26, 1799: Deed from Henry Hayes to James Weslock for 65 pounds, 100 acres on west side of Osborn's Creek beginning at a poplar at the mouth of a branch running west 26 chains to a post oak running south 37 chains to a black oak thence west 14 chains, Abel Nickleson's line, Joel Pendergrass's line.[8]

❖ Oct 23, 1799: Deed from Henry Hayes to Charles Coleman for 40 pounds, 35 acres on the west side of Osborne's Creek beginning at a white oak upon James Westlock's spring branch running north 40 chains to a red oak near the corner of the fence that formerly did belong to Joel Pendergrass, thence east 20 chains to a stake near the creek.[9]

In the 1790 U.S. Census, Henry was living in the 5th Company area of Wilkes County in a household with 1 free white male 16 years and upward (himself), 3 white males under 16, 4 free white females, and no slaves. In 1799, Henry had sold all the land he obtained and was probably living on land owned by Joshua Hayes on Bear Branch in Wilkes County. Henry and Keziah were early members of the Grassy Knob Baptist Church.[10] He died sometime before Feb 6, 1805, when his estate probate occurred. The inventory of his estate included one still with its utensils, 2 horses, 7 cattle, 21 hogs, 4 sheep, 13 geese, corn, bacon, 3 feather

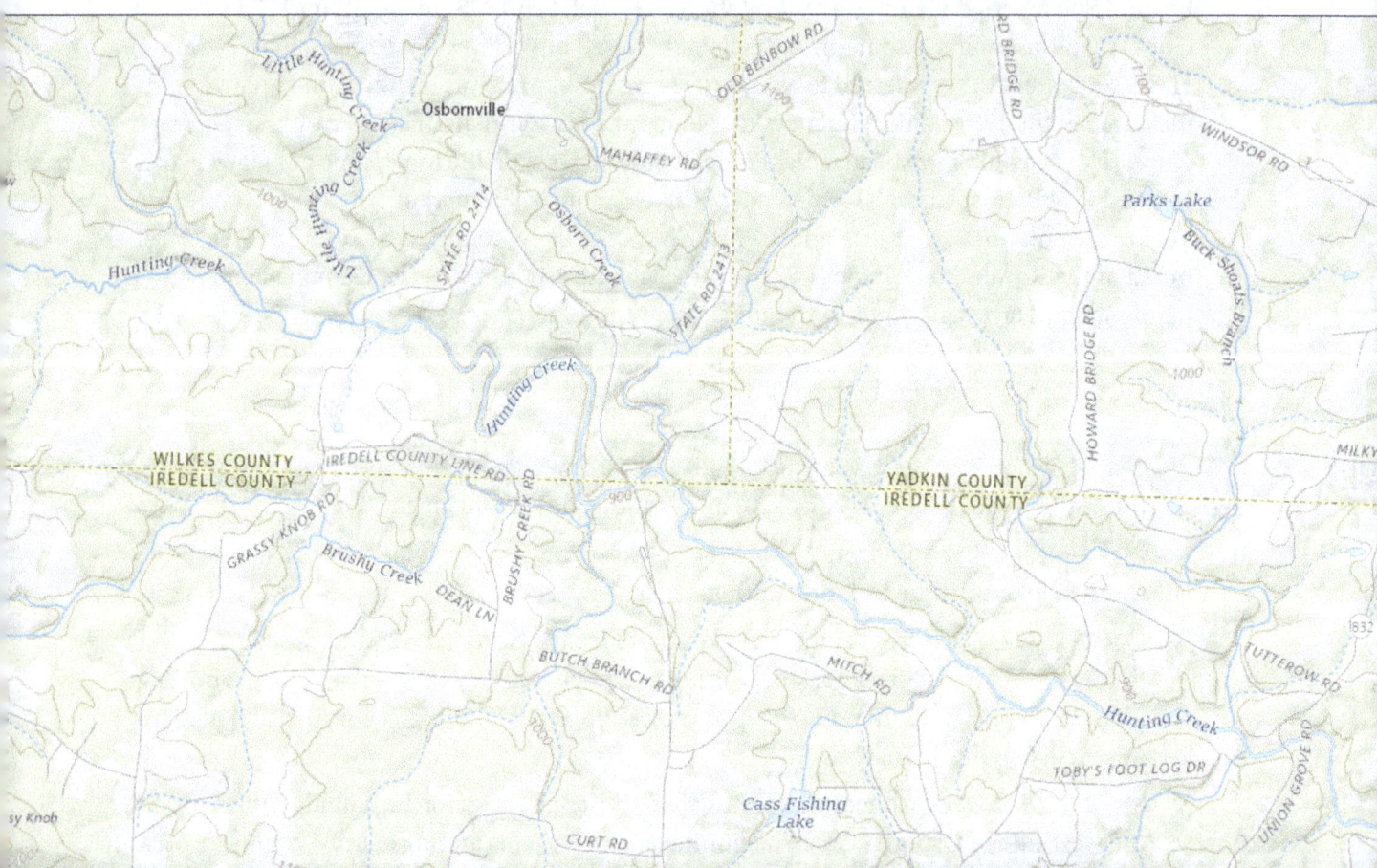

FIGURE 4.1 Current day map showing the area where Kiziah and Henry lived in Wilkes County near Osborn Creek, courtesy of Google Maps, Mar 30, 2025.

beds, 11 plates, 2 basins, 10 spoons, 7 tin cups, a set of knives and forks, an iron pot, a Dutch oven, a frying pan, 2 skillets, 1 Bible, 1 hymn book, 2 spelling books, 1 history book, sheep shears, tailor's sheers, and a long list of tools. Names mentioned in his estate included: Kezia Hayes (widow), Hartwell Hayes, Joshua Souther, Jonathan Hayes, Anthony Haden, John Stanley, John Marlow, Hix Combs, Archibald Loveless, Samuel Wilson, John Keaton, and Shadrach Stanley.[11, 14]

After 1830, Keziah moved to Hancock County, Indiana, where she died and probably is buried at the Hayes Cemetery in Hancock County.[12, 13, 14, 15, 16, 17, 18]

Keziah and Henry had 12 children, who were all born in Surry and Wilkes Counties. None of the children were mentioned in the *History of the Campbell Family* written in 1925.

JONATHAN HAYES

1.1.1   Jonathan Hayes (abt. 1775—aft. 1850) married Rachel Mitchel (1776–1860) on Oct 30, 1798, in Wilkes County.[2, 14, 19] Jonathan may have moved to Ketcher County, Kentucky, by 1850. Their children included the following:[20, 21]

1. Reubin Hayes Sr. (Dec 13, 1791–Nov 4, 1881), who married Tabitha Cornelius (Dec 30, 1800–Feb 16, 1852) in 1830 in Blount County, Alabama, where he was one of the original settlers. He later married Lucinda Thrasher (Jun 25, 1810–Jul 30, 1895) on Dec 26, 1852, in Marshall County, Alabama. Reuben was buried at the Little Cemetery in Houston, Winston County, Alabama. Tabitha was buried at the Hopewell United Methodist Church Cemetery in Blount County. Lucinda was buried at the Wesley Chapel United Methodist Church Cemetery in Lauderdale County, Alabama.[22]

2. Keziah Hayes (Jan 17, 1797–Dec 25, 1875), who married Thomas Gilbert Norris (Dec 25, 1793–Mar 14, 1884) in Jan 1813 in Wilkes County. They moved to Fentress County, Tennessee, before 1850, where they were buried at the Westfelt Cemetery.

SARAH HAYES

1.1.2   Sarah Hayes (1780–1855) married William Cary Mitchell Jr. (1778–1845) on Oct 30, 1798, in Wilkes County. This was a double wedding with her brother Jonathan. They lived near Brushy Mountain in Wilkes County.[23] Their children included:

1. Keziah Mitchell (Feb 2, 1800–Mar 1882), who married William Franklin Garris (1785–1833) in 1820 in Wilkes County. They had six sons and two daughters, including Uriah Samuel Garris (Nov 27, 1824–Feb 22, 1914) shown in Figure 4.2. William Garris was the owner of considerable land and other property in the state of North Carolina. In the year 1833, the family decided to move to Rush County, Indiana. Mrs. Garris brought the children to Rush County, while Mr. Garris stayed in North Carolina to dispose of his property and settle up his business before coming to Indiana to join his family. So,

Mrs. Garris, with her seven children, loaded in a one-horse wagon and made the entire trip and landed near Lewisville (on U.S. 40, Henry County, Indiana). After a long and tedious journey, they settled to await the arrival of her husband, who was expected to arrive within a few weeks. Before the time of his arrival, word was received that he was suddenly taken ill and died within 24 hours. Evidently, he was poisoned by someone who was interested in the settlement of his father's estate. His widow and her seven small children were without financial means, besides what she could make through her labor. No investigation was ever made by the family as to what became of the estate of her husband. She was left penniless and raised her children by her own manual labor. She never remarried and lived among her children until the time of her death in Hancock County.[24]

FIGURE 4.2 Uriah Samuel Garris, abt. 1900, Iowa.

2. John Henry Mitchell (Jun 15, 1804–Nov 9, 1892), who married Martha J. Bentley (May 1, 1809–Nov 29, 1850) on Aug 5, 1828, in Wilkes County. They moved to St. Francois County, Missouri. After Martha's death, he married Eglentine "Tinnia" Allen/Blackburn (Dec 10, 1820–Jun 21, 1883) on Jun 30, 1862, in St. Francois County, Missouri. Henry and both wives were buried at the Pendleton Cemetery in St. Francois County.

3. Rev. William Riley Mitchell (Mar 7, 1807–Apr 29, 1873), who moved to Macon County, Missouri. He married Mahala Thompson (Oct 14, 1812–Dec 16, 1852) on Jul 29, 1832, in Hardin County, Kentucky. He later married Martha Yoakum (Jan 11, 1807–Apr 20, 1873) on Aug 26, 1858, in Macon County, Missouri. According to family stories, Dr. Martha Yoakum was a well-known figure in the backwoods of Tennessee and Missouri. She was an old-time doctor, using herbs and Indian medicine to treat any and all people. She traveled the countryside on a mule, riding side-saddle on a beautiful

FIGURE 4.3 John Franklin Mitchell Sr., abt. 1910, Missouri.

hand-tooled saddle. One of William's children, John Franklin Mitchell (Jan 30, 1844–Jun 9, 1920), fought for the Union in Indiana during the U.S. Civil War (Figure 4.3).

4. Thomas Hicks Mitchell (May 11, 1808–Feb 2, 1897), who may have moved west and died in Jackson County, Oregon.

5. Rev. Hartwell Hayes Mitchell (Mar 25, 1816–Jan 24, 1884), who married Mary "Polly" Willis (Oct 4, 1818–Jan 19, 1877) on Aug 18, 1836, in Rush County, Indiana. They moved

to Missouri. After Mary died, Hartwell moved to Nebraska where his children had settled. Hartwell died in Harlan County, Nebraska, and was buried at the Republican City Cemetery. Mary died in Shelby County, Missouri, and was buried at the Pleasant Prairie Cemetery.

KEZIAH HAYES

1.1.3 Keziah "Kate" Hayes (Jun 1, 1782–Jun 2, 1866) married Thomas Hicks Combs (1783–bef. 1850) on Feb 3, 1801, in Wilkes County.[14,25] Their children were all born in Wilkes County. Theyp moved to Hancock County, Indiana, where Thomas died. Kate later moved to Monroe County, Iowa, before the Civil War with her oldest daughter, Sarah, and her son, Elias, and their families. Kate was buried at the Selection Cemetery in Monroe County Iowa.[26] Keziah and Thomas's children included:

1. William Thomas Combs (Jan 6, 1802–Sep 9, 1869), who married Asenath Ellis (Aug 8, 1800–Oct 19, 1880) on Jan 8, 1822, in Wilkes County. They died in Greene County, Indiana, and were buried at the Smith-Bethel Cemetery.

2. Sarah W. Combs (1804–1865), who married Jesse R. Anderson (1800–1870) in Wilkes County on Jan 1, 1822. Sarah died in Monroe County, Iowa, and was buried at the Allen Cemetery. Jesse died in Carroll County, Missouri, and was buried at the Trotter Cemetery.

3. Mary Margaret "Polly" Combs (Feb 18, 1807–May 1, 1894), who married John Jesse Souther (Jan 19, 1803–Feb 2, 1889) on Dec 7, 1824, in Wilkes County. They initially moved to Indiana but did not like the flat land there. Then, they moved to Alabama and later to Union County, Georgia, before 1836 for the free land there (Figure 4.4). They died in

FIGURE 4.4 John and Polly Souther's home, Union County, Georgia, built bef. 1857.

Union County, Georgia, and were buried at the New Liberty Cemetery where John had donated land for the church.

4. Nancy "Nanny" Combs (Jul 18, 1808–Aug 3, 1888) married Jabez Elza Hendren (Aug 4, 1805–Aug 27, 1888) on Mar 3, 1829, in Wilkes County (Figure 4.5). Their son, Jabez Elegy Hendren, died at the Battle of Gettysburg, while serving as a private with the 52nd North Carolina Infantry Regiment. Nancy and Jabez lived at the foothills of Brushy

(Left)
FIGURE 4.5 Jabez and Nanny Hendren, bef. 1888, Wilkes County.

(Right)
FIGURE 4.6 Hendren Mill on Rocky Creek.

Mountain in Wilkes County. Their Hendren Mill was located on Rocky Creek in Wilkes County (Figure 4.6). Nancy and her husband were buried at the Jabez Hendren Family Cemetery in Moravian Falls in Wilkes County.

5. Elizabeth Combs (Apr 23, 1814–Apr 26, 1839), who married Jehu "John" Hendren (Jan 17, 1809–Oct 13, 1888) on Jan 9, 1833, in Wilkes County. John's father, William Hicks Hendren Jr. (1779–Jan 7, 1868), ran the Hendren Mill on Rocky Creek near Brushy Mountain in Wilkes County (Figure 4.6). Elizabeth and John had a son, William Hicks Hendren (Jun 11, 1833–May 3, 1920), who lived in Arkansas and served as a captain with the 2nd Cherokee Mounted Volunteers, CSA, in Oklahoma during the U.S. Civil War. The Cherokee Volunteers were active in the Trans-Mississippi and Western Theaters and led by Brigadier General Stand Watie, the only Native American general in the Civil War.

FIGURE 4.7 Elizabeth Ann Steel, abt. 1900, California.

6. Jesse Combs (Jan 3, 1819–Oct 3, 1859), who left North Carolina and moved to Hancock County, Indiana, where he married Elizabeth Ann Steel (Nov 6, 1822–Jul 16, 1911) on Apr 1, 1841 (Figure 4.7). Jesse and Elizabeth left from there on May 5, 1852, for California by wagon train. It took them 5 months and 17 days to make the trip and they settled near Yreka, Siskiyou County, California. Jesse, in his letters from California, raved about the good farming and the cheap cost of goods. Jessie wrote in February 1854 that they had plenty to eat and plenty of gold—all they had to do was to dig it out of the ground. Gold had been discovered in Yreka in 1851. He was keeping a boarding house and digging gold, and he said that his average digging brought about five dollars a day, clear of all expenses. He died in Yreka, where he was buried at the City Cemetery. After Jesse's death, Elizabeth married Freeman Chandler (Sep 1828–Dec 10, 1900). She outlived both husbands and had at least 13 children.[27]

7. John Combs (Nov 9, 1821–Aug 18, 1900), who married Sarah Kennedy (Dec 13, 1832–Oct 6, 1900) on Jan 23, 1851, in Hancock County, Indiana. John was a farmer and moved with his parents to Hancock County between 1840 and 1850. John and Sarah were buried at the Hayes Cemetery in Hancock County.[18]

8. Jane Evelyn Combs (Feb 3, 1827–Jan 21, 1911), who married William Sparks McCray (May 29, 1824–Jul 20, 1878) on Dec 5, 1844, in Hancock County, Indiana. Jane and William died in Wilson County, Kansas, where they were buried at the Jackson Cemetery.

9. Elias Combs (Jul 11, 1830–Jan 12, 1871), who married Margaret R. Watson (Mar 4, 1837–May 18, 1883) on Jan 27, 1853, in Hancock County, Indiana. Elas was a captain in the Military Company of Monroe Township, Monroe County, Iowa, during the U.S. Civil War.

JAMES HAYES

1.1.4   James Hayes (abt. 1783–abt. 1850) married Sally Polard (1776–bef. 1850) on Apr 16, 1819, in Wilkes County. James obtained a land grant for 150 acres of land on Rocky Creek that the state issued to him on Jan 30, 1821. No additional information about James is known.[5, 28, 29]

WILLIAM S. HAYES

1.1.5   William S. Hayes (1785–aft. May 5, 1865) married Rachael Johnson (abt. 1796–aft. May 5, 1865) in Wilkes County on Oct 3, 1814. They may have moved to Carroll County, Ohio.[30, 31]

HARTWELL THURSTON HAYES

1.1.6   Hartwell Thurston Hayes Sr. (Feb 28, 1787–Dec 4, 1859) married Rebecca Elizabeth Brown (Mar 2, 1789–Sep 21, 1852) on Nov 5, 1805, in Wilkes County. They moved to Indiana by 1830 and to Marion County, Iowa, by 1850, where Hartwell obtained an Iowa land grant in Jasper County on Mar 1, 1850. They were buried at the Seay Cemetery in Monroe, Jasper County, Iowa.[32] See Figure 4.8 for a portrait of Hartwell. Their children included:

1. Clarissa A. Hayes (Nov 9, 1806–Apr 2, 1889), who married John Joseph Kimbrel (1806–Sep 14, 1854) on Dec 11, 1824, in Wilkes County. They moved to Franklin, Henry County, Indiana, by 1834, where they obtained an Indiana land grant. John died in Spiceland Township, Henry County. Clarissa died in Dodge City, Ford

FIGURE 4.8 Hartwell Thurston Hayes Sr., bef. 1859, Iowa.

County, Kansas, where she was living with her son, Joseph Taylor Kimbrel (1853–Oct 25, 1928). She was buried at the Concord Cemetery in Ford County.

2. James Thomas Hayes (Oct 13, 1808–Jun 1, 1880), who married Nancy Bucy (Sep 28, 1808–Nov 27, 1878) on May 13, 1831, in Wayne County, Indiana. James died in Henry County, Indiana. Their son, Mahlon Hayes (1835–Mar 26, 1862), died of disease in a hospital in Louisville, Kentucky, on Mar 26, 1862, while serving in the 36th Indiana Infantry Regiment.

3. John Hayes (Jun 8, 1811–Jun 1834), who married Martha Hooper (1794–1836) on Apr 2, 1829, in Wilkes County. The birth and death dates are uncertain, and nothing more is known about this couple.

4. William Hayes (Mar 2, 1814–Feb 10, 1896), who married Anna Jackson Wyatt (Sep 17, 1814–Apr 1, 1884) on May 2, 1836, in Hancock County, Indiana. They moved to the present town of Monroe, Iowa, in 1839, and later resided on a farm near Vandalia, Iowa. They were buried at the Vandalia Cemetery. Lewis's great-grandson, William Spencer Hayes (1917–1993), was president of Alice Lloyd College in Pippa Passes, Kentucky, from 1962 to 1977.[33]

5. Henry Hayes (Jan 27, 1817–Aug 2, 1852), who married Susan Elizabeth Guerin (Apr 30, 1822–Jan 6, 1905), possibly in 1839 in Indiana. Henry died on the Oregon Trail, 50 miles west of Fort Hall in Oregon Territory (now Idaho). See Figure 4.9. Susan continued to Marion County, Oregon. Susan may have married again in Oregon to Amos J. Ferris (1817–aft. 1900) in 1855.[34, 35]

6. Sarah "Sally" Hayes (Apr 12, 1824–Jul 22, 1863), who married David Daniel Spaw (Jul 22, 1817–Dec 18, 1897) on Jun 26, 1843, in Henry County, Indiana. She was buried at the Gifford Cemetery in Jasper County, Iowa. Daniel remarried to Emaline Fudge (1838–1904) in 1864 and moved to Nebraska to live with a daughter. He was buried at the Prospect Hill Cemetery in Madison County, Nebraska.

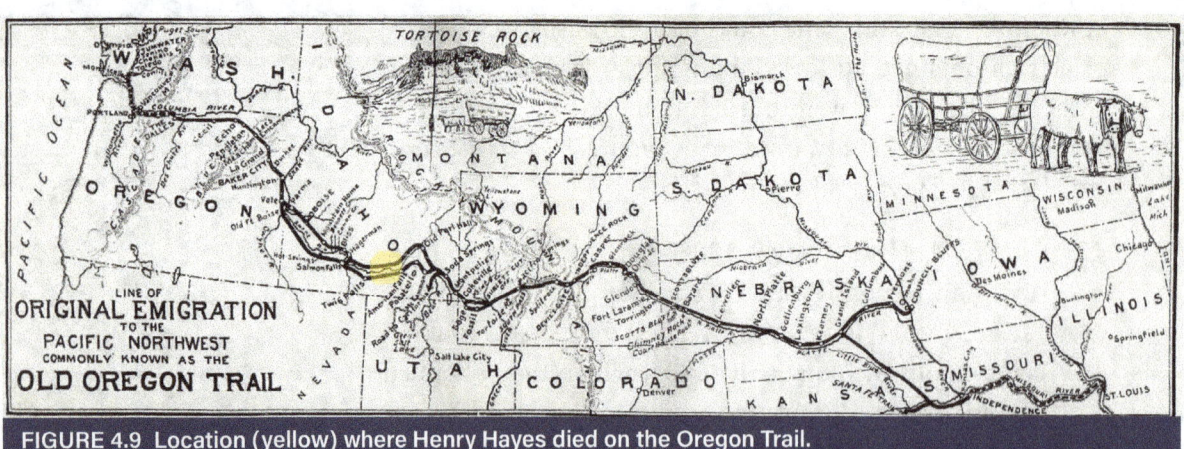

FIGURE 4.9 Location (yellow) where Henry Hayes died on the Oregon Trail.

7. Keziah Sophrone Hayes (Sep 17, 1826–May 13, 1886), who married Tarlton Parthena Duncan (Nov 1823–1910) in Marion County, Iowa, on Jan 11, 1849. They were buried at the Bowmans Grove Cemetery in Shelby County, Iowa.

8. Nancy Ann Hayes (Oct 30, 1828–1907), who married James F. Woody (Jan 30, 1832–Oct 1, 1868) on Nov 17, 1853, in Marion County, Iowa. They were buried at the Gifford Cemetery in Jasper County, Iowa.

9. James Hayes (May 12, 1831–unknown) was a twin of Hartwell Thurston Hayes Jr. Nothing more is known about him past the 1850 census record

10. Hartwell Thurston Hayes Jr. (May 12, 1831–Mar 29, 1876), who was born in Henry County, Indiana—the first sibling to be born outside of North Carolina. He is not known to have married. He was buried at the Vandalia Cemetery in Jasper County, Iowa. See Figure 4.10.

FIGURE 4.10 Hartwell Thurston Hayes Jr., bef. 1876, Iowa.

11. William A. Hayes (1838–Feb 1879), who married Lettie Camblin (1846–aft. 1879) in 1865 in Indiana. William served as a private in the 14th Indiana Infantry Regiment, Union Army, during the U.S. Civil War. He was buried at the Searsboro Cemetery in Poweshiek County, Iowa.

JOANNAH JEMIMAH HAYES

1.1.7   Joannah Jemimah Hayes (abt. 1789–Dec 1860) who married Turner Martin (1787–Jun 2, 1859) in Wilkes County on Dec 18, 1810. They died in Putnam County, Tennessee.[36] Their children may have included:

1. William Ellis Martin (Feb 19, 1817–Sep 1879), who married Nancy Warren Dodson (Feb 10, 1821–Jul 7, 1909) on Apr 18, 1843, in McMinn County, Tennessee. They died in Nashville, Davidson County, Tennessee.

2. James Martin (1824–aft. 1850), who was born in Wilkes County and died in Carter County, Tennessee.

3. Rebecca L. Martin (1825–Dec 26, 1888), who married John Lindley Murray (Oct 13, 1817–Dec 27, 1888) on Nov 27, 1851, in Washington County, Tennessee.

4. Elizabeth Evaline Martin (Sep 4, 1828–Sep 2, 1882), who was born in Tennessee and married Samuel Allen Patton (Apr 10, 1823–Aug 23, 1902) on Mar 14, 1845, in Carter County, Tennessee. They were buried at the Lannom Cemetery in Rutherford County, Tennessee.

ELIZABETH HAYES

1.1.8   Elizabeth "Betsy" Hayes (Jul 15, 1794–Jan 6, 1877) had a child out of wedlock with William Stanley (1795–1824) in Wilkes County before 1819.[37] She later married William on Jan 21, 1819, in Wilkes County and had another child with him. William moved out of Wilkes County before 1824 and died in Carroll County, Missouri. Elizabeth married William Rankin Dinwiddie Sr. (1795–Sep 18, 1872) in Rush County, Indiana, on Apr 2, 1841. Elizabeth did not have any children with William, but he did have seven children from previous marriages. By 1856, Elizabeth and William were living in Des Moines, Iowa. They died in Monroe County, Iowa, and were buried at the Selection Cemetery in Monroe County. Elizabeth's children were:

1. Richmond Hayes (1816–Dec 16, 1897), who married Elsie (McCord) Wissler (Jun 25, 1815–Aug 27, 1900) on Sep 4, 1847, in Indiana (Figure 4.11). They died in Wapello County, Iowa. Elsie was buried at the Westview Cemetery in Kirkville, Wapello County.

FIGURE 4.11
Richmond and Elsie Hayes, bef. 1897, Iowa.

2. Hilligas Hillah Hayes (May 29, 1819–Oct 5, 1909), who married Setha White (Aug 8, 1827–Jun 21, 1900) on Oct 26, 1845, in Hancock County, Indiana. See Figure 4.12. They died in Beeler, Ness County, Kansas, and were buried at the Beeler Cemetery.

JOHN FRANKLIN HAYES

1.1.9   John Franklin Hayes (Dec 10, 1795–May 3, 1872) married Mary Ann "Polly" Loving (Oct 7, 1799–Nov 27, 1875) in Burke County on Oct 17, 1820 (Figure 4.13). They moved to Bradley County, Tennessee, by 1840, and were buried at the Hayes-Shed Cemetery in Bradley County. Their children included:

1. William Sidney Hayes (Apr 18, 1822–Nov 16, 1871), who married Ellen Ophelia Hockenhull (May 1, 1835–Jul 2, 1917) on Jul 2, 1850, in Lumpkin County, Georgia. They lived in Bradley County, Tennessee. William was buried at the Hayes Shed Cemetery on Michigan Avenue in Cleveland, Tennessee. After his death, Ellen moved back to her family home in Georgia, where she married Starling Timonthy Coffey (Jul 23, 1829–Nov 27, 1909) on Feb 13, 1902, in Dawson County, Georgia. Ellen was born in Cheshire, England. She was buried at the Felton Cemetery in Montezuma, Georgia.

FIGURE 4.12 Hillah and Setha Hayes, bef. 1900, Kansas.

2. John Loving Hayes (1826–1857), who married Mary Louise Finley (May 18, 1826–Jul 19, 1906) in about 1847 in Bradley County, Tennessee, where they raised their family. John died in Murray County, Georgia. His burial location is not known. Mary was buried at the Whitefield Cemetery in Whitefield County, Georgia.

FIGURE 4.13 John Franklin and Polly Hayes, bef. 1872, Tennessee.

3. George Marion Hayes (Sep 2, 1827–Dec 17, 1894), who married Eleanor Gentry (Nov 17, 1828–1859) in 1848 in Tennessee. Eleanor died in Anderson County, Tennessee. George married Margaret Jane Hawk Cates (Dec 12, 1832–Jun 24, 1896) in 1853 in Carroll County, Arkansas. George and Eleanor were buried at the Bald Knob Cemetery in Boone County, Arkansas.

4. Franklin M. Hayes (Oct 11, 1832–Oct 1, 1900), who married Charlotte Jones (Mar 19, 1834–May 21, 1926) on May 6, 1857, in Sullivan County, Tennessee. They died in Sullivan County and were buried at the Crumley Cemetery.

5. James Bradford Hayes (Feb 13, 1834–Jan 12, 1877), who married Sarah A. Finley (1835–aft. 1870) in Tennessee in 1853. They moved to Henderson County, Illinois, in about 1869.

6. Franklin A. Hayes (Feb 13, 1834–Jan 12, 1883), who married Penelope "Eppi" Dobbs (1832–1864) in 1860 in Bradley County, Tennessee. He married Clarinda Dobbs (Jun 20, 1839–Feb 22, 1895) in 1860 in Bradley County. Clarinda and Franklin were buried at the Tasso Christian Church Cemetery in Bradley County.

7. James Frances Hayes (1836–aft. 1850), who was born in Tennessee. Nothing more is known.

8. Malissa "Millie" M. Hayes (1838–aft. 1880), who married David M. Bearden (1845–aft. 1880) in 1862 in Bradley County, Tennessee.

9. Henry Clay Hayes (Feb 1845–Dec 27, 1932), who married Martha "Mattie" Bennett Benard on Oct 9, 1873, in Fayette County, Tennessee. Henry and Martha were buried at the Mount Pleasant Cemetery in Haywood County, Tennessee.

10. Mary Elizabeth Hayes (Jan 2, 1848–Nov 2, 1929), who married William L. Lacewell (Sep 26, 1846–Nov 8, 1928) on Oct 16, 1866, in Bradley County, Tennessee. They were buried at the Chattanooga Memorial Park in Hamilton County, Tennessee. William served as a corporal in Seventh Tennessee Mounted Infantry Regiment, Union Army, enlisting on Sep 23, 1864.

HENRY HORNE HAYES

1.1.10 Henry Horne Hayes Jr. (Nov 15, 1796–Jun 2, 1888) first married Frances "Franky" Johnson (1803–Dec 14, 1857) on Dec 29, 1818, in Wilkes County. They had 10 children. After Franky died, he married Elizabeth "Betsy" Holland (1815–Jun 1, 1890) on Mar 1, 1858, in Wilkes County. Betsy and Henry did not have any children.[38] Henry and his first wife were buried at the Liberty Baptist Cemetery in Wilkes County. Henry's children were born near Brushy Mountain, Wilkes County, including:

1. William Parks Hayes (Jan 20, 1819–May 20, 1864), who married Mary "Puggy" Elizabeth Moore (Dec 20, 1820–Jul 27, 1895) on Jan 14, 1842, in Wilkes County. William

served as a Corporal in the 56thNorth Carolina Infantry Regiment, CSA, during the U.S. Civil War, and was killed at the Battle of Ware Bottom Church, Virginia. William and Mary were buried at the Old Anderson Cemetery in Moravian Falls, Wilkes County.

2. James Harrison Hayes (Jan 23, 1823–Nov 27, 1898), who married Elizebeth Estep (Apr 5, 1823–Aug 27, 1895) on Feb 8, 1843, in Wilkes County. They were buried at the James Hayes Family Cemetery in Moravian Falls Township, Wilkes County.

3. Mary "Polly" Hayes (Dec 26, 1825–Aug 13, 1905), who married Wilson K. "Deacon" Moore (Apr 25, 1823–Oct 21, 1911) on Mar 19, 1844, in Wilkes County (Figure 4.14). They were buried at the Old Hunting Creek Cemetery in Wilkes County.

4. Addison Harold Hayes (Dec 31, 1827–Apr 17, 1914), who married Mary "Polly" Estep (Oct 1, 1829–bef. 1857) in about 1856 in Wilkes County. Addison married Genetta Marlow (Aug 16, 1841–Apr 5, 1912) on Jan 15, 1858, in Wilkes County. Addison and Genetta were buried at the Liberty Baptist Cemetery in Moravian Falls, Wilkes County. Mary was buried at the Duncan-Estep Cemetery in Wilkes County.

5. Sarah Keziah Hayes (Jan 11, 1829–Nov 27, 1910), who married James Moore (Jul 6, 1825–May 8, 1893) on Feb 19, 1847, in Wilkes County. They were buried at the Liberty Baptist Church Cemetery in Wilkes County.

6. Elizabeth Sarah Hayes (Jun 1, 1831–Aug 10, 1924), who married Alexander Eli Parker (Aug 18, 1833–May 3, 1873) on Sep 28, 1855, in Wilkes County. Alexander was a private in the 37th North Carolina Infantry Regiment, CSA, during the U.S. Civil War. Eliza-

FIGURE 4.14 Mary Hayes and Wilson K Moore (bottom) with Rev. James Oliver Moore and probably his wife Martha Marlow, abt. 1888, Lovelace, Wilkes County.

beth and Alexander were buried at the Liberty Baptist Church in Moravian Falls, Wilkes County.

7. Martin Hayes (Jun 1, 1833–Jan 2, 1854), who died from a fever while living in the Brushy Mountains area of Wilkes County. He was the first to be buried at the Duncan-Estep Cemetery in Wilkes County.

8. Henry Houston Hayes (Oct 1, 1836–Oct 8, 1912), who married Sarah Emiline Cook (1838–Jun 23, 1916) on Sep 6, 1860, in Wilkes County. Henry was a private in the 55th North Carolina Infantry Regiment, CSA, during the U.S. Civil War. Henry and Sarah were buried at the Liberty Baptist Church in Wilkes County.

9. Mary Elizabeth Hayes (Sep 1838–abt. 1916), who married Aquilla L. Williams (1845–Nov 3, 1863) on Apr 19, 1859, in Wilkes County. Aquilla was a private in the 26th North Carolina Infantry Regiment, CSA, during the U.S. Civil War. He was captured in Falling Waters, Maryland, on Jul 14, 1863, and died of disease in prison at Point Lookout, Maryland, and was buried at the Confederate Cemetery in Scotland, Maryland.* After the Civil War, Mary married Lewis Greer (1823–1892) on Aug 16, 1873, in Watauga County.

10. Francis "Franky" R. Hayes (Sep 1840–Feb 1902), who married George J. Thornburg Sr. (Oct 2, 1808–Aug 6, 1900) on Oct 31, 1880, in Wilkes County. Franky was the second wife of George. His first wife was Elizabeth Mullis (Sep 1, 1811–Dec 9, 1878). George and Elizabeth were buried at the Liberty Baptist Church in Wilkes County.

11. Rebecca Louise Hayes (Dec 6, 1842–May 24, 1927), who married Melver Lloyd Marlow (May 26, 1842–Aug 22, 1922) on Jan 21, 1862, in Wilkes County. Melver (or Melvin) Marlow was a private in the North Carolina 55th Infantry Regiment, CSA, during the U.S. Civil War. Rebecca and Melver were buried at the Macedonia Methodist Church in Harmony Township. Note: There was an Adam Campbell (1789–Jan 1862) living in Iredell County, who was related to Rebecca's daughter, Lucille Marlow. Even though he lived near Perciphull Campbell, this Adam Campbell was descended from another Campbell family line, Matthew Campbell's.

12. Levisa "Lucy" Hayes (Jun 1, 1844–Jun 1, 1918), who married George J. Thornburg Jr. (abt. 1841–1910) in 1869 in Wilkes County. George was a private in the 13th North Carolina Infantry Regiment, CSA, during the U.S. Civil War.

13. Martha Evelyn Hayes (Aug 14, 1848–Nov 10, 1938), who married Preston Adolphus Mullies (Apr 25, 1852–Apr 23, 1903) on Nov 18, 1877, in Wilkes County. Martha and Preston moved from Wilkes County to Bates County, Missouri, before 1884. They were buried at the Woodfin Cemetery in Bates County, Missouri.

---

*Aquilla L. Williams was related to the wife of John R. Campbell (1.6.4), Lucy Williams, in Chapter 9.

HAREL HAYES

1.1.11 Harel Hayes (Mar 1798–Mar 1839) married Chloe Johnson (1796–Aug 22, 1875) on Nov 20, 1820, in Wilkes County. Harrel and Chloe were buried at the Anderson Family Cemetery in Lovelace Township, Wilkes County.[39] Harrel's children included:

1. George Washington Hayes (Nov 11, 1822–Feb 27, 1913), who married Mary "Polly" Riddle (Mar 1833–Dec 29, 1917) on Oct 28, 1851, in Wilkes County. George fought in the North Carolina 56th Infantry Regiment, CSA, during the U.S. Civil War. He died at age 90. George and Mary were buried at the Old Hunting Creek Cemetery in Lovelace Township, Wilkes County.

2. Mary "Polly" Hayes (Jul 13, 1826–Aug 13, 1905), who married Rufus Cyrus Mathias Parker (Oct 1822–May 7, 1890) in 1843 in Wilkes County. Rufus served as a private in the 1st North Carolina Infantry Regiment, CSA, during the Civil War. Mary and Rufus were buried at the Mountlawn Memorial Park and Gardens in Boone, Watauga County.

3. Sarah Hayes (1828–Jan 8, 1895), who married George Parks Johnson (Feb 1827–Aug 8, 1889) on Oct 4, 1877, in Wilkes County. George served in the 1st North Carolina Infantry Regiment, CSA, during the U.S. Civil War. Sarah was buried at the Mount Sinai Cemetery in Wilkes County. George was buried at the Anderson Family Cemetery in Wilkes County.

4. Elizabeth Hayes (1830–1870), who may have been a daughter born in Wilkes County and may have married Ambrose Johnson (abt. 1824–Mar 7, 1864) in about 1846 in Wilkes County.

5. Keziah Ciserarh Hayes (Oct 31, 1831–Sep 27, 1922), who married Robinette "Robert" Anderson (1809–Jan 4, 1871) in 1849 in Wilkes County. Five generations of her family are in the portrait in Figure 4.15. Keziah was buried at the Mount Sinai Cemetery in Wilkes County. Robert was buried at the Anderson Family Cemetery in Wilkes County. Robert had a previous wife, Rebecca Curry (1802–1847), whom he married in 1828. Rebecca was buried at the Anderson Family Cemetery.

FIGURE 4.15
Five generations of the Keziah (Hayes) Anderson's family. Son: Noah, Grandson: Ausborn, G-Grandson: Columbus, GG-Grandson: William Penn Anderson, 1918, Wilkes County.

JOHN D. HAYES

1.1.12 John D. Hayes (Mar 23, 1800–Jun 6, 1867) married Sarah E. Fagans (1814–after 1880) in Nov 9, 1836 in Henry County, Indiana.[40] A portrait of John is shown in Figure 4.16. John was buried at the Cadiz Friends Cemetery in Henry County.[41] They had the following children:

FIGURE 4.16
John D. Hayes,
abt. 1870, Blount
County.

1. Eaton Hayes (1839–Sep 8, 1866), who married Rebecca J. Osburne (Mar 16, 1844–Feb 16, 1932) on Feb 12, 1863, in Henry County, Indiana. Eaton died from wounds while serving in the Union Army, 140th Indiana Infantry Regiment during the U.S. Civil War. He was probably buried at the Cadiz Friends Cemetery in Henry County, Indiana.

2. Jeremiah Hayes (abt. 1842–aft. 1860), who may have died during the U.S. Civil War.

3. Noah Hayes, MD (Jun 21, 1844–Aug 6, 1929), who married Lucy M. Bogle (Oct 16, 1857–Mar 7, 1891) on Oct 12, 1887, in Lincoln County, Kentucky. Noah obtained a medical degree from the Georgetown University School of Medicine in 1876. He later married Libbie S. Swain (1857–1929) on Jul 6, 1899, in Holt, Mound City, Missouri. Noah served with the Union 30th Indiana Infantry Regiment during the U.S. Civil War and later as a

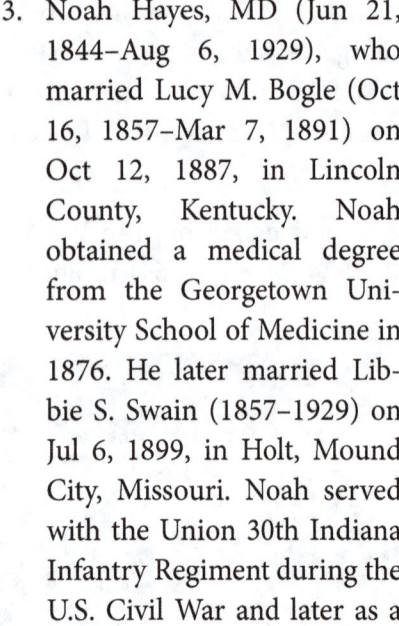

FIGURE 4.17 Noah Hayes, 1876, Washington, D.C

Navy seaman on the ship *Polaris* in 1871–1873 while attempting to reach the North Pole. Noah and his wives were buried at the Seneca City Cemetery in Seneca, Nemah County, Kansas.

4. Bennett Hayes (Jun 9, 1846–Aug 10, 1923), who married Martha Ellen Baughan (Dec 25, 1851–Oct 15, 1922) in 1869. Bennett served with the Union Army's 9th Indiana Cavalry during the U.S. Civil War. They were buried at the Blue Mound Cemetery in Seward County, Nebraska.

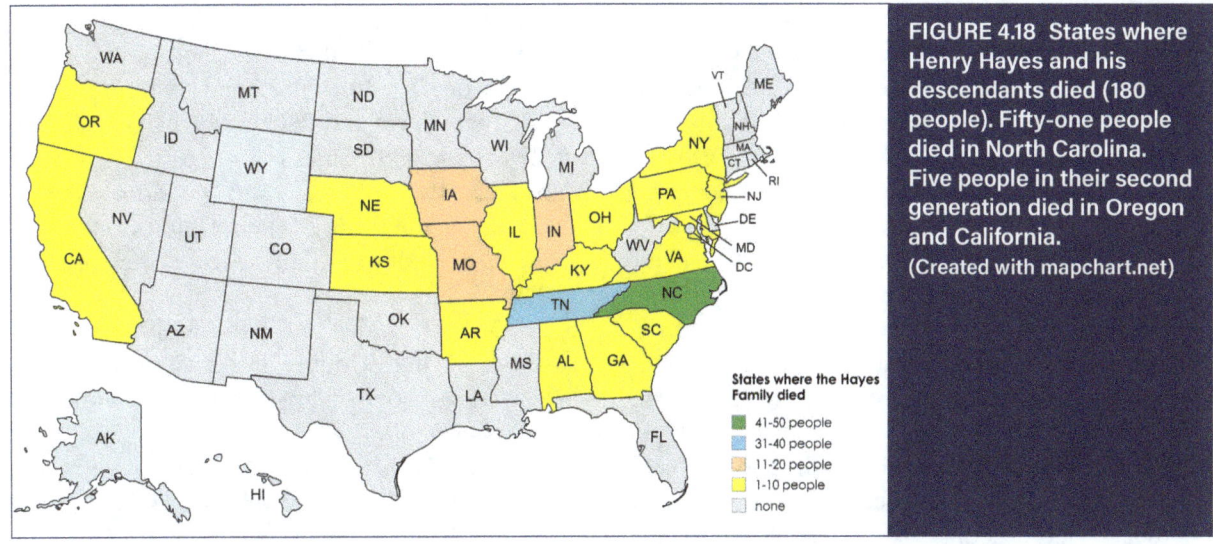

FIGURE 4.18 States where Henry Hayes and his descendants died (180 people). Fifty-one people died in North Carolina. Five people in their second generation died in Oregon and California.
(Created with mapchart.net)

States where the Hayes Family died

- 41-50 people
- 31-40 people
- 11-20 people
- 1-10 people
- none

5. Joshua Hayes (Jun 16, 1849–Oct 1921), who married Ida May Woods (Jun 3, 1855–Feb 16, 1939) on Dec 24, 1874, in Henry County, Indiana. They were buried at the Woodlawn Cemetery in Henry County.

6. David R. Hayes (Jan 8, 1855–Apr 18, 1918), who married and divorced Jean "Unknown Last Name." He died in Daviess County, Indiana.

CHAPTER 4 REFERENCES

1. Apr 9, 1833, Aug 23, 1843, "Revolutionary War Widows Pension Application for John Campbell, W-6616," transcribed by C. Leon Harris, https://revwarapps.org/w6616.pdf, access date Feb 20, 2025; John Campbell (1759-1834), a younger brother, states that he was born in Culpeper County, Virginia, so it is assumed that Kezia was also born there.

2. Sep 8, 1850, U.S. Federal Census, District 2, Letcher County, Kentucky, page 137, Jonathan Hayes, age 75, born in North Carolina.

3. Aug 1925, "Descendants of Pierce Campbell Holds Reunion," Statesville Morning Register, as well as handout given at the Reunion, History of the Campbell Family compiled by H. P. Vanhoy.

4. "Bob's Genealogy Filing Cabinet," Hayes Records in Wilkes County, 1777-1810, https://genfiles.com/hayes/hayes-records-in-wilkes-county-1777-1810/, access date Feb 3, 2025.

5. 2014, North Carolina Land Grant Images and Data, NC Historical Records Online, created by David McCorkly in 2014, various access dates in 2023 and 2024.

6. Oct 21, 1797, Wilkes County, North Carolina Deed Book 3, page 281.

7. Oct 27, 1797, Wilkes County, North Carolina Deed Book D, page 282.

8. Jan 26, 1799, "Wilkes County, North Carolina," Deed Book D, page 681.

9. Oct 23, 1799, "Wilkes County, North Carolina," Deed Book D, page 810.

10. 1801-1951, History, Membership, and Clerk's records of the Grassy Knob Baptist Church, Iredell County, North Carolina (1801–1951),

https://lfweb.co.iredell.nc.us/icpl/DocView.aspx?id=190&dbid=0&repo=Iredell-County-Library&cr=1, access date Feb 9, 2025, James Iredell Room, Iredell County Public Library.

11. 1800, U.S. Federal Census, Morgan District, Wilkes County, North Carolina, page 43, Henry Hays, 2112111629.

12. 1790, U.S. Federal Census, 5th Company, Wilkes County, North Carolina, page 155, Henry Hays, 134X.

13. 1800, U.S. Federal Census, Morgan District, Wilkes County, North Carolina, page 43, Henry Hays, 2112111629.

14. Feb 6, 1805, North Carolina Wills and Probate Records, Henry Hayes, deceased; probate date 1805, Wilkes County, North Carolina; executors Keziah Hayes, Jonathan Hayes, and Thomas Hicks Hays; signed by executors on Feb 6, 1805; *Wilkes County Will Book 2,* page 145.

15. Aug 6, 1810, U.S. Federal Census, Wilkesborough, Wilkes County, North Carolina, Kipiah Hays, page 862, 2121316.

16. Aug 7, 1820, U.S. Federal Census, Wilkes County, North Carolina, page 523, Keziah Hays, 11111133.

17. 1830, U.S. Federal Census, Wilkes County, North Carolina, page 391, Kessiah Hays, 2112144.

18. "Find a Grave," Hays Cemetery, Brown Township, Hancock County, Indiana, dates from headstones; a headstone for Kezia Hayes has not been found.

19. 1989, *Some Pioneers from Wilkes County,* North Carolina, by W. O. Absher, Southern Historical Press, Rachel Mitchel married Jonathan Hays, Henry Hays was bondsman, Oct 30, 1798, page 114, ISBN 0-89308-644-4.

20. 1800, U.S. Federal Census, Morgan District, Wilkes County, North Carolina, page 644, Jonathan Hays, 11113.

21. Aug 6, 1810, U.S. Federal Census, Knox County, Kentucky, page 644, Jonathan Hays, 1111224.

22. 1850, U.S. Federal Census, Subdivision 18, Blount County, Alabama, page 112, dwelling 320, family 321, Reuben Hays, born in North Carolina in about 1794, farmer; with Tabitha, Lettice, Luther, Pheby, and Asa Hays.

23. Oct 30, 1798, "North Carolina Marriage Bonds," Wilkes County, William Mitchell Jr. and Sarah Hayes on Oct 30, 1798, bond 000166651; and Jonathan Hayes and Rachel Mitchell on Oct 30, 1798, bond 000165628.

24. Jun 22, 1909, William and Keziah (Mitchell) Garris, *Tipton Daily Tribune,* Tipton County, Indiana, quoted from "Find a Grave," memorial ID 249895677.

25. Feb 3, 1801, "Index to North Carolina Marriage Bonds," Wilkes County, Hicks Combs and Keziah Hays, bonded by Henry Hays, bond no. 000164675.

26. Sep 14, 1850, U.S. Federal Census, Brown, Hancock County, Indiana, dwelling 194, family 197, page 355, Kesia Combs, age 69, born in North Carolina; along with John Combs, age 28, born in North Carolina; Elias Combs, age 20, born in North Carolina; and Betsey Farmer, age 23, born in Ohio.

27. 1985, *The Lives and Letters of the Combs Family,* by Ann Combs Krahn, Anundsen Publishing Company, Decorah, Iowa.

28. Apr 16, 1819, Wilkes County, North Carolina Marriage Bonds, record 01114, James Hayes and Sally Polard, bond no. 00016519, bondsman Joseph James, Witness, W W Martin.

29. 1820, U.S. Federal Census, Wilkes County, North Carolina, page 515, James Hays, age 16-25; one white female, age 16–25.

30. Oct 3, 1814, "North Carolina Marriage Bonds," Wilkes County, bond no. 000165634, Willaim S. Hays and Rachal Johnson, bondsman Lewis Johnson, witness W W Martin.

31. May 5, 1865, "Ohio Wills and Probate Records," Carroll County, William Hays, mentioning Rachel Hays and Josiah Dawns.

32. Aug 16, 1850, U.S. Federal Census, Marion County, Iowa, dwelling 13, family 13, page 229, Hartwell Hays, age 63, farmer; with Rebecca Hays, age 61, born in NC; Nancy Hays, age 21, born in NC; Hartwell Hays, age 19, born in IN; James Hays, age 19, born in IN; William A. Hays, age 12, born in IO; and Jammitte Wright, age 15, born in IN.

33. Apr 13, 1993, *Lexington Herald Leader*, "Hayes: Former Alice Lloyd president dies," Lexington, Kentucky.

34. "Find a Grave," entry by Peggy Bollenbaugh, Henry Hayes, 2022, memorial id 237879569, Buried on the Oregon Trail, 50 miles west of Fort Hall, near the Snake River.

35. 1907, *The Ox Team on the Old Oregon Trail 1852–1906, Map of the Oregon Trail*, by Ezra Meeker.

36. 1850, U.S. Federal Census, District 5, Carter County, Tennessee, page 186, dwelling 77, family 77: Joannah Martin, age 58; with Turner Martin, age 62; Rebeca L. Martin, age 25; and James Martin, age 26, blacksmith (all born in NC).

37. Mar 1, 1819, Wilkes County, North Carolina: State of North Carolina Wilkes County Superior Court of Law March Term, 1819.

38. Jun 11, 1880, U.S. Federal Census, Brush Mountain, Wilkes County, North Carolina, page 152, Henry Hayes, age 83, farmer, with Elizabeth Hayes, age 60; and Ellen Holland, age 18, all born in NC, including parents.

39. Sep 16, 1850, U.S. Federal Census, Wilkes County, North Carolina, page 326, dwelling 1125, Family 1125, Cloah Hayes, age 54; with George Hayes, age 27; Sally Hayes, age 16; and William Tedder, age 6; all born in Wilkes County.

40. Jul 25, 1850, U.S. Federal Census, Harison, Henry County, Indiana, page 345, dwelling 38, family 45, John D. Hays, age 50; with Sarah, age 37; Eaton, age 10; Jeremiah, age 8; Noah, age 5; Bennett, age 3; Joshua, age 0; and Nancy Hurst, age 67.

41. Nov 1, 1836, "Indiana Marriages, 1810-2001," FHL Film Number 001870202, John Hays and Sarah Fagans, marriage date Nov 1, 1836.

WILLIAM CAMPBELL

1.2   William Campbell (Aug 1, 1756–Jan 12, 1840) was the second of eight children of **Adam Campbell** (1735–1779) and **Elizabeth Morgan** (1735–1789) of Rowan and Iredell Counties, North Carolina. He was born in Culpeper County, Virginia, and moved with his family to Rowan County in about 1775, where his first child was born. The evidence that William was a son of Adam and Elizabeth Campbell is based on his census[1] and tax lists[2, 3, 4] in Rowan, Surry, and Iredell Counties, and his Revolutionary War pension application,[5] as well as the North Carolina land grants that he submitted for land on the north side of Hunting Creek in Rowan County, adjacent to Theophilus Morgan and Adam Simonton (Figure 5.1).[6] This land was part of Adam Campbell's land grant that was passed on to William after Adam died. William stated that he was born in Culpeper County, Virginia, in his pension application. William Campbell and his family did not appear in the 1925 *History of the Campbell Family* compiled by H. P. Vanhoy in Union Grove, North Carolina, probably because William had moved out of North Carolina before 1800.

William married Nancy Ann Hendren (abt. 1750–Aug 12, 1849), the daughter of John Hendren and Margaret (Jesper) Hendren, on Apr 3, 1792, in Rowan County.[7] Some genealogists show a middle name abbreviated as "R." He had a son whose middle name was Rice. He was referred to in public records as just William Campbell.

According to his pension statement, William was residing in Wilkes County, North Carolina, when he first served in the American Revolution. He gave the dates of his services as follows:[5, 8]

❖ 1775–1776: He served as a private under Capt. John Hamlin and Capt. (later promoted to Col.) Martin Armstrong in the Surry County Regiment of the North Carolina Militia, which was established on Aug 26, 1775. He fought with his unit at the Battle of Moore's Creek Bridge on Feb 27, 1775, in Currie, North Carolina.

❖ 1780: He was a private and scout under Capt. Benjamin Herndon (see Chapter 2) in the Wilkes County Regiment and Col. William Lee Davidson in the Mecklenburg County

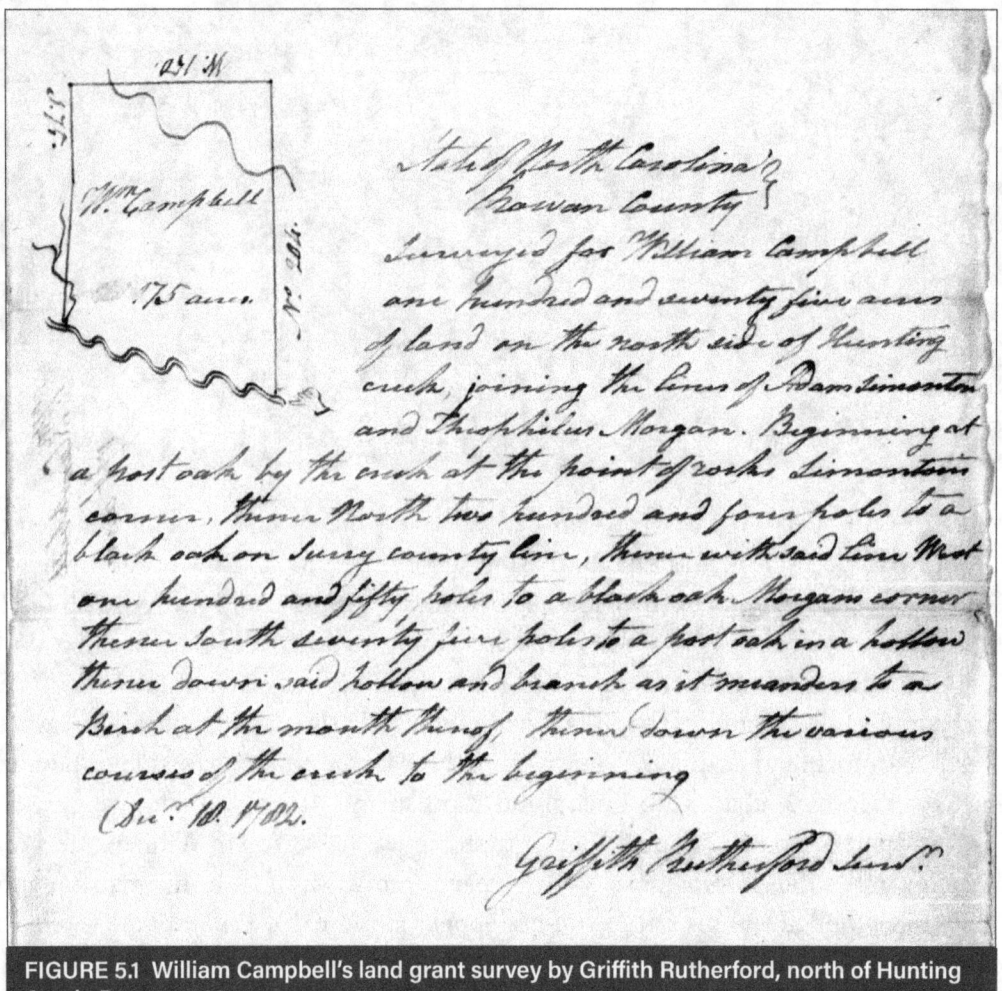

FIGURE 5.1 William Campbell's land grant survey by Griffith Rutherford, north of Hunting Creek, Dec 10, 1782.

Regiment. His unit fought at the Battle of Colson's Mill on Jul 21, 1780, and Kings Mountain on Oct 7, 1780.

❖ 1780: He was also a private under Capt. Jacob Nichols (see Chapter 2) in the Rowan County Regiment, which fought at the battles of Ramseur's Mill on Jun 20, 1780, Camden on Aug 16, 1780, Kings Mountain, and Shallow Ford on Oct 14, 1780.

❖ May 1781: He was a private under Capt. Alexander Brevard in the 1st North Carolina Regiment for 12 months. This Regiment was engaged in Battles in South Carolina, including Fort Motte on May 12, Siege of Ninety Six in May and June, Siege of Augusta in May and June, Eutaw Springs on Sep 8, and Hillsborough on Sep 12, 1781.

❖ Apr 28, 1782: When the militia discharged him, he was a shoemaker attached to the 3rd North Carolina Regiment at the Continental Factory in Rowan County, near what became Statesville.

The government gave William a pension of $40 per year, commencing on Mar 4, 1831, for one year of service as a private in the North Carolina militia. Dorothy Mae (Dowen) Bain (1922–1998), a descendant of William Campbell's daughter, Nancy (Campbell) Trowbridge (1.2.1), obtained membership in the Daughters of the American Revolution (DAR) based on his service record.[9]

William and Nancy lived in Wilkes County and Iredell County briefly after their marriage and then moved to Gerrard County, Kentucky, in 1796. While in Kentucky, on Nov 7, 1801, William sold his land on the north side of Hunting Creek in Iredell County to Thomas Huie. This was probably the land that he inherited from his father. In about 1785, William and Nancy moved to Crawford County, Indiana. In about 1843, they moved to Bureau County, Illinois, to live with their son Enos Rice Campbell. William and Nancy died in Bureau County.[5]

William and Nancy Campbell's first three children were born in Iredell County, North Carolina. The last child may have been born in Kentucky. None of the descendants of William Campbell, after the first generation, lived in North Carolina. The states with the largest number of births of his descendants were Kentucky (18) and Indiana (14). The largest number of deaths of his descendants were in Indiana (15) and Illinois (18). See Figure 5.2.

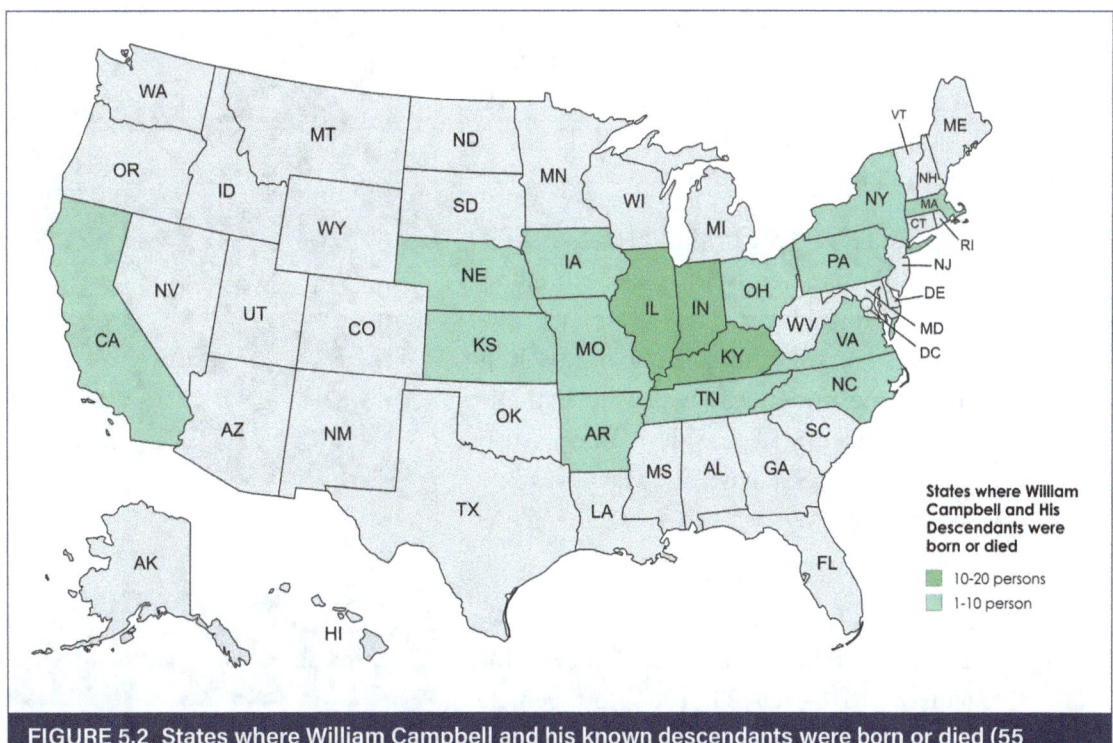

FIGURE 5.2 States where William Campbell and his known descendants were born or died (55 people). (Created with mapchart.net)

The following are the known descendants of William Campbell.[5]

NANCY CAMPBELL

1.2.1 Nancy Campbell (Apr 4, 1782–1856) married Isaac Trowbridge, II (1775–1832) in Lincoln County, Kentucky, on Dec 20, 1796. Isaac was born in Frederick County, Virginia, and emigrated to Kentucky with his older brothers, David and Jonathan. He first settled in Clark County, where he engaged in farming. He later lived in Washington, Lincoln, and Owen Counties. In about 1820, they removed to Indiana and settled on a farm near Orangeville, Orange County, in southern Indiana, where they died. Isaac and Nancy had seven children:[10, 11, 12, 13, 14, 15]

1. Jonathan Trowbridge (May 30, 1800–Jul 16, 1860) married Louisa Singleton (Apr 14, 1804–Nov 4, 1856) on Sep 15, 1820, in Lincoln County, Kentucky. He obtained a land grant in Putnam County, Indiana, in 1833. Some of his children moved to Emporia, Kansas. See Figure 5.3.

2. Mary "Polly" Trowbridge (1802–Feb 12, 1839) married Thomas C. Singleton (1790–1830) on Mar 6, 1819, in Lincoln County, Kentucky. Their son, James Hicks Singleton (Sep 21, 1819–Jun 5, 1908), served with the 10th Indiana Infantry Regiment, Union Army, during the U.S. Civil War. Mary and Thomas died in Parke County, Indiana. Their burial locations are not known.

3. Alexander F. Trowbridge (1804–aft. Oct 17, 1865) married Mary Elizabeth (Johnston) Young Hager (1809–Mar 14, 1894) on Oct 16, 1828, in Casey County, Kentucky. Alexander was a private with the 1st Kentucky State Cavalry, Union Army, during the U.S. Civil War. Mary was buried at the Pleasant Grove Cemetery in Washington County, Kentucky.

4. Ebenezer Trowbridge (Jun 20, 1808–Sep 22, 1875) married Lucinda "Lucy" Noel (Jun 8, 1818–Feb 23, 1901) on Feb 23, 1836, in Washington County, Kentucky. They were buried at the North Freedom Cemetery in Clay County, Illinois.

FIGURE 5.3 Jonathan Trowbridge's children: Malinda Jane, Lucinda Dove, and Granville Gaston; aft. 1872, Emporia, Kansas.

5. Margaret Trowbridge (Aug 14, 1810–1870) married Thomas Tolbert (1807–Jun 24, 1890) on Jun 15, 1830, in Orange County, Indiana. Their burial locations are not known.

6. Joseph James Trowbridge (Feb 24, 1812–Jan 1, 1894) married Martha Jane York Goode (Aug 25, 1816–Nov 6, 1863) on Feb 16, 1837, in Lincoln County, Kentucky. Joseph served with the 1st Kentucky Cavalry Regiment in the Union Army during the U.S. Civil War. He later married Maria Taylor (Jun 20, 1844–Sep 25, 1900) on Dec 1, 1864, in Boyle County, Kentucky. Jane was buried at the Goode Cemetery in Washington County, Kentucky. Maria and Joseph were buried at the Bethel Cemetery in Orange County, Indiana.

7. Thomas Merritt Trowbridge (1815–1900) married Priscilla (Head) Sorrels (1820–bef. 1867) on Dec 7, 1850, in Orange County, Indiana. Thomas married Mary A. Chadwick (Mar 1838–Jan 14, 1916) on Oct 1, 1867, in Adair County, Missouri. Priscilla died in Missouri. Thomas and Mary died in Ft. Smith, Sebastian County, Arkansas, where they were living with their oldest son, Merritt T. Trowbridge (1870–1937).

WILLIAM HENDREN CAMPBELL

1.2.2   William Hendren Campbell (1789–Feb 2, 1852) married Margaret Hendron (abt. 1790–bef. 1850) on Apr 7, 1832, in Crawford County, Indiana.[16] On May 7, 1852, William's brother, Enos Campbell, filed an affidavit in Bureau County, Illinois, stating that he was the only heir and surviving child of William Campbell, a revolutionary pensioner who died on Jan 19, 1840. No additional details about William are known at this time.[5, 17]

UNKNOWN MALE CAMPBELL

1.2.3   An unknown male Campbell (1791–bef. 1822) may have been born in Kentucky and had two daughters, Nancy Campbell (1808–aft. 1836) and Peggy Campbell (1811–aft. 1836). The daughters were born in Kentucky and died in Bureau County, Illinois.[5]

ENOS RICE CAMPBELL

1.2.4   Enos Rice Campbell (1792–Apr 17, 1870) married Mary Polly Carpenter (1791–1887) on Jul 4, 1811, in Overton County, Tennessee. Mary was born in Amherst County, Virginia. Enos Campbell claimed that he served in the War of 1812, although his pension application by his wife, Polly, was denied.[19] Enos Campbell came to Bureau County, Illinois, in 1843, and was an official in Mineral Township. Enos and Polly died on their farm in Mineral Township. Enos and Mary's burial locations are not known. Enos's son, William Campbell, stated in a letter supporting his father's pension application on Aug 8, 1881, that he was in possession of his father's family bible printed in 1816 that contained birth dates for Enos's 10 children.[18]

Enos and Polly Campbell's children were as follows:[19]

1. James Madison Campbell (Dec 25, 1812–1853), who was a Sheriff in Bureau County, Illinois. He married Ann H. Witt (1810–Apr 14, 1881) on Sep 2, 1832, in Crawford County, Indiana. Their son, Charles A. Campbell (Jan 28, 1839–May 5, 1898), served in the Union Army with the Illinois 139th Infantry Regiment during the U.S. Civil War and was buried in the Wymore Cemetery in Gage County, Nebraska. James and Ann were buried at the Sheffield Cemetery in Bureau County.

2. Benjamin Carpenter Campbell (Apr 15, 1815–Apr 23, 1901), who married Lucy McGehee (1819–May 18, 1875) on Aug 7, 1839, in Knox County, Illinois. He married Nellie Aseneath Johnson (1840–1898) on Mar 26, 1876, in Pulaski County, Illinois. Benjamin was a blacksmith.

3. John H. Campbell (Jan 28, 1817–Mar 25, 1906), who married Lucy Melvina Hotchkiss (Dec 1822–Feb 6, 1875) on Apr 10, 1842, in Knox County, Illinois. Lucy was buried at the Marengo City Cemetery, Iowa County, Iowa. John was buried at the Layton Township Cemetery, Pottawattamie County, Iowa. They had nine children, including Ida "Addie" (Campbell) Wendt (Aug 26, 1860–1934), with whom John lived after his wife died. See Figure 5.4.

FIGURE 5.4 *Bottom L to R:* Ida (Campbell) Wendt, John H. Campbell, Henry Wendt (Ida's husband); *Top L to R:* Fred Wendt (Ida's son), Harriet Wendt (Ida's daughter), abt. 1905, Iowa.

4. Sarah Campbell (Jan 29, 1819–unknown), who was born in Crawford County, Indiana, according to Enos's family bible quoted in his War of 1812 pension application.

5. Rosannah Campbell (Nov 25, 1822–aft. 1900) married Henry Wheeler Hotchkiss (abt. 1816–Nov 20, 1888) on Jan 9, 1842, in Knox County, Illinois. They died in Sheffield, Bureau County, Illinois.

6. William Madison Campbell Sr. (Apr 13, 1826–Mar 30, 1911), who married Deborah Louisa Humphrey (Jan 20, 1835–aft. 1880) on Dec 15, 1853 in Bureau County, Illinois.

7. Adelphia Loretta Campbell (Jan 6, 1828–1907), who married William H. Everson (Mar 20, 1820–May 13, 1913) on Aug 28, 1845, in Knox County, Illinois.

8. Lucinda Campbell (Mar 15, 1830–bef. 1840), who did not marry.

9. Enos Jackson Campbell (Aug 30, 1832–bef. 1900), who married Helen Marian Hotchkiss (Apr 7, 1836–Aug 7, 1915) on Sep 27, 1857, in Bureau County, Illinois. Helen was a dressmaker. They moved to Nevada by 1870 and then to Iowa by 1880, where they died. They had two daughters, one of whom, Mattie Esmetta Campbell (1858–1936), moved to Riverside, California.

10. Morgan W. Campbell (Apr 5, 1834–aft. 1863), who was not known to have married. He registered for the draft in Indiana during the U.S. Civil War.

CHAPTER 5 REFERENCES

1. 1790, U.S. Federal Census, Iredell County, North Carolina, page 396, William Campbell, 111xx; Elizabeth Campbell, x12xx; Perciphull Campbell, 111xx; John Camp, 143xx.

2. 1778, Rowan County Tax List for Capt. Nichols's District, Rowan County, North Carolina, Wm Campbell.

3. 1786, Surry County Tax List, Blackburn's District, Surry County, North Carolina; William Campble.

4. 1780, Surry County, North Carolina, William Campbel, listed on a petition, Jan 28, 1779, to the House of Assembly from inhabitants of Surry County seeking redress for the way titles for vacant lands are obtained.

5. Oct 13, 1822, "Southern Campaigns American Revolution Pension Statements and Rosters," transcribed by Will Graves, pension application of William Campbell, S32162, https://revwarapps.org/s32162.pdf, Crawford County, Indiana, access date Feb 14, 2025.

6. Sep 4, 1778, Rowan County, North Carolina state land grant; William Campbell, Certificate 771–1054, issued Oct 10, 1783, entered Sep 4, 1778; book 51, page 5, on the north side of Hunting Creek, 200 acres (surveyed at 175 acres on Dec 10, 1782), adjoining the Surry line and Theophilus Morgan and Simontons land.

7. Apr 3, 1792, "North Carolina Marriage Bonds," Rowan County, image 003578, record 03 029, William Campbell and Ann Hendren marriage bond 003578; John Hendren bondsman; Brice W. James witness.

8. "The American Revolution in North Carolina," by J. D. Lewis, https://www.carolana.com, access date Feb 20, 2025.

9. "DAR Descendants Database," William Campbell, Ancestor A012796, National Numbers 731194 and 738520, access date Feb 14, 2025; National Number 731194 DAR member Dorothy Mae Dowen Bain, (Note: Mary Trowbridge, daughter of Isaac Trowbridge, married Thomas

Singleton; son, James Hicks Singleton; daughter Susan Emeline (Singleton) Allen and her husband William Emory Allen).

10. 1908, *The Trowbridge Genealogy, History of The Trowbridge Family in America*, by Francis Bacon Trowbridge, New Haven, Connecticut.

11. Dec 20, 1796, "Kentucky Compiled Marriages, 1802-1850," Lincoln County, Isaac Trowbridge and Nancy Campbell.

12. Aug 6, 1810, U.S. Federal Census, Clark County, Kentucky, page 644, Isaac Trowbridge, 21111426.

13. Aug 7, 1820, U.S. Federal Census, Crab Orchard, Lincoln County, Kentucky, page 15; Isaac Trowbridge, 311111135288.

14. 1830, U.S. Federal Census, Orange County, Indiana, page 28, Isaac Trobridge, 21111466.

15. 1850, U.S. Federal Census, Northwest, Orange County, Indiana, dwelling 1067, family 1071, Nancy Trobridge, age 73, born in Virginia; with Meriton Trobridge, age 37; and Margaret Trobridge, age 6.

16. Apr 7, 1832, "Indiana Compiled Marriages," Crawford County, William H. Campbell and Margaret Hendron, microfilm 1377775.

17. Feb 2, 1852, *The Whig Press*, Middletown, New York, Feb 11, 1852, page 3, William Campbell, aged about 40.

18. Aug 8, 1881, Letter from William Campbell to Bureau County, Illinois, page 23–24, Fold3.com pension application.

19. 1881, "War of 1812 Pension Application Files Index," Enos Campbell, person no. WO41479, claim of widow for service pension, by Polly Campbell, including copy of names and dates of birth of family members from family bible of Enos Campbell, letter dated Aug 8, 1881.

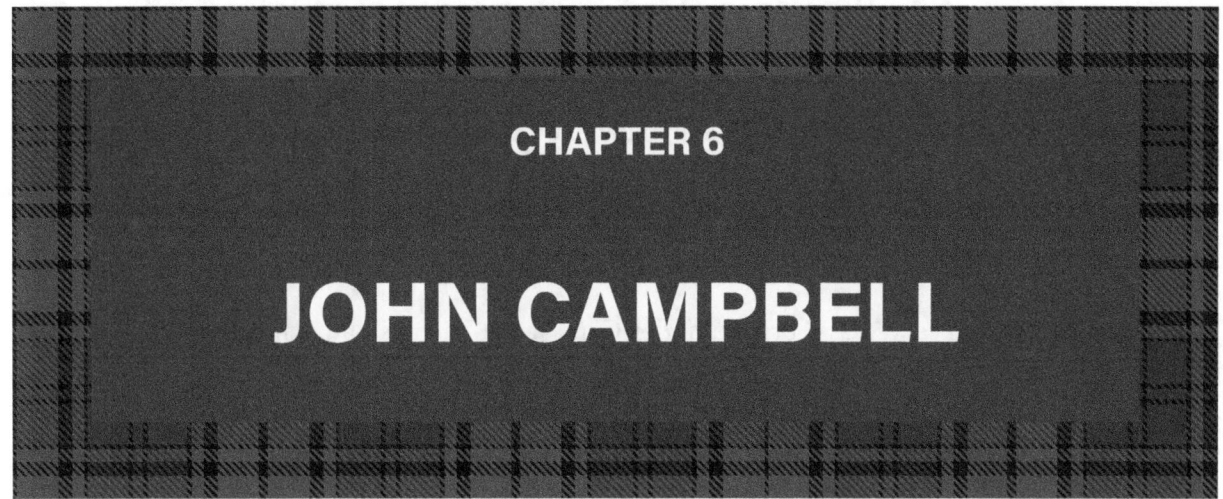

JOHN CAMPBELL

1.3   John Campbell (abt. 1759–Mar 23, 1834) was the third of eight children of **Adam Campbell** (1735–1779) and **Elizabeth Morgan** (1735–1789) of Rowan and Iredell Counties, North Carolina. He was born in Culpeper County, Virginia, and moved with his family to Rowan County in about 1775, where his first child was born. He married Cora or Carah Mullis (1760–aft. 1850) in Wilkes County in the latter part of 1785. Cora was the daughter of George Mullis (1722–1781) and his wife Sarah (1748–Feb 1800), who lived in Wilkes County and were buried at the Hendren-Mullis Cemetery in Wilkes County. Cora was born in Virginia, probably Culpeper County. She was living with her daughter, Nancy, and grandson, John Syrien, in Iredell County on Aug 27, 1850, when the U.S. Census was taken.[1, 2, 3, 4, 5, 6, 7, 8, 9, 10, 11, 12, 13]

John Campbell and his brother, William, served in the Rowan County Regiment during the American Revolution. The Rowan County Regiment was part of the North Carolina Militia, established by the Colony of North Carolina before the American Revolution as a local militia. The North Carolina Provincial Congress authorized the regiment on Sep 8, 1775, with Col. Griffith Rutherford as its commander. When John Campbell served in the regiment, it was commanded by Col. Francis Locke Sr.[14]

On Sep 9, 1833, John appeared before Samuel King, one of the Justices of Peace for Iredell County, to apply for a Revolutionary War pension. He stated in his application that he was born in 1759 or 1760 in Culpeper County, State of Virginia. He said that he was first called to service when he was living in Rowan County. The second and third times he was called to service, he was living in Wilkes County. He stated that he was generally living in Iredell County, formerly part of Rowan County, since the end of the war. He stated that General Gates was the principal continental officer when he joined the militia and General Rutherford was the brigade commander. On Aug 23, 1843, Carah Campbell, aged 83, applied for a pension stating that she married John Campbell in the latter part of 1785 and that John died on Mar 23, 1834. Percival Campbell (1.6), brother of John Campbell and an acting justice of the peace, deposed that he was present at their marriage in Wilkes County. Sarah Campbell (Perciphull's wife), aged 76, deposed that she had been a neighbor of John and Cary Campbell for 65 years, and that they had two small children by the time she was married in 1788.

Theophilus M. Campbell (1.6.3) assisted Carah Campbell in the preparation of her deposition. On Jan 12, 1844, Carah Campbell made another pension application in which her age was given as 82. On Jan 30, 1849, she made another application in which her age was given as 88.[1]

From these depositions and information about the Rowan County Regiment, John's service is as follows:[1, 14]

❖ 1779: John served as a private under Capt. Jacob Nichols and Capt. John George Lowman in the Rowan County Regiment of the North Carolina Militia. George Lowman was an adjutant under Col. Francis Locke in the Rowan County Regiment. Capt. Nichols was engaged in the Battle of Briar Creek in Georgia on Mar 3, 1779. John stated that he moved to Wilkes County in about 1780, implying that there was a break in his service.

❖ 1780: John served as a private under Capt. Benjamin Herndon, Capt. Joel Lewis, and Capt. William Nall. Capts. Herndon and Nall were part of the Wilkes County Regiment of Militia in 1780. John Campbell was taken prisoner at the Battle of Camden in South Carolina on Aug 16, 1780. Later, he escaped.

John Campbell appears as unmarried in Wilkes County on the North Carolina State Census in 1784. Others he served with in the military or would be related to his descendants and listed as heads of household in Capt. Gordon's District of Wilkes County on this list included Benjamin Herndon, Isham Harvell, William Hendren, Francis Vanhoy, Thomas Cook, and Sarah Mullis.[8]

John stated that his service record was intimately known by Col. Francis Young (1779–1854), John May Young (1776–1858), William Harbin, Esq. (1776–1844), and Martin Morgan (1758–1830). The two Young brothers were sons of Thomas Cadet Young (1733–1829), who lived near Houstonville in Iredell County where the Young Family Cemetery is located.* William Harbin donated the land on which the town of Williamsburgh was created in 1832.[15] Martin Morgan was the son of Theophilus Morgan Sr. (1720–1807), the father of John's mother.[1]

There are no DAR or SAR applications for John Campbell's service in the American Revolution. There was an inquiry from Mrs. Judie Brevard Reid of Shelby, North Carolina, in the 1920s to the National Archives about John's Revolutionary War service. Burial locations for John and Carah Campbell are not known. It is perplexing that there were no recollections of John Campbell or descendants in the *History of the Campbell Family* written for the 1925 reunion. In John Campbell's time, there was a close connection to Perciphull Campbell's family, as evidenced in their support in completing his pension application, which may not have been available or recalled by descendants in 1925. (Note: There was a John Campbells Sr. and a John Campbell Jr. living in Iredell County in the same time frame who were not

---

*See Chapter 2 for more information on the Sharpe and Young families.

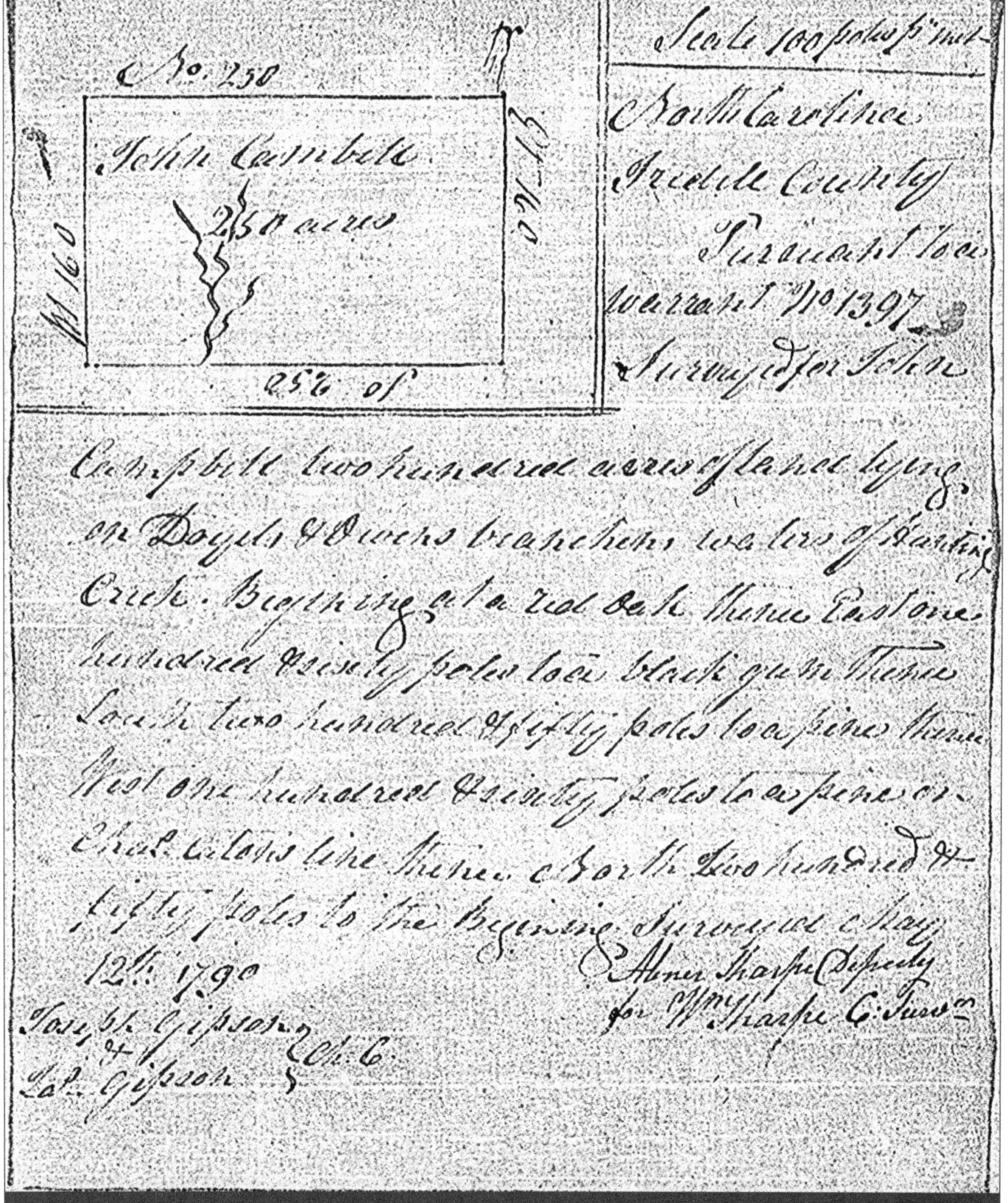

Scale 100 poles p^r inch

No. 250

John Cambell

250 acres

N 160

E 250

250 S

North Carolina
Iredell County
Pursuant to a
warrant No 1397
Surveyed for John
Campbell two hundred acres of land lying
on Dogels & Owens branches waters of Hunting
Creek. Beginning at a red oak thence East one
hundred & sixty poles to a black gum thence
South two hundred & fifty poles to a pine thence
West one hundred & sixty poles to a pine on
Chas. Wilsons line thence North two hundred &
fifty poles to the Beginning Surveyed May
12th 1790

Abner Sharpe Deputy
for Wm Sharpe C. Surv.

Joseph Gipson
&
Lat. Gipson
Ch. C.

FIGURE 6.1 John Campbell's land grant survey, May 12, 1790, Iredell County, signed by Abner Sharpe, Deputy for Wm Sharpe.

related. Land grant records indicated that these two Campbells lived on Cold Water Creek near China Grove in Rowan County.)

John Campbell was issued a North Carolina land grant for 250 acres on Jul 7, 1794, in Iredell County (Figure 6.1). It was located on Doyles and Owens branches of the Hunting Creek, most likely south of Hunting Creek. The original request for this land was entered on Apr 1, 1778, when the land was part of Rowan County. John's entry was made the same year that his father and brother made land grant entries (Adam Campbell's grant for 300 acres on both sides of Hunting Creek, and William Campbell's grant for 200 acres on the north side of Hunting Creek). Abner Sharpe surveyed John's land. Abner was a deputy of William Sharpe on May 12, 1790, when the land was part of the newly established Iredell County. The county issued John's land to him after they issued other lands to his brother William and mother, Elizabeth. The Campbell Family Cemetery is located very near Owens Branch in Iredell County. Basil Owens, the loyalist during the American Revolution discussed in Chapter 2, was probably the namesake for Owens Branch.[16]

John and Corah Campbell had two known children, Nancy and John M. Campbell. According to his pension, there may have been two other children of John Campbell and Cora Mullis, who would have been born in about 1786 and 1787, but no further information about these children has been found.[1]

NANCY CAMPBELL

1.3.1   Nancy Campbell (1792–aft. 1870) was either a daughter or daughter-in-law. At the age of 58, she was living in Iredell County with her mother, aged 91, and Syrien J. Campbell, aged 22, in 1850[11]; south of Hunting Creek at age 67; in Iredell County with her son John S. Campbell, aged 40, in 1860;[17] and at age 80 in Union Grove Township, Iredell County with John Campbell, aged 50, in 1870.[18] John Syrien Campbell (1820–aft. 1870) was her son from an unknown marriage. No other details about this family are known.

JOHN M. CAMPBELL

1.3.2   John M. Campbell (1801–aft. 1850) was a farmer living in Iredell County in 1830, 1840, and 1850 with Catharine Campbell (1810–aft. 1850), who was probably his wife, and his children. John M. Campbell owned three slaves in 1840. Catharine was born in Virginia in about 1810 and died after 1850, probably in North Carolina. Their children were born in North Carolina, according to the census records. John M. Campbell's family appeared next to the home of his mother and sister with her son Syrien in the 1850 U.S. Census.[19, 20, 21]

John and Catharine's known children were:[21]

1. Thomas Campbell (1825–aft. 1850), who was probably born in Iredell County.

2. Carolus (Carl) M. Campbell (1826–bef. 1900), who married Amanda Guy (abt. 1828–May 15, 1892) on Nov 24, 1853, in Iredell County. Carl was working at the sawmill in

Eagle Mills Township in 1870 and 1880. Carl married Sarah Jane Knight (Oct 5, 1857–Feb 10, 1934) on Aug 1, 1892, in Iredell County. Amanda and Carl were buried at Holly Springs Baptist Cemetery in Harmony. Sarah was buried at Winthrop Friends Meeting Cemetery in Harmony.

3. William Floyd Campbell Sr. (1830–1896), who married Malinda "Milly" Myers (abt. 1837–aft. 1898) on Jan 12, 1854, in Iredell County. They lived in New Hope Township. They had several children, including William Floyd Campbell Jr. (Apr 13, 1878–Apr 3, 1928), who married Annie Elizabeth Trexler (Dec 3, 1873–May 14, 1966) on Mar 21, 1896, in Rowan County; and Sina Estelle (Campbell) Atwell (Feb 15, 1878–Feb 8, 1940), who married Clark Alexander Atwell (Nov 21, 1878–Oct 10, 1946) on Apr 7, 1898 in Cabarrus County. William and Annie lived in Salisbury, Rowan County. William Floyd Campbell Jr. and Clark Atwell worked in cotton mills.

4. Mary Campbell (1835–aft. 1850), who was born in Iredell County.

5. F. M. Campbell (1838–aft. 1850), who was male and born in Iredell County.

CHAPTER 6 REFERENCES

1. Apr 9, 1833, Aug 23, 1843, "Revolutionary War Widow's Pension Application for John Campbell, W-6616," transcribed by C. Leon Harris, https://revwarapps.org/w6616.pdf, access date Feb 15, 2025.

2. 1790, U.S. Federal Census, Iredell County, North Carolina, page 396, John Camp [sic], 143xx; William Ball, 121xx; William Campbell, 111xx; Elizabeth Campbell, x12xx; Perciphull Campbell, 111xx.

3. 1800, U.S. Federal Census, Iredell County, North Carolina, Salisbury Census District, page 623, John Campbell, x1x1x5xx1xxx; Perciphull Campbell, 21x11xxx1xx1.

4. Aug 6, 1810, U.S. Federal Census, Iredell County, North Carolina, page 206, John Campbell, xx2xxx41xxxx.

5. 1815, Iredell County, North Carolina Tax List, Capt. Grant's Company; John Campbell, 13 ½ pounds, https://digital.ncdcr.gov/Documents/Detail/tax-lists-iredell-county-1815/358103?item=358191, access date Feb 15, 2025.

6. 1820, U.S. Federal Census, Iredell County, North Carolina, page 232, John Campbell, 3xx11x11xx2.

7. 1830, U.S. Federal Census, Iredell County, North Carolina, page 20–21, John Campbell Sen., 1 male 50–59, 1 female slave 36–54.

8. 1784–1787, North Carolina State Census, Wilkes County, page 8, John Campbell, head of household, one white male, 21–60; no others listed in household; Sarah Mullis on page 7, Thomas Cook and Isham Harvell on page 9.

9. 1793, North Carolina Census, Wilkes County, Campbells District, John Campbell.

10. 1787, North Carolina Census, Wilkes County, Gordons District, John Campbell.

11. Aug 27,1850, U.S. Federal Census, Iredell County, North Carolina, page 898, dwelling 529, family 536, Cary Campbell, age 91, birthplace Virginia, real estate valued at $45, cannot read or write; Nancy Campbell, age 58, born in NC; Syrien J. Campbell, age 22, born in NC.

12. 1986, *A History of the English-Speaking Mullis Family*, by Art Mullies, Etcetera Publishing Company.

13. 1790, U.S. Federal Census, Wilkes County, North Carolina, Sarah Mullis, 121x.

14. "The American Revolution in North Carolina," by J. D. Lewis, https://www.carolana.com/NC/

Revolution/nc_rowan_county_regiment.html, access date Feb 15, 2025.

15. "Williamsburgh, North Carolina," Wikipedia, https://en.wikipedia.org/wiki/Williamsburgh,_North_Carolina, access date Feb 16, 2025.

16. Apr 1, 1778, North Carolina land grant, Iredell County, file no. 111, John Campbell, recorded in Land Patent Book 82, page 284 as Iredell County Grant number 102, entered on Apr 1, 1778, issued on Jul 7, 1794; survey by Abner Sharpe, Deputy for William Sharpe, on May 12, 1790, https://www.nclandgrants.com/grant/?mars=12.14.76.111&qid=1142909&rn=8, access date Mar 4, 2025.

17. 1860, U.S. Federal Census. Union Grove Post Office, District South of Hunting Creek, Iredell County, North Carolina, page 25, Family 181, John S. Campbell, day laborer, aged 40; Nancy Campbell, mother, aged 67.

18. 1870, U.S. Census for Union Grove Postal Route, Union Grove Township, Iredell County, North Carolina, page 12, family 81, John Campbell, aged 50, Nancy Campbell, aged 70; page 19, family 138, Sampson Ball, Adeline Ball, Elijah Ball, Ann Eidson, Edmond Norman, Jane Ball.

19. 1830, U.S. Census for Iredell County, North Carolina, pages 9–10, Adam Campbell, George Campbell, John M. Campbell, John Campbell Sr.

20. 1840, U.S. Census for Iredell County, North Carolina, Sampson Ball, John M. Campbell.

21. Aug 27, 1850, U.S. Federal Census, Iredell County, North Carolina, page 898, dwelling 530, family 537, John M. Campbell, age 49, farmer; with Catharine, age 40; Thomas, age 25; Carolus, age 24; William, age 15; Mary, age 15; and F M Campbell, age 12; all born in North Carolina, except Catharine who born in Virginia.

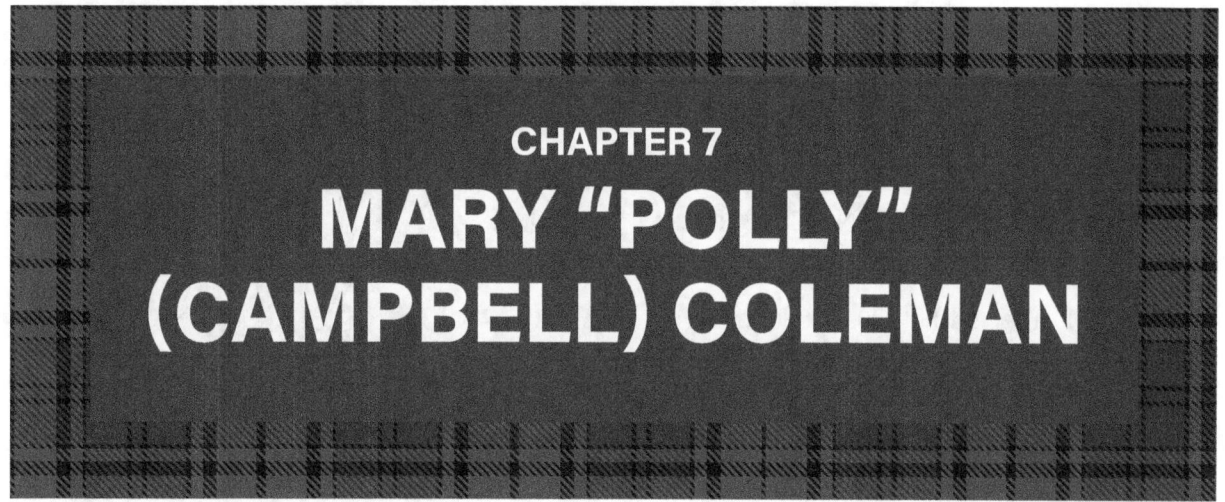

MARY "POLLY" (CAMPBELL) COLEMAN

1.4 **Mary "Polly" Campbell** (1760–aft. Sep 11, 1834) was the fourth of eight children of Adam Campbell (1735–1779) and **Elizabeth (Morgan) Campbell** (1735–1789) of Rowan County and Iredell County, North Carolina. Mary was born in Culpeper County, Virginia, and moved with her family to Rowan County in about 1775, where her first child was born. Mary married **Charles Coleman** (1756–May 23, 1826) in Wilkes County in about 1780. Charles owned 222 acres of land, including a mill, in Wilkes County on Osborn Creek near the Surry County line. Charles appeared on the 1784 Tax List for Wilkes County. Mary and Charles died in Wilkes County. Their burial locations are unknown but are probably in Wilkes County.[1, 2, 3, 4, 5, 6]

Five of Mary and Charles Coleman's 10 children were listed in the H. P. Vanhoy *History of the Campbell Family* in 1925.[7] Their known children are listed below.

JACKIE COLEMAN

1.4.1 **Jackie Coleman** (1781–unknown) is only mentioned but not profiled in the Campbell family history document. She may have died in Yadkin County.[7]

NANCY ANN COLEMAN

1.4.2 **Nancy Ann Coleman** (1782–Aug 24, 1870) married Asa Rash Sr. (1781–aft. Oct 30, 1828) in Wilkes County on Nov 12, 1800.[3] Asa was the son of Daniel Andrew Rash (1733–1836), a neighbor of Adam Campbell. Nancy and Asa lived in Wilkes County. Asa may have been buried at the Greenwell Cemetery in Johnson County, Tennessee, where he was visiting one of his children. His will was recorded and

Figure 7.1 Nancy Ann Coleman, bef. 1870, Wilkes County.

probated in Wilkes County. Nancy died in Somers Township, Wilkes County. See Figure 7.1. Asa and Nancy had 14 children:[7,8, 9, 10, 11, 12]

1. Charles Franklin Rash Sr. (1801–1831) married Lydia Cass (1805–Nov 1898) on Nov 18, 1820, in Wilkes County.[12]

2. Daniel Rash (1802–1870) married Sarah Rash (1800–aft. 1870) on Mar 9, 1824, in Wilkes County. They were living in Union Grove Township in 1870. Their oldest son, Asa Rash (Mar 28, 1823–Feb 5, 1888), married Martha J. Sheppard (Jan 26, 1827–Feb 4, 1881). See Figure 7.2. Asa and Martha were buried at the Cooper Cemetery in Hancock County, Indiana.[12]

3. Elizabeth Rash (1804–1850) married Beriam Byram Ball (Oct 7, 1802–aft. Sep 16, 1850) on Jan 18, 1825, in Wilkes County (see also 1.5.7). They died in Hancock County, Indiana, where Elizabeth was buried at the Cook Cemetery.[12]

4. Robert E. Rash (1805–1882) married Setha Leatha Bryant (Jan 31, 1805–Jul 31, 1880) on Aug 1, 1824, in Wilkes County. They remained in Wilkes County until 1835, when

FIGURE 7.2 Asa and Martha J. Rash, before 1881, Hancock County (colorized).

Left: FIGURE 7.3 Robert E. and Setha Rash, bef. 1882, Iowa.

Middle: FIGURE 7.4 Painting of Setha Leatha Bryant, abt. 1840, Wilkes County.

Right: FIGURE 7.5 Children of Robert and Setha Rash, Back, L to R: Watson, John, Melvin; Front, L to R: Amanda, Lewis, Nancy; abt. 1898–1900, Iowa.

they moved to Tennessee and then moved to Iowa in 1853. They died in Keokuk County, Iowa, and were buried at the Reed Cemetery.[12] See Figures 7.3, 7.4, and 7.5.

5. Lewis Levi Rash (1811–1854) married Rebecca Hamerner (1810–Apr 4, 1879) on Dec 24, 1928, in Wilkes County. They moved to Hancock County, Indiana, by 1840, where they died.[12]

6. Nancy Jane Rash (1811–Apr 1860) married Luke L. Rash (1808–1848) on Dec 3, 1837, in Wilkes County. After Luke died, Nancy moved to Watauga County, North Carolina, where she died.[12]

7. Phoebe E. Rash (Sep 28, 1814–Feb 3, 1877) married John William Morgan (1812–Sep 3, 1850) before 1832 in Putnam County, Indiana. After John died, she married George M. D. Paley (abt. 1815–aft. 1869) on Dec 28, 1869, in Hancock County, Indiana. Phoebe may have died in Nodaway County, Missouri.

8. Beverly Rash (1815–Dec 1851) married Mary Brown (1815–1849) on Jul 25, 1834, in Wilkes County. A jury in the Cabarrus County Superior Court found Beverly guilty of murdering his wife. Beverly kept a stillhouse and sold spirits. Spirituous liquor was at the bottom of the tragedy.[12, 13, 14]

9. Daniel Asa Rash Jr. (Mar 29, 1816–Nov 4, 1863) was a sergeant in the 55th North Carolina Infantry Regiment during the U.S. Civil War. He was captured at the Battle of Gettysburg and died. He was buried at Point Lookout, St. Mary's County, Maryland.

10. John Rash (1817–aft. 1860) was born in Wilkes County and married Ruth "Unknown Last Name" (abt. 1806–bef. 1860).[12]

11. Thomas Meredith Rash (1820–abt. 1870) may have moved to Indiana.[12]

12. Amos Rash (Aug 1821–Aug 28, 1907) married Rebeccah Coleman (abt. 1832–aft. May 14, 1861) on Sep 28, 1851, in Wilkes County. Amos and Rebeca moved to Johnson County, Tennessee, by 1860. Amos served as a private in the 12th and 13th Tennessee Cavalry Regiments in the Union Army during the U.S. Civil War. After Rebeca's death, Amos married Delilah E. Smith (Oct 1, 1842–Jun 15, 1894) in Johnson County on Aug 30, 1862. Amos, Rebeccah, and Delilah died in Johnson County. Delilah and perhaps Amos were buried at the Greenwell Cemetery in Johnson County.[12]

13. Mary Jane Rash (Jul 6, 1827–Nov 26, 1890) married Alfred Warren (Jun 24, 1813–Feb 5, 1903) on Sep 12, 1850, in Wilkes County. They lived near Osbornville in Wilkes County and were buried at Zion Baptist Church in Union Grove Township.[12]

EMMA COLEMAN

1.4.3 **Emma Coleman** (1783–unknown) may have married William Myers (1783–unknown). They may have died in Kentucky.[7]

ROBERT HENRY COLEMAN

1.4.4: Robert Henry Coleman Sr. (1785–1846) married Mary Elizabeth "Betsey" Rash (1785–aft. 1860) on Jun 2, 1805, in Wilkes County.[3] They had four children:

1. Ruth Coleman (1806–1840) married John Kemp (1805–bef. Sep 1891) on May 11, 1825, in Wilkes County.

2. John Ball Coleman (1808–Aug 28, 1889) married Rebecca Allen Brown (Dec 30, 1815–Sep 14, 1885) on Aug 14, 1829, in Wilkes County. Their son, Campbell Coleman (1834–Oct 22, 1863), fought with the 54th Infantry, CSA, during the U.S. Civil War and died of disease in Richmond, Virginia, where he was buried at the Oakwood Cemetery.

3. Mary Ann Coleman (1824–1850) married John Martin Laws (1820–aft. 1860) in Wilkes County on Feb 6, 1851.

4. Robert Henry Coleman Jr. (abt. 1845–Jun 30, 1862) married Mary Ann Jones (abt. 1825–aft. 1880) Sep 29, 1845, in Wilkes County. Robert was in the 37th North Carolina Infantry and died from wounds suffered at the Battle of Gaines' Mill in Virginia during the U.S. Civil War.[15]

JANE COLEMAN

1.4.5   **Jane Coleman** (1786–aft. May 1839) was mentioned in the Vanhoy Campbell History.[7]

AUGUSTUS COLEMAN

1.4.6   **Augustus "Gus" Coleman** (1787–aft. 1814) married Nancy Elmore (1787–unknown) before 1814. They may have had a child, Alfred H. Coleman (Aug 2, 1814–Oct 26, 1883), who lived in Georgia and fought for the CSA in Mississippi during the U.S. Civil War. He died in Ellis County, Texas. Alfred married Caroline Matilda Ingram (Jan 4, 1822–Mar 8, 1900) on Mar 2, 1837, in Talbot County, Georgia.[16]

BEVERLY C. COLEMAN

1.4.7   Beverly C. Coleman Sr. (Apr 3, 1788–May 1, 1872) married Rebecca Nicholson (1792–1844) on Dec 20, 1808, in Wilkes County and Tabitha Goodnight (1808–aft. 1880) on Dec 9, 1845, in Muhlenberg County, Kentucky. Beverly moved to Kentucky with his family by 1819. He obtained a land grant in Muhlenberg County in 1825. He died in Muhlenberg County and was buried at the Coleman Family Cemetery on land now owned by the Peabody Coal Company. He had nine children:[17, 18, 19]

1. James E. Coleman (Mar 21, 1815–Jun 4, 1877) was born in Wilkes County. He married Julia Ann Watkins (Nov 13, 1817–Apr 13, 1881) in Muhlenberg County, Kentucky. They were buried at the Coleman Cemetery in Muhlenberg County, Kentucky.

2. Mary Ann Coleman (Dec 28, 1816–Feb 27, 1891) was born in Wilkes County. She married Robert William Eades (Apr 25, 1816–Jun 21, 1907) on Apr 25, 1839, in Muhlenberg County, Kentucky. They were buried at the Evergreen Cemetery in Muhlenberg County.

3. Beverly H. Coleman (Jul 23, 1818–Nov 23, 1868) was born in Muhlenberg County. He married Catherine D. Ashbridge (Jan 6, 1825–Jul 13, 1915) in Caldwell County, Kentucky. Beverly was buried at the Coleman Family Cemetery in Muhlenberg County. Catherine was buried at the Yeargins Chapel Cemetery in Muhlenberg County.

4. Catherine Rebecca M. Coleman (Apr 11, 1820–Apr 1, 1887) was born in Muhlenberg County. She married Charles Watkins (Jan 11, 1815–Dec 4, 1876) on Aug 5, 1841, in Muhlenberg County. Charles was the brother of Julia Ann Watkins.

5. Archibald Cook Coleman (Jul 2, 1822–Oct 24, 1901) was born in Muhlenberg County. He married Mary Martha Powell (Aug 25, 1811–Feb 18, 1899) in Caldwell County, Kentucky, on Jan 14, 1846. They were buried at the Yeargins Chapel Cemetery in Muhlenberg County.

6. Charles E Coleman (1827–Apr 5, 1913) was born in Muhlenberg County.

7. Leroy P. Coleman (abt. 1829–aft. 1880) was born in Muhlenberg County.

8. William C. Coleman (1832–Nov 13, 1864) was born in Muhlenberg County. He married Amelia Rilley Asbridge (Jun 23, 1838–Jun 28, 1913) on Dec 2, 1854, in Eddyville, Lyon County, Kentucky. William was a Private in the 23rd Kentucky Infantry Regiment, Union Army, during the U.S. Civil War. He was killed in action, probably at the Battle of Bull's Gap in Tennessee. See Figure 7.6.

FIGURE 7.6 Pvt. William C. Coleman, abt. 1860, Chattanooga, Tennessee.

9. James Herrod Coleman (May 23, 1853–Jul 7, 1922) was the only child of Beverly C. Coleman Sr. by his second wife, Catherine "Tabitha" D. Goodnight. James married Drusilla Rhuehamer Bridges (Sep 8, 1854–Feb 4, 1926). See Figures 7.7 and 7.8. James and Drusilla were buried at the Yeargins Chapel Cemetery in Muhlenberg County, Kentucky.

Left:
FIGURE 7.7 James Herrod Coleman, abt. 1900, Muhlenberg County.

Right:
FIGURE 7.8 Drusilla Bridges, abt. 1880, Muhlenberg County.

PHOEBE COLEMAN

1.4.8: Phoebe Coleman (1790–abt.1865) married Lazarus Nicholson Sr. (1789–1855) on Mar 11, 1809, in Wilkes County.[3] Lazarus obtained a land grant in Sullivan County, Indiana, on May 25, 1841.[20] They lived near Jackson Hill in Sullivan County. Phoebe and Lazarus had 12 children, all born in Wilkes County:[21, 22, 23, 24]

1. Nancy Jane Nicholson (1801–1834) married Silas Elijah Lunsford (1806–aft. 1850) in about 1828 in Wilkes County.

2. Elizabeth Nicholson (Jun 19, 1813–Nov 6, 1864) married Wilborn "Ruben" Kemp (Sep 12, 1809–Mar 25, 1877) on Feb 21, 1832, in Wilkes County. They moved to Indiana before 1850 and died there.

3. John C. Nicholson (1814–Mar 1884) married Rebecca Zink (1827–Dec 1884) in about 1841, probably in Indiana. They were buried at the Bethel Cemetery in Sullivan County, Indiana.

4. Samuel Nicholson (1820–bef. 1880) married Jane McDonald (Aug 1833–Oct 20, 1917) on Mar 17, 1856, in Indiana. He may have married Judy Cox (1820–abt. 1850) in Indiana before Jane. Samuel died in Indiana, probably in Sullivan County.

5. Mary Ellen "Polly" Nicholson (1823–Aug 1880) married Ezekial Riley Sexton (Mar 4, 1823–Oct 20, 1903) in about 1840 in Indiana. She died of yellow fever in Linn County, Kansas. Ezekial served with the Missouri 12th Mounted Cavalry Regiment, Union Army

during the U.S. Civil War. Ezekial was buried at the Zoar Cemetery in Harrison County, Missouri. Mary Ellen died in Linn County, Kansas.

6. James Larena Nicholson (1824–Aug 1870) married Susan A. Piefer (1833–1861) in 1849 in Sullivan County. He died in Spencer County, Indiana.

7. Charles H. Nicholson (1826–1910) was born in Wilkes County and came to Hancock County, Indiana, as a young man. He married Mary "Polly" Cox (1830–1860) on Dec 26, 1850, in Vermillion County, Indiana. Charles was tall and possessed great physical strength. He helped to dig the Wabash and Erie Canals and later worked on the railroads. Charles and Polly were buried at the Union Cemetery in Hoosierville, Clay County, Indiana.[24]

8. Jacob J. Nicholson (Feb 20, 1826–Dec 25, 1883) may have died in Jasper County, Missouri, where he was buried at the Park Cemetery. He may have married Amanda Olive Hipsher (Feb 4, 1857–Apr 5, 1907) on Feb 7, 1772, in Sullivan County, Indiana. Amanda was buried at the Old Union Cemetery in Clay County.

9. Lazarus Nicholson Jr. (1829–1877) married Elizabeth Gabbard (1842–) on Sep 14, 1863, in Sullivan County.

10. Lydia Nicholson (Apr 5, 1830–Mar 1860) married Stephen John House (Jan 11, 1830–Sep 16, 1876) on Jul 15, 1859, in Sullivan County. They were both buried at the Coffman Cemetery in Sullivan County.

11. William Thomas Nicholson Sr. (Feb 1831–1908) married Telitha Elizabeth Thomas (Jul 12, 1837–Dec 1, 1911) in 1863 in Lafayette County, Missouri. William and Telitha were buried at the Cheyenne Valley Cemetery in Major County, Oklahoma.

12. Sarah Ann Nicholson (1836–1871/1875) married Lewis Mattox (May 28, 1846–Jul 3, 1934) on Mar 28, 1867, in Indiana.

ARCHIBALD COLEMAN

1.4.9: Archibald Coleman Sr. (1792–Sep 6, 1860) married Elizabeth D. Moorman (1798–1838) on Sep 6, 1812, in Wilkes County, and later married Elizabeth D. Roark (abt. 1798–Oct 2, 1860) in about 1840 in Hopkins County, Kentucky.[25] Archibald and his first wife moved to Hopkins County by 1815, where his children were born to his first wife:[26]

1. John Moorman Coleman (Jan 22, 1815–Jul 20, 1885) married Martha A. Oates (Nov 1817–Jan 14, 1884) on Mar 1, 1835, in Muhlenberg County, Kentucky.

2. Charles H. Coleman (1817–1867) married Marcella Pennington (1815–Jul 29, 1866) in about 1841 in Kentucky.

3. Jane Moorman Coleman (Jul 14, 1819–May 21, 1894) married William Madison Fox (Sep 22, 1814–Aug 23, 1883) on Oct 3, 1847, in Kentucky.

4. Beverly C. Coleman (Sep 15, 1821–Jan 3, 1874) married Sarah E. Teague (1827–1879) on Aug 22, 1843, in Hopkins County.

5. Archibald Coleman Jr. (Jul 1822–Sep 1905) died in Muhlenberg County, Kentucky.

6. Frances D. Coleman (1826–1863) married Ephraim Miller (1822–Aug 25, 1892) on Jul 5, 1847, in Hopkins County.

7. Andrew Jackson Coleman (Jun 30, 1829–Oct 1, 1894) married Rebecca Anne Harris (Oct 26, 1829–Feb 11, 1914) on Jan 19, 1851, in Muhlenberg County, Kentucky. Andrew was buried at the Earlton Cemetery in Neosho County, Kansas.

8. George Washington Coleman (abt. 1832–aft 1870) married Martha L. Bourland (abt. 1832–Apr 1880) on Dec 27, 1859, in Hopkins County, Kentucky.

9. Thomas Jefferson Coleman (Feb 1834–abt. 1905) married Mildred Ann Harper (abt. 1848–Nov 22, 1874) on Sep 16, 1867, in Mississippi County, Missouri. Thomas was a physician. Thomas served with the 43rd Ohio Infantry Regiment, Union Army, during the U.S. Civil War. After Mildred died, he married Mary Margaret Horn (Oct 1852–Apr 28, 1895) on Nov 10, 1875, in Mississippi County.

JOHN H. COLEMAN

1.4.10 John H. Coleman (1793–abt. 1880) married Susannah Felts (1793–aft. 1880) in Wilkes County on Dec 26, 1818.[3] John obtained a North Carolina land grant for five acres on Osborne Creek, issued on Nov 29, 1832.[27] Their eight children were all born in Wilkes County:[28, 29]

1. Elisha Coleman (1821–1873) died in Yadkin County.

2. Sarah Coleman (Mar 4, 1822–Jul 9, 1892) married Israel "Azel" M. Holland (Jun 10, 1820–Oct 10, 1880) on Apr 3, 1845, in Wilkes County.

3. Beverly Coleman (Oct 1825–Nov 29, 1900) married Nancy E. Norman (Dec 1825–aft. 1900).

4. Charles Coleman (1828–Jul 16, 1904) married Elizabeth Sparks (1825–aft. 1880) on Oct 3, 1851, in Yadkin County. Charles's headstone indicates that he served with the Union Army's 3rd Ohio Cavalry Regiment during the U.S. Civil War. He may also have married Dean Elora "Elvira" Brannoch (Feb 1834–Sep 2, 1920) in Surry County in about 1893. Charles was buried at the Rocky Ford Baptist Church Cemetery in Surry County.

5. Rebeccah Coleman (abt. 1832–aft. May 14, 1861) married Amos Rash (Aug 1821–Aug 28, 1907), her cousin and son of Asa Rash and Nancy Ann Coleman (1.4.2).

6. Aaron G. Coleman (1834–aft. 1880) may have served with the CSA during the U.S. Civil War.

7. William Coleman (1838–May 11, 1878) may have moved to Adair County, Kentucky.

8. Edmund J. Coleman (Mar 20, 1838–May 11, 1878) married Matilda J. Patterson (Dec 2, 1844–Jan 19, 1916) on Aug 4, 1866, in Christian County, Kentucky. Edmond and Matilda were buried at the Taylor-Wesley Cemetery in Adair County.

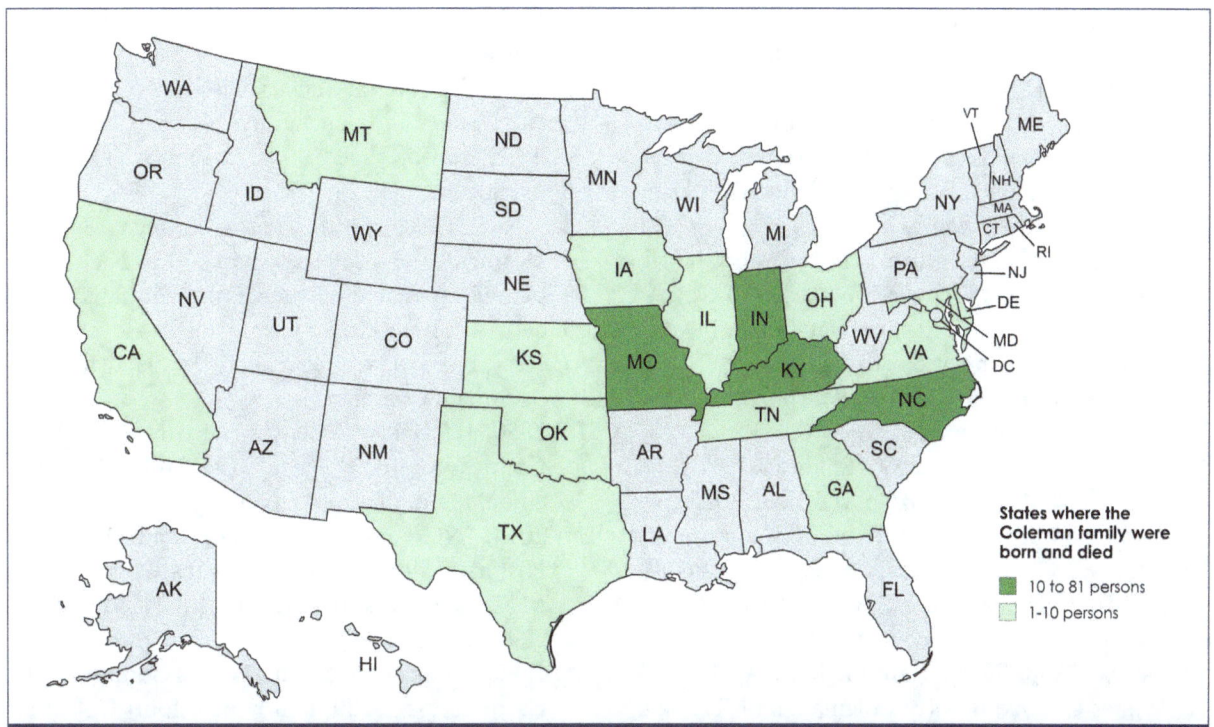

FIGURE 7.9 States where Mary Polly (Campbell) Coleman and her descendants were born and died (137 total people). The largest numbers were in North Carolina, 79 born and 37 died; Kentucky, 32 born and 34 died; Indiana, 9 born and 29 died; Missouri, 1 born and 10 died.

CHAPTER 7 REFERENCES

1. Aug 6, 1810, U.S. Federal Census, Wilkes County, North Carolina, page 876, Charles Coleman, head of household.

2. 1820, U.S. Federal Census, Wilkes County, North Carolina, page 497, Charles Coleman, head of household.

3. May 23, 1826, Estate Records, Wilkes County, North Carolina, Charles Coleman deceased, died on Osborn Creek, widow Mary Coleman, estate of 524 acres on Osborn Creek, plantation, and mill.

4. 1830, U.S. Federal Census, Wilkes County, North Carolina, page 382, Mary Coleman, head of household.

5. Sep 11, 1834, will of Mary Coleman, Wilkes County, North Carolina, probated Aug 1835.

6. 1784, Tax List, Wilkes County, North Carolina, image 15 of 28; Charles Coleman, 960 pounds.

7. Aug 1925, "Descendants of Pierce Campbell Hold Reunion," *Statesville Morning Register,* Aug 1925, as well as handout given at the reunion, *History of the Campbel Family,* compiled by H. P. Vanhoy.

8. Nov 12, 1800, Wilkes County, North Carolina marriage bond, Nansey Colmon and Asa Rash, Levey Rash Bondsman.

9. 1850, U.S. Federal Census for Wilkes County, North Carolina, page 541, family 294, Nancy Rash, aged 65.

10. 1860, U.S. Federal Census for Lower Division, Lovelace Post Office, Wilkes County, North Carolina, page 44, family 307, Nancy Rash aged 77, living with Daniel Rash, aged 61, family.

11. 1870, U.S. Federal Census for Sommers Township, Wilkes County, North Carolina, page 9, family 68, Nancy Rash, aged 81, living with Daniel Rash, aged 70, family.

12. Feb 1829, will of Asa Rash, Wilkes County, North Carolina, no. 4, 1821–1848, Wilkesboro.

13. May 15, 1851, The Carolina Watchman, Beverly Rash Story, Salisbury, North Carolina.

14. May 15, 1851, *The Carolina Watchman,* Beverly Rash Story, Salisbury, North Carolina.

15. Jun 30, 1862, "U.S., Civil War Soldier Records and Profiles, 1861–1865," Provo, UT, USA: Ancestry.com Operations Inc, Pvt. Robert Coleman.

16. Jun 8/9, 1880, U.S. Federal Cenus, Precinct 6, Ellis County, Texas; Alferd Coleman, dwelling 105, family 111, age 64, born in North Carolina.

17. Dec 20, 1808, "North Carolina Marriage Bonds," Wilkes County, Beverly Coleman, and Rebekah Nichelson bond 000164659.

18. Dec 9, 1845, "Kentucky County marriage Records, 1783-1965," Muhlenberg County, Beverly Coleman and Tabitha Goodnight, film no. 000557316.

19. "Find a Grave," Coleman Cemetery, Muhlenberg County, Kentucky, Beverly C. Coleman Sr., tombstone.

20. May 25, 1841, U.S. General Land Office Records, Vincennes Land Office, Sullivan County, Indiana.

21. Mar 11, 1809, "North Carolina, Marriage Bonds, 1741–1868," Wilkes County, Lazrus Nicholson married Phoebe Coleman, bondsman Beverly Coleman, witness Benjamin Martin, bond no. 000166745.

22. 1860, U.S. Federal Census, Louis Centerville Post Office, Jackson Township, Sullivan County, Indiana, page 207, family 1454, Pheba Nicholson, aged 68.

23. 1850, U.S. Federal Census, District no. 105, Sullivan County, Indiana, family 787, page 511, Phoeby Nicholson, aged 58 with family of Charles Nicholson, aged 24.

24. Jun 2, 1910, "Death Takes Pioneer," *Sullivan Democrat Newspaper,* Charels H. Nicholson, page 2, Hymera, Sullivan County, Indiana.

25. Sep 12, 1860, "Find a Grave" for Prospect Cemetery, Hopkins County, Kentucky, headstone for Archibald Coleman.

26. 1850, U.S. Federal Census, District 1, Hopkins County, Kentucky, page 122, family 187, Archibald and Elizabeth Coleman.

27. 2014, "NC Land Grant Images and Data," NC Historical Records Online, created by David McCorkle, access date various times in 2023 and 2024.

28. 1850, U.S. Federal Census, Wilkes County, North Carolina, page 539, family 280, John Coleman, aged 54; Susannah Coleman, aged 59; Elisha, aged 29; Beverly, aged 25; Charles, aged 22; Rebecca, aged 19; Aron, aged 16; William, aged 14; Edmond, aged 12.

29. Dec 26, 1818, "North Carolina Index to Marriage Bonds," Wilkes County, Susannah Felts and John Coleman, bondsman Charles Rash, witness Amelia Martin, bond no. 000164658.

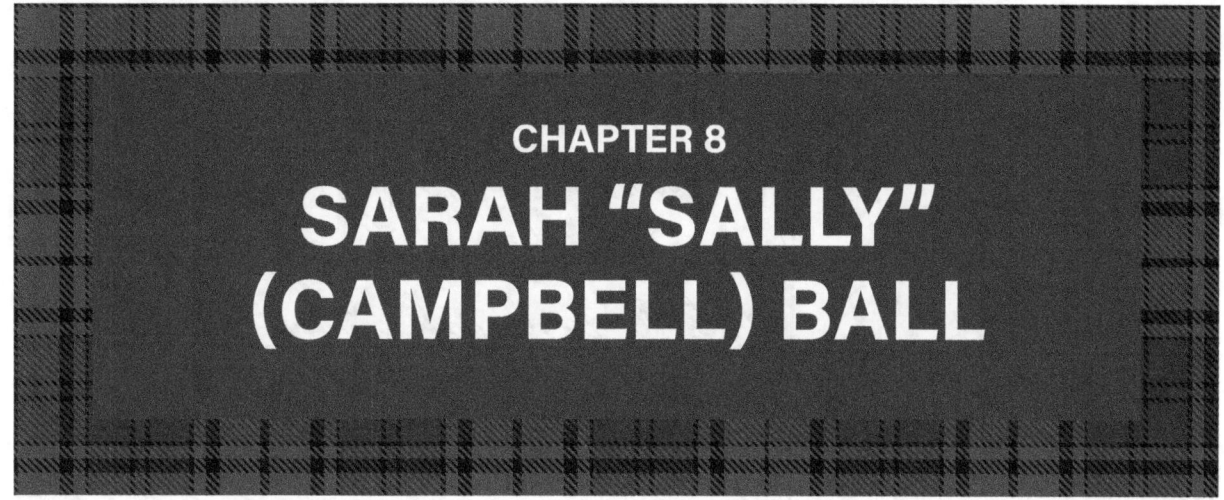

SARAH "SALLY" (CAMPBELL) BALL

1.5   **Sarah "Sally" Campbell** (Sep 9, 1763–Mar 23, 1844) was the fifth child of **Adam Campbell** (1735–1779) and **Elizabeth (Morgan) Campbell** (1735–1798) of Rowan County and Iredell County, North Carolina. Sarah was born in Culpeper County, Virginia, and moved to Rowan County with her parents in about 1775. Sarah married **William Ball Jr.**[1] (Jul 9, 1766–bef. Jan 30, 1844) on Sep 9, 1788, in Rowan County, in the part that became Iredell County on Nov 3, 1788[2, 3, 4, 5, 6, 7, 8, 9] Sarah and William lived on Ford's Branch of Hunting Creek in Iredell County near her brother, Perciphull Campbell, and Thomas Rash. In 1812, they moved to the area of Osborn's Creek in Wilkes County.

William Ball applied for the following North Carolina state land grants in Rowan and Iredell Counties:[10]

❖ 1780: 300 acres on Ford's Branch waters of Hunting Creek in Rowan County, issued by Rowan County in 1789. The land survey by Griffith Rutherford is shown in Figure 8.1.

❖ 1780: 100 acres on Hunting Creek issued by Iredell County in 1802.

❖ 1780: 50 acres on a branch of Hunting Creek, issued by Iredell County in 1802.

❖ 1823: 250 acres on the ridges between Hunting Creek and Rocky Creek adjoining Perciphull Campbell, Thomas Rash, and others, issued by Iredell County in 1825.

❖ 1812: 41 acres on Osborn Creek, issued by Wilkes County in 1814.

❖ 1836: 16 acres on Osborn Creek, issued by Wilkes County in 1837.

The first land grant applied for in 1780 may have been for William Ball Jr.'s father, William Ball Sr. (1745–1806), who was born in Middlesex County, Virginia. His great-grandfather was Edward Ball Sr. (1670–1726) of Christchurch Parish, Middlesex County, Colony of Virginia. His grandfather, Daniel Ball (1713–1794) came to Granville County, North Carolina, before the American Revolution. This Ball family has a Y-DNA project with a Haplogroup of R-BY191048 and English origins for this family line.[11] The William Ball Jr. family were early members of the Grassy Knob Baptist Church in Iredell County.[12, 13]

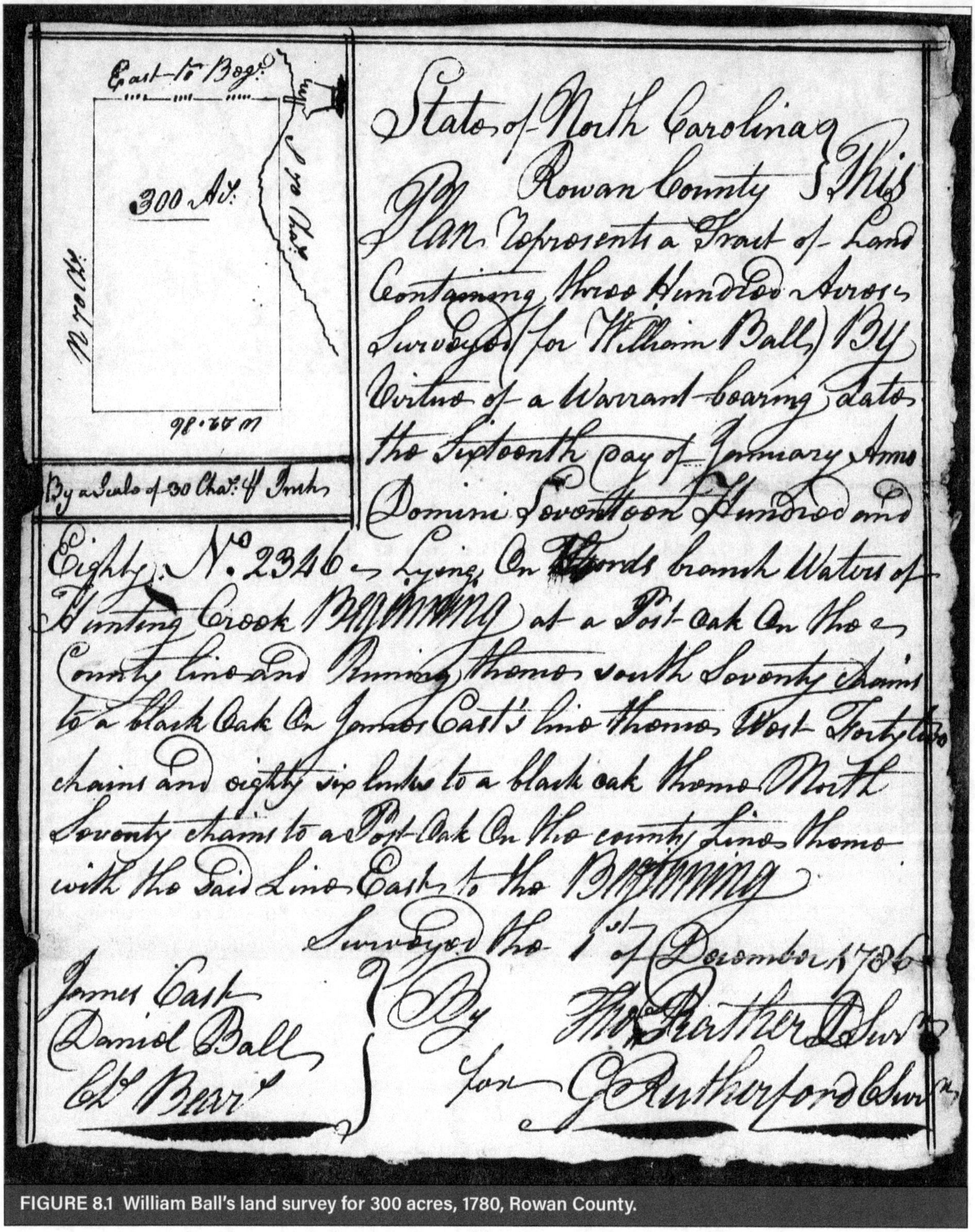

East to Begn.

S 70 Chs.

300 Acs.

N 70 Chs.

W 42.86

By a Scale of 30 Chas: 4 Inchs

State of North Carolina
Rowan County } This Plan represents a Tract of Land Containing three Hundred Acres Surveyed for William Ball By Virtue of a Warrant bearing date the Sixteenth day of January Anno Domini Seventeen Hundred and Eighty No. 2346 Lying On Heards[?] branch Waters of Hunting Creek Beginning at a Post Oak On the County line and Running thence south Seventy chains to a black Oak On James Cast's line thence West Forty two chains and eighty six links to a black oak thence North Seventy chains to a Post Oak On the county Line thence with the Said Line East to the Beginning

Surveyed the 1st of December 1786

James Cast
Daniel Ball
Chs. Barr[?] } By Thos. Rather D. Survr.
for G. Rutherford Survr.

FIGURE 8.1 William Ball's land survey for 300 acres, 1780, Rowan County.

William Ball may have served as a private in the War of 1812 under Maj. Tisdale's command in the North Carolina Militia.[14] William and Sarah probably died in Wilkes County. The executors of William's estate in 1844 were his son, Sampson Ball, and his son-in-law, Iredell Privette. William and Sarah's burial locations are not known, but could be on their land near Osborne's Creek in Wilkes County.

Only four of William and Sarah's eight children were listed in the 1925 Vanhoy *History of the Campbell Family*. See Figure 4.1 for a map showing the area along Hunting Creek where the Ball family lived. All eight children were born in Wilkes County, North Carolina, including those listed below.[1, 8]

SAMPSON HARRISON BALL

1.5.1 **Sampson Harrison Ball** (Jul 18, 1789–Apr 1, 1875) married Rosanna Norman (Sep 1792–Apr 25, 1860) on Oct 21, 1811, in Wilkes County.[15] Sampson was a millwright and owned and operated the Holten Mill in Iredell County. Sampson and Rosanna were buried at the Union Grove Methodist Church Cemetery.[16] Sampson served in the 48th North Carolina Infantry Regiment, CSA, during the U.S. Civil War. His sons who lived during the Civil War also fought for the CSA.[17] They had 13 children:[1, 18, 19, 20, 21]

1. William Franklin Ball (Apr 23, 1812–1870) married Margaret Martha Morris (1812–1877) on Aug 9, 1838, in Carroll County, Georgia. William served as a private in the 1st Regiment of the Texas Mounted Volunteers, CSA, during the U.S. Civil War. William and Margaret died in DeSoto Parish, Louisiana, and were buried at Mount Bethel Cemetery in Panola County, Texas.

2. Anna C. Ball (Jan 23, 1814–May 6, 1900) married William Spencer Eidson (1801–aft. 1860) in about 1835 in Iredell County. They were buried at the Morgan Hill Baptist Church in Buncombe County.

3. Sarah Jane R. Ball (Jan 23, 1816–Jun 19, 1889) married John Holmes Gentry (Mar 2, 1816–Jul 1907) in 1836 in Buncombe County, North Carolina. Sarah and John were buried at the Morgan Hill Baptist Church in Buncombe County.

4. Ruth M. Ball (Oct 16, 1817–1850) married Thaddeus Thomas Wooten (Jan 12, 1816–Aug 19, 1893) in 1840 in Iredell County. They were buried at Union Grove Methodist Church.

5. Elizabeth Ball (Jun 22, 1819–Dec 5, 1826) died as a child.

6. James William Ball (Jan 14, 1821–Jun 20, 1863) married Nancy Wooten (1827–Aug 1879) in 1851 in Iredell County.

7. Elijah Young Ball (Oct 4, 1822–May 18, 1902) married Lucinda Reid (Apr 22, 1824–Aug 7, 1886) on Dec 12, 1844, in Wilkes County. He married Critus Fletcher (1842–Jan 7, 1918) in 1874.

8. Mary Adeline Ball (Mar 22, 1824–Mar 5, 1901) did not marry. She was buried at Union Grove Methodist Church.

9. Margaret Emaline Ball (Nov 28, 1825–Apr 3, 1908) married Aaron Frazier (Jun 29, 1810–May 23, 1882).

10. Nancy Clementine Ball (Dec 21, 1827–May 9, 1889) married James Thomas Myers (Dec 29, 1831–Dec 2, 1899) on Apr 4, 1855, in Iredell County. They were buried at the Flat Creek Cemetery in Buncombe County.

11. Enoch J. Ball (May 7, 1829–Sep 13, 1830) died as a child.

12. Daniel Norman Ball (Jun 1, 1831–aft. Jun 1, 1900) married Minerva A. Lewis (1838–1867) on Jan 30, 1855, in Iredell County. He married Nancy M. Myers (Jan 1851–1900) on Nov 14, 1869, in Iredell County. Daniel was buried at the Morgan Baptist Church in Buncombe County.

13. Thomas Morris Ball (Aug 31, 1833–Aug 5, 1894) married Mary Julia Lazenby (Jun 25, 1843–Mar 2, 1928) on Feb 27, 1866, in Iredell County. Thomas was a corporal in the 4th North Carolina Infantry Regiment, CSA, during the U.S. Civil War. He was wounded at the Battle of Chancellorsville on Sep 14, 1862. Thomas and Mary were buried at the Morgan Hill Baptist Church in Buncombe County.

There may have been another child, Rebecca June Ball (Jun 18, 1841–1842), who died as an infant.

IMLAH BALL SR.

1.5.2 **Imlah "Imley" Ball Sr.** (Mar 27, 1791–Aug 26, 1848) married Lucy Johnson (Jan 26, 1791–Jan 1831) in about 1812 in Wilkes County. They had the following children (all born in Wilkes County):[1, 22, 23, 24]

1. Elsie Alcey Ball (Nov 11, 1816–Feb 12, 1899) married Elijah Oliver Felts (Jan 23, 1810–Feb 1, 1892) on Feb 26, 1833, in Wilkes County. See Figure 8.2. They moved to Winnebago County, Illinois, before 1850. Elijah served as a private in the 48th Illinois Infantry Regiment, Union Army, during the U.S. Civil War.

2. Nancy Ball (Nov 9, 1817–Jan 4, 1906) married John Armstrong (Aug 5, 1814–1846) in 1835 in Wilkes County. They moved to Hancock County, Indiana, where Nancy married Peleg "Pelly" Pritchard (abt. 1823–abt. 1858), after John died, on Feb 14, 1847, in Hancock County. She married a third time to George Rinewalt (abt. 1804–May 25, 1900) in Hancock County.

3. Edward Ball (1819–bef. Dec 1, 1862) married Matilda Barrett (1810–aft. 1861) on Feb 20, 1840, in Hancock County. Edward died while serving in the 39th Indiana Infantry, Union Army, during the U.S. Civil War. Edward was buried at the Woodlawn Cemetery in Vigo County, Indiana.

4. Charles Ball (Nov 6, 1821–Apr 17, 1879) married Thirsey Jackson (Aug 18, 1817–Mar 17, 1862) on Feb 9, 1843, in Hancock County. He married Miranda Adeline Atkinson (May 2, 1836–Nov 1, 1881) on Jun 23, 1863, in Moultrie County, Illinois. See Figure 8.3 Charles and Miranda were buried at the Pleasant Ridge Cemetery in Cass County, Missouri. Thirza was buried at the Keller Cemetery in Moultrie County.

5. Lucy Inez Ball (Jun 26, 1824–Sep 27, 1908) married Robert Matthew Jackson (Jan 12, 1815–Sep 19, 1901) on May 14, 1843, in Hancock County. They were buried at the Moline Cemetery in Frontier County, Nebraska.

6. Imlah Ball Jr. (Feb 21, 1825–Feb 26, 1825) died as an infant.

7. Sarah K. Ball (Oct 21, 1827–Aug 1, 1892) married Larkin Ferguson (1822–Apr 26, 1860) on Jul 15, 1843, in Hancock County. Sarah died in Winnebago County, Illinois. Larkin died in Mercer County, Illinois.

8. Hannah Arminta Ball (Mar 20, 1830–Dec 1896) married Roswell Wheeler Hurd (May 27, 1813–Apr 24, 1859) on Sep 20, 1854, in Winnebago County, Illinois. Roswell was the

Left:
FIGURE 8.2 Elsie and Elijah Felts, abt. 1885, Mt. Carroll, Illinois.

Right:
FIGURE 8.3 Charles and Miranda Ball with children: Andrew, Mary, Lucy, Benjamin, Elizabeth, abt. 1858, Cass County.

Left: **FIGURE** 8.4 James Alexander and Esther Ann Ball, abt. 1900, Nebraska.

Middle: **FIGURE** 8.5 Johnathan P. Gray, abt. 1885, Illinois.

Right: **FIGURE** 8.6 Elizabeth Ellen (Ball) Gray, abt. 1900, Illinois.

postmaster in Redding, Illinois, in 1846. Hannah may have married John Miller (1816–Oct 22, 1878) in about 1866 in Illinois. Hannah died in Winnebago or Fayette County, Illinois.

Imlah's second wife was Hannah Jarvis (Aug 3, 1804–Oct 12, 1855), whom he married in about 1835 in Wilkes County. Hannah and Imlah moved to Hancock County, Indiana, in about 1838 and may have been buried at the Gilboa Cemetery in Hancock County.[25] Imlah and Hannah had the following children:[26]

9. James Alexander Ball (Sep 21, 1936–May 18, 1915) married Esther Ann Jones (Sep 10, 1840–Aug 23, 1915) on Dec 4, 1860, in DeWitt County, Illinois (Figure 8.4). James served in the 51st Illinois Infantry Regiment, Union Army, during the U.S. Civil War. They died in Box Butte County, Nebraska, and were buried at the Hemingford Cemetery.

10. William Campbell Ball (Nov 28, 1838–May 4, 1959) did not marry. He died in Hancock County, Indiana

11. Elizabeth Ellen Ball (Sep 9, 1841–Mar 6, 1925) married Johnathan P. Gray (Oct 29, 1837–Jan 9, 1886) on Dec 1, 1859, in De Witt County, Illinois. See Figures 8.5 and 8.6. Jonathan served in the 26th Illinois Infantry Regiment, Union Army, during the U.S. Civil War. Elizabeth died in Macon County, Illinois, and Johnathan died in DeWitt County, Illinois. They were buried at the Evergreen Cemetery in DeWitt County.

12. Mary A. Ball (Aug 26, 1844–Sep 28, 1845) died as a child.

13. Tabitha Jane Ball (Jun 24, 1846–May 5, 1880) married John Wesley Sheets (Apr 14, 1843–Mar 9, 1929) on Feb 18, 1864, in DeWitt County. John served in the 68th Illinois Infantry

Regiment, Union Army, during the U.S. Civil War. They were buried at the Evergreen Cemetery in DeWitt County.

ELISABETH BALL

1.5.3   Elisabeth Ball (Mar 10, 1793–abt. 1820) married Charles Holland Jarvis (1791–1870) on Dec 17, 1811, in Wilkes County.[14] Mary died in Wilkes County. Mary and Charles had at least one child: Barbara Adaline D. Jarvis (abt. 1811–aft. 1860), who married Andrew Jackson Myers (abt. 1811–1908) on Dec 7, 1845, in Wilkes County and moved to Rush County, Indiana, before 1850. After Elizabeth Ball's death, her husband, Charles, married Sarah Ann "Sallie" Howard (1800–Jan 24, 1870), who was the daughter of John Howard of Wilkes County. Between 1840 and 1850, Charles and Sallie and their family moved to Howard County, Indiana, where they died.[1, 27]

LEVI LEE BALL

1.5.4   Levi Lee Ball Sr. (Jan 5, 1795–Aug 29, 1855) married Ailsy Alice Jarvis (Mar 5, 1796–1860), daughter of James Jarvis (1766–1840) and sister of Charles Holland Jarvis (1791–1870) of Wilkes County, on Aug 28, 1817, in Wilkes County. Their children included:[14, 28, 29]

1. Jane "Jincey" Ball (Apr 11, 1820–Apr 11, 1906), who married John William Privette[30] (1822–Jul 14, 1864). John served in the 42nd Infantry Regiment, CSA, during the U.S. Civil War.

2. John Campbell Ball (1824–1880), who married Paulina Vensa "Lina" Davis (1832–bef. 1896) on Nov 19, 1859, in Wilkes County.

3. Cynthia or Synthia Ball (Oct 30, 1829–Feb 3, 1907), who lived in Somers Township, Wilkes County. She may have married between 1880 and 1900.

4. Nancy Caroline Ball (Nov 13, 1829–Apr 25, 1885), who married Benjamin Moses Money (Nov 13, 1829–Jul 15, 1910) on Jan 22, 1851, in Wilkes County. Benjamin served as a private in the 55th North Carolina Infantry Regiment, CSA, during the U.S. Civil War. They died in Wilkes County and were buried at the Mount Vernon Baptist Church.

5. Mary "Polly" Ball (Mar 1830–aft. May 9, 1905), who married Abner Henderson (1841–aft. 1880) on Jan 17, 1867, in Wilkes County. Abner served as a private in the 42nd North Carolina Infantry Regiment, CSA, during the U.S. Civil War. They died in Wilkes County.

6. Lucy Ball (Mar 30, 1832–Oct 31, 1914)), who married Abraham Privette (Oct 31, 1831–Apr 14, 1864) on Feb 2, 1854 in Wilkes County. Lucy and Abraham were buried at the Prevett Cemetery in Yadkin County.

7. Rachel Ball (1838–Feb 28, 1913), who did not marry. She lived with her sister Cynthia in Wilkes County. She died in Wilkes County.

8. Tabitha Ball (abt. 1842–aft. 1880), who married Miles Nathan Gregory (1846–May 19, 1905) on Mar 18, 1866, in Wilkes County.

9. Levi Ball Jr. (1844–Mar 18, 1865), who served in the 44th North Carolina Infantry Regiment, CSA, during the U.S. Civil War. The Union Army captured him at Spotsylvania Court House, Virginia, on May 21, 1864. He was confined in the prison at Point Lookout, Maryland. The Union Army transferred him on Jul 8, 1861, to a prison in Elmira, New York, where he died of pneumonia and was buried at the Woodlawn National Cemetery.

JOEL BALL

1.5.5   Joel Ball (1799–1843) married Elizabeth Jarvis (1800–Dec 25, 1865), daughter of James Jarvis and Elizabeth Johnson, on Feb 17, 1820, in Wilkes County.[14, 31, 32, 33, 34] Elizabeth was the sister of Hannah Jarvis, the second wife of her brother, Imlah Ball (1.5.2). Joel died in Buncombe County. Their children included:

1. Noah H. Ball (Jan 16, 1825–Oct 22, 1906), who married Mary Ann Freeman (Jan 10, 1828–Aug 28, 1904) in 1845 in Buncombe County, North Carolina. Noah served as a private in the 64th North Carolina Infantry Regiment during the U.S. Civil War. Noah and Mary died in Madison County, North Carolina, where they were buried at the Ball Family Cemetery.

2. Marinda Ball (Oct 16, 1832–Apr 3, 1911), who married James Lunsford (Sep 29, 1829–Jan 18, 1901) on Mar 5, 1853, in Madison County, North Carolina. Marinda died in Madison County, where she was buried at the Ball Cemetery.

3. Celia Anne Senia Ball (Jul 16, 1833–Jun 28, 1860), who married Daniel Alexander Payne (Nov 8, 1831–May 21, 1891) on Mar 16, 1851, in Madison County, North Carolina. Daniel was a private in the 64th North Carolina Infantry Regiment, CSA, during the U.S. Civil War. They died in Madison County, North Carolina. Celia was buried at the Baxter Payne Cemetery in Madison County.

4. James Manly Ball (Aug 10, 1836–Nov 23, 1914), who married Sarah Lunsford (1836–1917) on Aug 10, 1855, in Madison County, North Carolina. He lived with his brother, Noah, after his father died. James served as a private in the 2nd North Carolina Mounted Infantry Regiment, CSA, during the U.S. Civil War. James and Sarah died in Madison County, North Carolina, where they were buried at the Ball Cemetery. See Figure 8.7.

FIGURE 8.7
James Manly
Ball, abt. 1900,
Madison County.

BERIAM BYRAM BALL

1.5.6   Beriam Byram Ball (Oct 7, 1802–aft. Sep 16, 1850) married Elizabeth Rash (abt. 1804–aft. Sep 16, 1850), daughter of Asa Rash and Nancy Ann Coleman (1.4.2), on Jan 18, 1825, in Wilkes County.[14] They moved to Hancock County, Indiana, in about 1830. Elizabeth was buried at the Cook Cemetery in Hancock County.[35, 36] Beriam and Elizabeth had four known children:

1.   John Ball (1822–bef. 1860) died in Indiana.

2.   Milton "Miles" William Ball (Jul 5, 1835–Jul 2, 1865) was born in Indiana and married Armilda Carolina Cunningham (Aug 20, 1832–Jun 24, 1913) on Mar 6, 1859, in Hancock County. Miles served as a private in the 30th Indiana Infantry Regiment, Union Army, during the U.S. Civil War. Miles and Armilda were buried at the Rossville Cemetery in Clinton County, Indiana.

3.   William Henry Ball (Jul 23, 1840–Mar 25, 1875) was born in Indiana and married Louisa Cass (Oct 18, 1848–Jun 7, 1928) on Sep 6, 1866, in Hancock County. William was a private and musician in the 116th Indiana Infantry Regiment, Union Army, during the U.S. Civil War. William died in Greenwood County, Kansas, and was buried at the Blakely Cemetery. After William died, Louisa married Thomas David Kelley (May 6, 1834–May 24, 1920) in 1877. Thomas and Louisa moved to Mesa, Colorado, in 1904. Louisa died in Dodge City, Kansas, and was buried at the Maple Grove Cemetery.

4.   Isaac James Ball (Sep 25, 1842–Dec 20, 1896) was born in Indiana and married Mary Abigail Cass (Dec 17, 1840–Aug 6, 1928) on Aug 25, 1864, in Hancock County. Mary and Louisa were sisters. Isaac was a private in the 116th Indiana Infantry Regiment, Union Army, during the U.S. Civil War. Isaac and Mary were buried at the Eden Cemetery in Hancock County.

MARY "POLLY" BALL

1.5.7   **Mary "Polly" Ball** (Oct 2, 1804–aft. 1870) married Iredell Privette (abt. 1807–1868) on Jul 28, 1827, in Wilkes County. Iredell may have been buried at Grassy Knob Baptist Church in Union Grove Township.[1, 8, 14, 37, 38] They had two children:

1.   Cader Calvin Privette (May 1835–Dec 9, 1903) married Martha Wooten (1833–1874) in 1865 in Iredell County. Cader later married Angeline Elliott (1836–Jun 13, 1894) on Nov 5, 1874, in Iredell County. Cader died in Eagle Mills Township and was buried at Union Grove Methodist Church. Cader and both wives were buried at the Union Grove Methodist Church in Union Grove Township.

2.   Nancy L. Privette (Jul 10, 1844–Mar 23, 1926) married Hiram Speaks (1833–Feb 15, 1905) on Apr 14, 1863, in Wilkes County. Nancy and Hiram lived on the farm of Perciphull

Campbell Jr., as referred to in Vanhoy's Campbell family history. Nancy was buried at Grassy Knob Baptist Church in Union Grove Township.

SARAH BALL

1.5.8   **Sarah "Sally" Ball** (Oct 2, 1804–1805) was a twin of Mary and died as an infant.[1]

There may have been another son, James Jerod "Cruther" Ball (1797–May 3, 1855), who was born in Wilkes County and died in Rhea County, Tennessee. The relationship to William Jonas Ball and Sarah Sally Campbell has not been verified. James married Jemina E. Brinkley (1800–1870) on Aug 4, 1821, in Orange County, North Carolina. Jemina died in Benton County, Arkansas.

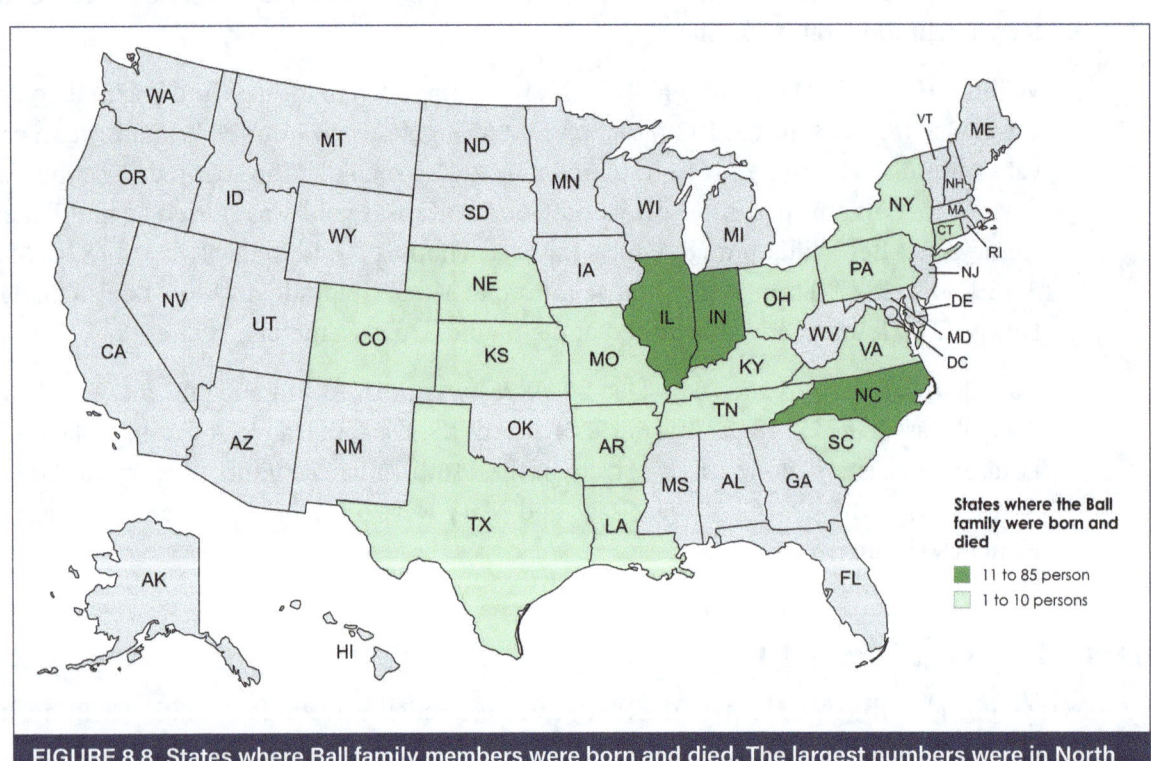

FIGURE 8.8 States where Ball family members were born and died. The largest numbers were in North Carolina, 86 births and 65 deaths; Indiana, 11 births and 20 deaths; Illinois, 2 births and 12 deaths.

CHAPTER 8 REFERENCES

1. Some genealogists speculated that William Ball Jr. may have had a middle name of Silas, but no sourcing has been found that shows his middle name.

2. Aug 1925, "Descendants of Pierce Campbell Holds Reunion," *Statesville Morning Register*, as well as handout given at the reunion, *History of the Campbell Family*, compiled by H. P. Vanhoy.

3. 1790, U.S. Federal Census, Iredell County, North Carolina, page 396, William Ball, 121X.

4. 1800, U.S. Federal Census, Iredell County, North Carolina, page 720, William Ball, 31211338.

5. 1810, U.S. Federal Census, Wilkes County, North Carolina, William Ball, 1121211429.

6. 1820, U.S. Federal Census, Wilkes County, North Carolina, page 542, William Ball, 11121122266.

7. 1830, U.S. Federal Census, Wilkes County, North Carolina, page 377. William, Ball, 111133.

8. 1840, U.S. Federal Census, Capt. Biecknells District, Hunting Creek, Wilkes County, North Carolina, page 22, William Ball, 21xxxxxxx1xxx-|xxxxx1xx1, 6 total, 2 person employed in agriculture.

9. Jan 30, 1844, Wilkes County, North Carolina Estate Records; Sampson Ball and Iredell Privett bound with $200 as administrators of the estate of William Ball, deceased.

10. 2014, "NC Land Grant Images and Data," NC Historical Records Online, created by David McCorkle in 2014, access date various times in 2023 and 2024.

11. "Ball Family of North Carolina, USA and Bedfordshire, England DNA Research Project," https://www.facebook.com/groups/352843345291838, Haplogroup R-DF27, access date Jan 2025.

12. 1989, *Some Pioneers from Wilkes County, N.C.*, compiled by Mrs. W. O. Absher, Southern Historical Press, ISBN 0–8308–644–4.

13. 1804–1951, "History, Membership and Clerk's records of Grassy Knob Baptist Church," compiled by L. T. Queen, https://lfweb.co.iredell.nc.us/icpl/DocView.aspx?id=190&dbid=0&repo=Iredell-County-Library&cr=1, access date Feb 9, 2024; James Iredell Room, Iredell County Public Library.

14. War of 1812 Service Records, Roll Box 9, Microfilm M602, Pvt. William Ball.

15. "North Carolina Marriage Records," Wilkes County: Biram Ball and Elizabeth Rash, Joel Ball and Elizabeth Jarvis, Sampson Ball and Rosanna Norman, Levi Ball and Alce Jarvis, Charles Jarvis and Elizabeth Ball, Iredell Prevatt and Mary Ball.

16. "Find a Grave," Union Grove Methodist Church Cemetery, Iredell County, dates from headstones.

17. "Confederate Soldiers Compiled Service Records," Pvt. Harrison Ball, born abt. 1840, enlisted Aug 8, 1862, place Petersburg, Military Unit 48th Infantry.

18. Aug 7, 1820, U.S. Federal Census, Iredell County, North Carolina, Sampson Ball, 114115177.

19. Aug 14, 1850, U.S. Federal Census, Iredell County, North Carolina, Sampson Ball, age 61, occupation millwright, dwelling 223, family 224, with Rosana, Anna C., Mary A., Margaret M., Nancy O., David N., Thomas M., and Rebeca G. Ball.

20. Jul 9, 1860, U.S. Federal Census, Iredell County, North Carolina, Sampson Ball, age 70, occupation millwright, dwelling 488, family 460, with Mary A., Margaret E., Thos M., and Rebecca J. Ball, and Robt Brown.

21. Sep 5, 1870, U.S. Federal Census, Union Grove Post Office, Iredell County, North Carolina; Sampson Ball, age 82, occupation farmer, dwelling 145, with Adeline, Elijah, and Jane Ball; and Edmond Norman.

22. Aug 7, 1820, U.S. Federal Census, Wilkes County, North Carolina, Imlah Ball, 112113155.

23. 1830, U.S. Federal Census, Wilkes County, North Carolina, Imlah Ball, page 382, X111X1.

24. 1840, U.S. Federal Census, Green, Hancock County, Indiana, page 388, Imlah Ball, 11111121126299.

25. "Find A Grave," Gilboa Cemetery, Hancock County, Indiana, dates from headstones.

26. Sep 15, 1850, U.S. Federal Census, Green, Hancock County, Indiana; Hannah Ball, age 45, page 548, dwelling 932, family 9957, with James A., William C., Elizabeth E., and Tabitha J. Ball.

27. Aug 12, 1850, U.S. Federal Census, Center Township, Rush County, Indiana, dwelling 88, family 90, Charles Jarvis, age 59, occupation farmer, with Sarah, Cornelius, John, Imlah, James F., Noah, and Wesley Jarvis.

28. Aug 14, 1850, U.S. Federal Census, Wilkes County, North Carolina, Levy Ball, age 52, occupation farmer, dwelling 584, family 584, with Alice, Nancy, Cynthia, Mary, Lucy, Tabitha, Rachael, and Levy Ball.

29. Sep 28, 1860, U.S. Federal Census, Lower Division, Wilkes County, North Carolina, Ailsy Ball, age 63, occupation farmer, dwelling 1084, family 1084, with Cynthia, Mary, Tabitha, Rachel, and Levi Ball (age 15).

30. "Privette" is sometime spelled "Prevett" or "Privett." "Privette" is used for consistency.

31. 1820, U.S. Federal Census, Wilkes County, North Carolina, Joel Ball, page 507, 11122.

32. 1830, U.S. Federal Census, Buncombe County, North Carolina, Joel Ball, page 259, 11213255.

33. 1840, U.S. Federal Census, Northern Division, Buncombe County, North Carolina, Joeb Ball, page 190, 1111121216288.

34. Some genealogists have Joel Ball as a child of Benjamin W. Ball (1775–1841), a brother of William Ball Jr.

35. 1830, U.S. Federal Census for Iredell County, North Carolina, page 30, Beram Ball, 11112244.

36. 1850, U.S. Federal Census, Green Township, Hancock County, Indiana, Beriam Ball, occupation farmer, born in NC, age 49; Elizabeth, born in NC, age 46; Milas, age 15; William H., age 13; Isaac J, age 58; and John, age 28.

37. Jul 29, 1850, U.S. Federal Census, Wilkes County, North Carolina, dwelling 296, family 296, Iredell Privett, age 43, occupation farmer; Polly, age 44; Calvin, age 15; and Nancy, age 6; all with last name Privett.

38. Jul 4, 1860, U.S. Federal Census, Lovelace Post Office route, Lower Division, Wilkes County, North Carolina, dwelling 303, family 303, Iredell; age 53, occupation farmer; Mary, age 54; De Cater, age 24; Nancy, age 16.

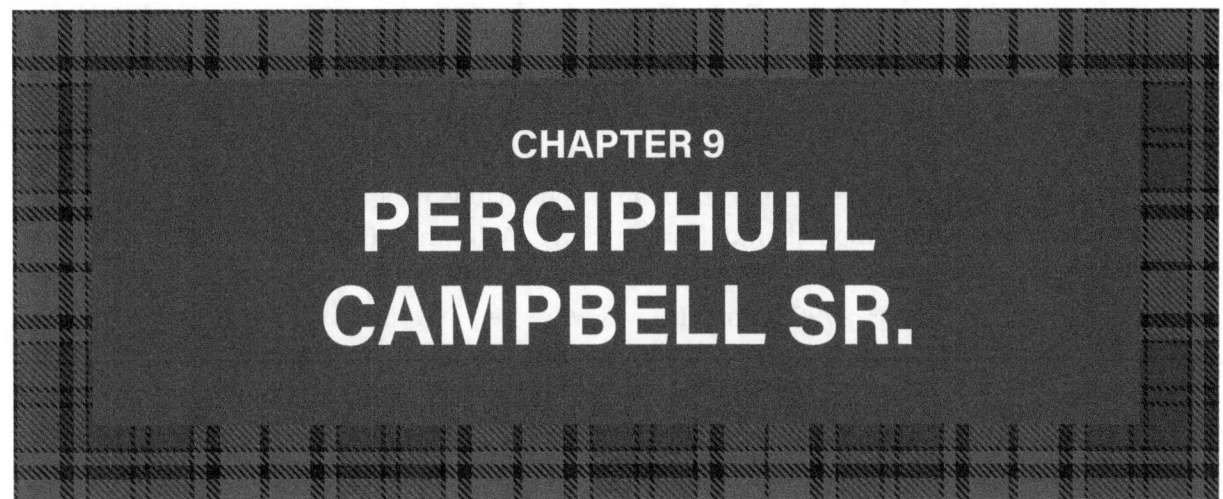

CHAPTER 9
PERCIPHULL CAMPBELL SR.

1.6 **Perciphull Campbell Sr.** (Apr 18, 1767–Jun 6, 1853) was the sixth child of **Adam Campbell** (1735–1779) and **Elizabeth (Morgan) Campbell** of Rowan and Iredell County, North Carolina. He was born in Culpeper County, Virginia, and moved to Rowan County with his parents in about 1774. Perciphull married **Sarah "Sally" Elizabeth Cook** (Jun 2, 1767–Feb 28, 1848) in 1788 in Iredell County. Sarah was probably the daughter of Abraham Cook and Elizabeth (Cass) Cook and was born in Culpeper County as well. According to his headstone, Perciphull was a Mason (Figure 9.1). Both Perciphull and Sarah, along with at least one child (**Perciphull Campbell Jr.**) and perhaps two other children (**Theophilus M. Campbell** and **Mary Polly [Campbell] Parks**) were buried at the Campbell Family Cemetery near their home in northern Iredell County south of Hunting Creek.[1, 2, 3, 4, 5, 6, 7, 8, 9, 10]

FIGURE 9.1
Headstones: Perciphull and Sarah Campbell, Campbell Family Cemetery, Iredell County, 1982.

LAND HOLDINGS OF PERCIPHULL CAMPBELL SR.

Perciphull was too young at age nine in 1776 to be a soldier in the American Revolution. When Rowan County issued the land grant that his father originally applied for to his mother after his father's death, Perciphull was probably living on this land with his mother and sister, **Sarah Campbell**, until Sarah married **William Ball** on Sep 8, 1788. His mother, **Elizabeth Campbell**, sold 100 acres of land on a creek in Iredell County to Perciphull for 20 pounds on Jun 15, 1795.[11] This sale was witnessed by Miller Wood Jr. and Miller Wood Sr. The witness, Miller Wood Sr., may have been the husband of his possible sister, Malinda Mae Campbell. On May 15, 1798, Elizabeth Campbell sold an additional 200 acres of land opposite Point of Rocks on a creek (probably Hunting Creek) in Iredell County to Perciphull.[12] Theophilus Campbell, John Morgan, and Nimrod Lunceford witnessed this deed. The witness, Theophilus Campbell, may have been Perciphull's younger brother. Perciphull's mother died shortly after May 15, 1798, since there are no additional records of her after this date. Perciphull bought several tracts of land (250, 151, and 20 acres) on Hunting Creek on Feb 25, 1819.[13] On May 10, 1822, Perciphull bought an additional 160 acres of land on Hunting Creek from Alexander Hall and Stephen Sharpe for $200. In 1828, he bought a parcel of land on Hunting Creek from Martin Morgan, a son of Theophelus Morgan, for $100. In 1837, he bought 750 acres on Big Rocky Creek for $4,000 from Sandy R. White.[14] This deed was witnessed by his two sons, **John R. Campbpell** and **Perciphull Campbell Jr**. Perciphull lived on this larger parcel of land until his death in 1853. His home on Big Rocky Creek was called the **John Pierce Bolin** (1.6.5.3) homeplace in the H. P. Vanhoy *History of the Campbell Family* in 1925.* Perciphull's son, Perciphull "Pierce" Campbell Jr., would occupy the land and mill on Hunting Creek after Perciphull moved to his Rocky Creek home. Figures 9.2 and 9.3 are paintings made by an artist who lived in Harmony, North Carolina, Esther Elizabeth (Gaither) Campbell (1924–2012). She painted the mill and bridge from memories and old photographs of the mill and covered bridge over the Hunting Creek at the Campbell Mill. Esther was not related to Adam Campbell. The mill was built of local stone (Figure 9.4). Figures 9.5 to 9.8 are exterior and interior views of Perciphull Campbell's house on Hunting Creek.

Perciphull deeded two acres of land for $10 to School District Number 4 on Sep 8, 1843.[15] This school was the earliest known public school in northern Iredell County and continued until 1909 when it was replaced by the Union Grove School.

Perciphull was a witness to the will of his neighbor, Theophilus Morgan, on Feb 13, 1807, in Iredell County. Theophilus's grandson, **Barlett Morgan,** would marry Perciphull's daughter, **Sarah**, in 1830.[16] Perciphull Campbell Sr. built a home in about 1810 to 1820 near the Campbell Mill on Hunting Creek. This house included a smoke house, main house in the I-frame style, grist mills powered by Hunting Creek using tubs, slaves, and later a covered

---

*The John Pierce Bolin home and Campbell Mill are shown on the 1917 Map of Union Grove Township (Figure 9.158).[68]

FIGURE 9.2 The covered bridge across Hunting Creek at the Campbell Mill.

FIGURE 9.3 The Campbell Mill on Hunting Creek.

FIGURE 9.4 Stone from the wall of the Campbell Mill.

Top left: FIGURE 9.5 Front porch of the Campbell home.

Top right: FIGURE 9.6 Stairway to the second floor inside the home.

Bottom: FIGURE 9.7 Perciphull Campbell's House in 1982. It is located just north of the Campbell Mill on Hunting Creek and was originally built in about 1820. It was added to the National Register of Historic Places in 1980.

FIGURE 9.8 End views of the Perciphull Campbell home near the mill on Hunting Creek, 2020.

bridge over Hunting Creek. The principal crops on the estate were wheat, rye, oats, and corn. There was severe flooding in Iredell County in Aug 1848 that left only three mills operating, the Campbell Mill, Jennings' mill, and the Diffy mill. The Perciphull Campbell House is still standing and is on the National Register of Historic Places in Iredell County. The mill and a bridge over Hunting Creek were standing until the 1930s.[17]

THE TOWN OF WILLIAMSBURGH

At the time that Perciphull moved to Rowan County with his family, there were no towns in northern Iredell County. After Iredell County was created from Rowan County in 1778, the legislature designated an area near the Fourth Creek Congregation as the county seat and named it Statesville. In the 1800 U.S. Census, there were only 95 people in Statesville. Early settlers in northern Iredell County felt a need to have a county seat closer to where they lived. In 1815, the North Carolina General Assembly appointed a commission to lay out a new town in northern Iredell County, which would be called Williamsburgh. The legislature named Perciphull Campbell Sr., Amos Sharpe, Reuben Morgan, and John Cowden as commissioners to set up this new town. This was the second town to be established by a legislative act in Iredell County. Williamsburgh was established on lands owned by William Harbin (Sep 13, 1776–May 11, 1844) and James Moody.[18] After 1832, the town was referred to as Williamsburg instead of Williamsburgh.

Williamsburgh included a horse-racing tract on the land of John McLelland, located east of the current Tabor Road. There was also a mustering ground for the militia northwest of Williamsburg that was used between the War of 1812 and the U.S. Civil War. In 1819, there was a dance hall in Williamsburgh in John Howard's assembly room. The town also contained a tavern, a post office, and the Macedonia Methodist Church, which is still in existence. In 1847, a petition was presented to the North Carolina General Assembly by 114 local women to establish a new county by the name of William with Williamsburgh as its county seat and a female academy to be located in Williamsburgh.[18]

The assembly did not approve the request for a new county or the academy. In 1860, the population of Williamsburg (renamed in 1832 to omit the "h" in Williamsburgh) was 139 people in about 38 families. By 1860, the population of Union Grove had grown to about 850 people. Even Eagle Mills, with a population of 476, and Houstonville, with a population of 276, were larger than Williamsburg. After the U.S. Civil War, the town of Williamsburg was overshadowed by the communities of Harmony and Union Grove. The Williamsburg post office lasted until 1905. The 1917 map of Iredell County shows a Williamsburg School (Figure 9.158 at the end of this chapter).[68] Eventually, the charter for the forgotten town of Williamsburg was repealed by the General Assembly in 1971.[18]

SLAVES OF PERCIPHULL CAMPBELL SR.

In addition to his large land holdings, Perciphull Campbell Sr. owned African American slaves, which he acquired after the 1790 Census was taken. He owned 1 slave in 1800, 4 slaves in 1810, 1 slave in 1820, 2 slaves in 1830, 19 slaves in 1840, 24 slaves when his will was written in 1844, and 21 slaves (12 male and 9 female slaves, ages from 1 to 55) in 1850. After his house and mills were completed and operating, he acquired more slaves and was one of the larger slave owners in Iredell County.[3, 4, 5,6, 7, 8, 19, 20]

In his will that he signed on Nov 1, 1854, Perciphull listed land, money, and 24 slaves willed to his children or their heirs. The will was proved by jury in the August Term 1854. His wife, Sarah, predeceased him. The terms of the will included the following:[21]

1. Heirs of his eldest son, **William R. "Billy" Campbell** (1790–1844), i.e., **Alfred Campbell** (1819–1860) and **Thersy Campbell** (1820–aft. 1860, living in Izard County, Arkansas, at the time), were to receive $100 each.

2. His Second son, **Perciphull Campbell Jr.** (1792–1862) was to receive all his land on the north side of Hunting Creek and "negroes" Big Isaac, Susannah, Marion, and Canah.

3. His son **Theophilus M. Campbell's** (1797–1855) heirs were to receive 300 acres of land adjoining Elijah Salmons and four "negroes", James, Peter, Silva, Andrew, when the heirs become of age. Theophilus M. Campbell was to have neither title nor claim to the said property.

4. His son **John R. Campbell** (1802–1872), living in Iredell County, was to receive 500 acres of land on the south side of Hunting Creek on the waters of Rocky Branch, as well as "negroes" Nelson, Betty, Lee, and Mirandy.

5. His son **William Rutherford Campbell** (1813–1883) was to receive 550 acres of land on the waters of Rocky Creek, including, the house that he lived in, and four "negroes," named Bryant, Frank, Burton, and Rachael.

6. His oldest daughter, **Sarah "Sallie" (Campbell) Morgan** (1801–1870), was to receive six "negroes": Huldey (Hulda), Jane, Eli, Catherine, Emily, and Sarah. Sarah's husband, Barlett Morgan, was to have neither title nor claim to these slaves, and Sarah was to "dispose" of these slaves as she saw proper at her death.

7. The heirs of his second-oldest daughter, **Mary Polly (Campbell) Parks** (1806–1844), i.e., **Dabney W. Parks**, **John P. Parks**, and **Theophilus C. Parks**, were to receive $1 each. After Mary Polly (Campbell) Parks died, her husband, **Gabriel Parks** (1798–1880), moved to Georgia. Gabriel was well-to-do and had his own slaves in Georgia.

8. His third and youngest daughter, **Frances (Campbell) Dobbins** (1809–1846), was to receive his mills and all machinery thereunto belonging, and additionally 250 acres of land adjoining said mill and a "negro boy" Little Isaac and a "negro girl" Miry.

Of the 15 African American families in Union Grove Township in the 1870 Census, only Hulda Morgan, Sarah Redman (probably Sarah Campbell, age 70), and Lewis Campbell's families took the last name of Campbell or Morgan. There were several African American Dobbins families living in Olin Township, but no Isaac or Miry/Mary Dobbins families were in the area. The former slaves could have taken other last names, moved to other counties or states, or may have died before 1870.

Some of the Campbell and Morgan slaves continued to stay in the area after the Civil War ended and the emancipation took place. A female slave named Hulda (Jun 1824–Feb 18, 1905) took the last name Morgan and was living near the Campbell Mill in Union Grove in 1870 with three young boys: Jack or Jackson Morgan (Jun 1843–Jun 17, 1917), Dick or Richard Morgan (1854–unknown), and Albert Burton Morgan (1858–Jul 9, 1926). Her son, Albert Burton, was too young to be the slave mentioned in Perciphull's will. Hulda later moved to Statesville, where she was living in 1900 with her son Jackson. Hulda was buried at the Green Street Cemetery in Statesville. In her obituary in the Statesville newspaper, she was referred to as Aunt Huldy Morgan, one of the few remaining "old-time colored women and a slave of the Morgan family" in Union Grove Township.[22]

The female slave Catherine (abt. 1840–aft 1870) also took the last name Morgan and was a domestic servant in the house of **Ema (Buxton) Campbell** (**Leolin V. Campbell's** estranged wife) and William Buxton (Ema's father) in 1870.[23]

John R. Campbell had one slave in 1840 and 1850. In 1860, he had one female slave (aged 70) and two male slaves (ages 70 and 22). Mirandy may have been the older female slave, born in 1790. Nelson could have been the older male slave born in 1790 and Lee could have been the younger male slave born in 1838. In 1870, there were no African Americans living in **John R. Campbell's** household in Union Grove Township. John R.'s wife's brother, Aquilla Williams Jr. (aged 63), and Leolden Shaver (aged 12) were living with **John R. Campbell's** family in 1870. However, there was a "mulatto" farmer, Lewis Campbell (Jul 1836–aft. 1923) living with his wife, Epsy (Spann) Campbell (1841–Jan 4, 1923), and family in Union Grove Township in 1870, who was the former slave named Lee (aka Lewis or Lou). Lewis and his parents were born in North Carolina. Epsy and her parents were born in South Carolina. Epsy and Lewis were buried at the Mount Nebo Baptist Church Cemetery in Harmony, Iredell County.[24, 25]

Isaac Morgan's Descendants

Although **Perciphull Campbell Sr.** willed slaves to his daughter **Sally "Sallie" (Campbell) Morgan (1.6.5)**, he spelled out in his will that her husband **Bartlett** was not to get any slaves. This might support speculation that **Bartlett Morgan** fathered a child, Isaac "Ike" Morgan (1837–aft. 1885), from one of the slaves of **Perciphull Campbell Sr**. Ike may have been the Big Isaac referred to in his will. Ike was living in the Cypress Creek District of Jones County, North Carolina, in 1850. Isaac fought with the 115th U.S. Colored Infantry during the U.S. Civil War. He moved to Lamar County, Texas, after the war. Ike married Millie Rucker in about 1862. One of their daughters was Joanna (Morgan) Lee (May 20, 1879–Jun 22, 1967), who married Arthur Douglas Lee (Jan 21, 1879–Mar 14, 1956) on Mar 25, 1895, in Lamar County, Texas. Joanna (Figure 9.9) traces her roots back to **Perciphull Campbell Sr.'s** slaves. Joanna and Arthur were buried at the Tahoma Cemetery in Yakima, Washington.[26, 27, 28]

FIGURE 9.9
Joanna (Morgan) Lee, Grayson County, Texas, abt. 1960.

Sarah "Sallie" Campbell, Slave of Perciphull Campbell

There was a slave, Sarah "Sallie" Campbell, born in about 1776 in North Carolina, most likely in Rowan County near the area of Hunting Creek that became Iredell County in 1788. She was born into slavery and was one of the original slaves of **Perciphull Campbell Sr**. bought during the War of 1812. Sarah was previously owned by an Unknown Green in about 1812 and later sold to an Unknown Rash, who failed to pay for her when Perciphull bought her. She was hired out in 1853 to an H. Hartmon in 1853, along with another slave, Charles, for $44 per year. She was sold on Dec 12, 1854, to **John Pettis Parks Sr**. for $380, along with another slave, Martha, for $525. John was living with his grandfather, **Perciphull Campbell Sr.**, in the 1850 Census in Iredell County on the Williamsburg Postal Route. Sarah may also have been owned by **John R. Campbell**. According to her story that appeared in the Statesville Landmark in 1880, she was manumitted (set free) when **Perciphull Campbell Sr.** died. She appears in Perciphull's will as being bequeathed to his daughter **Sarah (Campbell) Morgan**. According to her own accounts, Sarah had two children by 1812. In 1880, at age 104, Sarah was the oldest person in Iredell County. She had a grandson, Frank Fraley, born in Sep 1823 or 1825 in North Carolina, with whom she was living in Olin Township in 1880.

She died around Jan 12, 1888, in Iredell County, and her coffin was paid for by the Iredell County Commissioners.[29]

An article in the Statesville Landmark on May 21, 1880, said the following about Sarah Campbell:

"Near Olin, this county, upon Calvin Bowles' land, resides a negro woman, Sarah Campbell, with her grand-son, Frank Fraley, who doubtless from all accounts is the oldest inhabitant of Iredell County, whether white or colored. She was originally owned by ___ Green, who stole a horse during the war of 1812, and in consequence thereof fled the country [*sic*]. Before running away Green sold her to ___ Rash, who, failing to pay for her, sold her during the war of 1812 to Pearce Campbell, the grandfather of Williamson and L. V. Campbell. At the time she was purchased by Pearce Campbell, she had two children, all she ever had, and she claims to have been thirty years old then. She also states that she carried a crock of butter to be used at the wedding of the father of the late Dr. Richard M. Parks, who died a few years since, over eighty years old. Pearce Campbell died about 1859, over 80 years old, and manumitted this woman at his death. She is still quite active and hearty, with mind unimpaired and memory good and retentive when pertaining to matters and events of early life. She is a great talker and when once asked about the war of 1812, her tongue runs like the flutter-wheel of a saw mill. She gives the names of different persons who lived in North Iredell, who either volunteered or were drafted, and of those who went to the front and remained, or rearward and to the bushes. She names certain families who skulked military service and "bushed it" in the war of 1812, and who then had the reputation of not perceiving the difference between meum and tuum, but were openly charged with stealing sheep. For the truth of the above we cannot vouch, but it is a singular coincidence that persons of the same name, (claimed by Sarah to be grandchildren), in the unpleasantness would neither volunteer nor go to the front when drafted, but bushed it during the war, and were charged with a fondness for other people's mutton whilst deserters. Some of the same name have been prosecuted in court for sheep stealing."

WILLIAM R. "BILLY" CAMPBELL

1.6.1   **William R. "Billy" Campbell** (1790–1844) married **Jensie Jane Morgan** (1791–1865) in Iredell County, in about 1818. William R. and Jensie moved to Tennessee and then Izard County, Arkansas. Jensie and her children died in Franklin Township, Izard County, Arkansas. It is not known where William R. Campbell died, but is most likely Arkansas. William R. died before his father, Perciphull. William and Jensie had two children:[1,30, 31, 32]

1.6.1.1   **Alfred Campbell** (1819–Apr 1860) was born in Tennessee. He purchased a homestead in Independence County, Arkansas, on Mar 1, 1855. He married Susan Ann Givens (1829–

FIGURE 9.10
William Franklin Campbell, back row with white hair standing next to Saucy and his family and members of the Shell family, at the Shell family home near Sage, Izard County, abt. 1920.

1880) before 1850, in Izard County, Arkansas. Susan was born in Alabama. Alfred's mother and sister were living with them in Union Township, Izard County in 1850. Susan continued to run a farm in Franklin, Izard County after Alfred died. Alfred and Susan's burial location is not known. They had four children:[32]

1. Sarah Jane Campbell (Jul 1853–aft. 1910) married Isaac Harrison Jones (Jan 1850—aft. 1930) in 1872 in Izard County. They were buried at an unmarked grave at the Upper Reed Cemetery in Izard County.

2. William Franklin "Bully" Campbell (Feb 15, 1856–Mar 15, 1927) married Nancy Ellen "Saucy" Shell (Dec 16, 1869–Sep 18, 1954) on Oct 2, 1887, in Izard County. See Figure 9.10. They were buried at the Campbell Cemetery in Zion, Izard County.*

3. Tabitha Carrie Campbell (Feb 1858–Mar 28, 1927) married James Monroe Arnold (Aug 3, 1858–Apr 7, 1951) in 1876 in Arkansas. They lived in Ruddell, Independence County, Arkansas, and were buried at the Oaklawn Cemetery in Batesville.

4. Alfred William Campbell (Sep 6, 1859–May 18, 1909) married Mary L. "Last Name Unknown" (1866–aft. 1910) in Arkansas in 1886. Alfred was buried at the Campbell Cemetery in Zion, Izard County.

1.6.1.2 **Thersy or Thurza Campbell** (abt. 1820–after 1860) was born in Kentucky or Tennessee and died in Izard County. Thurza (aged 35) was living with her grandmother (Jane Campbell,

---

*A great-grandson of William Franklin "Bully" Campbell is part of the Adam Campbell Y-DNA Project.

aged 67) on the Big Spring Postal route in Franklin Township, Izard County, in 1860. Jane's occupation was domestic.[33]

PERCIPHULL "PIERCE" CAMPBELL JR.

1.6.2 **Perciphull "Pierce" Campbell Jr.** (Aug 18, 1792–Oct 22, 1862) married **Tabitha Morgan** (Jul 7, 1797–Sep 29, 1879) in Iredell County in about 1815. Their home was referred to in the Vanhoy history as the **Hiram Speaks** place on Hunting Creek, about one-half mile above the Campbell Mill on Hunting Creek. Perciphull Campbell Jr. and Tabitha were buried at the Campbell Family Cemetery in Union Grove Township. Perciphull Jr. and Tabitha had five children.[1]

1.6.2.1 **Williamson H. Campbell** (Dec 17, 1815–May 4, 1881) married **Flossie Jemima Mayberry** (Feb 18, 1812–Mar 16, 1881) on Oct 1, 1835, in Iredell County. They lived in Union Grove, Iredell County, until after the U.S. Civil War, when they moved to Somers Township, Wilkes County. Williamson was appointed and bonded as a constable for Iredell County in 1859. They were buried at Zion Baptist Church, along with their children, except for James.[34, 35] Their children included:

1. **Sarah Ann Campbell** (Apr 6, 1836–Dec 22, 1898), who married Rev. **Thomas Lawson Jennings** (Oct 8, 1829–Sep 23, 1910) on Sep 14, 1854, in North Carolina. During the U.S. Civil War, Thomas was a private in the 52nd NC Infantry Regiment, CSA, and imprisoned at Burgess' Mill, Virginia. He was a farmer and ran a general store in Union Grove Township. Their children were **Margaret Emily (Jennings) Weisner** (Jul 29, 1855–Aug 31, 1933), Augustus Jennings (1859-abt. 1870), **Alice Elizabeth (Jennings) Doss** (1864–abt. 1900), **Josephine Adeline "Minnie" (Jennings) Davis** (Jul 4, 1865–Jan 6, 1919), **Martha A. (Jennings) Myers** (Sep 17, 1867–Mar 9, 1915), John W. Jennings (May 1870–Nov 25, 1871), **James Turner (J. T.) Jennings** (Nov 10, 1872–Apr 20, 1956),* and Thomas F. Jennings (Mar 1876–Apr 29, 1877).

2. **Martha Emily Campbell** (Nov 21, 1837–Dec 26, 1886), who married Sylvanus Timotheus Crater (Apr 13, 1832–Apr 16, 1887) in about 1855 in Iredell County. Sylvanus was the son of Jacob Crater Jr. (1801–1890) and was a private in the 5th North Carolina Cavalry, CSA, during the U.S. Civil War.

3. **Nancy Emily Campbell** (Nov 29, 1839–Jun 20, 1906), who married **Jacob Jeremiah Crater** (Apr 2, 1834–Mar 1, 1920) in about 1866 in Iredell County. Jacob was the brother of Sylvanus Timotheus Crater, her sister's husband. The Vanhoy *History of the Campbell Family* also mentions their children: James P. (Apr 20, 1868–Jun 10, 1896), John Williamson (Dec 4, 1869-Nov 4, 1935), Augusta Ellen (Crater) Parks (Apr 27, 1871–Aug 25, 1957), Newton Gwyn (Oct 26, 1875–Nov 30, 1949), and Jacob Williamson (Apr

---

* J. T. Jennings took over the store from his father. He married Dovie Huie, 1.6.4.4.5.

26. 1979–Jul 14, 1944) Crater. Nancy and Jacob were buried at the Winthrop Friends Cemetery in Union Grove Township.

FIGURE 9.11 Monument of Confederate War Dead in the Hollywood Cemetery, erected in 1869, Richmond, Virginia.

4. **James P. Campbell** (1842–Jul 12, 1864), who did not marry. He was a private in the 4th North Carolina Infantry Regiment, CSA. He was wounded at the Battle of Antietam in Sharpsburg, Maryland, on Sep 17, 1862. He died in captivity and was buried at the Hollywood Cemetery in Richmond, Virginia (Figure 9.11).

5. Augustus Franklin Campbell (Jan 29, 1844–Mar 14, 1863), who did not marry. He was a private in the CSA 4th Infantry Regiment. He was wounded at the Battle of Seven Pines, Virginia, on May 31, 1862, and died at the Battle of Fredericksburg. He was buried at Zion Baptist Church.

6. **Arminda Jennings Campbell** (Jan 20, 1846–Feb 12, 1886), who married **William Marius Cooper** (Oct 30, 1844–Aug 11, 1907) on Mar 10, 1866, in Iredell County. The Vanhoy Campbell family history also mentions their children: **Della V. Cooper** (Mar 1, 1867–Jun 12, 1882), **Augusta Cooper** (Jul 21. 1968–Sep 5, 1879), **Rufus Agustus Cooper** (Oct 12, 1870–Feb 28, 1941), **William W. Cooper** (abt. 1873–Jun 20, 1913), **Ella Cordie Cooper** (Nov 26, 1874–Sep 4, 1894), **Josephine E. (Cooper) DeVane** (Dec 25, 1876–Sep 22, 1943), **Rowena Bell (Cooper) Orr** (Apr 1879–Feb 21, 1939), **Etta Campbell (Cooper) Setzer** (Jan 21, 1881–Mar 7, 1927), and **Mae Cooper** (Jan 1884–Dec 21, 1920). After Arminda died, William married Bertha Lee Drake (Jul 27, 1864–Oct 20, 1955) in Jun 1886 in Statesville. Arminda was buried at Zion Baptist Church. William and Bertha were buried at Oakwood Cemetery in Statesville.

1.6.2.2 **Reuben Campbell** (1818–1830) was mentioned in the Vanhoy Campbell family history. He died at age 12 and was probably buried at the Campbell Family Cemetery in Iredell County.[1]

1.6.2.3 **Sarah Eve Campbell** (1820–Nov 1849) married Capt. **Uriah J. Douthit** (Jul 1816–Dec 25, 1867) in about 1839 in Surry County. After Sarah's death, Uriah married again, to Sarah Matilda Smith (Oct 29, 1826–Oct 29, 1912), on Aug 16, 1851, in Wilkes County. In about 1854, Uriah left North Carolina for Lawrence County, Arkansas. During the U.S. Civil War, Uriah went north and fought for the Union Army in the 47th Missouri Infantry. He was involved in marauding homes in Arkansas during the war. After the war, he returned to Lawrence County, where he was murdered on Christmas Day in 1867. See Figure 9.12.

His second wife returned to Wilkes County, North Carolina. Mary E. and Columbus C. Douthit remained in North Carolina and were living with their grandparents, Perciphull and Tabitha Campbell, in 1860. There is a record of Uriah's children in Piney Fork, Lawrence County, Arkansas, in 1860, including Uriah J. (age 49), Sarah (age 32), Uriah A. (age 13), Sarah A. (age 12), Julius C. (age 6), and Ellen Douthett (age 4). Sarah Eve may have been buried at the Campbell Family Cemetery in Iredell County. Uriah was probably buried at the Evening Shade-Sharp Cemetery in Sharp County, Arkansas.

Uriah and Sarah Eve's children were all mentioned in the Vanhoy history, including:[1]

1. **Mary E. Douthit** (Feb 29, 1841– Oct 16, 1870), who married Daniel Thomas Crouse/Krouse (May 19, 1836–Nov 28, 1903) on Nov 7, 1865, in Davidson County. Daniel was a Moravian and lived in Salem, Forsyth County. Moravians were pacifists, so during the U.S. Civil War he served in the Regimental Band of the CSA's 26th North Carolina Infantry Regiment (Figures 9.13 and 9.14). He enlisted in March 1862 and served until its capture in Apr 1865 at Amelia Court House, Virginia. Except for a month's leave in Feb 1864, the band was actively engaged, enduring defeat, hunger, and fatigue at Gettysburg and later in the Wilderness. When not in battle, the band provided hard-pressed troops both entertainment and distraction from the horrors of combat. After the war, Daniel was director and captain of the Salem Moravian Band. Daniel and Mary were both buried at the Salem God's Moravian Acres in Winston-Salem.[36]

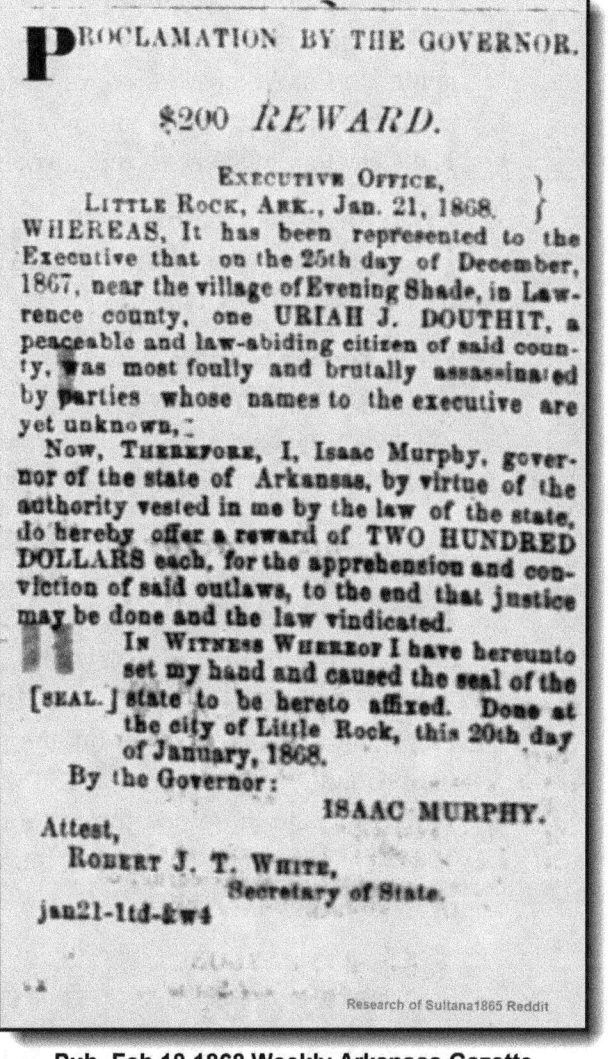

PROCLAMATION BY THE GOVERNOR.

$200 REWARD.

EXECUTIVE OFFICE,
LITTLE ROCK, ARK., Jan. 21, 1868.

WHEREAS, It has been represented to the Executive that on the 25th day of December, 1867, near the village of Evening Shade, in Lawrence county, one URIAH J. DOUTHIT, a peaceable and law-abiding citizen of said county, was most foully and brutally assassinated by parties whose names to the executive are yet unknown,

Now, THEREFORE, I, Isaac Murphy, governor of the state of Arkansas, by virtue of the authority vested in me by the law of the state, do hereby offer a reward of TWO HUNDRED DOLLARS each, for the apprehension and conviction of said outlaws, to the end that justice may be done and the law vindicated.

IN WITNESS WHEREOF I have hereunto set my hand and caused the seal of the [SEAL.] state to be hereto affixed. Done at the city of Little Rock, this 20th day of January, 1868.

By the Governor:

ISAAC MURPHY.

Attest,
ROBERT J. T. WHITE,
Secretary of State.

jan21-1td-&w4

Research of Sultana1865 Reddit

Pub. Feb 18 1868 Weekly Arkansas Gazette Little Rock, Arkansas

FIGURE 9.12 News clipping about Arkansas Governor Isaac Murphy's reward for apprehension of outlaws who assassinated Uriah J. Douthit, Jan 21, 1868.

2. **Frances "Fannie" L. Douthit** (Jan 15, 1841–Sep 1925), who married Jefferson Cave Johnson (Oct 20, 1838–Jul 2, 1891) in about 1854 in Arkansas. Cave was a sergeant in the 38th Arkansas Infantry, CSA. Fannie and Jefferson were buried at the Ash Flat Cemetery in Sharp County, Arkansas.

3. **Uriah Augustus Douthit** (1845–aft. 1864), who did not marry. He served in the Union Army in the Missouri 46th and 47th Infantry during the U.S. Civil War.

4. **Sarah Adeline Douthit** (Nov 24, 1847–Sep 26, 1914), who married Hollon Smith Baldwin Carter (Oct 8, 1845–Mar 28, 1912) in Lawrence County, Arkansas, on Nov 17, 1867. Sarah was buried at the Oakland Cemetery in Dallas, Texas.

5. **Columbus C. Douthit** (Sep 4, 1848–Oct 30, 1915), who married Susan Amanda (Baker) Genaw Rainwater (Nov 5, 1844–Sep 12, 1926) on Feb 20, 1876, in Labette County, Kansas. Columbus and Susan were living in Newton County, Missouri, in 1880, with Elvira Jane Rainwater (1864–1954) and Kattie Rainwater (1861–1885), children from Susan's previous marriage to William Columbus Rainwater (1838–1872). Columbus Douthit purchased land in Pottawatomie County, Oklahoma, on Aug 1, 1901. Columbus and Susan were buried at the Union Cemetery in Pottawatomie County.

FIGURE 9.13 Capt. Daniel Crouse.

FIGURE 9.14 The Regimental Band of the 26th North Carolina Infantry Regiment, CSA, L to R: S. T. Mickey, A. P. Gibson, J. O. Hall, W. H. Hall, A. L. Hauser, D. T. Crouse, J. A. Leinbach, and James M. Fisher, between 1861 and 1865.

1.6.2.4 **Mildeon G. Campbell** (Dec 7, 1826–May 30, 1854) married **Rachel Clementine Huie**[*] (Apr 9, 1827–Dec 13, 1909) in about 1846 in Iredell County. Mildeon's headstone is at the Campbell Family Cemetery. Rachel may have been buried there, as well, but no headstone has been found. They had two children:

FIGURE 9.15 Mary Elizabeth Campbell and husband Charles Romulus York (1886–1965), Union Grove Township, abt. 1950.

1. **Leolin Davidson Campbell** (Jan 1847–aft. 1900) married **Mary Elizabeth Feimster** (Oct 5, 1843–Jul 18, 1884) on Jan 29, 1872, in Iredell County. They both may have been buried at the Campbell Family Cemetery, but no headstones have been found. Their children were **Cora Lee (Campbell) Hodgson** (Jan 2, 1873–Mar 16, 1934), **Thomas David Campbell** (Aug 26, 1875–Mar 6, 1925), **Marie Esther Campbell** (Jun 1878–aft. 1900), **Nannie Mary Earl "Etter" (Campbell) Stroud** (Aug 22, 1879–Apr 4, 1940), and **Mary Elizabeth (Campbell) York** (Dec 22, 1882–Sep 13, 1960) (Figure 9.15).

2. **Preston Clifford Campbell** (Apr 19, 1849–Nov 12, 1921) married **Martha Geneva Carrigan**[**] (Sep 29, 1955–Dec 17, 1925) on Dec 27, 1877, in Iredell County. Preston was a farmer and textile worker (Figures 9.16 and 9.17). He served in the Army in World War I. Preston and Martha were living in Jerusalem, Davie County, in 1920. Preston was buried at the Legion Memorial Park in Cooleemee, Davie County. Preston and Martha

---

[*]An alternate spelling for "Huie" is "Huey."
[**]The *Vanhoy History of the Campbell Family* refers to Martha Geneva Carrigan as "Miss Spann."

FIGURE 9.16 Preston Clifford Campbell, abt. 1910, Davie County.

FIGURE 9.17 Martha Geneva Carrigan, wife of Preston Clifford Campbell, abt. 1910, Davie County.

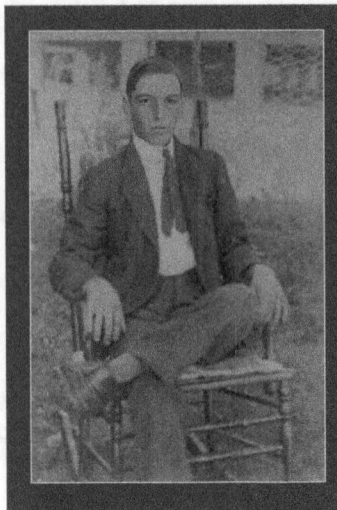

Left:
FIGURE 9.18 Milden Oscar Campbell Sr. as a young man, abt. 1900, Iredell County.

Right:
FIGURE 9.19 Clark Clifton Campbell and his wife, Cordie (Goodman) Campbell, abt. 1960, Davie County.

had the following children: Mary Alice Campbell (Jan 26, 1878–Jan 21, 1881), **Milden Oscar Campbell** (Mar 19, 1881–May 25, 1962), **Virginia Genevia (Campbell) Gregory** (Oct 25, 1884–Jan 16, 1985), **Lela Mae (Campbell) Howard** (May 2, 1888–Feb 13, 1950), **Clark Clifton Campbell** (May 31, 1892–Apr 14, 1964), **Clifford Preston Campbell** (Mar 4, 1895–Apr 29, 1939), and **Annie Clementine (Campbell) Miller** (Sep 12, 1898–Apr 2, 1992). See Figures 9.18, 9.19, and 9.20.

1.6.2.5 Leolin Vanhook Campbell (Nov 16, 1827–May 20, 1888) married **Ann Clementine Dent** (May 1823–Sep 2, 1856) on Jun 3, 1851, in Iredell County. They had three children:

1. **Emma C. Campbell** (Jun 30, 1851–Aug 8, 1856) died as a child.

2. **Alice C. Campbell** (Mar 5, 1855–Jan 21, 1936) did not marry. She lived at the Perciphull Campbell House that her father inherited until her death. She was the last in this Campbell line to live at the Campbell house. Alice was buried at the Campbell Family Cemetery in Iredell County, along with her two siblings. See Figure 9.21.

3. **Turner Campbell** (Jan 18, 1856–Aug 18, 1856) died as an infant.

After Ann Clementine's death, Leolin married **Margaret Emma "Emily" Buxton** (Mar 16, 1839–Feb 4, 1907) in about 1861 in Iredell County. She was living with her son, William Buxton Campbell, in the Perciphull Campbell House when she died in the measles epidemic in 1907. She was buried at Moss Chapel in Iredell County. Leolin and Emily had two children:

FIGURE 9.20 Milden Oscar Campbell and wife, Molly (Shore) Campbell, abt. 1950, Davie County.

FIGURE 9.21 Alice C. Campbell with dog at the Perciphull Campbell House, abt. 1930.

4. **William Buxton Campbell** (Feb 2, 1862–Apr 28, 1942) married Adelia Emily Sale (Apr 7, 1864–Oct 14, 1947) on Jan 30, 1898, in Iredell County. William and Adelia were buried at Zion Baptist Church. William was the only child of Leolin to have a family. He and Adelia had eight children, including: Nettie Mae Campbell (May 4, 1886–Apr 23, 1943), James Rex Campbell (Jul 39, 1888–Jan 28, 1913), Ruby Cole Campbell (May 7, 1900–Mar 16, 1986), Nola May (Campbell) Lowe (Aug 27, 1901–Jan 18, 1972), Viola F. Campbell (1903–Jul 11, 1926), Olean (Campbell) Knight (Mar 26, 1903–Sep 7, 1999), Grace Gwyn (Campbell) Freeze (Dec 20, 1904–Feb 10, 1971), and William Frances Campbell (Dec 11. 1906–Jul 12, 1979). See Figure 9.22.

5. **Della Pearl Campbell** (Jan 28, 1864–May 28, 1884) did not marry. She was buried at Moss Chapel at 20 years old.

FIGURE 9.22 Nola May Campbell with husband, William Albert Lowe, abt. 1960, Harmony, Iredell County.

THEOPHILUS MARION CAMPBELL

1.6.3   **Theophilus Marion Campbell*** (1797–Dec 14, 1855) married **Tabitha Renee "Arena" Allen** (1816–1880) in Iredell County on Aug 12, 1832.[37] While records show that he went by Theophilus M. Campbell, his middle name was most likely Marion. Their home was known in 1925 as the Rev. Edmond Mitchell (1842–1920)** home place on Hunting Creek. See Rev Mitchell on the 1917 map of Union Grove Township in Figure 9.158.[1, 68]

Theophilus was one of three delegates from Iredell County to the 1836–1837 session of the North Carolina House of Commons. The other two delegates were James A. King and Solomon Lowdermilk. Theophilus was elected on Aug 11, 1836, and reported for duty as a delegate on Nov 22, 1836. The Vanhoy history included a story about how Theophilus would pull off his shoes and walk to Raleigh barefoot and set them under his seat and make a fiery speech in the Legislative Hall. The Campbell history also related how Theophilus left Winston-Salem at sunrise and walked to where J. T. Jennings lived and got there just as the sun was setting—a distance of 50-odd miles.[38]

In the 1835 North Carolina State Constitutional Convention, the constitution was rewritten to give a greater number of delegates to more populous counties. Previously, there were two delegates from each county. By the Antebellum South period, the western counties had grown to cover a larger area and were growing faster in population than in the east. In 1836, counties were represented for the first time by one to four delegates, based on population. Among the acts passed by the General Assembly were the creation of Davie County, an act that enrolled all free white males between the ages of 18 and 45 in the state militia, and a law defining the qualifications and duties of the North Carolina justice of the peace.[39]

During Theophilus's time in the legislature, they did not meet in the original North Carolina State House that was built on Union Square in Raleigh between 1792 and 1796. During construction at the state house to fireproof the building on Jun 21, 1831, workers accidentally set the roof on fire. From 1833 to 1849, a new North Carolina State Capitol was built on the same site.[40] From 1831 to 1838, the General Assembly met in the Government House in Raleigh, temporarily displacing the governor, who moved into rented quarters. The Government House was the state-owned residence of the governor at the south end of Fayetteville Street, built in about 1815.[41]

Theophilus Campbell and his father, Percival Campbell, were part of a gathering on May 12, 1835, that met in Statesville in response to dissatisfaction with President Martin Van Buren's role in electing a presidential candidate in Baltimore and in support of Hugh L. White, a native of Iredell County and then a Senator in Congress from Tennessee. The meeting consisted of 350 to 400 individuals from all parts of the county, including James A.

---

* "Theophilus" is sometimes spelled "Theophelus." It is spelled with an "i" here for consistency. This Theophilus Marion Campbell should not be confused with 1.8.0, who was born in 1777 and lived his life in Mississippi.

**Rev Mitchell died in the state hospital in Morganton. His wife was Rebecca Howard (1846–1910).

King, John M. Young, William King, John Gaither, Hosea Redman, Theophilus Williams, Col. Milton Campbell, Col. Sol. Lowdermilk, John Feimster, Gracey Templeton, Rufus Reid, James Campbell, Sampson Ball, and J. P. Caldwell.[42]

On Jun 15, 1850, Theophilus Campbell was elected chairman of a committee to nominate a candidate to represent the 89th Regiment district of Iredell County in the next General Assembly of North Carolina. The meeting took place in Williamsburg, which was a town Perciphull had helped create. The committee members included Greenbury Gaither, Pierce Campell Jr., J. L. Nisbitt, Z. Albea, Capt. Journey, Asel Dickens, Capt. H. Allen, Theo Marshall, Milus Dobbin (probably Milas Dobbins, his brother-in-law), T. Redman, John Jennings, Capt. Martin Jacks, Joseph Revis, and Sampson Ball (Sampson Harrison Ball, a cousin). The committee offered the name of Col. Charles Reynolds Jones as their choice of candidate. Col. Jones resigned his seat as chairman of the meeting, and Theo M. Campbell, Esq., was called to chair.[43] Some of the resolutions of the committee included:

❖ "That we will stand by the constitution always, and our motto shall be, the union of the States "now and forever.""

❖ "That (we see with sorrow and regret that the Congress of the U. States has not yet been able to settle the great question now agitating the whole country,) the thanks of this meeting are due to Senator's Webster (Daniel Webster), Clay (Henry Clay), and all other Senators and Representatives in Congress, who are disposed to do justice to the South. May heaven's choicest blessings smile upon their efforts, and we would say to them, God speed you, go, cease not your efforts until this dangerous question of slavery is settled forever according to the true spirit of the constitution."

❖ "That his glorious Union, established by the sufferings and blood of our gallant fathers, may stand firm and unimpaired as long as time shall last; and may the names of all those who lay down party spirit and devote their energies and influence to an honorable adjustment of this disgraceful question, be handed down to posterity as bright examples, worth of imitation, and may their names be loved and cherished by millions yet unborn, while those who continue to agitate and endeavor to create a sectional feeling in regard to this matter, and who labor to prevent a settlement of this question, be they northern or southern men, may sink into oblivion, 'unwept, un-honored, and unsung.'"

❖ "That we respect the President of these United States (Zachary Taylor, Whig Party) for the able and firm manner in which he discharges the duties of his office."

The Col. Charles R. Jones (1815–1857), who was at the meeting with Theophilus, lived in Williamsburg, North Carolina. He was a veteran of the Mexican American War and later became a general in the local militia. Tradition places a mustering ground for the militia northwest of Williamsburg, south of the Smith Road, presumably during the period between the War of 1812 and the U.S. Civil War. They usually met for two weeks of training along with horse racing, dancing, and other activities. The mustering ground was owned by William Harbin until the 1840s, then by Col. Charles R. Jones and his wife, Sarah L. Jones (1820–1873), whose estate left the income from the property to Macedonia Church until purchased by Jesse E. Fraley (1817–1903) in the 1870s.[19]

Theophilus and his wife, Arena, were living in separate households in 1850. Family historians speculate that this separation may have been due to Theophilus's gambling debts from involvement in horse racing at Williamsburg, his fiery lifestyle, or the 19-year age difference between them. On Aug 29, 1850, Arena (aged 33), and her children Sarah (aged 14), Fanny (aged 11), Caroline (aged 6), John (aged 4), and Isabella (one month old) were living in Iredell County in a separate household.[44] Two days earlier, on Aug 27, 1850, Theophilus (aged 53) was occupied as a teacher and living in the household of his nephew, Williamson H. Campbell (aged 34). Theophilus is believed to have died on Dec 14, 1855, in Iredell County. Although there is no tombstone, Theophilus may have been buried at the Campbell Family Cemetery.[45]

Arena moved to Arkansas after her youngest daughter was born in 1850 and before the U.S. Civil War. On May 1, 1860, Tabitha R. Campbell of Fulton County, Arkansas, was issued a patent for 80 acres of land in Arkansas. The land was described as the south half of the southwest quarter of section 22, in township 18, north of range 8 west, in the district of lands subject to sale at Batesville, Arkansas (1 S1/2SW 5th PM No. 18N 8 W 22). Arena was probably buried at the Reeves Cemetery in Izard County.[46]

Theophilus and Arena had six children (William Marion and Isabella were not mentioned in the Vanhoy history). Several of their children moved west with Arena.

1.6.3.1 **Mary E. "Polly" Campbell** (1834–abt. 1874) married **Rev. Andreas "Andrew" Edwin Rominger** (May 13, 1824–1874). Polly and "Mr. Romanger" appear in the Vanhoy history with three unnamed children, which some genealogists believe to be Gus, Jane, and Emma Rominger. There is an Andrew (a carpenter) and Mary Rominger with a child Ellen Cole Rominger in Forsyth County in the 1850 Census. In the 1860 Census and 1870 Census, an Anderson Rominger appears with a wife, Antoinett Rominger, in Forsyth County.

1.6.3.2 **Sarah "Sallie" Ann Lodema Campbell** (1836–1874) married Jonathan Leviticus Litten Mize (1835–1891) in about 1852 in Iredell County. Sallie appears in the Vanhoy history, but it was said that she married a Gilreath. Sarah and Jonathan had moved to Lawrence County, Arkansas, by 1860. Jonathan served in the 27th Arkansas Infantry Regiment, CSA, during the U.S. Civil War. Jonathan was a blacksmith. Sarah and Jonathan were buried at the Mize-Painter Cemetery in Wild Cherry, Fulton County, Arkansas. See Figure 9.23. Their children were:

FIGURE 9.23
Jonathan Leviticus Mize, abt. 1885. Fulton County, Arkansas.

1. Mary Lodema Mize (Jul 15, 1853–May 1, 1909), who married Thomas Littleton Wallace (Jul 15, 1852–Jan 26, 1892) on Jan 19, 1873, in Fulton County, Arkansas. Mary later married Thomas Henry Martin (abt. 1840–Mar 10, 1909). Mary and Tom were buried at the Moten Cemetery in Fulton County. See Figures 9.24 and 9.25.

2. Miranda Jane Mize (Feb 1860–May 21, 1932), who married Elisha Vines (May 15, 1857–Dec 1938) in 1877 in Jefferson County, Alabama.

3. Parthenia Elizabeth Mize (May 25, 1862–Aug 17, 1945), who married James Monroe Elliott (Jul 23, 1863–Oct 3, 1925) in about 1883 in Fulton County, Arkansas. They were buried at the Mize-Painter Cemetery in Wild Cherry, Fulton County. See Figure 9.26.

4. Tabitha Ann Mize (Jul 19, 1864-Nov 27, 1948), who married Rev. Thomas Graham Hawkins (Dec 2, 1847–Mar 27, 1917) in 1882 in Fulton County. Thomas served in the 35th Kentucky Infantry Regiment, Union Army, during the U.S. Civil War. He was a preacher. They lived in Cleveland and Benton Townships, Fulton County.

5. John William Mize (abt. 1866–Apr 5, 1945), who married Marie Florence Munsch (Sep 21, 1871–Aug 14, 1916) in 1904 in Wood County, Texas. Marie was born in Alsace-Lorraine. Marie was previously married to Gaspard G. Koenig (Apr 1824–Oct 17, 1903), with whom she had three children. John was born in Arkansas and moved to Wood County after 1900. John and Marie moved to Lake County, California, by 1910, where John was a fruit farmer.

6. Martha Lucinda "Mattie" Mize (Oct 11, 1867–Sep 21, 1908), who married Phillip Bradley LaFevers (Jan 25, 1858–Dec 20, 1938) in Fulton County in 1889. They were buried

Left: FIGURE 9.24 Mary Mize and Thomas Wallace, abt. 1890, Fulton County.
Middle: FIGURE 9.25 Mary Mize and Thomas Martin, abt. 1900, Fulton County.
Right: FIGURE 9.26 James Monroe Elliott and Parthenia Elizabeth Mize, abt. 1900, Fulton County, Arkansas.

Left:
FIGURE 9.27 Charles Edward Davis and Harriett Cordelia Mize, abt. 1887, Lake County, California, from tintype.

Right:
FIGURE 9.28 George Alexander Cagle and Harriet Corde Alia Mize, abt. 1900, probably Marion County, Alabama.

at the Mount Pisgah Cemetery in Fulton County. Phillip had two other wives: Nettie Brown (1873–1941), whom he married on May 13, 1909, in Izard County; and Martha Leticia Cole (1860–1884), whom he married in 1878.

7. Sarah Carolina Mize (abt. 1869–aft. 1880), who was born in Fulton County.

8. Harriett Cordelia Mize (Sep 27, 1871–Jan 1, 1940), who was born in Fulton County. She first married Charles Edward Davis (Nov 1867–Jan 28, 1922) on Oct 27, 1887, in Lake County, California, where she was probably staying with her older brother, John. She gave birth to her daughter, Retta Leola (Davis) Adams (1890–1984) in Fulton County, probably after a separation from her marriage to Charles. She married George Alexander Cagle (Oct 20, 1861–Jun 14, 1933) on Feb 11, 1894, in Marion County, Alabama. Harriet and George were buried at the Bethel Cemetery in Franklin County, Alabama. See Figure 9.27 and 9.28.

In about 1878 in Fulton County, Jonathan married Mary Elizabeth Harley (Aug 18, 1842–Mar 18, 1918), with whom he had two additional children:

9. Minnie Mize (Jun 23, 1879–Jun 17, 1960), who married Henry Fred Geara (Jun 1862–abt. 1939) and moved to California. Henry was born in Germany and was a resident of the United States for 51 years and a rancher in California for 31 years. Minnie and Henry died in Kings County, California.

10. Lula May Mize (Aug 5, 1881–Oct 25, 1965), who married Harold "Harley" Ross Murphy (Jul 24, 1876–Jan 10, 1945) on Oct 22, 1902, in Gila County, Arizona. Lula and Harley died in San Bernadino County, California.

1.6.3.3 **William Crawford Campbell** (Sep 10, 1836–Sep 28, 1901) married **Lucy Catherine Ross** (Feb 3, 1838–aft. 1880) in 1858 in Fulton County, Arkansas. William served in the Arkansas 2nd Cavalry Regiment, Union Army, during the U.S. Civil War. William was buried at the Witt Baptist Church Cemetery in Hamblen County, Tennessee. William and Lucy had seven children:

1. Mary Caroline Campbell (Dec 8, 1858–Oct 16, 1914) was born in Fulton County, Arkansas. She married Darnadus Leweldan Kemp (Jan 25, 1856–Nov 8, 1922) on Nov 12, 1876, in Franklin County, Washington. They were buried at the Woodlawn Cemetery in Snohomish County, Washington.

2. Martha Emmaline Campbell (abt. 1860–Nov 16, 1933) was born in Arkansas and married Martin Oscar Wright (Apr 8, 1854–Jul 23, 1957) on Feb 4, 1877, in Wilkes County. See Figure 9.29. They died in Lane County, Oregon.[47]

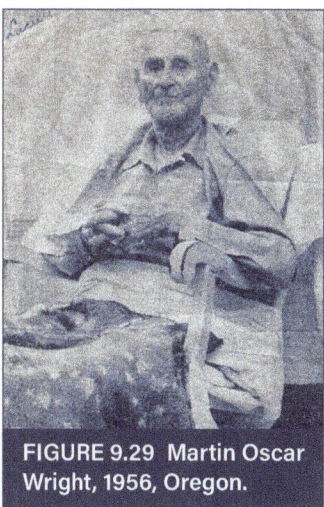

FIGURE 9.29 Martin Oscar Wright, 1956, Oregon.

3. Adaline Campbell (abt. 1863–unknown) was born in Arkansas.

4. William L. Campbell (1866–abt. 1880) was born in Missouri.

5. John D. Campbell (abt. 1868–Mar 24, 1924) was born in Missouri and married Nina Dee Berry (Sep 9, 1867–Jan 11, 1956) on Dec 20, 1893, in Columbia County, Washington. They died in King County, Washington.

6. Estella M. Campbell (abt. 1873–aft 1880) was born in Missouri.

7. Bytha L. Campbell (abt. 1876–unknown) was born in Missouri.

   Lucy either died or left William for another man after 1880. William married **Nancy Jane Croxdale** (Jan 1, 1854–Jan 25, 1935) on Jun 25, 1882, in Hamblen County, Tennessee. William and Nancy had four children:*

8. Hilda J. Campbell (Apr 1884–aft. 1910) was born in Hamblen County, Tennessee, and married George W. Gregory (abt. 1856–1920).

9. Ethel Suetta Campbell (Jul 8, 1885–Dec 24, 1974) married a Baptist minister, Rev. John Edward Harris (Sep 1, 1879–Feb 15, 1960) on Jun 18, 1893, in Dickson County, Tennessee. See Figure 9.30. They were buried at the Bookwalter Cemetery in Knoxville.

FIGURE 9.30 Rev John Edward Harris and Ethel Suetta Campbell, abt. 1940, Tennessee.

10. Lucy Kansas Campbell (May 23, 1890–Oct 5, 1959) married George Robinett Hudgens Sr. (Aug 14, 1883–Mar 25, 1918) in 1909 in Tennessee. She

---

* The Vanhoy *History of the Campbell Family* only indicated three children from William C. Campbell's marriage to Nancy Jane Croxdale. The children were not named.

divorced George and married Benjamen Levi White (Sep 2, 1886–Jul 6, 1953) on Sep 28, 1920, in Hamblen County. Lucy died in an automobile accident. Lucy and George were buried at the Witt Baptist Church Cemetery in Hamblen County.

11. Florence A. Campbell (Aug 2, 1893–Dec 18, 1928) married William Elliot Gibson (Dec 2, 1883–May 11, 1949) on Apr 3, 1911, in Hamblen County.

1.6.3.4 **Frances "Fannie" Elizabeth Campbell** (May 20, 1839–Jan 20, 1922) married **John Wanta Redman** (Apr 14, 1836–Apr 18, 1883) in 1859 in Iredell County. John enlisted as a 3rd sergeant in the 54th North Carolina Infantry Regiment, CSA, on May 5, 1862. John was murdered by his cousin, Hosea Columbus Redman (Oct 28, 1849–Apr 13, 1891), whose father, Absolum Redman (1817–1892), was a Baptist minister. See Figure 9.31. Hosea was convicted of manslaughter and released after three

FIGURE 9.31
Hosea Columbus Redman and his wife, Lula Williams, abt. 1890, Iredell County.

years in prison. Fannie was buried at Saint Lukes Evangelical Lutheran Church Cemetery in Mount Ulla, Rowan County. Fannie and John's children included:

1. James R. Redman (Jun 1860–bef. Jul 1860), who died as an infant and may have been a twin of Dabney B. Redman. In the 1860 Census taken on Jul 10, there was only one one-month-old male infant (Dabney B. Redman) living with J.W. and Fanny E. Redman on the New Hope Postal Route in the Taylor Spring District of Iredell County. An 11-year-old female African American servant of mixed Black and white ancestry, Keziah Ivins, loaned to them by their neighbor, I. F. Wright, was also living with them. John Wanta's grandparents, Hose and Lucretia Redman, were living nearby.

2. **Dabney B. Redman** (Jun 1860–bef. 1910), who married Matilda B. Mayberry (Mar 29, 1860–Jun 26, 1947) on Nov 13, 1879, in Iredell County. Matilda was buried at Oakwood Cemetery in Statesville. Dabney's burial location is unknown.

3. **John Beauregard Redman** (Aug 3, 1861–Jun 15, 1944), who married Laura Temperance Crews (Mar 22, 1863–Nov 14, 1936) on Jun 7, 1885, in Stokes County. John and Laura had a family of four girls (Mary, Jennie, Gillie, and Eva) and five boys (Osborn, Samuel, Joseph, Luther, and Willie). See Figure 9.32. John and Laura were buried at the Woodlawn Cemetery in Rockingham County.

4. **William Preston Redman** (May 12, 1863–Jul 4, 1940), who may have married Ella Salmons (1861–Dec 6, 1898) on Feb 14, 1886, in Iredell County. He married Cora Lee Dixon (Oct 3, 1878–Jun 1, 1908) on Aug 26, 1898, in Rowan County. He married Dora Belle Foster (Jul 8, 1880–Dec 28, 1975) on Apr 18, 1908, in Davie County, North

FIGURE 9.32
John Beauregard
Redman Family.
Bottom L to R: Willie,
Samuel, Gillie, Eva,
Laura, Joe, John;
Top L to R: Osborn,
John, Mary, Jennie,
abt. 1905, Leaksville,
North Carolina.

Carolina. See Figure 9.33. William and Cora were buried at Ebenezer Methodist Church in Rowan County. Dora was buried at the Carolina Memorial Park in Cabarrus County.

5. **Dewitt David Clinton Redman** (1866–aft. 1880), who was born in Iredell County and moved to the Cleveland area of Rowan County before 1880.

6. **Hosea E. Redman** (Mar 21, 1869–Jun 1, 1897), who married Elmira Myra "Maurey" Salmons (abt. 1864–Nov 17, 1895) on Jun 17, 1888, in Iredell County. Myra was a sister of Ella Salmons, both of whom were daughters of James Calvin Salmons (1834–1880) and Elizabeth Elliott (1834–1882). Hosea was buried at Oakwood Cemetery.

7. **Lillie Idocus "Callie" Redman** (Feb 3, 1872–May 3, 1964), who married George Wilhelm Hunter (Jul 14, 1868–Feb 18, 1918) on Aug 20, 1894, in Iredell County.

FIGURE 9.33 William Preston and Dora Belle Redman, abt. 1920, Rowan County.

George was a farmer and carpenter. See Figure 9.34. Lillie was buried at the Westminster Gardens Cemetery in Greensboro. George was buried at the Cedar Tree Cemetery in Barium Springs, Iredell County.

8. **James Robert Redman** (Mar 22, 1877–Jan 18, 1901), who served in Capt. Flannigan's Company, 1st North Carolina Regiment, during the Spanish– American War. He was buried at the Campbell Family Cemetery in Iredell County.

FIGURE 9.34
Lillie Idocus Redman, 1956, Guilford County.

9. Marshall Clemons "Mash" Redman (Mar 20, 1879–Sep 4, 1945), who married Margaret Caroline Graham (Nov 3, 1876–Jul 31, 1951) on Mar 27, 1907, in Rowan County. Marshall and Margaret were buried at St. Luke's Evangelical Lutheran Church in Rowan County.

10. **Romulus "Raum" Z. Redman** (Oct 31, 1881–Apr 14, 1919), who married Lura Scates (Feb 25, 1889–Oct 30, 1976) on Mar 18, 1908, in Gaston, North Carolina. He served in the 19th Infantry, U.S. Army, from 1901–1904. After the war, he was a night watchman at the Norcott Mill in Concord. He was shot and killed in a dispute during a union strike rally at the mill. He may have gone by a nickname, "Woodie." He was buried at the West Concord Cemetery in Cabarrus County. After his death, Lura married Ernest Victor Dry (Feb 12, 1888–Feb 16, 1967) before 1930 in North Carolina.

1.6.3.5 **John Price Campbell Sr.** (May 21, 1842–Feb 4, 1878) married **Isa "Icy" Ann Elkins** (Aug 13, 1843–Feb 17, 1932) in 1866 in Izard County, Arkansas. He served as a private in the 4th North Carolina Infantry Regiment, CSA, during the U.S. Civil War, and was wounded on Dec 13, 1862, at the Battle of Fredericksburg. After John's death in Izard County, Icy married Samuel Zachariah Dover (Apr 9, 1835–Aug 16, 1908) on Jul 20, 1893, in Sharp County, Arkansas. See Figure 9.35.

FIGURE 9.35
Icy Elkins and 2nd husband, Samuel Dover, abt. 1900, Izard County.

Samuel was buried at the Finley Creek Cemetery in Izard County. After Samuel's death, Icy moved with her daughter, Martha Carolyn (Campbell) Lawhorn, to Le Flore County, Oklahoma, where she died and was buried at the Witteville Cemetery. John and Icy's children were:

1. Christian Elkins Campbell (1869–abt. 1895), who married Sarah Rebecca Roten (Jan 10, 1871–Jan 28, 1946) on Dec 15, 1889, in Izard County. They had two children: James Andrew Campbell (Jul 2, 1891–Oct 5, 1954) and Roxie Tennessee Campbell (Dec 22, 1894–Sep 28, 1965), both born in Izard County. James was a private in the U.S. Marine Corps in World War I. Christian's burial location is unknown. After Christian died,

Sarah married George Newton Howell (Dec 9, 1877–Aug 2, 1944) on Dec 16, 1899, in Jasper County, Missouri. George and Sarah were buried at the Fairview Cemetery in Jasper County.

2. Martha Carolyn "Mattie" Campbell (Nov 23, 1870–Apr 12, 1967), who married Thomas Martin Lawhon (Mar 4, 1858–Mar 30, 1958) on Mar 12, 1885, in Sharp County, Arkansas. They were buried at the Memorial Park Cemetery in Oklahoma City, Oklahoma. See Figures 9.36 and 9.37.

3. Sarah Frances "Sallie" Campbell (Jan 30, 1873–May 17, 1942), who married Robert Ham "Uncle Bunk" Caldwell (Jan 5, 1870–Feb 15, 1956) in 1893 in Sharp County, Arkansas. They were buried at the Witteville Cemetery in Le Flore County, Oklahoma.

FIGURE 9.36 Icy Elkins and Mattie Campbell, abt. 1930, Arkansas.

4. Rufus William Campbell (Dec 15, 1873–Jul 8, 1955), who married Eva Tabitha Josephine "Josie" Jordan (Feb 1, 1876–Nov 24, 1929) on Nov 28, 1897, in Sharp County, Arkansas. See Figure 9.38. Rufus married Iva Nona Bowden (Sep 25, 1906–Feb 26, 2001) in about 1937 in Tarrant County, Texas. See Figure 9.39. According to family, Rufus was an abusive person. Rufus and Eva were buried at the Shannon Rose Hill Memorial Park in Tarrant County, Texas. Iva was buried at the Rosehill Cemetery in Johnson County, Texas.[48]

FIGURE 9.37 Thomas Lawhon Family, *Front L to R:* Lucinda, Thomas, Mattie, and Jasper; *Back L to R:* Effie, Herbert, Curtis, and May; abt. 1959, Oklahoma.

FIGURE 9.38 Rufus William Campbell, abt. 1930, Ballinger, Texas.

FIGURE 9.39 *Front L to R:* Iva holding son Ralph Huron, Rufus William holding son Rufus Robert; *Back L to R:* Step-daughters Ethel Elizabeth *(left)* and Nona Celeste Graham *(right),* 1939, Handley, Texas.

5. Lucinda A. Campbell (1874–1879), who may have been a daughter who died as a child.

6. John Price Campbell Jr. (Mar 10, 1878–1950), who married Mary Leanna "Mollie" Battles (Mar 10, 1883–Apr 10, 1926) on Jun 26, 1897, in Sharp County, Arkansas. They were buried at the Fairmount Cemetery in Harmon County, Oklahoma. See Figure 9.40.

1.6.3.6 **Tabitha Caroline "Carrie" Campbell** (1844–aft. 1910) married **George Washington Williams** (1835–Aug 12, 1917) in about 1855 in Iredell County. Caroline and Wash Williams appear in the Vanhoy history, where it was said they moved out west. They moved to David-

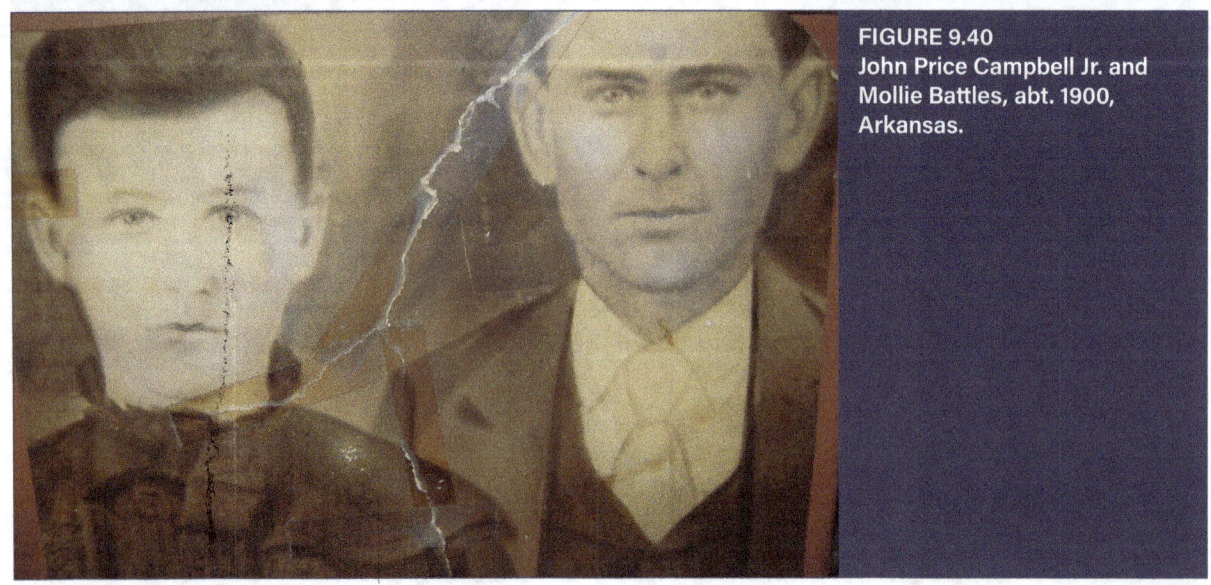

FIGURE 9.40 John Price Campbell Jr. and Mollie Battles, abt. 1900, Arkansas.

son County, Tennessee, by 1870, and then to Laclede County, Missouri, by 1900. George was a private in the 24th Missouri Infantry Regiment, Union Army, during the U.S. Civil War. Carrie and George probably died in Laclede County, Missouri. Their children were:

1. Dora "Bell" J. Williams (1861–Mar 3, 1839), who was born in Iredell County. She married Henry Coleman Rice (Dec 28, 1868–Jan 25, 1955) in 1895, probably in Missouri. Dora and Henry died in Nashville, Davidson County, Tennessee, and were buried at the Mount Olivet Cemetery in Nashville.

2. Theophilus Williams (1863–aft. 1880), who was born in Iredell County and probably died in Davidson County, Tennessee.

3. Barbara L. Williams (Nov 7, 1867–Dec 10, 1925), who married John G. Griggs Sr. (Jan 7, 1847–Feb 13, 1933) on Jul 30, 1883, in Davidson County, Tennessee. They were buried at the Turner Family Cemetery in Davidson County.

4. Hugh Richard Williams (1868–aft. 1880), who was born in Iredell County and probably died in Davidson County, Tennessee.

5. Thomas Benjamin Williams (Oct 1, 1870–Aug 21, 1948), who married Emma Rhetus Marshall (Aug 4, 1883–Apr 28, 1958) in 1901 in Marshall County, Kentucky. They were buried at the Briensburg Baptist Church Cemetery in Marshall County. See Figures 9.41 and 9.42.

FIGURE 9.41 Thomas Benjamin Williams, abt. 1900, Kentucky.

FIGURE 9.42 Emma Rhetus Marshall, abt. 1900, Kentucky.

6. John E. Williams (1874–Sep 10, 1882), who was born and died in Davidson County, Tennessee.

7. Hattie Elizabeth Williams (Sep 22, 1876–Jul 17, 1956), who married Samuel Washington Dunn (Oct 27, 1874–Jun 9, 1957) on Jan 13, 1896, in Marshall County, Kentucky. Hattie and Samuel were buried at the Briensburg Baptist Church Cemetery in Marshall County.

8. Ivy "Iva" Lula Williams (Oct 5, 1878–Nov 29, 1953), who was born in Davidson County and died in Marshall County, Kentucky. She did not marry. She was living with her sister Hattie's family since 1910 in rural Marshall County, Kentucky. She was buried at the Briensburg Baptist Church Cemetery in Marshall County.

1.6.3.7 Isabella M. Campbell (Apr 15, 1850–Oct 27, 1928) was born in Iredell County and moved with her mother to Izard County, Arkansas. She married James Henry Clay Harvell (Aug 6, 1944–Dec 21, 1918) in 1867 in Arkansas. James was a private in the Missouri Artillery, CSA, during the U.S. Civil War. See Figures 9.43 and 9.44. James's great-grandfather, Isham John Harvell Sr. (1756–1813), lived in Wilkes County in 1778, where he married Matilda Harriet Cass (1762–1815) in 1781. Isabella died in Lunenburg, Izard County, Arkansas. She and James were buried at the Reeves Cemetery in Melbourne, Izard County, Arkansas.49, 50, 51, 52 Isabell and James had the following children:[53]

FIGURE 9.43
Isabella Campbell and James Henry Clay Harvell, abt. 1880, Izard County.

1. Isabella Tabitha "Mariah" Harvell (Nov 1869–Mar 1906) married George Thomas Anderson (Mar 19, 1866–Mar 13, 1944) on Sep 21, 1890, in Izard County, Arkansas. Mariah died in Izard County. George was buried at the Heber Springs City Cemetery in Cleburne County, Arkansas. See Figure 9.45.

FIGURE 9.44 Isabella M. Campbell, abt. 1900, Izard County.

George and Mariah (nee Harvell) Anderson Family

1. GEORGE T. ANDERSON
2. ALLEN ANDERSON
3. JAMES ANDERSON
4. EDNA ANDERSON
5. TOM ANDERSON
6. MARY ANDERSON
7. MARIAH (HARVELL) ANDERSON
8. MADLINE ANDERSON

FIGURE 9.45 George and Mariah Anderson Family, abt. 1903, Izard County.

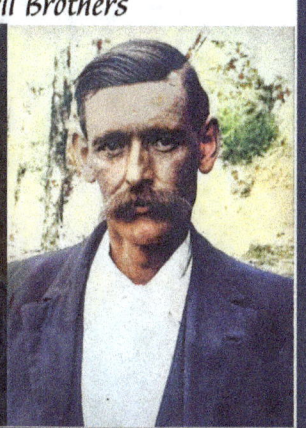

Left: **FIGURE 9.46** Emma Malone and William Thomas Harvell, abt. 1900, Texas.

Right: **FIGURE 9.47** William Thomas and Samuel Henry Harvell, abt. 1900, Arkansas.

2. William Thomas Harvell (Nov 1870–Dec 17, 1921) married Viola Goldie "Dolie" Shoemaker (abt. 1874–unknown) on Dec 31, 1891, in Izard County, and Cynthia Emeline "Emma" (Malone) Hayes (Aug 16, 1876–Nov 22, 1923) on Jul 2, 1899, in Collin County, Texas. See Figure 9.46 and 9.47. They were buried at the Pecan Grove Cemetery in Collin County. George B. Harvell (abt. 1872–abt. 1895) died of typhoid as a child.

3. Samuel Henry "Little Sam" Harvell (Apr 10, 1877–May 17, 1965) married Samantha Elmira Moser (Mar 8, 1878–Feb 10, 1912) on Jun 6, 1898. in Lunenburg, Izard County. He married Rose Etta Sipes (Dec 14, 1885–Nov 22, 1966) on Nov 29, 1916, in Izard County. Samuel had three children by Samantha: Zilla Mary "Lilla" Harvell (Aug 26, 1905–Nov 29, 1990), John Henry Owen William Harvell (Sep 12, 1908–Feb 7, 1993), and Della Ada Harvell (Jul 5, 1910–Nov 25, 1998). He did not have any children by Rose. Samuel and Samantha were buried at the Reeves Cemetery in Izard County. Rose married Harvey Adam Pool (Sep 3, 1889–Oct 15, 1969) on Sep 19, 1906, in Cleburne County, Arkansas. Rose moved out west after 1930 and was buried at the Hillcrest Memorial Park Cemetery in Josephine County, Oregon. See Figures 9.48 and 9.49.

FIGURE 9.48 Little Sam Harvell with children, Zilla, Della, and John Henry Harvell, abt. 1960, Izard County.

4. Sarah Margarette Harvell (Feb 10, 1878–bef. 1900) married James Addison Kelley (Jan 1, 1874–1928) on Sep 27, 1894,

THE IZARD COUNTY

Historian

Volume 9   July, 1978   Number 3

Samuel Harvell, Samantha Moser Harvell and daughter Zilla M. Harvell Johnson. 1907

FIGURE 9.49 Samuel Harvell, Samantha Moser Harvell, and daughter Zilla M. Harvell Johnson, 1907, Izard County.

FIGURE 9.50 James Addison Kelly and Sarah Margarette Harvell, abt. 1900, Izard County.

FIGURE 9.51 Kelley Family: *Back L to R:* Joseph, Annie, James A., Margaret (Harvell), Francis Marion, George T.; *Front L to R:* Joshua Franklin, Lovie, Dora Elizabeth (Kelley) Brooks, Eugene, William Franklin, Eva, Nancy Catherine (Horton), Euphie, Mary (Kelley) Coleman, Bertha, Mary (Harvell), Genella; abt. 1903, Izard County.

in Izard County. James was born in Gordon County, Georgia. Sarah died of typhoid in Izard County. She was buried at the Reeves Cemetery in Izard County. See Figures 9.50 and 9.51.

1. Mary L. Harvell (Feb 1881–abt. 1911) married George T. Kelley (Aug 1878–bef. Apr 1910) on Oct 22, 1899, in Gid, Izard County. They were buried at the Reeves Cemetery in Izard County.

JOHN R. CAMPBELL

1.6.4   **John R. Campbell** (Sep 18, 1802–Aug 23, 1872) married **June Lucy Williams** (Dec 4, 1815–Jan 26, 1901) in about 1836 in Iredell County. See Figure 9.52. John R. Campbell's middle name may have been Randolph or Rutherford, although direct sourcing for this name has not been found.

According to an article that appeared in the Statesville newspaper in 1977, George Washington Reid (Apr 29, 1914–Aug 3, 1989) lived at the home of John R. and Lucy Campbell (Figure 9.53). George's father, Augustus Reid (Mar 6, 1844–May 1, 1936), moved to the house in 1920. George said that the two-story home, with the original chimneys, was 181 years old in 1977. This would imply that the home was built in about 1796. Although the house was destroyed by a fire in the 1980s, a couple of pictures of the house have survived (Figures 9.54 and 9.55).

Augustus Reid (1844–1936) was a U.S. Civil War veteran who had 20 children by 3 wives. Augustus and his last wife, Eliza Mae (Rash) Reid (1878–1960), and 2 of his sons,

FIGURE 9.52 June Lucy Williams, abt. 1900, front porch of her house.

FIGURE 9.53 Augustus and son, Martin L. Reid, on porch of John R. Campbell's house, abt. 1930, Union Grove Township.

FIGURE 9.54 John R. Campbell's house, Union Grove Township, 1982.

FIGURE 9.55 John R. Campbell's house, abt. 1985, Union Grove Township.

George Washington Reid (1914–1989) and Wilborn Reid (1887–1918), as well as one grandson, Dwight David Reid (1953–1953), are buried at a small cemetery near the site of his former home (Figure 9.56). The cemetery is called the Augustus Reid Cemetery. His son Wilborn Reid died in northern France, just weeks before the end of World War I. See Figure 9.57. He was buried in Varennes, France. In 2012, family members placed a memorial marker in this cemetery next to his father.

John R. and Lucy Campbell were the first ones to be buried at the Augustus Reid Cemetery (Figures 9.58 and 9.59). This cemetery is located on Mitch Road in Union Grove Township. To reach the cemetery, you walk down from the paved road to a gravel road and continue down that road for about a mile. The cemetery is visible on the right. The current owners of the property have kept up the cemetery.

1.6.4.1 **Tabitha C. "Bitha" Campbell** (May 19, 1837–Sep 19, 1874) married **Hamilton C. "Ham" Somers*** (Jul 10, 1830–Sep 4, 1878) in about 1857 in Iredell County. See Figure 9.60. Hamilton was the son of John A. Somers (1806–1887) and Frances Sturdivant (1806–1878) of

*All known records show his name as Hamilton C. Somers or Ham Somers. Some genealogists show the middle name as Calvin. Hamilton did have a younger brother Calvin Somers, who was living in Hamilton's house at the time of the 1870 U.S. Census.

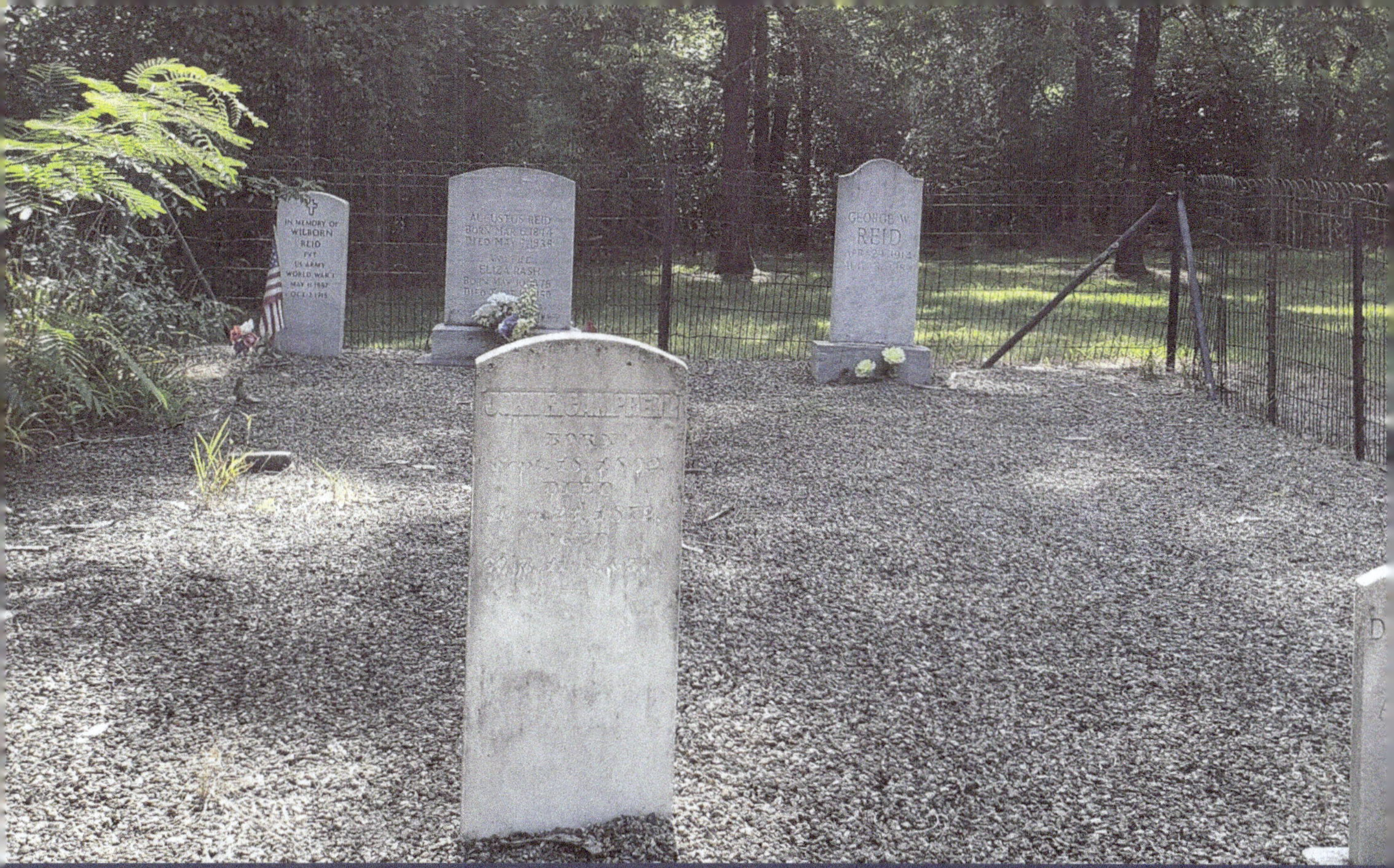

FIGURE 9.56 August Reid Cemetery, abt. 1980, Union Grove Township.

FIGURE 9.57
Wilborn Reid, abt. 1918, probably France.

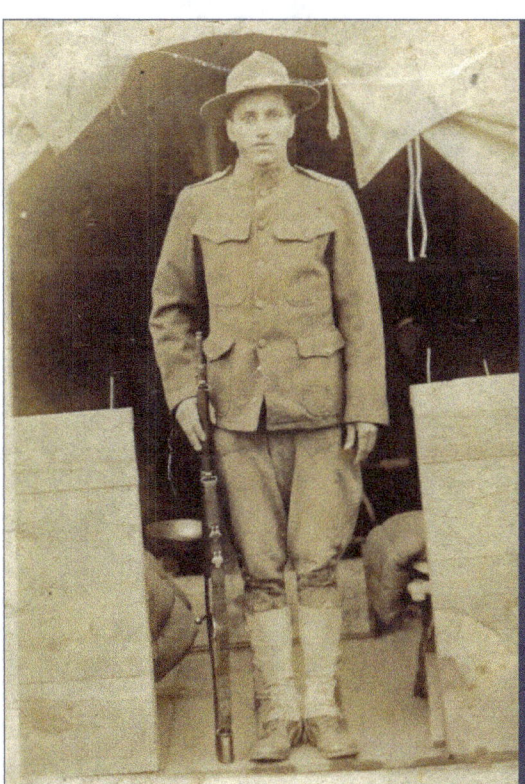

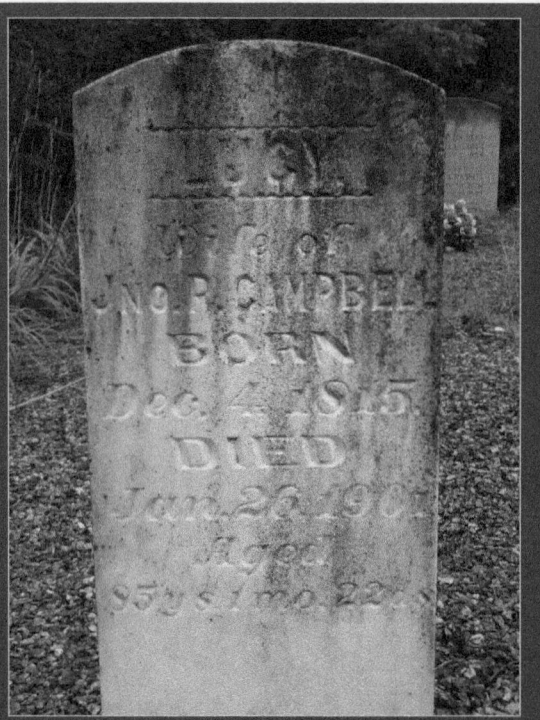

Left: FIGURE 9.58 John R. Campbell's headstone, abt. 1980, Augustus Reid Cemetery.

Right: FIGURE 9.59 Lucy Williams Campbell's headstone, abt. 1980, Augustus Reid Cemetery.

FIGURE 9.60 Hamilton C. Somers and Tabitha C. Campbell, abt. 1870, Wilkes County.

Wilkes County. He was born in Rowan County (in the area that became Davie County in 1836) and moved to Wilkes County with his family by 1850. Hamilton and Tabitha owned a farm less than a mile southeast of Hamilton's father's home in Osbornville, Wilkes County. Hamilton was a farmer, miller, and distiller. They lived on Osborne Creek, just upstream of what is now Hunting Creek Road in Wilkes County. The family, his younger brother, Calvin (age 22), and a Black farmhand, Alexander Somers (age 20), were living on the Lovelace Postal Route in Somers Township, Wilkes County, on Jul 29, 1870. At that time, his real estate and personal property were valued at $4,000 and $1,000, respectively. The two older sons were attending school. Hamilton divorced Tabitha in 1873, but they were buried side by side at the Union Baptist Church Cemetery in Wilkes County.

Tabitha and Hamilton had five children. At the time of Hamilton's death, the oldest child was 19 and the youngest was only 10. They had to fend for themselves without parents.

1. **John W. Somers** (abt. 1859–May 1897) was living with his brothers Gaston and Lee Preston on the family farm in Somers Township in Wilkes County in 1880. John served in the U.S. Army 2nd Artillery between 1881 and 1892. John W. married Paulina E. Nicholson* (Mar 26, 1860–Oct 13, 1918) in Wilkes County in about 1892. He left Paulina in Wilkes County near Osbornville and went to Point a la Hache, Louisiana, where he died in jail after drinking heavily. Paulina filed for a pension based on his service in 1897. Paulina was buried at the Sweet Home Baptist Church Cemetery in Wilkes County.

2. **Gaston Turner Somers** (Jun 4, 1860–Apr 1, 1893) married Sarah Ann Hampton (Jan 30, 1864–Dec 4, 1959) in Yadkin County on Dec 16, 1891. Gaston worked as a farmer in 1880 and as an inspector for the Internal Revenue Service in Osbornville in 1885. Sarah and Gaston were buried at the Oakdale Cemetery in Surry County.

3. **Emma J. Somers** (Jul 25, 1863–Sep 9, 1941) was living with her uncle, John Franklin Somers (Nov 15, 1834–Nov 23, 1907) in 1880. James Franklin Somers was the sheriff of Wilkes County from 1868 to 1870. Emma married Soloman David Swaim "Swim" Lewis (Nov 5, 1857–Mar 6, 1948) in North Carolina in about 1882. They were living in Somers Township in Wilkes County in 1900. Solomon was a farmer and sewing machine mechanic. Emma and Soloman divorced before 1910 and Emma was probably running a rooming house with her son, Hamilton D. Lewis, in Wichita, Kansas, in 1910. Soloman died in the Moore County home in Carthage, North Carolina. Emma had three children: Commie Swaim Lewis (1883–1910), Hamilton Dee Lewis (1888–1977), and Maude "Minnie" Lewis (1893–aft. 1920). See Figure 9.61. Hamilton was a piano tuner and died in Fond Du Lac, Wisconsin. Emma may have lived in Tulsa, Oklahoma, in 1934, and then moved to Orange County, California. She may have been buried at the

---

*Paulina used the last name of her mother, Mary Elizabeth "Polly" Nicholson, as did her other siblings. Her father was Ezekiel Benjamin Cass.

Loma Vista Memorial Park in Fullerton, California.

4. **Lee Preston "L. P." Somers,** MD (Sep 12, 1864–Apr 16, 1932) married Mina "Minni" Dell Couch (May 15, 1873–Aug 19, 1937) on Jan 28, 1892, in Yadkin County. L. P. farmed in the summer and attended local subscription schools in the winter. At the age of 16, he walked the 25 miles to attend Moravian Falls Academy in Wilkes County (Figure 9.62). He worked for his tuition and lived alone in a log cabin while attending the academy, from which he grad-

FIGURE 9.61 *(L to R)* **Hamilton, Soloman, Commie, Emma, and Maude Lewis family, abt. 1900, Wilkes County.**

uated in 1884. After graduation, he read medicine under Dr. J. C. Wilcox in Jefferson, North Carolina. With financial help from his uncle William Howard Somers (1832–1888), he was able to attend lectures at the University of Baltimore, which he entered under the "pauper plan," which required him to pay only half the regular fees. After medical school, he served as a doctor in Southwest Wilkes County for over 40 years. See

FIGURE 9.62 Moravian Falls Academy, abt. 1900, Wilkes County.

Figures 9.63 and 9.64. Lee was buried at the Somers Cemetery in Iredell County. The day of his funeral, some 5,000 people came to pay their respects. Minnie was buried at Zion Baptist Church.[54]

L. P. found time for community affairs and financed the building of roads and bridges in the area. He had an active interest in business and politics. In 1906, he accepted the nomination to represent his district composed of Wilkes, Yadkin, and Davie counties in the state senate. He received the largest vote majority that any candidate had ever received. The day after the election, the one person who voted for the opposing candidate came and apologized, saying he was drunk and did not realize what he was doing.[54]

President William McKinley appointed L. P. Somers as the U.S. Examining Surgeon. He served as president of the U.S. Pension Board at Wilkesboro for 16 years. He was instrumental in seeing that all widows of both the Confederate and Union army soldiers received pensions and that all deceased soldiers of both armies had grave markers.[54]

He was a 32nd-degree Mason, a Shriner, and he was responsible for many deserving children being placed in the Oxford Orphanage. Likewise, he saw to it that all the blind babies he delivered attended the school for blind children. He did the same for children who were deaf.[54]

5. **Sarah A. "Sissy" Somers** (Oct 24, 1866–Apr 24, 1957) married Lemuel Esau Wallace (May 11, 1859–May 26, 1938) on Aug 27, 1888, in Iredell County. Lemuel was a millwright. Sarah was buried at Oakwood Cemetery in Statesville. Lemuel was buried at the Wesley United Methodist Church Cemetery in Union Grove, Iredell County.

Left:
FIGURE 9.63
L. P. Somers, abt. 1910, Wilkes County.

Right:
FIGURE 9.64
Minnie Dell Couch, abt. 1920, Wilkes County.

1.6.4.2 **Theophilus "Offie" Campbell** (Nov 6, 1839–Jun 11, 1906) married **Mary Louisa Somers** (Jan 15, 1843–Jan 11, 1867) in about 1865, probably in Wilkes County. Mary was the sister of Hamilton C. Somers. Theophilus did not have any children by Mary Louisa. Theophilus Campbell enlisted during the U.S. Civil War in the 44th North Carolina Infantry Regiment at Camp French, Prince William County, Virginia, on Nov 12, 1862. The 44th Regiment served with the Army of Northern Virginia under General Robert E. Lee and surrendered at Appomattox on Apr 9, 1865.

FIGURE 9.65 Theophilus Campbell and Rebecca C. Minish, abt. 1880, Union Grove Township.

After Mary Louisa's death in 1867, Theophilus married **Rebecca C. Minish** (Jan 8, 1850–Apr 11, 1920) in Iredell County. Rebecca was the oldest of five children of **Capt. John C. Minish** (Sep 25, 1818–aft. Jun 12, 1880) and Margaret (Salmons) Minish (abt. 1817–Aug 1870). See Figures 9.65 and 9.66. Theophilus and Rebecca were buried at Zion Baptist Church in Union Grove Township.

Theophilus and Rebecca Minish had eight children:

1. **Mary Louisa Campbell** (Jan 25, 1870–Feb 2, 1940) married Iram Green Reid (Feb 7, 1868–Feb 11, 1954) on May 2, 1892, in Iredell County. They were buried at Zion Baptist Church in Iredell County. See Figures 9.67, 9.68, and 9.69.

2. **Celia Angaline Campbell** (Nov 8, 1871–Jun 14, 1899) married Daniel Asbury "Did" Mullis (May 24, 1867–Jan 21, 1932) on Sep 27, 1893, in Iredell County. Did was a blacksmith and ran a lumber mill. After Celia died, Did married twice again. Celia and Did were buried at Zion Baptist Church. See Figure 9.70.

FIGURE 9.66 Campbell Family: (*L to R*) Evelyn Octavia Mullis, Johnny Campbell, Mary Louisa Campbell, Iram Reid, Ezra Campbell, Daniel Asbury Mullis, Joseph Franklin Dobson, Tabitha Campbell, Henry Columbus Bennett, Lucy Paulina Campbell; seated: Rebecca Minish; abt. 1910, Union Grove Township.

FIGURE 9.67 Mary Louisa Campbell and Iram Green Reed, abt. 1930, Union Grove Township.

Left:
FIGURE 9.68 Iram Reid and granddaughter Mary Joanna Leonhardt, abt. 1938, Harmony.

Right:
FIGURE 9.69 Mary Louisa Campbell and Mary Joanna Leonhardt, abt. 1935, Harmony.

FIGURE 9.70 Daniel Asbury Mullis with grandchildren, abt. 1930, Harmony.

3. **John "Johnny" Dodredge Campbell** (Jun 19, 1874-Nov 25, 1940) married Evelyn Octavia "Arkie" Mullis (Jan 15, 1872–Oct 7, 1956) on Oct 4, 1896, in Iredell County. Arkie was the sister of Did Mullis. Johnny was a farmer, a carpenter, and store owner. See Figures 9.71 and 9.72. Johnny and Arkie were buried at Zion Baptist Church.*

FIGURE 9.71 Johnny Campbell, abt. 1900, Union Grove Township.

4. Pierce Americus Campbell (Jun 16, 1877–May 8, 1878) died as a child.

5. **Ezra Wilford Campbell** (Mar 16, 1881–Jun 21, 1959) married Doshie Precilla Shore (May 28, 1880–Aug 29, 1939) before 1907 in Iredell County. After Doshie died, Ezra married Julia Oakley "Oakie" Moose (Oct 18, 1879–Apr 30, 1961) on Nov 30, 1948, in McDowell County, North Carolina. (Oakie had previously married William Milas Campbell, 1.6.4.8.) Ezra and Doshie were buried at Zion Baptist Church. Oakie was buried at Union Grove Methodist Church next to her first husband, William Milas Campbell.

FIGURE 9.72 Arkie Mullis and Garry E. Moore (author), 1951, Union Grove Township.

6. **Lucy Paulina "Plina" Campbell** (Dec 28, 1881–Oct 24, 1948) married Henry Columbus "Lum" Bennett (May 27, 1865–Jul 2, 1938) on Sep 15, 1910, in Iredell County. Lucy had a child, Zeda Carr Campbell Sr. (Aug 22, 1906–Mar 9, 1972), before her marriage to Henry. Zeda was raised by his grandmother, Rebecca (Minish) Campbell, and later by his uncle Ezra W. Campbell. Lucy's son Henry Woodrow Bennett (Jul 2, 1913–Nov 22, 1944) was killed while serving with the 18th Infantry Regiment in Germany during World War II. He was buried at the Henri-Capelle Cemetery in Liege, Belgium. Lucy and Henry were buried at Union Grove Methodist Church. See Figures 9.73 and 9.74.

7. Winfield Dent Campbell (Oct 5, 1884–Jul 17, 1886) died as a child.

FIGURE 9.73 Lucy Paulina Campbell, abt. 1940, Union Grove Township.

---

*Three great-grandsons of John Dodredge Campbell are participants in the Adam Campbell Y-DNA Project.

8. **Tabitha Ann Campbell** (Jun 11, 1888–Feb 22, 1949) married Joseph Franklin Dobson Jr. (May 31, 1886–Feb 8, 1942) on Oct 4, 1908, in Iredell County. After Frank died, Tabitha married Ephraim James Stack (Jun 10, 1878–Oct 13, 1956) on Apr 29, 1947, in Iredell County (Figures 9.75 and 76). Frank and Tabitha were buried at Zion Baptist Church. Ephraim was buried at the Harmony City Cemetery in Iredell County.

FIGURE 9.74 Henry Woodrow Bennett, 1940, Union Grove Township.

FIGURE 9.75 Tabitha Ann Campbell, abt. 1900, Union Grove Township.

FIGURE 9.76 Ephraim James Stack and his first wife, Sarah Jurney's family (Laura Anne, Dave, and Amy), and African-American servant, abt. 1903, Eagle Mills Township, Iredell County; Ephraim married Tabitha Ann Campbell in 1947, his third of four wives.

1.6.4.3 **Mary "Polly" Campbell** (Apr 2, 1843–Nov 26, 1891) married **Reuben A. Morris Jr.** (Mar 8, 1837–Aug 9, 1863) on Jan 1860 in Iredell County. Reuben owned one 10-year-old male slave in 1860. Reuben served in the 4th North Carolina Infantry Regiment during the U.S. Civil War and was wounded in the Battle at Chancellorsville. Mary and Reuben had one child:

1. **John Jackson G. Morris** (Oct 8, 1860–Sep 12, 1926) married and divorced between 1900 and 1910. He lived on Campbell Mill Road with his cousins **Alice C. Campbell**, Berlie Jurney, and **Ruby Ann Vanhoy** in 1910 and 1920. He worked as a miller at the Campbell Mill, grinding corn and wheat. He was buried at the Union Grove Methodist Church.

    After Reuben's death, Mary Polly married **James William Bolin** (Oct 24, 1844–May 10, 1908) in about 1861 in Iredell County. James also served in the 4th North Carolina Infantry Regiment during the U.S. Civil War. After Mary Polly died, James married Senia Speaks (Aug 12, 1865–May 14, 1960) on Dec 24, 1895, in New Hope Township, Iredell County. Polly, Reuben, and James were buried at Moss Chapel in Iredell County. Senia moved to Winston-Salem by 1920 and was buried at the Forsyth Memorial Park in Winston-Salem. Mary Polly and James had 12 children:

2. **Sarah Roxann Bolin** (Feb 23, 1862–Aug 29, 1903) did not marry. She was buried at Moss Chapel in Iredell County.

3. Nancy Bolin (1865–bef. 1880) died young.

4. **John Pierce "Johnnie" Bolin** (Jan 21, 1869–Aug 15, 1933) first married Sarah D. Henderson (Nov 24, 1869–Dec 16, 1903) in 1889 in New Hope Township, Iredell County. He married Bertha Mae Rash (Aug 8, 1883–Jan 2, 1965) on May 1, 1905, in New Hope Township. See Figures 9.77 and 9.78. Johnny and Bertha were buried at Union Grove Methodist Church in Iredell County. Sarah was buried at Grassy Knob in Iredell County.[55]

5. Sophia E. Bolin (May 19, 1871–Dec 13, 1877 died as a child and was buried at Moss Chapel.

6. Dora C. Bolin (Sep 12, 1873–Dec 16, 1877) died as a child and was buried at Moss Chapel.

7. **William T. Bolin** (Dec 5, 1875–Aug 17, 1896) did not marry. His cousin, **Edward Clinton Vanhoy,** stabbed William in the side while

FIGURE 9.77 John Pierce Bolin and Bertha Mae Rash with children Sandy Bolin and Lucy Bolin, abt. 1913, Union Grove Township.

FIGURE 9.78 Bertha Mae (Rash) Bolin and children: Tracy Jewell, Gordon, Lucy, Raby Pierce, Leah Grace, Helen Ruth, and Betti Jean, abt. 1950, Catawba County.

drinking near the Smith Chapel church. He died the next day.56 He was buried at Moss Chapel at 21 years old.

8. **Mary Cornelia "Mollie" Bolin** (Oct 15, 1879–Jan 26, 1971) first married Wesley Columbus Henderson (abt. 1879–Nov 15, 1914) on Dec 23, 1897, in Iredell County. She later married Lewis Pleasant Mikles (Dec 17, 1872–Nov 4, 1957) on Oct 15, 1923, in Guilford County. She was buried at the Floral Garden Memorial Park in High Point, North Carolina. Wesley was buried at Union Grove Methodist Church. Lewis was buried at Oakwood Cemetery in High Point, North Carolina.

9. **Joseph Cornelius Bolin** (Oct 15, 1879–Mar 8, 1953) did not marry. He was buried at Moss Chapel. He and Mary Cornelia were twins.

10. **Emma Campbell Bolin** (Apr 22, 1881–Jul 28, 1956) married James Preston Henderson (Jul 26, 1876–Jul 15, 1965) on May 31, 1903, in Iredell County. They lived in Yadkin County and were buried at the Shiloh Missionary Baptist Church.

11. **Fannie M. Bolin** (Apr 1883–Dec 7, 1920) married Thomas Mack Henderson (Jun 5, 1887–Nov 20, 1961) on May 3, 1907, in Iredell County. Fannie was buried at the Union Grove Methodist Church. Thomas was buried at the Iredell Memorial Gardens in Statesville.

12. **Lillie Jewel Bolin** (Jul 24, 1883–May 20, 1913) married Ransom Vance Jurney (Nov 3, 1882–Apr 17, 1912) on Oct 12, 1902, in Iredell County. They lived in Union Grove Township and were buried at the Union Grove Methodist Church.

13. Grover C. Bolin (Sep 14, 1885–Jan 13, 1887) died as a child and was buried at Moss Chapel.

1.6.4.4 **Paulina Campbell** (Oct 8, 1845–Mar 18, 1923) married **John Robey Huie** (Jun 30, 1846–Apr 23, 1926) on Mar 1, 1866, in Union Grove Township. John was a private in the North Carolina 8th Battalion of Mounted Infantry of the Junior Reserves, CSA, during the U.S. Civil War. There are also records of John R. Huie enlisting in the 2nd Mounted Infantry Regiment, Union Army in Boone, North Carolina, in 1864. John and Paulina were buried at Mount Vernon Baptist Church Cemetery in Iredell County.

Paulina and John Robey Huie had the following children:[34, 57]

FIGURE 9.79
James Calloway Fletcher, abt. 1900, Iredell County.

1. **Fannie Luiza Huie** (Dec 15, 1866–Mar 18, 1927) married John Pinkney Howard (Nov 1, 1863–Aug 23, 1919) on Feb 26, 1889, in Iredell County. They lived in Union Grove Township and were buried at Zion Baptist Church.

2. **Sarah H. Huie** (Aug 20, 1868–Jan 14, 1906) married James Calloway Fletcher (Jun 2, 1862–Jul 20, 1942) on Jun 17, 1888, in Iredell County. James was a schoolteacher for 40 years in Iredell County. See Figure 9.79. James and Sarah lived in Eagle Mills Township. James and Sarah were buried at the Mount Vernon Baptist Church in Iredell County.

3. **Amanda "Mandy" Huie** (Nov 10, 1870–Jun 10, 1900) married James Walker Bowles (Apr 23, 1862–Apr 18, 1930) on Oct 1, 1890, in Iredell County. See Figure 9.80. James was a carpenter. His son, Henry Clay Bowles (May 9, 1896–Aug 7, 1961), served in World War I (Figure 9.81). Amanda was buried at the Mount Vernon Baptist Church.

FIGURE 9.80 James Walker Bowles with children: Henry Clay, Douschka "Lucy," and Lois Puog, abt. 1904, Iredell County.

FIGURE 9.81
Cpl. Henry Clay Bowles, 1918.

James married Minnie Messick (Jul 15, 1878–Nov 2, 1932) from Eagle Mills Township after Amanda died. He moved to Winston-Salem after Mandy died.

4. **Samuel Huie** (May 21, 1873–Aug 11, 1941) married Susan Lenora Fletcher (May 21, 1876–Jan 12, 1970) on Dec 23, 1897, in Iredell County. They lived in Union Grove Township and were buried at Mount Vernon Baptist Church.

5. Dovie Huie (Apr 12, 1875–Dec 3, 1943) married **James Turner Jennings** (Nov 10, 1872–Apr 20, 1956) on Nov 20, 1893, in Iredell County. They lived in Union Grove Township and were buried at Zion Baptist Church. James operated Jennings General Store in Union Grove (Figure 9.82). James's parents were Thomas Lawson Jennings and Sarah Ann Campbell (1.6.2.1.1).

6. **Myra Leyra Huie** (May 1, 1878–Jan 15, 1959) married Charlie Sanford Sloan (Nov 24, 1876–Dec 7, 1946) on Dec 18, 1902, in Iredell County. They lived in Turnersburg Township and were buried at Mount Vernon Baptist Church.

7. **Flake Huie** (Feb 28, 1879–Jul 10, 1946) did not marry. He lived on Jennings Road in Union Grove Township. He was buried at Mount Vernon Baptist Church.

8. **Lucy Pussy Huie** (Oct 24, 1880–Jan 4, 1899) did not marry. She lived in Union Grove Township and was buried at Mount Vernon Baptist Church.

9. **Lavica "Lovie" Huie** (Jul 9, 1882–Oct 3, 1918) married Edgar Elisha "Eli" Robertson (Nov 3, 1877–Jan 4, 1947) on Dec 24, 1904, in Iredell County. They lived in Union

FIGURE 9.82
Jennings General Store, 2025, Union Grove.

Grove Township and were buried at Mount Vernon Baptist Church. Edgar was a general store merchant in Union Grove.

10. **George Washington Huie** (Apr 6, 1884–Apr 17, 1918) married Eva Lee (Journey) Huie Hedrick (Feb 5, 1888–Apr 12, 1953) on Oct 10, 1906, in Iredell County. They lived on Huie Mill Road in Union Grove Township. They were buried at the Mount Vernon Baptist Church.

11. **Lela "Lealer" Huie** (Dec 17, 1886–Mar 30, 1983) did not marry. She lived with her brother Flake and was buried at Mount Vernon Baptist Church.

12. **Ina Campbell Huie** (Mar 6, 1888–Jan 21, 1973) married Robert Cromwell Sloan (Feb 28, 1884–Apr 17, 1971) on Nov 23, 1911, in Iredell County. Robert was a farmer and mail carrier. They lived in Union Grove Township and were buried at Mount Vernon Baptist Church Cemetery.

13. **Anna Angie Huie** (Jan 1, 1890–Jun 10, 1927) married Dr. Henry Clay Salmons (Nov 16, 1882–Feb 28, 1954) on Dec 17, 1908, in Iredell County. Henry was educated in county schools. He took his premedical work at Davidson College, subsequently attending the North Carolina Medical College at Charlotte, from which he graduated in 1904. He did further study at North Carolina Polyclinic, New York Post Graduate School of Medicine, John Hopkins University, George Washington University, and Barnes Hospital in St. Louis, Missouri. They lived in Union Grove Township. Dr. Salmons practiced medicine in Jonesville in Yadkin County and Elkin in Surry County. He was appointed health officer of Jonesville in 1905 and operated a drug store in connection with his general practice from 1908–1916. He was a member of the Yadkin County Board of Health in 1912, and served on Jonesville Board of Commissioners and was elected mayor of Jonesville in 1941. In 1919, he moved to Elkin to practice medicine and surgery. In 1924, he, along with Dr. Robert R. Garvey, who was practicing medicine at State Road, opened the first hospital in Elkin, which they operated from 1924 to 1928. Later, Dr. Salmons went to Europe to study at clinics in London, Edinburgh, Stockholm, Upsala University, Berlin, Vienna, Heidelberg University, and Paris. After Angie died, he married Cyrene Willie Gertrude Michael (Apr 14, 1899–Feb 22, 1954) of Kernersville.[58] Henry and both wives were buried at the Hollywood Cemetery in Surry County.

1.6.4.5 **James W. Campbell** (Nov 6, 1846–Jul 31, 1898) married **Arminda C. "Minda" Privette** (Feb 7, 1851–Feb 23, 1920) on Mar 12, 1874, in Iredell County. James was a farmer and lived in Union Grove Township. Both James and Arminda were buried at Grassy Knob Baptist Church. James and Arminda had four children:

1. **Vallie Daisy Campbell** (Aug 19, 1878–Jan 27, 1953) married Oliver Curtis Barnard (Sep 1, 1872–Feb 10, 1961) on Sep 19, 1907, in Iredell County. They lived in Statesville. See Figures 9.83 and 9.84. Oliver died at Broughton Hospital in Morganton, Buncombe

County. Daisy and Oliver were buried at Grassy Knob Baptist Church.

2. **Charles W. Campbell** (Jun 21, 1880–Jun 4, 1927) married Maud E. "Maudie" Mitchell (Oct 16, 1886–Mar 15, 1950) on Mar 15, 1911, in Wilkes County. They lived on Zion Road in Union Grove Township. Their son, Zebra James Campbell (Jun 2, 1906–May 22, 1972), was a chief machinist mate in the U.S. Navy during World War II (Figure 9.85). Zebra married Raby Pierce Bolin, daughter of John Pierce Bolin. See Figures 9.86 and 9.87. Charles and Maudie were buried at Union Grove Methodist Church.

FIGURE 9.83 The Vallie Daisy (Campbell) Barnard family, *(L to R)* John William, Daisy holding Helen Gertrude, Sallie May, Arminda (Privette) Campbell, Virginia Ethel, and James Royal, abt. 1906, Eagle Mills Township.

Left: FIGURE 9.84 Zebra Campbell, 1940, Union Grove Township.

Middle: FIGURE 9.85 (*Front L to R*) Curtis and Daisy Barnard; (*Back L to R*) Children: McDonald (1918–2013), Lucile, Helen, Ethel, John William, James Royal, abt. 1940, Statesville.

Right: FIGURE 9.86 Charles W. Campbell and wife, Maudie Mitchell, holding Lessie, and Zebra James in front, abt. 1913, Union Grove Township.

FIGURE 9.87 Maud (Mitchell) Campbell and Children, Front L to R: John Clayton Campbell, Lucy Inez Doby, Tobitha Trivette, Maude, Ida Gray, Cornelius Campbell, Curtis Campbell; Back L to R: Zebra Campbell, Lessie Knight, Jimmy Campbell, Jackson Campbell, Lealdon Campbell, Weldon Campbell, 1948, Harmony.

3. **Mack Campbell** (May 14, 1883–Mar 15, 1900) did not marry. He was buried at Grassy Knob Baptist Church at age 17.

4. **Williams R. Campbell** (May 22, 1887–Dec 21, 1901) died as a child. He was buried at Grassy Knob Baptist Church.

1.6.4.6 **Sarah A. Campbell** (Mar 5, 1850–Jun 30, 1934) married **William Ashley Vanhoy** (Mar 13, 1849–Feb 11, 1917) on Oct 6, 1875, in Iredell County. William was born in Surry County and was one of eight children of Edward F. Vanhoy (Jun 30, 1821–Apr 14, 1898) and Nancy Johnson/Johnston (Aug 4, 1819–Nov 22, 1896). Edward F. Vanhoy served during the Mexican American war in the North Carolina Militia as a drummer and as a private with the 66th North Carolina Infantry Regiment, CSA, during the U.S. Civil War. He was a POW in Richmond in 1865.

Sarah was known far and wide for her sterling honesty, strong mind, and firm convictions. Born 10 years before the outbreak of the Civil War, and in a slave-owning family, she recalled clearly the principal events of that period and its resultant hardships. She was a devoted reader of the Bible all her life and a champion of the causes of education and good government. See Figure 9.88.

Sarah and William were buried at Union Grove Methodist Church.[59] They had nine children.

1. **Milas Leoldan "Chig" Vanhoy** (Jul 1, 1876–Apr 6, 1926) married McCollis Brown (Feb 12, 1884–Jul 6, 1950) on Feb 2, 1905, in Wilkes County. They lived in Union Grove Township. Chig committed suicide near his home. He was distressed about illnesses in the family. See Figure 9.89. Chig and McCollis were buried at Union Grove Methodist Church.

FIGURE 9.88
Sarah A. (Campbell) Vanhoy; Elizabeth Jane (Vanhoy) Ireland, sister of William Ashely Vanhoy; Sarah Christine (Durham) Vanhoy; and husband, Joseph Leander Vanhoy, brother of William Ashely Vanhoy, abt. 1926, probably Union Grove Township.

FIGURE 9.89 McCollis Brown and Milas Vanhoy, abt. 1910, Yadkin County.

2. **Edward Clinton Vanhoy** (Dec 9, 1877–Feb 27, 1967) was also known as Daniel Mason. As noted above, Edward murdered his cousin, William T. Bolin, in 1896. He fled to Kentucky, where he took on a new identity as Daniel Mason and raised a family with his wife Lillie May Williamson (Apr 16, 1886–Mar 15, 1960) after 1900 in Frankfort, Franklin County, Kentucky. See Figure 9.90.

FIGURE 9.90
Edward Clinton Vanhoy, aka Daniel Mason, abt. 1950, Franklin County.

He died in Midway, Woodford County, Kentucky, where he was buried at the Sunset Memorial Gardens and Mausoleum.[56]

3. **John Webster Vanhoy Sr.** (Aug 28, 1880–Jun 24, 1943) married Nettie Paris Casey (Jul 18, 1892–Jun 8, 1977) on Jun 18, 1913, in Mecklenburg County. John was a farmer and public schoolteacher in Iredell County. He attended Wake Forest College, where he graduated in 1910. See Figure 9.91. He later attended Georgetown Law School in Washington, D.C., for three years. He was appointed assistant title attorney in the U.S. Department of Agriculture from 1913 to 1923, where

FIGURE 9.91
John Webster Vanhoy, abt. 1910, Iredell County.

his duties included examining titles of land acquired for the forest reserve. He was a Democrat and served for a time as secretary for a member of Congress in 1915 and 1916, as well as clerk on the House Committee on Expenditures in the Department of Agriculture. After his government service, he practiced law in Louisiana, representing the interests of oil companies, and served as an attorney for the Arkansas Bar Association. In 1930, he returned with his family to live in Iredell County and practice law in Statesville. John Webster did much of the research for the Campbell family history presented at the 1925 Campbell Family Reunion in Union Grove. His namesake son, John Webster Vanhoy Jr. (Oct 2, 1915–Apr 5. 2003), attended Mars Hill College and the U.S. Military Academy at West Point, where on Nov 2, 1943, he married Joan O. Whitney (May 15, 1917–Feb 22, 2002) of New York, who was a member of Women's Army Corps. John Webster Jr. obtained the rank of colonel in the U.S. Army. John Webster Vanhoy Sr. and Nettie were buried at Zion Baptist Church in Union Grove Township.

4. **Alice Campbell Vanhoy** (Nov 30, 1882–Oct 21, 1956) married **Wilburn Burchard Tutterrow** (Oct 16, 1876–Apr 2, 1963) on Aug 24, 1911, in Iredell County. They lived on Campbell Mill Road in Union Grove Township. Her mother lived with them after her

father died. See Figure 9.92. Alice and Wilburn were buried at the Zion Baptist Church.

5. **Henry Price (H. P.) Vanhoy** (Jan 22, 1887–Jul 19, 1976) married Ada Jane Casey (Nov 10, 1896–Oct 13, 1989) on Dec 10, 1914, in Iredell County. They first met at the Union Grove School. Ada played guitar and Henry played fiddle. Henry attended Eupeptic Springs Academy, Harmony High School, and Appalachian University in Boone, North Carolina. Henry was a public schoolteacher in Union Grove in 1920, the treasurer and tax collector for Iredell County from 1828 through 1932, bridge construction foreman for the State Highway Department in 1940, a farmer, and an amateur fiddle player. He was most widely known for organizing and managing the "World's Champion Old Time Fiddler's Convention" that was held yearly in Union Grove. The convention was founded on the Saturday before Easter in 1924 to benefit Union Grove

FIGURE 9.92 Wilburn Burchard Tutterow, abt. 1950, Union Grove Township.

High School, where it was first held and where he was the principal. He was a member of the Board of Trustees of Iredell Memorial Hospital. See Figures 9.93, 9.94, and 9.95.

6. William Luther Vanhoy (Dec 31, 1889–Feb 24, 1891) died as an infant.

7. **Pauline Iona "Polly" Vanhoy** (Nov 19, 1891–Apr 18, 1923) married John Cleveland Sharpe (Aug 22, 1886–Dec 30, 1943). See Figure 9.96. They lived in Union Grove. John was a graduate of the Wake Forest Law School and practiced law in Statesville. Pauline and John were buried at the Union Grove United Methodist Church.

8. **James Pierce Vanhoy** (Sep 2, 1894–Sep 22, 1915) did not marry. See Figure 9.97. He lived near Jennings in Iredell County and died of tuberculosis. He was buried at the Union Grove Methodist Church at 19 years old.

9. **Ruby Ann Vanhoy** (Mar 7, 1899–Nov 30, 1927) did not marry. She lived in Statesville and died from tuberculosis. See Figure 9.96. She was buried at the Union Grove Methodist Church.

1.6.4.7 **John Pierce Campbell** (Jul 28, 1855–May 14, 1925) married **Elizabeth Isabel Mitchell** (Mar 3, 1845–Apr 2, 1916) in about Aug 1874 in Iredell County. Elizabeth was the daughter of Moses H. Mitchell Jr. (Oct 1811–1910) and Olive Elizabeth Speaks (Apr 12, 1824–bef. 1900). John's farm was near Rocky Creek in Union Grove Township. See Figure 9.99. John and Elizabeth were buried at Grassy Knob Baptist Church in Union Grove Township. They had four children:

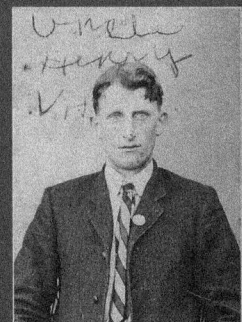

Left:
FIGURE 9.93 Henry Price Vanhoy, abt. 1960, Iredell County.

Middle:
FIGURE 9.94 Ada (Casey) Vanhoy, abt. 1940, Union Grove.

Right:
FIGURE 9.95 Henry Price Vanhoy, abt. 1910, Iredell County.

Left:
FIGURE 9.96
John Cleveland Sharpe, abt. 1930, Union Grove Township.

Right:
FIGURE 9.97
H.P. Vanhoy's son James Pierce Vanhoy (right) waits to close a performance during the 1951 fiddler's convention in the Union Grove School Auditorium.

Left:
FIGURE 9.98
Ruby Vanhoy, abt. 1920, Union Grove Township.

Right:
FIGURE 9.99
John Pierce Campbell, abt. 1880, Union Grove Township.

1. **Margaret Ellen "Maggie" Campbell** married James Robert "Bob" Walker (Oct 5, 1876–Sep 21, 1948) on Dec 15, 1895, in Iredell County. They lived in Taylorsville, Alexander County. See Figure 9.100. They were buried at Moss Chapel in Iredell County (Figure 9.101).

FIGURE 9.100 Maggie Campbell, abt. 1900, Union Grove Township.

FIGURE 9.101 Moss Chapel, built abt. 1800, site of Methodist Camp meetings.

2. **Smith Armfield Campbell** (Aug 4, 1879–Jul 25, 1953) married Lessie May Webb (Nov 23, 1884–Feb 3, 1951) on Dec 24, 1912, in Iredell County. Smith attended Mars Hill College and taught in Iredell County schools for several years. He was also a road surveyor. In his final years, Smith and Lessie lived in Florida for 35 years, where Smith managed a pecan grove and dairy farm. He died in Union Grove while visiting his sister, Dessie. Smith and Lessie were buried at Grassy Knob Baptist Church. See Figure 9.102. They did not have any children.

3. **Odessa "Dessie" Campbell** (Aug 17, 1882–Jul 4, 1970) married Ernest Burton Sharpe (1890–Sep 19, 1964) on Apr 9, 1919, in Wilkes County. They lived on Mitch Road in Union Grove Township. They were buried at Grassy Knob Baptist Church.

4. **Isom Campbell** (Sep 9, 1885–Jun 13, 1977) married Maude Belle Myers (May 10, 1899–Mar 3, 1981) on Apr 3, 1924, in Iredell County at the residence of Alice Campbell (Perciphull Campbell House) by his uncle, Jackson G. Morris, justice of the peace. Isom was a farmer and lived on Howard's Bridge Road in Union Grove Township. See Figures 9.103 and 9.104. Isom and Maude were buried at Grassy Knob Baptist Church. They had six sons.[60]

1.6.4.8 **William Milas Campbell** (May 13, 1858–May 18, 1936) married **Sarah Ann Mitchell** (Mar 13, 1964–Jan 9, 1887) on Dec 28, 1880, in Iredell County. He married **Julia Oakley "Oakie" Moose** (Oct 18, 1879–Apr 30, 1961) on Jul 29, 1906, at the home of J. D. Moose in Sharpsburg Township, Iredell County. The Rev. J. G. Weatherman officiated. William settled at the home place of his father, **John R. Campbell**, and lived there for a while. He later sold the home and land and moved out west. He later moved back to Union Grove Township and

1789–1894 (Depictions, not actual sketches)

FIGURE 9.102 *Left:* Grassy Knob Baptist Church, 1894–1953; *Right:* depictions of earlier church, Union Grove Township.

FIGURE 9.103 Isom and Maudie Campbell's home, abt. 1975, Union Grove Township.

lived on the Capt. John Minish farm place, near Howard's Ford. The location of this farm is shown as the W. M. Campbell farm on the 1917 map of Union Grove Township (See Figure 9.159 in the Maps section at the end of this chapter.).[68] According to the Vanhoy family history, "William Milas was a great trapper and hunter and had killed more hawks and caught more minks than any man in Iredell County. Though crippled, he had been classed the best one-horse farmer in Iredell County."[1] William and both of his wives were buried at Union Grove Methodist Church. William and Sarah had the following children:

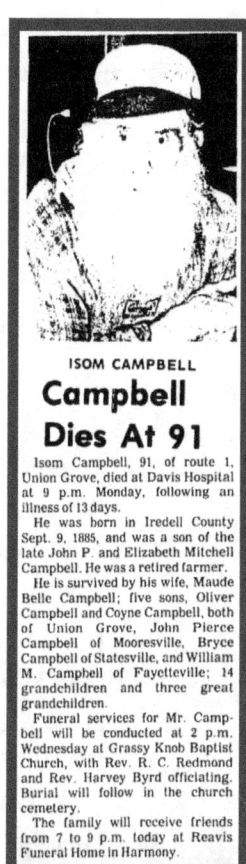

ISOM CAMPBELL

Campbell Dies At 91

Isom Campbell, 91, of route 1, Union Grove, died at Davis Hospital at 9 p.m. Monday, following an illness of 13 days.

He was born in Iredell County Sept. 9, 1885, and was a son of the late John P. and Elizabeth Mitchell Campbell. He was a retired farmer.

He is survived by his wife, Maude Belle Campbell; five sons, Oliver Campbell and Coyne Campbell, both of Union Grove, John Pierce Campbell of Mooresville, Bryce Campbell of Statesville, and William M. Campbell of Fayetteville; 14 grandchildren and three great grandchildren.

Funeral services for Mr. Campbell will be conducted at 2 p.m. Wednesday at Grassy Knob Baptist Church, with Rev. R. C. Redmond and Rev. Harvey Byrd officiating. Burial will follow in the church cemetery.

The family will receive friends from 7 to 9 p.m. today at Reavis Funeral Home in Harmony.

FIGURE 9.104 Obituary for Isom Campbell, 1977, Statesville.

1. **Ella B. Campbell** (Sep 20, 1882–Feb 5, 1948), who married William James Allen (Aug 22, 1882–Oct 29, 1950) on Apr 14, 1910, in Wilkes County. They lived in North Wilkesboro. James owned the Orpheum Theater of North Wilkesboro. They were buried at the Mountlawn Memorial Park in Wilkes County.

2. **Sarah "Sallie" Campbell** (Mar 27, 1883–May 19, 1950), who married Thomas Marvin Jurney (Oct 1, 1875–Oct 23, 1936) on Oct 1, 1902, in Iredell County. Thomas was a farmer in Union Grove Township. Sarah and Thomas were buried at Union Grove Methodist Church.

3. **Fannie Lee Campbell** (Jan 1, 1885–Nov 29, 1940), who married James Monroe Templeton (Dec 13, 1874–Sep 12, 1939) on Feb 4, 1904, in Forsyth County. They lived on South Trade Street in Winston-Salem, Forsyth County, where James worked as a machinist in a mattress factory and cotton mill. They were buried at the Union Ridge United Methodist Church in Winston-Salem.

SARAH "SALLIE" CAMPBELL

1.6.5   **Sarah "Sallie" Campbell** (1805–aft. Aug 31, 1870) married **Bartlett "Bart" Morgan** (abt. 1790–aft. Aug 31, 1870) in about 1824 in Iredell County. Bartlett was the son of Martin Morgan (1758–1830) and grandson of Theophilus Morgan Sr. (1720–1807).[1] Bart bought several books, including a *History of the World*, *Acts of the Assembly*, and the Campbell family bible at Perciphull Campbell Sr.'s estate sale on Oct 17, 1853. Sally Morgan (age 60) and Bartton Morgan (age 72) were living with Mary Douthit (age 30) and a child, Augustus Douthit (age 3), in Union Grove Township on Aug 31, 1870. The burial locations for Sarah and Bart are not know but are probably in Iredell County.

Sarah inherited slaves (Huldey, Jane, Eli, Catherine, Emily, and Sarah) from her father, Perciphull Campbell. Her husband, Bartlett, had six slaves in 1860. Bartlett's real estate was valued at $1,000 and personal estate at $6,130 in 1860. In 1870, his real estate in Union Grove Township was valued at only $100.

Sarah and Bart had eight children:

1.6.5.1 **Holeman Morgan** (1808–bef. 1860) appears in the Vanhoy history. There was a Holman or Hilman Morgan (age 42) and Permelia Morgan (age 44) living in Iredell County in 1850, near Aquilla Williams. Holeman's or his mother's birth date could be incorrect since she would have only been 11 when Holeman was born. Permelia could have been Permelia Redman (1806–aft. 1880). Holeman and Permelia had two children according to census records:

1. Thomas L. Morgan (1836–aft1880) was living north of Rocky Creek in Iredell County with his mother, Permelia, in 1860. He enlisted in the 4th North Carolina Infantry Regiment, CSA, on Mar 1, 1862, at Williamsburg in Iredell County. He was wounded at the Battle of Seven Pines in Virginia. He mustered out (was discharged) at the surrender at Appomattox Court House on Apr 9, 1865. He may have married sometime during the Civil War and had a daughter, Cathrine Morgan (1863–aft. 1880).

2. John T. Morgan (May 1836–Mar 30, 1921) married Mary Bettie "Last Name Unknown" (1862–bef. 1921). John was a farmer and horse doctor. They may have had a daughter, Susie Morgan, born in Jun 1892. John died at the Broughton State Hospital in Morganton, Burke County, where he was admitted to between 1910 and 1920. He did not have any known living relatives at the time of his death. He was buried at the Broughton Hospital Cemetery.

1.6.5.2 **Polly Morgan** (1825–unknown) may have married or died before the 1850 U.S. Census. Nothing more is known.

1.6.5.3 **Pierce Morgan** (1828–aft. 1860) was living with his parents north of Hunting Creek on the Eagle Mills postal route in 1850 and 1860. Nothing more is known.

1.6.5.4 **Reuben R. Morgan** (1831–aft. 1880) married Mahaley "Aley" Shoemaker (abt. 1830–Apr 8, 1907) before 1860. Reuben was a private in the 4th North Carolina Infantry Regiment, CSA, during the U.S. Civil War. He was wounded at the Battle of Seven Pines on May 31, 1862. He mustered out on Apr 21, 1865, in Farmville, Virginia. He was living in Buck Shoals Township, Yadkin County, in 1880. Rueben and Aley had three children:

1. Zeno Columbus Morgan (Jul 11, 1860–Mar 20, 1944) married Mary Victoria Shoemaker (May 5, 1864–Nov 7, 1935) on Dec 9, 1883, in Iredell County. They moved to Winston-Salem by 1900. Zeno was a cobbler and weaver. They were buried at the Salem Moravian God's Acre in Winston-Salem, Forsyth County. Zeno's grandson, James Pierpont Morgan (Sep 29, 1918–Oct 2, 2011), was a trombonist in an orchestra in Greensboro, Guilford County, in 1940.

2. Sarah Jane Morgan (Sep 10, 1863–Jan 19, 1950) married William Green Rowe (May 1859–1920) on Nov 21, 1900, in Iredell County. Sarah was buried at the New Prospect Baptist Church Cemetery in Statesville.

3. Emily S. "Emma" Morgan (Feb 1867–bef. 1930) married Harrison Hopson (Mar 1860–bef. 1930) on Nov 17, 1882, in Carter County, Tennessee, where they died.

1.6.5.5 **William J. Morgan** (1833–aft. 1880) was living with his parents in Iredell County in 1850. There was a William J. Morgan, born in North Carolina, living with his own family in Saline County, Arkansas, in 1860, but a definitive connection has not been made. This William J. Morgan had moved to Arkansas by 1852. He married Elizabeth Eskridge (Jan 15, 1823–bef. 1900) on Jul 20, 1854, in Saline County. William served as a private in Carlton's 48th Arkansas Cavalry Regiment, CSA, during the U.S. Civil War. He was wounded at the Battle of Seven Pines and mustered out at the Battle of Appomattox Courthouse. Their children were:

1. Benjamin C. Morgan (1852–aft. 1870), who was born in Arkansas.

2. Arkansas Morgan (1855–1860), who was female and living with her parents in Saline County, Arkansas, in 1860.

3. Rufus Oliver Morgan (Jul 18, 1857–Apr 18, 1932), who married Virginia Pocohontas Mashburn (Aug 1, 1865–Jun 12, 1911) on Oct 10, 1880, in Saline County, Arkansas. They were buried at the McPherson Cemetery in Saline County.

4. Mary Elizabeth Morgan (1859–1938), who married James Scott West on Jan 7, 1877, in Saline County. They were buried at the McPherson Cemetery in Saline County.

5. Sarrah Laurine Morgan (Apr 21, 1861-Nov 3, 1909), who married Zachariah N. Hill (Aug 29, 1858–1883) on Nov 14, 1880, in Saline County; and William Daniel Green (Nov 3, 1853–Jun 15, 1928) on Oct 23, 1887, in Saline County.

1.6.5.6 **Gabriel Barry Morgan** (Jul 19, 1839–May 18, 1890) may have married Caroline Young (abt. 1840–unknown) on Apr 8, 1866, in Davidson County, North Carolina. See Figure 9.105. Gabriel may have died in Lamar County, Texas, and may have been buried at the Tigertown Cemetery. No additional information about Caroline has been found.[61] They may have had a son, John Barton Morgan (Feb 18, 1867–Nov 10, 1895), who married Margaret Melinda Fults (Jan 31, 1873–Apr 30, 1933) on Dec 7, 1887, in Bonham, Fannin County, Texas. See Figure 9.106.

Left:
FIGURE 9.105 Gabriel Barry Morgan, abt. 1890, Texas.

Right:
FIGURE 9.106 John Barton Morgan, son of Gabriel Barry Morgan, abt. 1880, Texas.

1.6.5.7 **John B. Morgan** (abt. 1840–Jun 19, 1862) was a private in the 4th North Carolina Infantry Regiment, CSA, during the U.S. Civil War. He died in Richmond, Virginia, from wounds incurred at the Battle of Seven Pines in Virginia on May 31, 1862. He was buried at the Hollywood Confederate Cemetery in Richmond. He did not marry.

1.6.5.8 **Joseph Milden Morgan** (about 1843–May 31, 1862) was a private in the 4th North Carolina Infantry Regiment, CSA, during the U.S. Civil War. He was killed in action on May 31, 1862, at the Battle of Seven Pines. He did not marry.

MARY POLLY CAMPBELL

1.6.6 **Mary Polly Campbell** (1806-Nov 1844) married **Gabriel B. Parks** (Feb 20, 1798–Feb 27, 1880) in about 1824 in Iredell County. Although there is no tombstone, Mary may have been buried at the Campbell Family Cemetery. Since Mary died before her father, each of her children was named in her father's will and given $1 each plus their mother's share of the estate proceeds. The Vanhoy *History of the Campbell Family* mentions Polly and Gabriel and their children Pettis, Dabney, Richard, and Theophilus. After Mary died, Gabriel moved to Monroe County, Georgia. Gabriel married Martha Matilda (Jernigan) Burch (Apr 6, 1806–Jun 8, 1885) on Sep 14, 1845, in Harris County, Georgia. See Figure 9.107. Gabriel and Martha were buried at the Parks Family Cemetery near Forsyth, Monroe County, Georgia. See Figures 9.108 and 9.109.

FIGURE 9.107 Martha Matilda Jernigan, abt. 1880, Harris County, Georgia.

FIGURE 9.108 Headstone of Gabriel Parks, Monroe County.

FIGURE 9.109 Parks Family Cemetery, Monroe County, Georgia.

Gabriel's father, Benjamin Parks Sr. (1746–1839), and his wife, Elizabeth Branch (1758–1815), lived in Wilkes County. Benjamin was an ensign, captain, and lieutenant in the Surry County Regiment during the American Revolution. He fought at the Battle of Shallow Ford during the American Revolution. After the war, Benjamin obtained North Carolina land grants for property in Burke County on the Upper Creek and in Wilkes County on the Buggabo Creek. At some point before 1828, the Parks family moved to Georgia. The brother of Gabriel Parks, Benjamin Parks Jr. (Oct 27, 1802–Mar 5, 1895), had discovered gold in Dahlonega, Georgia, in 1828.[62]

Gabriel owned 18 slaves in 1850 and 26 slaves in 1860 in Monroe County.[63] See Figure 9.110.

Gabriel had five children—four by his first wife, Mary Polly, and one, Melville, by his second wife, Martha:

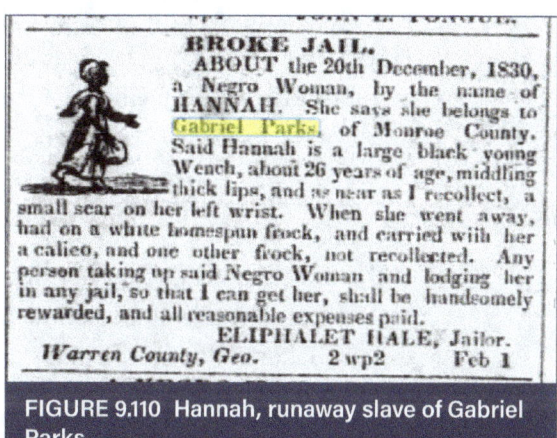

BROKE JAIL.
ABOUT the 20th December, 1830, a Negro Woman, by the name of HANNAH. She says she belongs to Gabriel Parks, of Monroe County. Said Hannah is a large black young Wench, about 26 years of age, middling thick lips, and as near as I recollect, a small scar on her left wrist. When she went away, had on a white homespun frock, and carried with her a calico, and one other frock, not recollected. Any person taking up said Negro Woman and lodging her in any jail, so that I can get her, shall be handsomely rewarded, and all reasonable expenses paid.
ELIPHALET HALE, Jailor.
Warren County, Geo. 2 wp2 Feb 1

FIGURE 9.110 Hannah, runaway slave of Gabriel Parks.

1.6.6.1 **Dr. Richard M. Parks** (1826–Jan 6, 1871) became a medical doctor and moved to Gwinnet County, Georgia. He married Sarah Elizabeth Allen (Sep 9, 1828–May 28, 1861) on Sep 9, 1845, in Habersham County, Georgia. They lived in Norcross, Gwinnett County, Georgia. Dr. Parks represented Gwinnett County as a representative in the 80th Georgia General Assembly in 1869. This post-Civil War legislature was the first to meet in Atlanta after a new Georgia Constitution was written. Dr. Parks died in Atlanta, Georgia.[64] Sara was buried at the Allendale Family Cemetery in Banks County, Georgia. They had two known children:

1. John Richard Parks (Sep 13, 1846–Jul 26, 1893) married Amanda Isabell "Sadie" Singleton (Mar 25, 1849–Sep 5, 1921) on Feb 14, 1872, in Fulton County, Georgia. They lived

in Atlanta. John was a private in the 16th Georgia Infantry, CSA, and was at Appomattox Court House when the South surrendered. John and Sadie were buried at Oakland Cemetery in Atlanta.

2. Sarah Parks (1853–aft. 1860) was born and died in Georgia.

1.6.6.2 **John Pettis Parks Sr.** (Sep 1827–1913) married Mary Ann Smith/Utzman (Mar 19, 1832–Jan 15, 1917)* on Dec 29, 1851, in Rowan County. See Figure 9.111. They lived on the Williamsburg Postal Route in Iredell County and moved to Cook County, Texas, by 1880. They were buried at the Hulver Cemetery in Hall County, Texas. John Pettis Parks Sr. and Mary Ann had six children who were all born in Iredell County:

FIGURE 9.111 Mary Ann Smith, abt. 1915, Hulver Hall County, Texas.

1. Alice Helen Parks (Nov 21, 1852–Feb 5, 1888) married John Gaither Tomlinson (Jan 9, 1849–Mar 12, 1914) on Aug 2, 1872, in Iredell County. John and Alice were buried at the Era Cemetery in Denton County, Texas.

2. Mary Eugenia "Mamie" Parks (May 20, 1854–Jun 15, 1896) married Wilfred Columbus Hayes (Nov 25, 1852–Dec 5, 1920) on Feb 6, 1873, in Iredell County. They were buried at Tabor Presbyterian Church Cemetery in Iredell County.

3. Dewitt Clinton Parks (Apr 15, 1858–Oct 9, 1918) married Catharine Clyde "Kitty" Robinson on Dec 26, 1880, in Cooke County, Texas. Kitty was buried at the Era Cemetery. After her death, Dewitt moved to California and was buried at the Union Cemetery in Bakersfield, California.

4. Dora A. Parks (Jan 12, 1860–Apr 19, 1948) married James Madison Williams (Jun 6, 1858–Sep 24, 1932) on Dec 16, 1884, in Cooke County. They were buried at the Hope Cemetery in Clay County, Texas.

5. Laura Ella Parks (Jan 22, 1862–Jan 28, 1945) married Thomas Jones Boswell (Jan 13, 1860–Apr 1, 1951) on Dec 9, 1879, in Fayette County, Tennessee. They were buried at the Macon Cemetery in Fayette County, Tennessee. See Figure 9.112.

FIGURE 9.112 Annie Boswell with parents, Thomas Boswell and Laura Parks, abt. 1930, Fayette County, Tennessee.

*Mary Ann's parents (John Utzmann and Mary Smith) were never married. Mary Ann used the last name of her mother.

6. John Pettis Parks Jr. (Jan 9, 1870–May 30, 1959) married Lilly Mae Collier (May 10, 1880–Nov 2, 1941) on Nov 10, 1902, in Harris County, Texas. They were living in Chaves County, New Mexico, in 1930. Lillie was buried at the Woodbine Cemetery in Eddy County, New Mexico. After her death, John moved to San Diego, California, to live with his daughter, Jannette Irene (Parks) White (Nov 20, 1912–Jan 6, 1976). He was buried at the Woodbine Cemetery.

1.6.6.3 **Dabney W. Parks** (1831–1863) was a captain in the 54th North Carolina Infantry Regiment, CSA, during the U.S. Civil War. He was living in Wilkes County when he enlisted. He died on Jun 12, 1863, from wounds at the Second Battle of Fredericksburg in May 1863. His headstone is at the Mount Pisgah Baptist Church Cemetery in Wilkes County. He did not marry.

FIGURE 9-113
Marcus Parks, abt 1900, Hamilton County, Tennessee.

1.6.6.4 **Theophilus Campbell Parks** (1835–1903) married Ollie Bell Laura Williams (Jul 1834–aft. 1910) on Nov 6, 1856, in Wilkes County. He served in 54thNorth Carolina Infantry Regiment, CSA, during the U.S. Civil War. Theophilus was appointed postmaster of the Poplar Bridge Post Office (formerly Boyden) in Iredell County on Mar 12, 1861. The exact location of this post office is not known. Theophilus and Ollie had nine children:

1. Laura Sarah Parks (Sep 29, 1857–Oct 31, 1946) married Wesley Osborn Anderson (1858–Jul 14, 1931) in North Carolina in about 1880. They were buried at the Antioch Baptist Church in Madison County, North Carolina.

2. Marcus Richard "Mock" Parks (Mar 31, 1860–May 29, 1944) married Florence Melinda Marshall (Oct 13, 1857–May 4, 1925) in about 1862 in Tennessee. See Figure 9.113.

3. Mary Lula Parks (Feb 23, 1865–Aug 21, 1956) married Romulus Milton Johnson (Feb 25, 1856–Nov 13, 1928) on Mar 21, 1882, in Wilkes County. They were buried at the Woodland Cemetery in Mecklenburg County, Virginia.

4. Robert Boyd Parks (1859–Dec 22, 1938) married Nora Levina Owenby (Oct 14, 1879–Dec 23, 1916) in 1902 in Union County, Georgia. After her death, he married Lillian A. Nix (Aug 1, 1878–Jan 22, 1962) in about 1910 in Georgia. Robert and Nora were buried at the Mount Pleasant Cemetery in Union County. Lillian was buried at the Corinth Cemetery in Union County.

5. Lolena Parks (1869–bef. 1880) may have died as a child.

6. John Dabney Parks (Feb 1, 1869–Oct 12, 1944) married Nancy Callie Adeline York (Jul 28, 1877–Jun 8, 1949) in about 1897 in North Carolina.

7. Flora Zell Parks (Oct 3, 1871–Oct 6, 1968) married Sanford J. York (1867–Aug 11, 1901) on Dec 24, 1889, in Buncombe County. She later married William Josiah Winchester (Nov 3, 1871–Mar 7, 1951) on Feb 24, 1898, in Clay County, North Carolina. See Figure 9.114. Flora and William were buried at the Hayesville Baptist-Presbyterian Cemetery in Clay County. Sanford was buried at the Oak Grove United Methodist Church in Surry County.

FIGURE 9.114 Flora and Josiah Winchester, abt. 1920, Clay County.

8. Amanda Mae Parks (Feb 22, 1874–Nov 2, 1950) married William Taylor Herbert (Sep 29, 1876–Oct 16, 1936) on Feb 2, 1897, in Clay County. William was a county attorney of Lincoln County, Montana, and founder of the Herbert Gold Mining Company and the Golden West Mining Company in Montana. William Taylor Herbert robbed a Mexican sheepherder of $477, near Baggs, Wyoming, in 1897, and stole a horse and $350 from a member of Butch Cassidy's gang (Elzy Lay) at Powder Springs, Wyoming. He was caught in the state of Washington for stealing a horse, acquitted of the charge, and sent back to Wyoming, where he was convicted of attempted murder and robbery. He served four years in the Wyoming State Penitentiary. He feigned insanity and was pardoned by the governor and was escorted back to Chattanooga, Tennessee. See Figure 9.115. Amanda was buried at the Old Auburn Cemetery in Placer County, California. William was buried at Libby Cemetery in Lincoln County, Montana.[65]

FIGURE 9.115 William Taylor Herbert, abt. 1898, Laramie, Wyoming.

9. Joshua G. Parks (abt. 1878–unknown) may have moved out of North Carolina before 1900.

1.6.6.5 Melville Jernigan Parks (Nov 12, 1849–Nov 6, 1919) was the child of Gabriel and his second wife, Martha Matilda Jernigan. He married Miranda Amanda Holland (Jan 9, 1861–Jul 31, 1944) in 1880 in Monroe County, Georgia. See Figure 9.116. He died in Clyde, Callahan County, Texas, where he and Miranda were buried at the Ross Cemetery.

FIGURE 9.116 Melville Jernigan Parks, abt. 1900, Texas.

FRANCES "FANNY" CAMPBELL

1.6.7 **Frances "Fanny" Campbell** (May 2, 1809–Feb 23, 1846) married **Milas Dobbins** (Dec 27, 1800–Nov 24, 1862) on Oct 2, 1827, in Iredell County. Frances inherited two African-American slaves from her father (a oy" by the name of Little Isaac and a girl by the name of Mary). After Frances died, Milas married Lamira Reid (Jan 26, 1805–Oct 12, 1897) on Feb 21, 1856, in Iredell County. Milas and both of his wives were buried at the Bethany Presbyterian Church in Bethany Township, Iredell County. Frances and Milas had six children:

FIGURE 9.117 Alfred Milas Campbell Dobbins, abt. 1870, Fayette County, Tennessee.

1.6.7 **Dr. Alfred Milas Campbell Dobbins** (May 4, 1828–Sep 15, 1878) was born in Iredell County. He received his medical training at the University of Pennsylvania Medical School in 1847–1848. Alfred married Jane Ann Carlton (1827–Jan 1, 1860) in about 1849, in Tennessee. Jane was born in Virginia. He immigrated to Tennessee for a time prior to 1850. He then moved to Cache Township, Monroe County, Arkansas, where he settled at Clarendon in Monroe County and followed his medical profession until 1857 before moving to Evening Shade, Sharp County, Arkansas. See Figures 9.117, 9.118, and 9.119.

After his wife, Jane Ann, died in 1860 in Evening Shade, he moved back to North Carolina, where he enlisted on Apr 26, 1861, in Davie County to serve as a private and later 3rd lieutenant and doctor in the 13th North Carolina Infantry during the U.S. Civil War. He was at the Battle of Seven Pines, where he received a gunshot wound.

He was taken prisoner at the Second Battle of Fredericksburg and confined at Rock Island and later Johnstown Island, Illinois. He was paroled in Jun 1865 and returned to North Carolina.

In 1867, he moved to Fayette County, Tennessee, to engage in his medical practice. He also served as the postmaster in Williston, Fayette County, Tennessee.

Alfred married Rosana Tennessee Roark (Aug 1842–Oct 10, 1917) on Mar 3, 1873, in Fayette County, Arkansas (Figure 9.120). His death in 1878 was caused by yellow fever. Alfred and his second

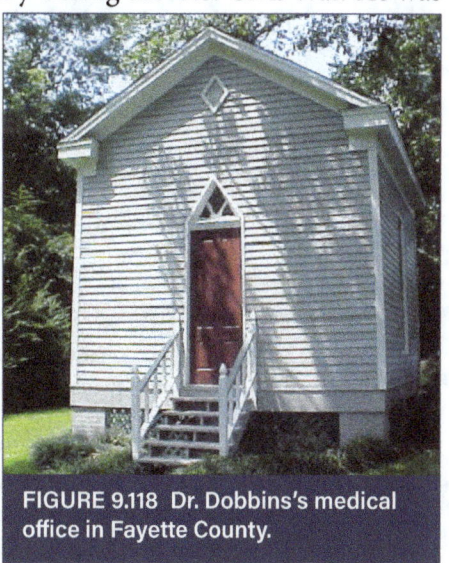

FIGURE 9.118 Dr. Dobbins's medical office in Fayette County.

FIGURE 9.119 University of Pennsylvania Medical School, 1842, Philadelphia.

FIGURE 9.120 Rosana Tennessee Roark, abt. 1910, Fayette County, Tennessee.

wife, Rosana, were buried at the Shady Grove Cemetery in Fayette County. His first wife, Jane, was buried at the Smyrna Cemetery in White County, Arkansas.[66] Alfred's children included (the first three were with his first wife):

1. **Frances Ann "Fanny" Dobbins** (May 1850–Mar 13, 1934), who married Daniel Stewart Baxter (Mar 27, 1848–Aug 13, 1904) on Sep 26, 1871, in Fayette County. Daniel was a farmer. They moved to Hunt County, Texas, by 1900. See Figure 9.121. They were buried at the Sonora Cemetery in Hunt County.

2. **George Wood Dobbins** (Jul 12, 1851–Jul 5, 1938), who married Elizabeth Hamblen Deener (Feb 8, 1855–Jun 27, 1936) on Aug 26, 1873, in Fayette County. George was educated in the schools of North Carolina and clerked in a store for two years. He attended Olin College in Iredell County in 1869 and went to Fayette County, Tennessee, in 1870, where he was again engaged

FIGURE 9.121 Daniel Baxter and Frances Dobbins, Oct 1900, Hunt County, Texas.

in clerking. He purchased a 180-acre farm in White County, Arkansas, in 1877. He was the county assessor in 1888. George and Elizabeth were buried at the Smyrna Cemetery.

3. **John Milas Dobbins** (Dec 25, 1859–Dec 27, 1905), who married Mary Tabitha "Mollie" Gaither (Oct 7, 1861–Dec 6, 1903) on Nov 30, 1880, in Fayette County. John worked at the W. C. Crawford General Merchandise in Williston, Fayette County.

4. David "Davie" Dobbins (Jan 22, 1875–Jan 27, 1915), who was the son of Alfred and Rosana. He married Mary Elizabeth "Bessie" Morton (Feb 24, 1882–Aug 9, 1977) on Oct 17, 1906, in Fayette County, Tennessee. See Figure 9.122. David was filling in for a deputy sheriff in Fayette County, Tennessee, when he sustained a fatal gunshot as he was ambushed in a posse to apprehend burglary suspects. He was honored on the Memorial Wall for Fallen Officers in Washington, D.C. After his death, his family moved in with Bessie's father, John David Morton (Aug 23, 1849–Apr 8, 1924), in Williston, Tennessee. David and Bessie were buried at the Ebenezer Cemetery in Fayette County. Of note, his grandson was Eugen David "Gene" Dobbins (Mar 19, 1934–Nov 23, 2008), who was a famous American country music songwriter and arranger, and one of the arrangers of the 1985 song "I'm Gonna Leave You Tomorrow," as well as others.

FIGURE 9.122
David Dobbins and Bessie Morton, Oct 1906, Fayette County.

5. Arva Una M. Dobbins (Apr 1878–bef. 1910), who was the daughter of Alfred and Rosana. She lived in Memphis, Tennessee, and worked as a salesclerk. She is not known to have married. Her burial location is not known.

1.6.7.2 **Theophilus E. Dobbins** (Mar 13, 1830–1861) married **Emiline Falcion*** (Mar 20, 1830–Feb 21, 1860) in Iredell County in about 1855.** Theophilus enlisted in the 13th Tennessee Infantry Regiment, CSA, on Jun 1, 1861. Theophilus may have died in Fayette County, Tennessee. Their two known children died young and were buried at the Bethany Presbyterian Church in Statesville alongside Emiline: Frances Dobbins (1856–May 25, 1858) and William Dobbins (Nov 1, 1858–Jul 27, 1859). See Figure 9.123.

1.6.7.3 William W. Dobbins (Mar 7, 1834–Nov 24, 1851) did not marry. He was buried at Bethany Presbyterian Church in Iredell County.

1.6.7.4 Adelia Dobbins (Sep 20, 1836–Apr 16, 1838) died as a child and was buried at Bethany Presbyterian Church.

---

*She appears as Miss Forcum in the 1925 *Vanhoy History of the Campbell Family.*
**The Vanhoy *History of the Campbell Family* refers to a Miss Forcum vice Falcion as the wife of Theo Dobbins.

1.6.7.5 **David P. Dobbins** (Jun 29, 1839–Aug 29, 1861) did not marry. He enlisted on Jun 7, 1861, as a corporal in the 4th North Carolina Infantry Regiment, CSA, during the U.S. Civil War. He died from wounds incurred at the First Battle of Bull Run in Prince William County, Virginia. He was buried at Bethany Presbyterian Church.

1.6.7.6 **Augustus A. Dobbins** (Mar 14, 1843–Mar 2, 1901) married **Sarah "Sally" Davis Clegg** (Jul 8, 1849–Nov 14, 1929) on Mar 31, 1870, in Iredell County. They did not have any children. Augustus was a farmer in Olin Township. Sally's father was **Maj. George**

FIGURE 9.123 Bethany Presbyterian Church, originally built in 1777, an offshoot of the Fourth Creek Congregation, Bethany Township, Iredell County.

Washington Clegg (Jan 31, 1826–Feb 5, 1910). Augustus was buried at Bethany Presbyterian Church and Sarah was buried at Oakwood Cemetery in Statesville.

WILLIAM RUTHERFORD CAMPBELL

1.6.8 **William Rutherford Campbell** (Jun 17, 1813–Jun 8, 1883) married **Mary Polly Howard** (Feb 16, 1815–Jul 1, 1894) on Nov 26, 1835, in Iredell County.[68] William and Mary moved to Arkansas before 1858. William inherited four slaves from his father (Bryant, Frank, Burton, and Rachel). They moved to Arkansas before the U.S. Civil War in about 1858. The census shows that he owned one 16-year-old male slave in Iredell County in 1850 and one 10-year-old female slave in Izard County in 1860. William and Mary were buried at the Campbell Family Cemetery in Zion, Izard County, Arkansas. William and Mary's 11 children included (all but the last child, Alice, were born in Iredell County):

1.6.8.1 **James Alfred Campbell** (Nov 21, 1836–Jan 22, 1884), who married Sarah Cecelia Scribner (Apr 15, 1842–Sep 15, 1926) in about 1858 in Independence County, Arkansas. Sarah was born in Maury County, Tennessee, but was living in Arkansas by 1850. James served in the 14th Regiment, Arkansas Infantry, CSA, during the U.S. Civil War. Although there is no headstone, James may have been buried at the Campbell Cemetery in Zion Izard County, Arkansas. Sarah was buried at the Flora Cemetery in Fulton County, Arkansas.[67] They had eight children, including:

1. Mary Jane Campbell (Jul 1858–Aug 21, 1933), who married Harden Decalbe Hopper (1854–Dec 20, 1914) on Aug 14, 1873, in Independence County, Arkansas. Harden was a farmer and born in Mississippi. Mary and Harden were buried at the Flora Cemetery in Fulton County, Arkansas.

2. William Washington Campbell (1862–1948), who married Nancy Jean Slaughter (Nov 18, 1867–Jun 9, 1957) in 1887 in Fulton County. They were buried at the Flora Cemetery in Fulton County. See Figure 9.124.

3. James Campbell (1864–bef. 1880), who died in Independence County.

4. Louisa G. Campbell (Apr 23, 1867–Aug 20, 1873), who was buried at the Claxton Cemetery in Independence County, Arkansas, at six years old.

5. Ophelia "Mamie" Campbell (1871–bef. 1879), who died as a child.

6. Nancy Elizabeth "Nonnie" Campbell (Jun 15, 1872–Sep 21, 1952), who married James Edmond Barrett (Aug 4, 1867–Dec 23, 1963) on Jul 28, 1889, in Fulton County. See Figure 9.125. They were buried at the Hurst Cemetery in Fulton County.

FIGURE 9.124 Nancy Jean Slaughter, grandson JW Webb, and William Washington Campbell, abt. 1945, Fulton County.

FIGURE 9.125 James Barrett and Nonnie Campbell, abt. 1950, Fulton County.

7. Charles Edward Campbell (Nov 22, 1875–May 3, 1959), who did not marry. He was a farmer. His mother lived with him after his father died. He was buried at the Flora Cemetery in Fulton County.

8. Emma Campbell (Feb 12, 1877–Apr 22, 1936), who married Thomas Lindsey Hayes (Oct 9, 1873–Mar 5, 1949) on Jan 2, 1895, in Sharp County, Arkansas. Ema was the U.S. postmaster in Zion, Izard County, Arkansas, from 1892 to 1930. Thomas was a farmer and born in Mississippi. See Figure 9.126. Emma and Thomas were buried at the Shady Grove Cemetery in Monroe County, Arkansas.

FIGURE 9.126 Thomas Hayes and Emma Campbell, abt. 1930, Sharp County.

1.6.8.2 **William Washington "Wash" Campbell** (Dec 9, 1838–Aug 5, 1898) was born in Iredell County.[67] He moved with his parents to Arkansas in about 1858, where he married Hiley Jane/Juna Walker (1838–1863) in Izard County in about 1860. Hiley and Wash were probably buried at the Campbell Family Cemetery in Izard County. Wash and Hiley had one child:

1. William Pierce Campbell (Mar 21, 1862–Apr 10, 1916) married Frances J. Miller (1869–Jan 6, 1943) in 1888 in Arkansas. They had one child, Grover Cleveland Campbell (Nov 7, 1888–Sep 7, 1911). William and Frances were buried at the Violet Hill Cemetery in Izard County.

    After Hiley's death, Wash married Hiley Jane Hightower (1842–1876) in about 1864 in Izard County. During this marriage, Wash and Hiley had two children:

2. Sarah Ann Campbell (1866–aft. 1900) did not marry.

3. Martha J. Campbell (1869–aft. 1880) married Conrad Donahue (1858–aft. 1894) on Jul 15, 1894, in Izard County.

Wash married a third time in 1883 in Izard County to Caroline E. (Jones) Smith (Jan 1858–Dec 5, 1932), with whom he had seven children. After Wash died, Caroline married for a third time to John William McCormick (Nov 4, 1835–Oct 10, 1919), with whom she raised the children she had with Wash:

4. Edward Ramon Campbell (Mar 29, 1884–Mar 5, 1956) married Prudence Leonard (May 1890–Dec 12, 1929) on Jun 2, 1907, in Izard County.

5. Augustus Arthur Campbell (Feb 1886–Feb 13, 1953) married Lula Ellen Cooper (Dec 6, 1886–1964) on Aug 20, 1905, in Izard County.

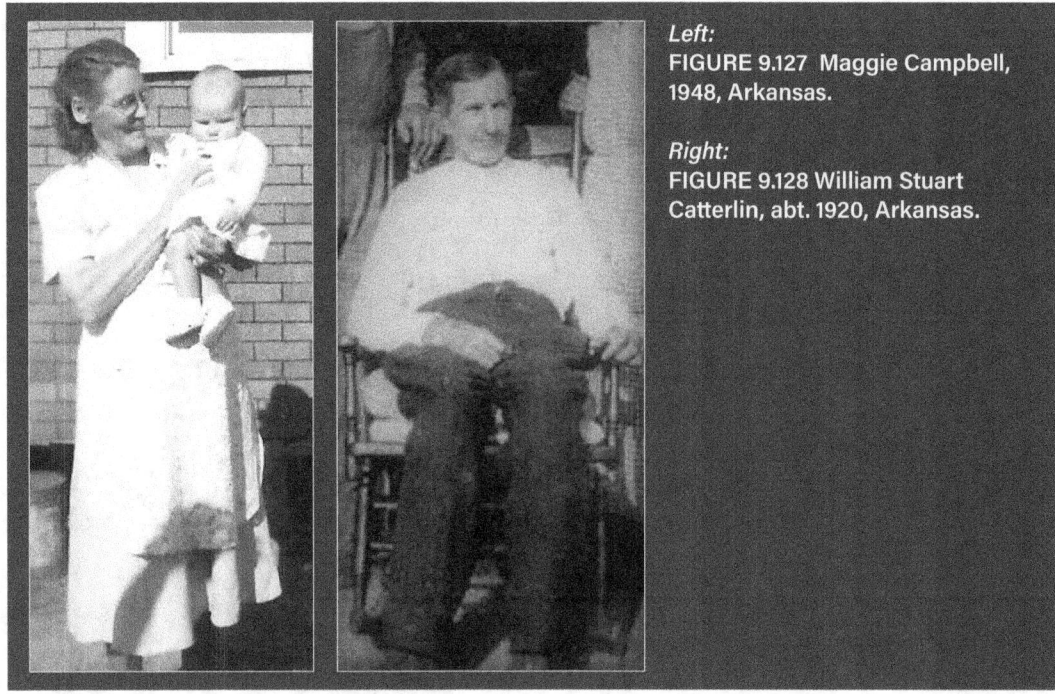

Left:
FIGURE 9.127 Maggie Campbell, 1948, Arkansas.

Right:
FIGURE 9.128 William Stuart Catterlin, abt. 1920, Arkansas.

6. Maggie Orelia Campbell (Jan 18, 1889–1953) married William Stuart Catterlin (1867–1924) on Aug 19, 1906, in Izard County. See Figures 9.127 and 9.128. They were buried at the Pleasant Plains Cemetery in Independence County, Arkansas.

7. Robert Horton Campbell (Apr 5, 1890–Oct 19, 1957) married Effie Gaines (May 1888–aft. 1930) on Mar 3, 1912, in Baxter County, Arkansas. Robert was buried at the Pleasant Plains Cemetery.

8. Maud Eburne Campbell (Oct 1891–aft. 1950) married John Wesley Hall (Feb 8, 1875–Jun 24, 1958) on Dec 21, 1910, in Independence County, Arkansas.

9. Jessie Campbell (Oct 1893–aft. 1900), like her other siblings, was born in Izard County. Nothing more about her is known.

1.6.8.3 **Sarah Ann Caroline Campbell** (Jan 11, 1841–Feb 11, 1872) married Leander Thomas Jennings (Apr 14, 1837–Mar 5, 1900) in about 1861 in Izard County, Arkansas.[67] Leander had moved to Izard County, Arkansas, from North Carolina with his family by 1857. His parents were Dennis Dempsey Jennings (Oct 24, 1811–Oct 28, 1881) and Elizabeth "Mahala" Johnson (May 15, 1815–Nov 20, 1892). See Figure 9.129.

FIGURE 9.129 Dennis Dempsey Jennings, abt. 1881, Izard County.

His family lived on Hunting Creek in Wilkes County before moving to Arkansas. Leander served as a fifer, private, and sergeant with the 14th and 21st Arkansas Infantry Regiments, CSA, during the U.S. Civil War. After Sarah died, Leander married Nancy E. Foster (abt. 1848–Jul 11, 1924) in about 1872 in Izard County. Leander had an additional four children with Nancy. Leander, Sarah, and Nancy were buried at the Campbell Cemetery in Zion, Izard County, as where his parents. Sarah and Thomas, had five children:

1. Williams Marion Jennings (1862–1874) died as a child. He was buried at the Campbell Cemetery in Izard County.

2. Preston W. Jennings (1866–1951) married Alice Zilpha Stone (Sep 8, 1863–Jun 7, 1905) on Dec 31, 1889, in Sharp County, Arkansas. He later married Rosa Lee (Adams) March-
ant (Aug 28, 1870–Mar 31, 1958) on Dec 22, 1927, in Izard County. Preston and Alice were buried at the Antioch Cemetery and Rosa was buried at the Melbourne Cemetery in Izard County.

Left: FIGURE 9.130 Carrie Jennings, abt. 1930, Izard County.

Right: FIGURE 9.131 William Muncy, abt. 1930, Izard County.

3. Carrie Lee Jennings (Jan 18, 1868–1950) married William Luther Muncy (Dec 1859–1930) on Jul 18, 1884, in Sharp County, Arkansas. William owned the Muncy hotel in Melbourne, Izard County. See Figures 9.130 and 9.131. Carrie and William were buried at the Melbourne Cemetery in Izard County.

4. Mary C. "Mollie" Jennings (Apr 1869–Nov 28, 1953) married George Washington Gray (Oct 19, 1865–Sep 15, 1960) in 1888 in Arkansas. See Figure 9.132. They were buried at the Oak Forest Cemetery in Lawrence County, Arkansas.

5. Sarah Florance Jennings (Jan 11, 1872–Oct 15, 1872) died as an infant.

1.6.8.4 Frances Rebecca Campbell (Mar 30, 1843–Jul 29, 1845) died as an infant in North Carolina.

1.6.8.5 **Augustus William "Gus" Campbell Sr.** (Aug 30, 1845–Aug 25, 1936) married Almira Melinda Baker (Jun 24, 1850–Apr 13, 1906) on Nov 10, 1867, in Lacrosse, Izard

FIGURE 9.132 George Gray, abt. 1910, Arkansas.

Left: FIGURE 9.133 Augustus Campbell and Malinda Baker, abt. 1880, Izard County.

Right: FIGURE 9.134 Brothers Augustus, and Henry Fraley Campbell, abt. 1920, Izard County.

County, Arkansas.[67] See Figures 9.133 and 9.134. Almira's parents were from Wilkes County, but she was born in Missouri. Gus served in Ford's Mounted Infantry, Missouri Cavalry, during the U.S. Civil War. Gus and Almira lived in Lacrosse, Izard County, where they raised 13 children:

1. Robert Edward Lee Campbell (Oct 1868–1917) married Sarah Elizabeth Blue (Oct 1872–Aug 17, 1948) on Oct 16, 1892, in Fulton County, Arkansas. See Figure 9.135. They were buried at the Harmony Cemetery in Fulton County, Arkansas.

2. Mary Matilda "Mollie" Campbell (Jan 26, 1870–Apr 1, 1956) married William Grant Caldwell (Oct 1865–Feb 28, 1948) on Dec 12, 1889, in Fulton County. See Figure 9.136. They were buried at the Harmony Cemetery in Fulton County, Arkansas.

3. William Nelson Campbell (Aug 12, 1871–Aug 10, 1874) died as a child and was buried at the Campbell Cemetery in Izard County.

4. Margaret A. "Maggie" Campbell (Mar 22, 1873–Nov 1874) died as a child and was buried at the Campbell Cemetery in Izard County.

5. Albert Sidney Campbell (Feb 7, 1875–Oct 19, 1876) died as a child and was buried at the Campbell Cemetery in Izard County.

FIGURE 9.135 Robert Campbell and Sarah Blue, abt. 1892, Fulton County.

6. Ada Eldora "Dora" Campbell (Aug 27, 1877–Nov 25, 1954) married Marian Luther Montgomery (Sep 16, 1876–Apr 20, 1914) on Apr 28, 1901, in Fulton County. Later, she married James Lee Acklin (1861–Mar 23, 1939) on Sep 7, 1919, in Fulton County. Ada and Marian were buried at the Morriston Cemetery in Fulton County.

7. Hampton Burton Campbell (Aug 7, 1879–May 7, 1958) married Eva Arella Painter (Oct 16, 1878–Nov 8, 1972) on May 1, 1903, in Fulton County. They were buried at the Union Cemetery in Fulton County.

8. Sarah A. "Sallie" Campbell (Sep 14, 1881–Nov 20, 1900) did not marry. She was buried at the Harmony Cemetery in Fulton County at 19 years old.

FIGURE 9.136 William Caldwell and Mollie Campbell, abt. 1945, Fulton County.

9. Laura Melinda Campbell (Feb 18, 1884–Sep 23, 1959) married Pinkney Green "Pink" Felts (Mar 29, 1882–Mar 17, 1978) on Feb 18, 1903, in Fulton County. See Figure 9.137. They were buried at the Salem Cemetery in Fulton County.

10. James Alfred Campbell (Feb 23, 1886–Apr 14, 1967) married Mary Iona Barnett (May 14, 1889–Aug 15, 1983) on Sep 1, 1907, in Fulton County. James was a farmer and was working as a guard in the Missouri State Prison in 1950. They died in Wyandotte County, Kansas, and were buried at the Chapel Hill Memorial Gardens.

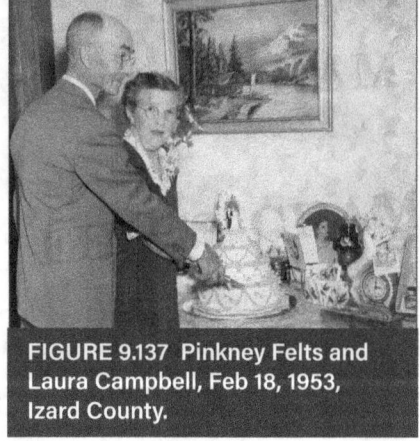

FIGURE 9.137 Pinkney Felts and Laura Campbell, Feb 18, 1953, Izard County.

11. Henry Cooper Campbell (Mar 12, 1888–Sep 20, 1955) married Zella E. Allison (Nov 5, 1892–Oct 25, 1975) on Mar 24, 1912, in Izard County. Henry was a schoolteacher for 16 years. Henry lived in Oklahoma for 33 years and worked for the U.S. Post Office for 28 years in Seminole and Chouteau, Oklahoma. They were buried at the Little Cemetery in Seminole County, Oklahoma.

12. Augustus William "Ray" Campbell Jr. (Jul 9, 1890–Nov 9, 1952) married Ruth Cleveland Moore (May 30, 1893–Jun 1973) on Dec 24, 1911, in Fulton County. They were buried at the Fairlawn Cemetery in Payne County, Oklahoma.

After Almira died, Augustus married Maggie Dow Newman (Jul 14, 1870–Feb 28, 1948) on Mar 21, 1907, in Fulton County. See Figure 9.138. Augustus and his first wife,

FIGURE 9.138
Augustus Campbell home, and 2nd wife Maggie Newman, possibly Andy Campbell and other family, abt. 1915, Fulton County.

FIGURE 9.139 Susie Blevins and Andy Campbell, abt. 1930, Fulton County.

Almira, were buried at the Harmony Cemetery in Fulton County. Maggie was buried at the Bexar Cemetery in Fulton County. Augustus and Maggie had one child:

13. Andy Richie Campbell (Jan 3, 1909–Dec 12, 1981) married Susie Myrtle Blevins (Feb 5, 1906–Sep 20, 2005) on Jun 15, 1930, in Oregon County, Missouri. See Figure 9.139. They were buried at the Ava Cemetery in Douglas County, Missouri.

1.6.8.6 **Dr. Henry Fraley Campbell** (Jan 11, 1848–Jul 6, 1925)[67] married Mary Elizabeth Helm (Jul 22, 1855–Mar 7, 1889) in Arkansas in about 1874. See Figure 9.140. Henry was a medical doctor in Violet Hill, Izard County. After Mary's death, Henry married Mary Ann Riggs (Apr 12, 1859–Jul 1, 1923). See Figures 9.142 and 9.143. Henry and both wives were buried at Violet Hill Cemetery in Violet Hill, Izard County. Henry and Mary had seven children:

1. Mary Emmaline "Emma" Campbell (May 9, 1875–Jun 28, 1935) married George William Bray (Oct 29, 1850–Jul 15, 1928) on Sep 2, 1917, in Fulton County. See Figure 9.143. Mary was buried at the Violet Hill Cemetery in Izard County. George was buried near his first wife, Martha Ann Cornelius (Jan 20, 1851–Jan 21, 1916), at the Union Cemetery in Fulton County.

2. Joseph Shelby Campbell (May 6, 1878–Apr 19, 1921) married Mary Jeffie Nicks (Jan 23, 1881–Oct 6, 1942) on Nov 27, 1898, in Izard County. They were buried at the Violet Hill Cemetery in Izard County.

Left: FIGURE 9.140 Henry Fraley Campbell and Mary Helm, abt. 1880, Izard County.

Right: FIGURE 9.141 Stepdaughter's wedding photo: Emma, Fannie, Mary Alice, Sallie Campbell with mother Mary Ann Riggs, 1911, Izard County.

Left: FIGURE 9.142 Henry Fraley Campbell and Mary Ann Riggs (2nd wife) with grandchildren: Grace, William Henry, Mildred, and Claudie, 1919, Izard County.

Right: FIGURE 9.143: George Bray and Emma Campbell, abt. 1920, Izard County.

3. William Relford Campbell (Oct 16, 1879–Mar 14, 1955) married Myrtle "Mertie" Wilson (Apr 13, 1887–Jan 6, 1974) on Jan 2, 1907, in Izard County. They were buried at the Wenatchee City Cemetery in Chelan County, Washington.

4. Fannie Lee Campbell (Oct 1881–Jul 12, 1964) did not marry. She was buried at the Violet Hill Cemetery in Izard County.

5. Mary Alice Campbell (Dec 1883–Aug 15, 1973) did not marry. She was buried next to her sister, Fannie, in the Violet Hill Cemetery.

6. Sarah "Sallie" Victoria Campbell (Jul 13, 1886–Feb 17, 1939) married David Franklin Davidson (May 1878–1917) on Jul 16, 1911, in Izard County. David died of influenza. See Figures 9.144 and 9.145. They were buried at the Violet Hill Cemetery in Izard County.

FIGURE 9.145 David Franklin Davidson, abt. 1911, Izard County.

7. James Thurman Campbell (Aug 1, 1888-Nov 16, 1968) married Ruth May Lackey (Oct 15, 1901–Jan 8, 1944) on Sep 4, 1918, in Stone County, Arkansas. He served in World War I (Figure 9.146). He married Ethel (Speaks) Benbrook (Feb 19, 1901–May 31, 1990) on Aug 20, 1951, in Izard or Independence County, Arkansas. James and his first wife were buried at the Historic Cemetery of Mountain View in Stone County. His second wife was buried at the Roselawn Cemetery in Izard County.

1.6.8.7 Martin Howard Campbell (Feb 4, 1850–Jul 29, 1854) died as a child in Iredell County.[67]

1.6.8.8 **Mary Elizabeth "Polly" Campbell** (Jan 18, 1852–Aug 31, 1934) married Elisheba Puckett (Jun 22, 1851–Apr 9, 1898) on Dec 10, 1872, in Izard County. See Figures 9.147 and 9.148. Mary moved to McCain County, Oklahoma, by 1930, where she died and was buried at the Hillside Cemetery. Elisheba was buried at the Campbell Cemetery in Izard County. Polly and Elisheba had 10 children:

FIGURE 9.146
James Thurman Campbell, 1918, Izard County.

1. Cora Lee Puckett (abt. 1874–Nov 21, 1939) married Robert Phillip Walker (Aug 30, 1872–Apr 8, 1933) on Jul 20, 1895, in Sharp County, Arkansas. They were buried at the Memorial Park Cemetery in Oklahoma City, Oklahoma.

2. William Hartwell Puckett (Oct 29, 1875–Mar 14, 1921) did not marry. He was buried at the Hillside Cemetery in McClain County, Oklahoma.

3. Pettis Josephus Puckett (Aug 29, 1877–Sep 21, 1938) married Mary Ida (Caruthers) Boler on Nov 12, 1922, in Garvin, Oklahoma. See Figure 9.149. They were buried at the Hillside Cemetery in McClain County, Oklahoma.

Left: FIGURE 9.147 Mary Elizabeth Campbell, 1934, Izard County.

Right: FIGURE 9.148 Family of Elisheba Puckett: Front L to R: Thomas, Margaret, Henry; Back L to R: Pettis, William, Elisheba and wife Mary, Edward, Cora Lee and husband Bob Walker, abt. 1940, Izard County.

Left: FIGURE 9.149 Mary Caruthers and Pettis Puckett with children George and Bonnie, abt. 1930, McClain County, Oklahoma.

Middle: FIGURE 9.150 Myrtle (Boler) Puckett, abt. 1905, Izard County.

Right: FIGURE 9.151 Mary Alice Puckett, abt. 1930, McClain County.

4. Edward Newton Puckett (Sep 20, 1879–May 7, 1954) married Myrtle L. Boler (Aug 12, 1882–Dec 14, 1918) on Aug 20, 1905, in Izard County and Sarah Amanda Pankey (Dec 4, 1891–Sep 21, 1968) on Feb 12, 1922, in Texas County, Oklahoma. See Figure 9.150.

5. Mary Alice Puckett (Dec 1, 1881–Nov 6, 1968) married George Alexander Rose (Dec 26, 1880–Dec 30, 1962) on Dec 11, 1904, in Izard County. Her mother was living with her in 1930 in Wayne, McClain County, Oklahoma. See Figure 9.151. Mary and George were buried at the Hillside Cemetery in McClain County, Oklahoma.

6. Earnest Pucket (Oct 22, 1884–Nov 15, 1887) died as a child.

7. Henrietta Della Puckett (Dec 21, 1886–Jul 1, 1931) married James Robert Lee Waggoner (Feb 2, 1879–Jun 23, 1960) on Nov 20, 1907, in Izard County. They were buried at the Violet Hill Cemetery in Izard County.

8. Thomas Howard Puckett (Aug 6, 1889–Sep 3, 1968) married Mary Leah Helm (Jul 6, 1890–Oct 30, 1977) on Feb 6, 1910, in Izard County. They were buried at the Resthaven Gardens Cemetery in Oklahoma City, Oklahoma.

9. Margaret Elizabeth Puckett (Aug 18, 1892–May 11, 1945) did not marry. She was living with her mother and two siblings, William and Pettis, in Arkansas in 1920 before they moved to Oklahoma. She was in the Central Oklahoma State Hospital in 1940. She was buried at the Hillside Cemetery in McClain County, Oklahoma.

1.6.8.9 **Samuel Pettus Campbell** (Apr 17, 1856–Apr 7, 1906) married Manerva E. Walker (Aug 1862–1934) in about 1881 in Izard County. Samuel and Manerva were buried at the Salem Cemetery in Fulton County. They had three children:

1. Tobitha "Bitha" Campbell (Dec 1882–1906) married Dr. Samuel Bridgewater Richmond (Dec 27, 1857–May 12, 1921) on Aug 13, 1905, in Fulton County, Arkansas. Samuel was a physician at the Boys' Industrial School. They were buried at the Salem Cemetery in Fulton County, Arkansas.

2. James Theophilus Campbell (Feb 11, 1889–Mar 7, 1965) was in the U.S. Army and moved to Seattle, Washington, where he died. He married Agnes Benbrook Schmidt (Mar 1892–Jun 3, 1941) in about. 1925 in Washington state. Agnes was born in Minnesota, and her parents were German. After Agnes died, Theophilus married a widow, Geneva Augusta (Timmons) Arcus Peterson (Sep 15, 1907–Feb 15, 1992), on Apr 19, 1945, in Seattle, King County, Washington. See Figures 9.152, 9.153, and 9.154.

3. Robert Forrest Campbell (May 1891–1911) did not marry. He was buried at the Salem Cemetery in Fulton County, Arkansas, at 20 years old.

1.6.8.10 **Preston Brooks Campbell** (Jul 30, 1856–Feb 27, 1936) married Malinda Lynn Lawhon (Sep 9, 1865–Nov 29, 1944) in about 1880 in Izard County. See Figures 9.155 and 9.156. Preston and Malinda were buried at the Violet Hill Cemetery in Izard County. Their children included:

1. Mary Lou "Mollie" Campbell (Oct 3, 1882–Aug 11, 1972), who married James Leonard Shaver (Feb 28, 1876–Dec 4, 1942) on Oct 9, 1898, in Izard County. They were separated and James moved to Texas and remarried. Mollie married a widower, Thomas Marvin Standerford (Jul 19, 1883–Jul 12, 1943), on Oct 4, 1928, in Fulton County, Arkansas. Mollie Lou was buried at the Violet Hill Cemetery in Izard County.

Left: FIGURE 9.152 James Theophilus Campbell, abt. 1960, King County.

Middle: FIGURE 9.153 Geneva Timmons, abt. 1960, Oregon.

Right: FIGURE 9.154 Agnes Benbrook Schmidt, abt. 1905, Minnesota.

Left: FIGURE 9.155 Preston Brooks Campbell and Malinda Lawhon, abt. 1930, Izard County.

Right: FIGURE 9.156 Preston Brooks Campbell Family: *(Back L to R)* Norah B., Mary Lou, Willie; *(Middle L to R)* Eddie, James Alfred, Preston, Lillie Mae, Malinda Lynn, Claude E. in Malinda's lap; *(Front)* George William, 1898, Izard County.

2. Willie Campbell (Jul 30, 1883–May 21, 1933), who married Ransom Adophus Nelms (Apr 28, 1877–Feb 10, 1940) on Jan 14, 1917, in Izard County. They were buried at the Violet Hill Cemetery in Izard County.

3. Norah B. Campbell (Aug 1885–1905), who did not marry. She was buried at the Campbell Cemetery in Izard County at 20 years old.

4. George William Campbell (Jul 4, 1886–Mar 8, 1955), who married Cora Hope Beaver (Sep 24, 1887–Jun 21, 1979) on Sep 13, 1914, in Fulton County, Arkansas. They were buried at the Violet Hill Cemetery in Izard County.

5. Eddie Campbell (Mar 12, 1889–Oct 21, 1954), who married Mildred Tate (Jun 30, 1901–Mar 12, 1992) on Dec 30, 1916, in Independence County, Arkansas. They were buried at the Oaklawn Cemetery in Independence County, Arkansas.

6. Lillie Mae Campbell (Jan 3, 1892–Feb 1978), who married Loran Oman Craig (1895–1965) on Mar 13, 1921, in Izard County. They were buried at the Violet Hill Cemetery in Izard County.

7. James Alfred Campbell Sr. (Nov 3, 1893–Dec 29, 1964), who married Lillie Mae Ritchey (Feb 25, 1894–Jul 4, 1940) in about 1917. James served in the U.S. Army in World War I and died in Gregg County, Texas, where he was living with his son, Leo Alfred Campbell (Dec 23, 1920–Oct 16, 1984). His son was a veteran of World War II. James was buried at the Lakeview Memorial Gardens in Gregg County.

8. Claud E. Campbell (Mar 4, 1897–Apr 10, 1929), who married Bertha Clara Ruminer (Oct 5, 1901–Feb 1, 1990) on Nov 6, 1927, in Sharp County, Arkansas. Claud was buried at the Violet Hill Cemetery in Izard County. Bertha married Samuel Wetzel Draper (1902–1976) after Claud died. She was buried at the Barren Fork Cemetery in Izard County.

9. Leonard Lonzo Campbell (Jan 1, 1899-Nov 22, 1976), who married Beulah Alberta Lewis (1906–Jun 13, 1995) in about 1926 in Izard County. They were separated and Beulah moved to California, where she married a baker, Edward Purdy Giles (1889–1976). Leonard married Margie Ann Coleman (Jan 22, 1908–Mar 26, 2009) on Oct 27, 1962, in Izard County. Leonard served in the U.S. Army during World War II. Leonard and Margie were buried at the Reeves Cemetery in Izard County.

10. Harvey Campbell (1902–1904), who died as a child and was buried at the Campbell Cemetery in Izard County.

11. Homer Eldon Campbell (Nov 11, 1904–Dec 27, 1978), who did not marry. He served in the U.S. Army during World War II. He was buried at the Violet Hill Cemetery in Izard County.

12. John Wayne Campbell Sr. (May 6, 1909–Apr 21, 1984), who married Pearl Mae Parish (Jan 15, 1915–Aug 12, 2002) on Jun 26, 1948, in Independence County, Arkansas. He served as a sergeant in the U.S. Army Air Corps in World War II. They were buried at the Rosewood Funeral Home and Cemetery in Harris County, Texas.

1.6.8.11 **Alice Catherine Campbell** (Oct 3, 1858–Oct 9, 1940) was born in Franklin, Izard County, Arkansas. She married Amos Ladd Felts (Apr 20, 1854-Nov 8, 1899) in Arkansas in about 1877. After Amos died, Alice married **John C. Storey** (Feb 8, 1843–Aug 5, 1927) on Feb 25, 1904, in Fulton County, Arkansas. John was born in Jackson County, Georgia, and moved to Arkansas after the Civil War, in which he served with the CSA in Georgia. Alice and Amos were buried at the Violet Hill Cemetery in Izard County. John C. Storey was buried at the Old Philadelphia Cemetery, where his parents were buried. His father, Rev. William Harvey Storey (1813–1870), was a Methodist minister and moved from Georgia to Izard County in 1869. Alice and Amos had two children:

1. George Rutherford Felts (Dec 9, 1879–Ot 17, 1909) married Francis Asberene Hutchison (Dec 15, 1881–May 7, 1966) on Jan 28, 1900, in Izard County. George married Callie Ducon Waller (Nov 3, 1874–Feb 19, 1965) on Apr 12, 1903, in Izard County. After George died, Francis married Lewis L. Horton (1882–1948) on Jun 21, 1920, in Sebastian County, Arkansas. George was buried at the Violet Hill Cemetery in Izard County. Francis and Lewis were buried at Greenhill Cemetery in Le Flore County, Oklahoma.

2. Thomas F. Felts (Mar 19, 1885–Nov 16, 1899) was buried at the Violet Hill Cemetery in Izard County at 14 years old.

1925 CAMPBELL FAMILY REUNION

The following history of the Campbell family was handed out at the Campbell Family Reunion in Union Grove, Iredell County, North Carolina in August 1925.[1] See Figure 9.157. The newspaper reported the events as follows.

DESCENDANTS OF PIERCE CAMPBELL HOLDS REUNION

The reunion of the descendants of Pierce Campbell, pioneer North Iredell settler will be made an annual affair and is expected to become the big celebration days of this section. The first of these reunions was held at Union Grove Church, about twenty miles north of here, on Thursday of this week and some 2,500 people were present. In historical interest, Henry P. Van Hoy's reading of a sketch of the Campbell family from the first pioneers to the present stood out in the day's program. In entertainment, Hon. Loomis Klutz, Catawba member of the North Carolina House of Representatives, was the high mark in his address on the subject of Iredell County, its progress and citizenship. But in all round enjoyment the big dinner, served on a crescent shaped table, surpassed every other feature of the day and that dinner will be remembered long in the community history of North Iredell. There was fried chicken, deviled eggs, fried country ham, boiled, baked and barbecued ham, roast beef, canned sausage, dainty cakes and pies and custards. There on the table was found peaches, apples, cantaloupes, watermelons, and other fruits in piles and that there was not enough room on the table for all the good things they brought in their baskets and the men and boys complained because they couldn't eat all they would like to. They simply had to say that there had to be a limit to the capacity of the human body to consume food and try to be content. J. T. Jennings, a grandson of Williamson Campbell was chairman of the day's proceedings. The program was opened with a song, "America," and devotional exercises were conducted by E. W. Campbell. The Greensboro quartet consisting of Messrs....Brady, Boyles, and Jarvis sang several songs. H. P. Van Hoy, a grandson of John R. Campbell, delivered the address of welcome and this was responded to by Rev. R. N. Garner, of Wilkes County. A mixed quartette, made up of Miss Sloan, Miss Harris, Messrs. Sloan and Henrich, sang several selections during the program. The address of Mr. Kluttz was of an eloquent nature and he paid high tribute to Iredell County and the progressiveness of the people here. The listeners decided that Mr. Kluttz would like to live in Iredell. The historical sketch was read by Mr. Van Hoy and as he went along, he told several old stories about various Campbell families and boys of the old days. The afternoon was given over to songs, various refreshments, and stories of old times in North Iredell. People came for miles and miles and all promised support for a reunion to be held each year. The committee on arrangements for the day was composed of H. P. Van Hoy, Dr. L. P. Somers, J. T.

Jennings, and Mrs. W. B. Tutterow. The latter acted as corresponding secretary. The reunion will be held the latter part of August each year. Last week in making the announcement of the coming reunion, it was stated that Pierce Campbell, the first, gave the land for Union Grove Church and school house.

The following history of the Campbell family was handed out at the Campbell Family Reunion in Union Grove, Iredell County, North Carolina in August 1925.[1] See Figure 9.157. The newspaper reported the events as follows.

A seven-page handout was given to participants in the reunion as they listened to H. P. Vanhoy read it and give his own stories. This is the earliest known written family history and has been invaluable in constructing the Adam Campbell Family History. It is included verbatim in its entirety below with the contemporary comments by Garry E. Moore in parentheses.

HISTORY OF THE CAMPBELL FAMILY
COMPILED BY: H. P. VANHOY IN 1925

1. It is not known when the Campbells of Scotch-Irish decent came to this country, but sometime prior to 1795. The oldest deed on record in Iredell County shows that Pierce Campbell the first, purchased a tract of land from Elizabeth Campbell in 1795. It is believed that Pierce Campbell took up some grants from the State prior to 1795, but if he did the records are in Rowan County. Iredell County was separated from Rowan County in 1787 and all records prior to this time are on record in Rowan.

2. The Campbell family is one of the old pioneer families that helped settle Iredell County. It has been handed down from father to son that this family was known as "Bells in Scotland", and being very strict to their religious views; and not believing in the state church,

FIGURE 9.157
1925 Campbell Family Reunion in Union Grove, North Carolina.

they held their Camp Meetings and on account of this they were called "Campbells". The Pioneer settlers, who settled North Carolina were classed in three classes:

1st. Those who were driven out on account of Religious Persecution, and it seems that the Campbells were in this class.

2nd. Those who followed farming for an occupation and were looking for better farming lands.

3rd. Those who like to live by themselves and gain their living by hunting wild game.

3. The following record is given by the oldest living decendents [*sic*] of the Campbell family. This record is not complete but is the best that can be had at this time. If this reunion is made an annual affair, which is probable, we hope to add to this record until a full history of this family can be had.

4. Pierce Campbell the first (*Adam Campbell*), originally from Scotland married Miss Betty Morgan, originally from Ireland. These young people settled, the exact date not known, but prior to 1795, at what is now known as the John P. Campbell home place. To this union were born the following: Polly, Sally, Kizzie, and Pierce the second.

5. Pierce Campbell the second (*Pericphull* [*sic*] *Campbell Sr.*), son of Pierce the first, married Miss Sally Cook and settled at what is known as the J. P. Bolin place on Hunting Creek, adjoining the land of his father. To this union were born the following children: Billie, Pierce the third, Theophelus the first, Fannie, Sallie, Polly, John R. and William R.

6. Billie Campbell, son of Pierce Campbell the second, married Miss Jensie Morgan. Two children were born to this couple: Alfred and Teresa. This family moved to Arkansas, and no further record of them can be had at this time.

7. Pierce Campbell the third, son of Pierce the second, married Tobitha Morgan and settled at what is known as the Hiram Speaks place on Hunting Creek about ½ mile above Campbell Mill. (*The newspaper report also includes the following: Five children were born in this home: Williamson, Mildon, Sally, Reuben, who died at age 12, and Leolin V.*)

8. Theophelus Campbell the first, son of Pierce the second, married Miss Rena Allen and settled at what is now known as the Edmond Mitchell home place, on Hunting Creek. To this union, the following children were born: Polly, Sallie, Fannie, Carolina, William C, and John.

9. Theophelus Campbell the first, represented this section in the Legislature about 1830. Conveyance at that time was very poor and it has been handed down that he would pull off his shoes and walk to Raleigh barefooted. I have also heard that he would pull off his shoes and set them under the seat and make a fireing [sic] speech in the Legislative Hall bare footed. He said he left Winston-Salem at sun rise and walked to were J.T. Jennings now lives and got there just as the sun was setting, a distance of 50 odd miles.

10. John R. Campbell, son of Pierce the second, married Miss Lucy Williams and settled at his father's home place, the J. P. Bolin farm. The following children were born to this union: Tobitha, Theophelus the second, Polly, Paulina, James W., Sarah, John P., and William Milas.

11. William R. Campbell, son of Pierce Campbell the second, married Polly Howard, and the following children were born in this home: Alfred, Washington, Sarah Ann, Henry, Augustus, Preston, Pettis, Mary, and Alice. This family moved to Arkansas, and we cannot give a complete record of them. A letter from Mrs. Alice Story [sic] daughter of William R. Campbell, said that when Dr. Henry Campbell, son of William R. Campbell, died the family was all together and owing to conditions they would not be able to attend this reunion.

12. Williamson Campbell, son of Pierce Campbell the third married Miss Mimie Mayberry and settled 1 ½ miles south of Union Grove at what is known as the Jacob Crater Place, now owned by N. G. Crater. To this union were born the following children: Sarah; Emily; James P., who died in the Civil War; Nancy; and Arminda.

13. Mildeon Campbell, son of Pierce Campbell the third, married Clementine Huie, and settled at what is now known as the Davison Campbell Home Place. To this union were born the boys Davidson and Preston.

14. Leolin V. Campbell, son of Pierce Campbell the third, was married twice. First, (he was married) to Ann Clementine Dent. The following children were born by the first marriage: Emma, Turner, and Alice. Second, (*he was married*) to Miss Emma Buxton and had two children by this union: William B. and Della Pearl. L.V. Campbell settled at the Campbells [sic] Mill.

15. William Campbell, son of Theophelus Campbell the first, married Miss Lucy Ross first. Seven children were born to this union. Second, (*he married*) Miss Jany Croxdale, and three children (*were born*) to this union. The family moved out west, and we are unable to give further history on them.

16. John C. Campbell, son of Theo the first, married Icy Ann Elkins and located in the west. (*There has been*) no record from them since [*sic*].

17. Theophelus Campbell the second, son of John R. Campbell, was twice married, first to Miss Louisa Somers, and there were no children [*sic*]. Second, [he was married] to Miss Rebecca Minish, and the following children were born to this union: Louisa, Celia, Johnny, Ezra, Paulina, and Tobitha. He settled east of Union Grove, about two miles where Ezra Campbell now lives.

18. 18. James W. Campbell, son of John R. Campbell, married Arminda Privette and settled north of Union Grove about 1 mile [*sic*]. The following children were born in this home: Daisy, Charles W., William R., and Mack.

19. 19. John P. Campbell, son of John R. Campbell, married Elizabeth Mitchell and settled at the home place of the old original Pierce Campbell. To this union were born the following: Maggie, Smith, Dessie, and Isom.

20. William Milas Campbell, son of John R. Campbell, was twice married. First [he was married] to Miss Sara Mitchell. Three girls were born to this union: Ella, Sallie and Fannie. He settled at the home place of his father and lived here for a while. Finally, he sold out and moved west, again later moving back here. Several years after his first wife died, he married Miss Julia Oakie Moose. No children (*were had*) by this marriage. Uncle Milas, as everybody calls him now, lives on the Capt. Minish farm, near Howard's Foard [*sic*]. Uncle Milas, following the tradition of his forefathers, has been a great trapper and hunter, and has killed more hawks and caught more minks than any man in Iredell County. Though crippled, he has been classed the best "One Horse Farmer in Iredell County."

21. Davidson Campbell, son of Mildeon Campbell, married Miss Mary Femister, to this family were born the following: Cora, Tom, Esther, Nan, and Eliza.

22. Preston Campbell, son of Mildeon Campbell, married a Miss Spann, and to this union were born the following children: Oscar, Geneva, Lula, Clark, Clifton, and Annie.

23. Polly Campbell, daughter of Pierce the first, married Chas. Coleman. (*They had*) Two children: Jackie and Nancy. In his home: Emma, Jane, and Gus.

24. Sallie Campbell, daughter of Theo the first, married a Gilreath. (*There is*) No record [of this couple].

25. Fanny Campbell, daughter of Theo the first, married John Redmond. Children Dab, John, Pres, Clint, Hosea, Robert, Lillie [*sic*] and Woodie.

26. Carolina Campbell, daughter of Theo the first, married Wash Williams and went west. (*There is*) No record (*of this couple*).

27. Sarah Campbell, daughter of Williamson Campbell, married Thomas L. Jennings and the following children were born: Margret, Alice, Minnie, Martha, and James Turner.

28. Emily Campbell, daughter of Williamson Campbell, married Jacob Crater. Children (*are*) Jim, John W, Newton G., W.J., and Augusta.

29. Arminda Campbell, daughter of Williamson Campbell, married W. M. Cooper. Children are Della, Augusta, Will, Rufus A., Cordia, Josephene, Roena, Etta, and May.

30. Tobitha Campbell, oldest daughter of John R. Campbell, married W. Ham Somers. And to this union the following children: L. P., Gaston, Johny, Sissie, and Emma.

31. Sallie Campbell, daughter of Pierce the first, married Billy Ball. Four children: Sampson, Imlah, Sally, and Polly.

32. Kizzie, daughter of Pierce the first, married a Hayes, no record at this time.

33. Fannie Campbell, daughter of Pierce the second, married Milas Dobbins. Four boys were born to this union: Thee married a Miss Forcom and died without any children. Alfred married a Miss Carlton and had three children, Fanny, John, and George. David died in the Civil War, and Gus married Sally Clegg, daughter of Major C. W. Clegg. No children were born to them.

34. Sally Campbell, daughter of Pierce Campbell the second, married Bartlet Morgan. The following named children were born: Polly, William, Holeman, Gabriel, Reuben, Pierce, John, and Mildeon.

35. Polly Campbell, daughter of Pierce Campbell the second, married Gabriel Parks. Four children: Pettis, Dabney, Richard, and Theophelus.

36. Sally Campbell, daughter of Pierce the third, married Uriah Douthit and had five children: Mary, Fanny, Sarah, Gus, and Columbus.

37. Polly Campbell, daughter of Theo the first, married Andy Romanger. Three children.

38. Polly Campbell, daughter of John R. Campbell, was twice married, first to R. A. Morris. Jackson G. Morris was the only child born to this union. second to J. W. Bolin, and to this union the following: Johnny, Will, Joe, Roxann, Mollie, Emma, Fanny, Lillie.

39. Paulina Campbell, daughter of John R. Campbell, married John R. Huie. Their children were Sara, Manda, Fannie, Myra, Lovie, Ina, Puss, Angie, Lela, Samuel, Flake, and George.

40. Sarah Campbell, daughter of John R. Campbell, married William A. Vanhoy. To this union the following (*were born*): Milas L., Edward C., John Webb, Alice C., Henry P., Polly, James Pierce, Ruby.

1917 MAP OF IREDELL COUNTY

A 1917 Map of Iredell County, showing families, roads, churches, schools, and other features as they existed in 1917, depicts where many of the members of Adam Campbell's family were living just before the 1925 Reunion (Figure 9.158).[68] Shown on the map are locations of several Campbell landmarks, including the Campbell Mill, Campbell School (which later became Union Grove School), Jennings, Jenning's Mill, Jenning's Store, Williamsburg

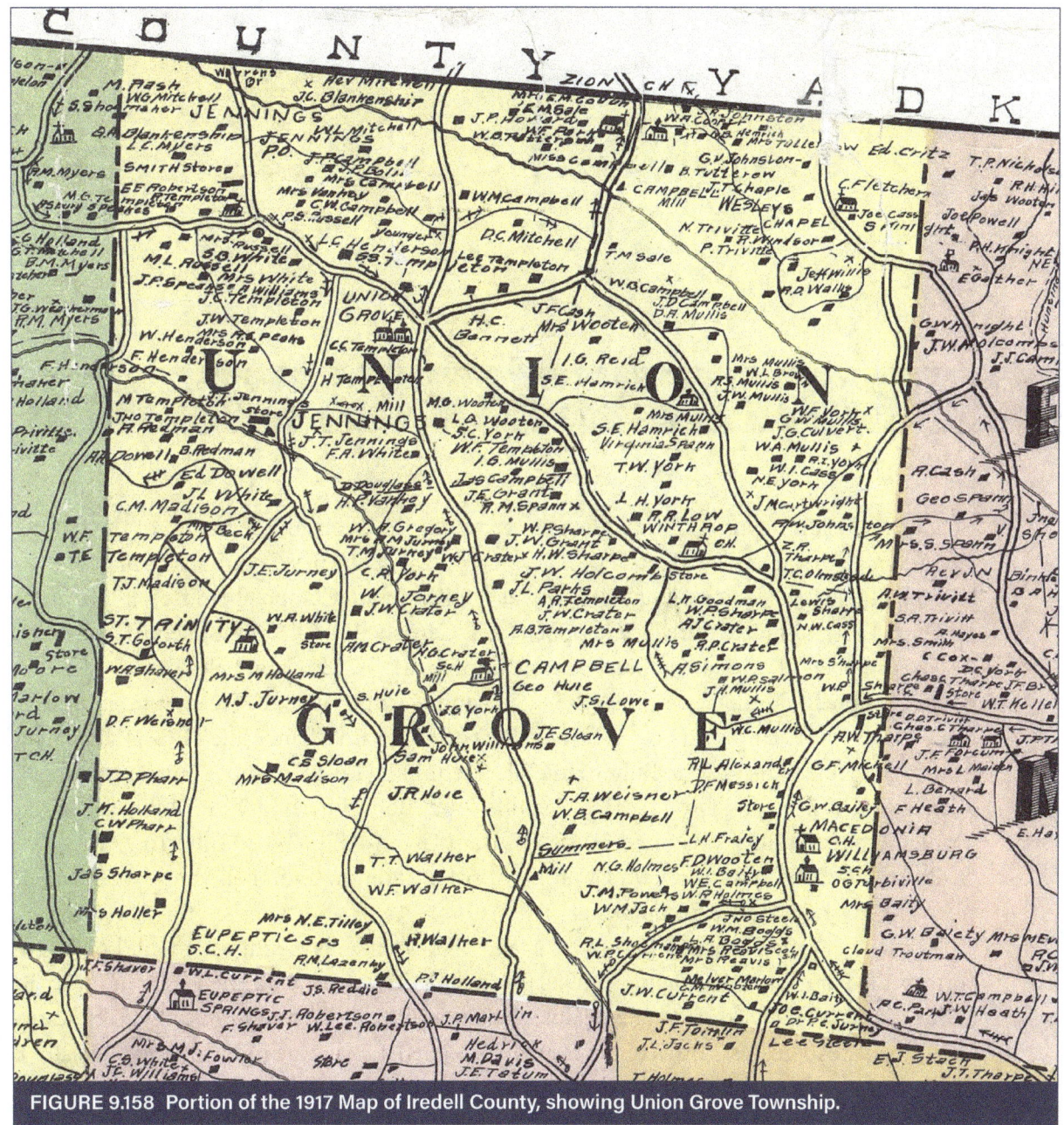

FIGURE 9.158 Portion of the 1917 Map of Iredell County, showing Union Grove Township.

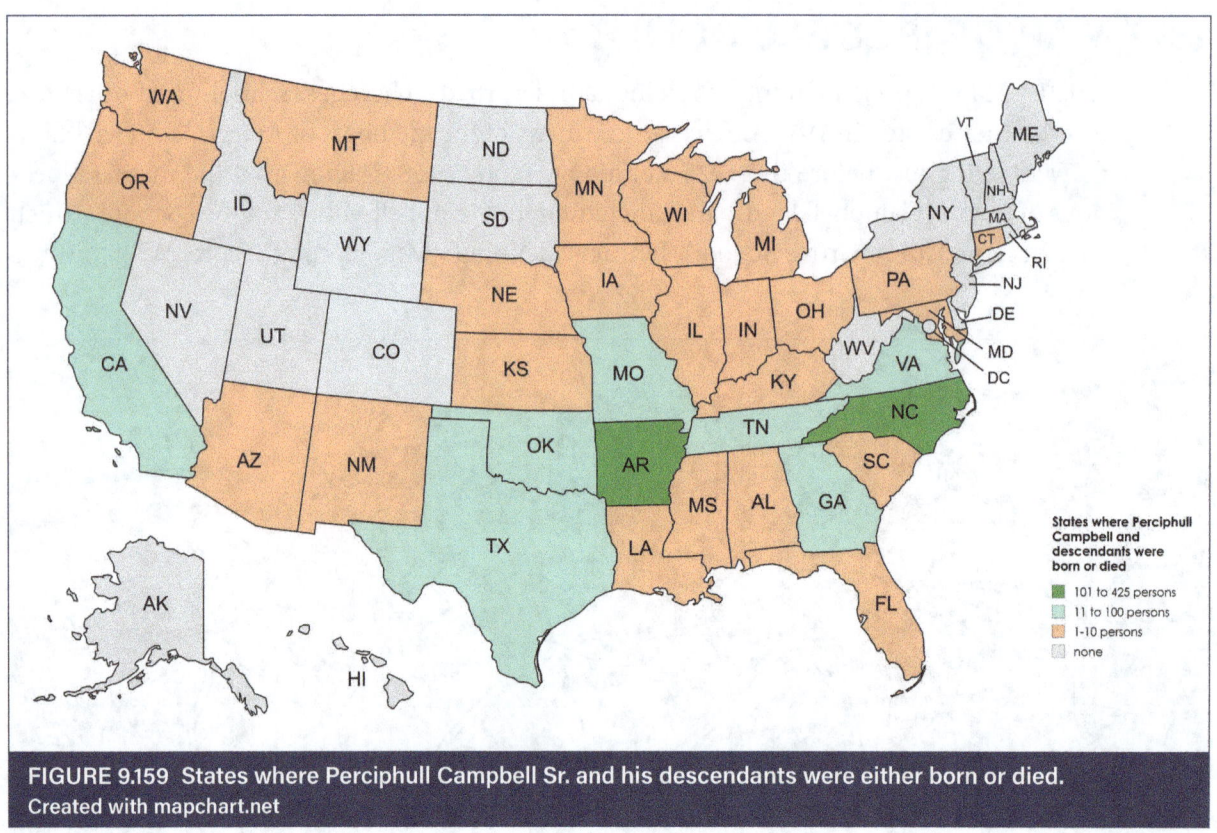

FIGURE 9.159 States where Perciphull Campbell Sr. and his descendants were either born or died. Created with mapchart.net

School, and Zion Baptist Church. The map shows the locations of the homes of the following Adam Campbell descendants: H. C. Bennett (1.6.4.2.6, Henry Columbus Bennett), Miss Campbell (1.6.2.5.2, Alice Campbell living at the Perciphull Campbell House), J. D. Campbell (1.6.4.2.3, Johnnie Dodredge Campbell), J. P. Campbell (1.6.4.7, John Pierce Campbell), W. B. Campbell (1.6.2.5.4, William Buxton Campbell), W. M. Campbell (1.6.4.8, William Milas Campbell), N. G. Crater (1.6.2.1.3.4, Newton Gwyn Crater), C. Fletcher (1.5.1.7, Critus Fletcher), J. P. Howard (1.6.4.4.1, John Pinkney Howard), Sam Huie (1.6.4.4.4, Samuel Huie), J. R. Huie (1.6.4.4, John Robey Huie), J. T. Jennings (1.6.4.4.5, James Turner Jennings), Mrs. R. M. Jurney (possibly 1.6.4.3.1.12, Lillie Jewel Bolin Jurney), D. A. Mullis (1.6.4.2.2, Daniel Asbury Mullis), I. G. Reid (1.6.4.2.1, Iram Green Reid), W. B. Tutterrow (1.6.4.6.4, Wilburn Burchard Tutterrow), Mrs. Vanhoy (1.6.4.6, Sarah A. Campbell Vanhoy), and C. R. York (1.6.2.4.1.5, Charles Romulus York).

The states where Perciphull Campbell Sr. and his descendants mentioned in this book were born or died are shown in Figure 9.159. This included 33 states with the largest number in North Carolina (424 births and 332 deaths), Arkansas (181 births and 179 deaths), Tennessee (41 births and 40 deaths), Texas (6 births and 36 deaths), Oklahoma (4 births and 32 deaths), Virginia (11 births and 12 deaths), California (1 birth and 17 deaths). Descendants were also born or died in Alsace-Loraine (1), France (2), Germany (2), India (1), and Ireland (3).

CHAPTER 9 REFERENCES

1. Aug 1925, "Descendants of Pierce Campbell Holds Reunion," *Statesville Morning Register*, as well as handout given at the reunion, *History of the Campbell Family*, compiled by H. P. Vanhoy, a descendant of Sarah Campbell, the daughter of John R. Campbell who married William A. Vanhoy.

2. "Find a Grave," Campbell Family Cemetery, Union Grove Township, Iredell County, North Carolina, dates from headstones personally document in 1981 by G. Moore and W. Campbell.

3. 1790 U.S. Federal Census for Iredell County, North Carolina, page 396, William Ball, William Campbell, Elizabeth Campbell, and Penniful/Perchull Campbell.

4. 1800 U.S. Federal Census for Iredell County, North Carolina, page 149: Perciphull Campbell, 21x11xxx1xxx1; John Campbell, x1x1x5xx1xxx; Daniel Ball, 2112x31x11xx.

5. Aug 6, 1810, U.S. Federal Census for Iredell County, North Carolina, page 206: John Campbell, xx2xxx41xxxx; page 176: Purciphull Campbell, 1111x3x11xxx4.

6. Aug 7, 1820, U.S. Federal Census for Iredell County, North Carolina, page 234: Sampson Ball; John Campbell; Purciphul Campbell, Esq; Adam Campbell; Perciphull Campbell Sr.; John Campbell; Reuben Fletcher; Mary Fletcher; James Fletcher; Reuben Morgan.

7. 1830, U.S. Federal Census for Iredell County, North Carolina, page 28/30: Percival Campbell Sr.; Percival Campbell Jr.; John Campbell, Sr.; Biram Ball; Sampson Ball.

8. 1840, U.S. Federal Census for Iredell County, North Carolina, page 184: Pierciful Campbell (26 persons, including 19 slaves), Hannah Campbell, Wm Campbell, Wm Hays, Charles Hays.

9. 1850, U.S. Federal Census for Iredell County, North Carolina, page 440, Family 544: P. Campbell, age 81, born in Virginia; John P. Parks, age 22; Theos C. Parks, age 15; Family 542: Milon Campbell, age 24; Clementine Campbell, age 23; Leolen D. Campbell, age 3; Preston C. Campbell, age 1.

10. "Perciphull Campbell," Wikipedia, https://en.wikipedia.org/wiki/Perciphull_Campbell, access date: Jan 27, 2025.

11. *Iredell County Deed Book B*, page 314, filed Nov 11, 1795.

12. *Iredell County Deed Book C*, page 118, filed May 15, 1798.

13. *Iredell County Deed Book J*, pages 575–576 (250 acres for $400 from Eli Lunceford, 151 acres for $301 from Reuben Morgan), page 705 (20 acres for $30 from Thomas Rash), Feb 25, 1819.

14. *Iredell County Deed Book T*, page 94, 750 acres for $4,000, filed.Sep 5, 1836

15. *Iredell County Deed Book W*, page 183, 2 acres for $10 to School District #4, filed Sep 8, 1843.

16. Jun 19, 1790, will of Theophilus Morgan; probated Feb 13, 1807 in Iredell County, North Carolina.

17. Feb 4, 1980, "Perciphull Campbell House," National Register of Historic Places—Nomination and Inventory, by Laura A. W. Phillips, https://files.nc.gov/ncdcr/nr/ID0012.pdf, access date Jan 27, 2025.

18. "Williamsburgh, North Carolina," Wikipedia, https://en.wikipedia.org/wiki/Williamsburgh,_North_Carolina, access date Jul 20, 2024.

19. Nov 1976, *Iredell Piedmont County*, with illustrations by Louise Gilbert and maps by Mildred Jenkins Miller, by Home M. Keever, Iredell County Bicentennial Commission, Brady Printing Company, pages 113, 130, 154, 180.

20. 1850, U.S. Federal Census, Slave Schedules, Iredell County, North Carolina, P. Campbell, 21 slaves; P. Campbell, 10 slaves; John R. Campbell, 1 slave; Williamson Campbell, 1 slave; B. Morgan, 2 slaves.

21. "Will of Perciphull Campbell," signed Nov 1, 1844 by Perciphull Campbell Sr.; probated in Jul 1853; executors were Percival Campbell Jr. and Milus Dobbins.

22. Feb 24, 1905, *Statesville Landmark*, Local Department, Minor Matters, "Aunt Huldy Morgan, one of the few remaining old-time colored women, died."

23. Sep 5, 1870, U.S. Federal Census, Union Grove Township, Iredell County, North Carolina, dwelling

167, page 22, William Buxton, age 57; Ema Campbell, age 31; William Campbell, age 8; Sis Campbell, age 6; Catherine Morgan, age 30, domestic servant; all born in North Carolina.

24. 1870, U.S. Federal Census, Union Grove Postal Route, Union Grove Township, Iredell County, North Carolina, page 25, dwelling 191, family 179, Lewis Campbell, age 36, working on farm, born in North Carolina; Epsey Campbell, age 24, born in South Carolina; Maggie Campbell, age 5, born in North Carolina; Jacob Campbell, age 2, born in North Carolina; all classified as "mulatto"; neighbor, family 178, Mary Span, age 48, born in Virginia.

25. Jan 13, 1920, U.S. Federal Census, Olin Road, Union Grove Township, Iredell County, North Carolina, dwelling 115, family 116, page 6B, Lee Campbell, age 89, head; Epsie Campbell, age 73, wife; Flake Somers, age 16, grandson.

26. 1850, U.S. Federal Census, Cypress Creek, Jones County, North Carolina, dwelling 251, family 243, race "Black," James Morgan, age 57; Sarah Morgan, age 57; Isaac Morgan, age 16; Alexander Morgan, age 13; Zacheus Morgan, age 11.

27. 1864, "U.S. Colored Troops Military Service Records," Isaac Morgan, age 24, private, 115th US Colored Infantry, age 24; military service date 1864.

28. Jun 22, 1967, "Texas Death Certificates. 1903-1982," Grayson County, father Ike Morgan; mother Millie Rucker; child Jo Anna Lee; usual residence: Seattle, Washington; date of birth: May 20,1880, place of birth: Texas, race: "Negro", informant: Lorine Carter (daughter).

29. Statesville Landmark, Statesville, North Carolina; articles about Sarah "Sallie" Campbell; May 21, 1880: "An Aged Negress," May 21, 1880, Feb 9, 1888: "Coffin paid for by Commissioners, "Jan 12, 1888: "Death of Sallie Campbell"

30. 1838, Arkansas Compiled Census and Census Substitutes Index, Tax List for 1838, William R. Campbell, Union County, Arkansas, page 7.

31. Arkansas Homestead and Cash Entry Patents, Will R Campbell, 103.14 acres, issued Jun 1, 1932 in Little Rock Land Office; description: 1 SE 5TH PM Yes 10S 1E 27.

32. 1850, U.S. Federal Census, Union Township, Izard County, Arkansas, Jane Campbell, age 58, born in North Carolina, living with: Alfred Campbell, age 31; Susan A Campbell, age 21; and Tirza Campbell, age 21.

33. 1860, U.S. Federal Census, Franklin Township, Izard County, Arkansas, page 98.

34. "Find a Grave," Zion Baptist Church Cemetery, Iredell County, dates from headstones.

35. U.S. Civil War Soldier Records and Profiles, 1861-1865.

36. Jun 2015, "The 26th NC Regiment Band," A Storm in the Land: Sothern Moravians in the Civil War, courtesy of the Moravian Music Foundation; also "26th North Carolina Infantry Regiment," Wikipedia, access date Mar 20, 2025.

37. Aug 29, 1832, Marriage announcements in The Greensboro Patriot, Greensboro, North Carolina, In Iredell County, on the 12th ult. (sic), Capt. Theophilus M. Campbell to Miss Tabitha R. Allen.

38. Journal of the Senate and House of Commons of the General Assembly of North Carolina 1836-1837, https://www.carolana.com/NC/Legislators/Documents/Journal_of_the_House_of_Commons_of_the_General_Assembly_of_North_Carolina_1836_1837.pdf, cited by J. D. Lewis, access date Jan 21, 2024.

39. NCPedia, "It needed to change before the state could grow: North Carolina's Constitutional Convention of 1835," by Thomas E. Jeffrey, https://www.ncpedia.org/1835-consitutional-convention, access date Jan 21, 2024.

40. "North Carolina State House," Wikipedia, https://en.wikipedia.org/wiki/North_Carolina_State_House, access date Jul 4, 2024.

41. Nov 1, 2011, For History's Sake: The Preservation and Publications of North Carolina History 1663-1903, pages 88-90, by H. G. Jones, originally published in 1966, UNC Press.

42. May 29, 1835, "Meeting of the Friends of Judge White, in his Native County," Newbern Spectator, New Bern, page 2.

43. Jun 27, 1850, "Public Meeting in Iredell," Carolina Watchman, Salisbury, North Carolina, page 3, meeting on Jun 15, 1850.

44. Aug 29, 1850, U.S. Federal Census for Iredell County, North Carolina, page 443, dwelling 580, family 587, A. Campbell, age 33, born in North Carolina.

45. 1850, U.S. Federal Census, Iredell County, North Carolina, page 438; Thomas M. Campbell, born 1797, occupation, teacher; living with W. Campbell, age 34; and Jemima Campbell, age 37; dwelling 525; family 532.

46. U.S. General Land Office Records, Land Office in Batesville, Arkansas; Tabitha R Campbell; issued on

Mar 1, 1860, accession number AR0710__.058, document number 12030.

47. 1956, "Oldster Celebrates at 102," *Register-Guard*, Eugene, Oregon, news clipping.

48. Stories relayed to the author by descendants of Rufus William Campbell.

49. Jul 7, 1880, U.S. Federal Census, Lafferty Creek Township, Izard County, Arkansas.

50. "Find a Grave," Reeves Cemetery, Melbourne, Izard County, Arkansas, dates from headstones.

51. Jul 20, 1870, U.S. Federal Census for Big Creek Township, Fulton County, Arkansas.

52. Jun 16, 1900, U.S. Federal Census, Lunenburg Township, Izard County, Arkansas.

53. Names and dates for the family of Isabella M. Campbell family were provided by Roger Harvell of Izard County, Arkansas, in Mar 2024.

54. 1982, *Heritage of Wilkes County*, by W. O. Absher, Wilkes County Genealogical Society, family 0998, page 419, article by Mr. L. P. Somers Jr..

55. 1804–1951, "History, Membership and Clerk's records of Grassy Knob Baptist Church," compiled by L. T. Queen, https://lfweb.co.iredell.nc.us/icpl/DocView.aspx?id=190&dbid=0&repo=Iredell-County-Library&cr=1, access date Feb 9, 2024, James Iredell Room, Iredell County Public Library.

56. Aug 25, 1893, *Statesville Record and Landmark*, "The Murder was in Iredell," page 3.

57. "Find a Grave," Mount Vernon Baptist Church, Iredell County, dates from headstones.

58. Mar 2, 1954, *News and Record*, Greensboro, North Carolina, page 10, obituary for Mrs. Vance Gertrude Salmons.

59. "Find a Grave," Union Grove Methodist church, Union Grove, Iredell County, North Carolina, dates from headstones.

60. Jun 14, 1977, "Campbell Dies at 91," *Statesville Record & Landmark*, Statesville, North Carolina, page 8-A.

61. Apr 8, 1866, "North Carolina Index to Marriage Bonds, 1741-1868," Davidson County, Gabriel Morgan, and Caroline Young, bond no. 000039108.

62. "An Illustrated History of the Georgia Gold Rush and the United States Branch Mint at Dahlonega, George," by Carl N. Lester, https://www.goldrush-gallery.com/dahlmint/c_history_outline.html, access date Mar 1, 2024.

63. Feb 21, 1831, "Negro Woman, Hannah," *Constitutional Whig*, page 4, Richmond, Virginia, from Eliphalet Hale, Jailer, Warren County, Georgia.

64. Jan 8, 1871, *The Atlanta Constitution*, page 4.

65. "Held Up a Mexican," *The Rawlins Republican*, Rawlins, Wyoming; Jul 30, Aug 13, Aug 20, 1897.

66. 1890, *Biographical and Historical Memoirs of Eastern Arkansas*, Goodspeed Publishing Company.

67. 1960, *The Descendants of Claiborne Howard, soldier of the American Revolution*, by Gerald Wilson Cook (1932–), https://archive.org/details/descendantsofcla00cook/page/30/mode/2up?q=Campbell, 929.2 H830C, Mary Howard and Williamson R. Campbell, (son of John R. Campbell) and children James A. Williamson W., Sarah C., Augustin, Henry F., and Martin H., pages 30–31, 41, 150; Piercihull Campbell, Esq, pages 14; Pauline Campbell and John Pinkney Howard, page 42.

68. Jan 1, 1917, *Map of Iredell County*, showing families, roads, churches, schools, and other features as they existed in 1917, North Carolina Map Collection, drawn by N. E. Kinney, C. E., Lexington, North Carolina, George F. Cram Company, Chicago, https://dc.lib.unc.edu/cdm/singleitem/collection/ncmaps/id/413/rec/16, access date Mar 31, 2025, cropped to show only Union Grove Township.

MALINDA MAE (CAMPBELL) WOOD

1.7   Malinda Mae (Campbell) Wood (Dec 1776–Sep 4, 1838) was possibly the seventh of eight children of **Adam Campbell** (1735–1779) and **Elizabeth (Morgan) Campbell** (1735–1789) of Rowan and Iredell Counties, North Carolina. She would have been born in Rowan County, North Carolina, after her parents moved from Culpeper County, Virginia, to Rowan County in about 1774. She married Miller A. Wood (Nov 11, 1769–Nov 29, 1838) in about 1796. Some genealogists report that they were married in Long Island, Queens, New York, and that Miller was born in Bristol County, Massachusetts, as the son of Seth Wood (Feb 6, 1731–Apr 4, 1815) of Swansea, Bristol County, Massachusetts.[1] A Miller Wood Sr. and Miller Wood Jr. were witnesses on a deed between **Perciphull Campbell** and **Elizabeth Campbell** in Iredell County.[2] Malinda and her family are not mentioned in the 1925 Vanhoy *History of the Campbell Family* that was distributed in Union Grove, North Carolina.

While the connection directly to Adam Campbell is not well documented, the history of the family of Miller and Malinda is extensively documented by her son, Miller Chapman Wood. Miller and Malinda moved from North Carolina to Kentucky and lived in Logan County, Kentucky, until 1832, when they moved to Illinois. They died in Macoupin County, Illinois, and were buried at the Sulphur Springs Cemetery in Atwater, Illinois.[3, 4, 5, 6, 7, 8]

Malinda and Miller Wood had six children, listed as follows.

MARTHA WOOD

1.7.1   Martha "Patsy" Wood (1795–1855) was born in North Carolina and moved to Kentucky with her parents, where she married Davis P. Bagby (1792–Mar 31, 1865) in Warren County on Oct 7, 1817. They had six children. Davis Bagby fought for the 56th Illinois Infantry in the Union Army in the U.S. Civil War. While he was returning home, he drowned as the ship he was on, the steamer *General Lyon*, sank off the coast of Cape Hatteras. See figure 10.1. Martha died in Atwater, Illinois, and was buried at the Sulphur Springs Cemetery near her parents.[9,10, 11, 12]

FIGURE 10.1 USS General Lyon (1862–1865).

REV. BLATCHLEY CAMPBELL WOOD

1.7.2   Rev. Blatchley Campbell Wood, MD (Nov 5, 1797–Jan 16, 1887), was born in North Carolina and was a Methodist clergyman and physician. He married Nancy McCaw (1795–Oct 15, 1882) in Pulaski County, Kentucky, on Sep 22, 1823. They had four children. In the *History of Greene County, Illinois*, it is stated that Rev. Wood's grandfather and brothers "emigrated from England in about 1690 and settled on what is called Wood's Neck, Long Island." His great grandfather "emigrated from Scotland about the same time." Blatchley and Nancy were buried at the Carrollton Cemetery in Greene County, Illinois.[13, 14, 15]

WILLIAM C. WOOD

1.7.3   William C. Wood (1805–1844) married Sarah "Polly" Cloud (1805–aft. 1832) on Jul 16, 1829, in Morgan County, Illinois. He died in Jefferson County, Ohio.[16, 17]

MARY WOOD

1.7.4   Mary "Polly" Wood (1808–1838) was born in North Carolina. She married John K. Felts (1805–Jul 26, 1887) on Mar 1, 1833, in Warren County, Kentucky.[18, 19] John was the brother of Susannah Felts, wife of John H. Coleman (1.4.10).

FRANCES A. WOOD

1.7.5   Frances A. Wood (1814–1836) was born in Kentucky and died in Macoupin County, Illinois. She did not marry and was buried at the Sulphur Springs Cemetery in Atwater, Macoupin County.

MILLER CHAPMAN WOOD

1.7.6   Miller Chapman Wood (Aug 4, 1818–Mar 23, 1889) was born in Logan County, Kentucky. See Figure 10.2. He married Minerva A. Deatherage (Oct 10, 1823–Mar 21, 1853) on Mar 16, 1843, in Morgan County, Illinois.[20] He had seven children with Minerva. After Minerva died, he married Lucinda Suzanne Rogers (Nov 27, 1837–Feb 25, 1916) on May 11, 1854, in Montgomery County, Illinois.[21] See Figure 10.3. Lucinda and Miller had 13 children. He left his native state of Kentucky in 1832 with his parents and settled in Illinois, and was one of the earliest settlers in that region. In 1864, he moved to Nicollet County, Minnesota. A year later, he moved to Meeker County, Minnesota, and settled on a farm in Union Grove Township. In 1879, he moved to Manannah Township in Meeker County and settled on a farm in section 20 of the township, where he had 80 acres for light general farming and raising stock. In political matters, Miller was affiliated with the Democratic Party and was a Southern sympathizer. There is a story that he used to sit on the fence railing and harass the Union soldiers after the Civil War. He named one of his

Left: FIGURE 10.2 Miller Chapman Wood, abt. 1870, Meeker County.

Right: FIGURE 10.3 Lucinda Rogers, abt. 1870, Meeker County.

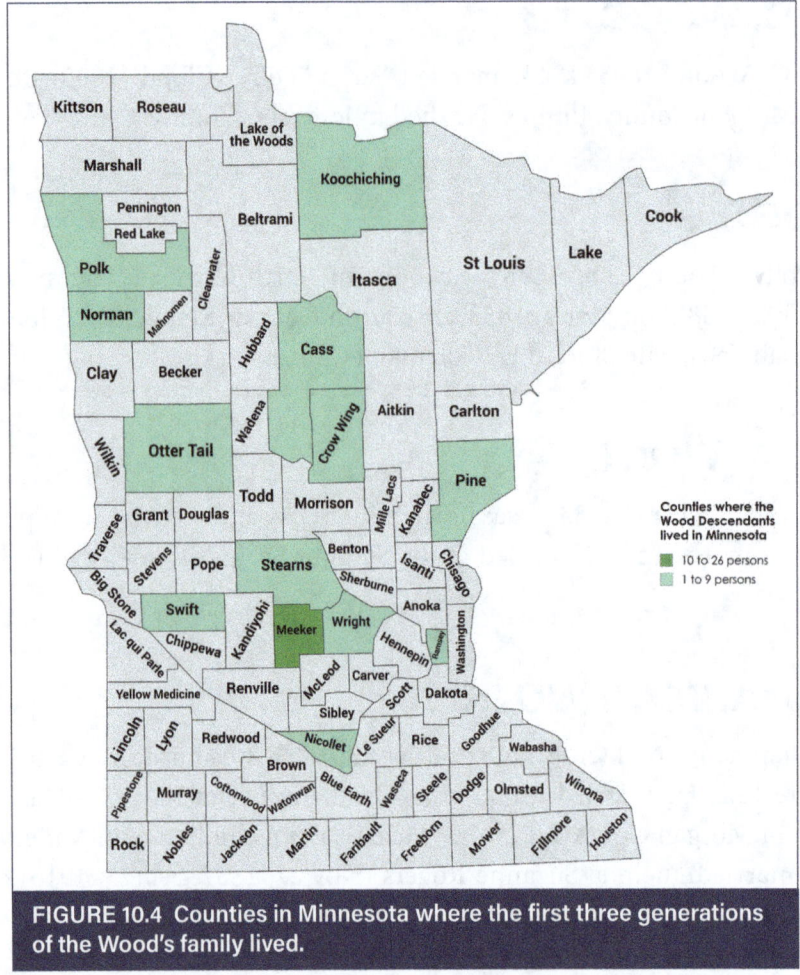

FIGURE 10.4 Counties in Minnesota where the first three generations of the Wood's family lived.

sons Robert Edward Lee Wood (Apr 27, 1869–Aug 1949) in support of the South. Miller and Lucinda were buried at the Eden Lake Cemetery in Stearns County, Minnesota.[4, 22, 23, 24]

Counties in Minnesota where the first three generations of Malinda (Campbell) Wood's descendants lived in Minnesota are shown in Figure 10.4. The largest number (26 people) lived at some point in their lives in Meeker County. States where the first three generations of Malinda Mae (Campbell) Wood's family (79 people) were born or died are shown in Figure 10.5. This includes 19 states with the largest numbers in Illinois (21 births and 18 deaths), Kentucky (19 births and 0 deaths), and Minnesota (15 births and 19 deaths). Some descendants moved to Canada.

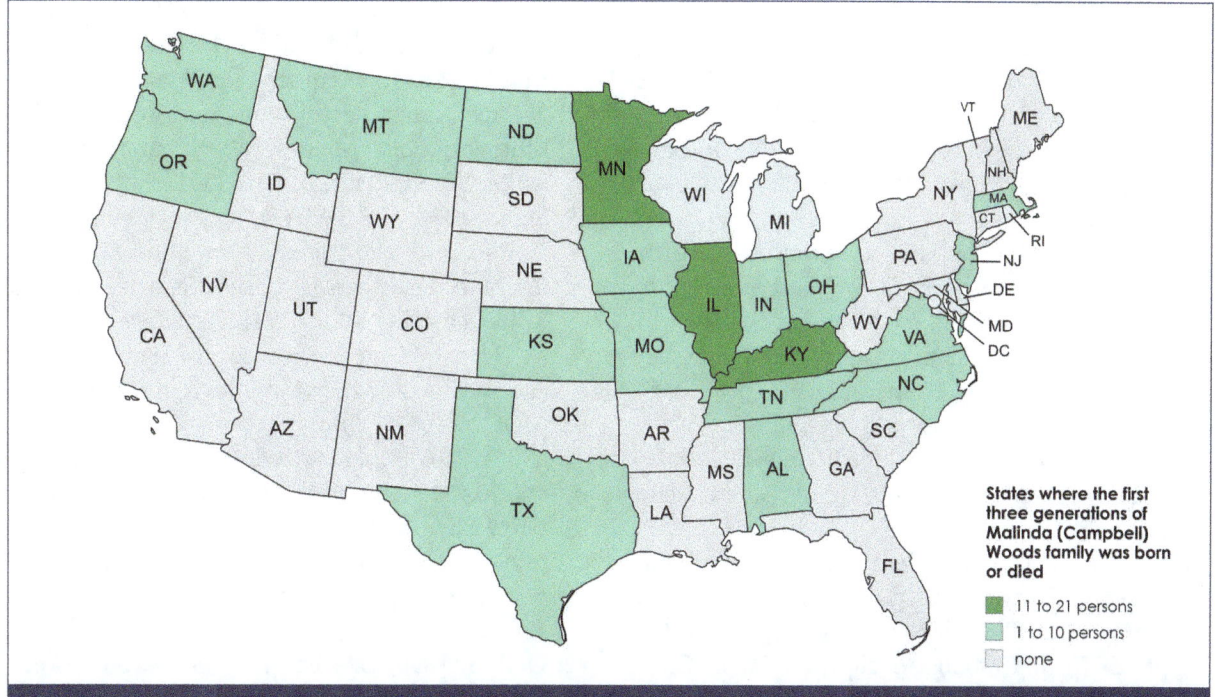

FIGURE 10.5 States where the first three generations of Malinda (Campbell) Wood's family were born or died. (Created with Mapchart.net)

CHAPTER 10 REFERENCES

1. "Find a Grave," Mount Hope Cemetery, Swansea, Bristol County, Massachusetts, Seth Wood, Sr. (Feb 6, 1731–Apr 4, 1815), headstone with dates.

2. 1795, *Iredell County Deed Book B*, page 314, Elizabeth Campbell sold 100 acres of land in Iredell County for 20 pounds to Perciphull Campbell, located on a creek in Iredell County, witnessed by Miller Wood, Miller Wood Sr., with Nimrod Lunceford as Jurat, filed on Jun 15, 1795, signed on Nov 11, 1795.

3. 1800, U.S. Census Index, Garrard County, Kentucky, Miller Woods.

4. 1988, *Album of History and Biography of Meeker County, Minnesota*, published in Chicago, Alden Ogle & Company, section: Biography of Miller Chapman Wood, son of Miller and Melinda (Campbell) Wood, https://tile.loc.gov/ storage-services/public/gdcmassbookdig/albumofhistorybi00alde/albumofhistorybi00alde. pdf, access date Feb 21, 2025.

5. Aug 6, 1810, U.S. Federal Census, Warren County, Kentucky, page 259, Millier Wood, 312211174"11".

6. Aug 7, 1820, U.S. Federal Census, Warren County, Kentucky, page 35, Miller Wood; 311213121382 14 14.

7. 1830, U.S. Federal Census, Warren County, Kentucky, page 92, Miller Wood, 111111114288.

8. Dec 13, 1836, Illinois Public Land Purchase Records, Section E2NE, 1.25 per acres, volume 339, page 138, township 11N, range 5W.

9. Oct 8, 1816, "Kentucky County Marriage Records," Warren County Patsy Wood and Davis Bagby, Film 000339890.

10. 1850, U.S. Federal Census, Southwest, Montgomery County, Illinois, page 331, dwelling 1033, family 1057, Martha Bagsby, age 55, born in North Carolina; inferred husband Davis Bagsby, age 58, born in North Carolina; Julia Bagsby, age 24, born in Kentucky; Francis Bagsby, age 22, born in Kentucky.

11. Mar 31, 1865, "U.S. Civil War Soldier Records and Profiles," Davis P. Bagby, Enlisted Nov 6, 1861, rank, Corporal, mustered Feb 27, 1862 in Illinois, 56th Regiment, mustered out Mar 31, 1865 from Steamer "General Lyon" (drowned), residence: White County, Illinois.

12. "USS *General Lyon*," Wikipedia, https://en.wikipedia.org/wiki/USS_General_Lyon, access date Mar 7, 2025.

13. Nov 27, 1850, U.S. Federal Census, Carrollton, Greene County, Illinois, page 160, dwelling 1091, family 1103; Blatchley C. Wood, age 52, birthplace North Carolina, occupation M. E. Clergyman; Nancy Wood, age 55, born in Virginia; Martha M. Wood, age 27, born in Kentucky; Amanda Wood, age 20, born in Kentucky.

14. Aug 13, 1822, "Kentucky County Marriage Records," Pulaski County, Blatchley Woods and Nancy McCaw, film no. 001912849.

15. 1879, *History of Green County, Illinois*, published in Chicago by Donnelley, Gassette & Loyd, https://ia804506.us.archive.org/10/items/historyofgreenec00clap/historyofgreenec00clap.pdf, access date Feb 21, 2025, pages 504–505.

16. Jul 16, 1829, "Illinois Compiled Marriages," Morgan County, William C. Wood and Polly Cloud, Family History Library Microfilm 1317641.

17. Apr 14, 1844, "Ohio Wills and Probate Records," Jefferson County, William Wood, probate on Apr 14, 1844, Record of Wills, vol. 4–5; mentions William, Sarah, Rasselas Castner, Catherine Wood, Sarah Mears, Benjamin Mears, Alicia Spencer, Catherine Castner, Joseph C. Spencer, David Moodey, and Nathaniel Dike.

18. Mar 1, 1833, "Kentucky Marriage Records," Warren County, Polly Wood and John K. Felts, mother of Polly: Malinda Wood, father of Polly: Miller Wood, film no. 000164003.

19. Sep 3, 1850, U.S. Federal Census, Union, Wells County, Indiana, page 330, dwelling 27, family 27, Mary Feltz, age 43, born in North Carolina; John, age 45; C. W., age 21; Elisha, age 13; A. E., age 11; E. M., age 7; Rebecca, age 18; Christiana, age 5; Almeda, age 3; and John Jones, age 20.

20. Mar 16, 1843, "Illinois Compiled Marriages, 1790-1860," Morgan County, Miller C. Wood, and Minerva A. Deatherage, Family History Library Microfilm 1317641.

21. May 11, 1854, "Illinois Marriage Index," Montgomery County, Miller C. Wood, and Lucinda S. Rodgers.

22. Oct 28, 1850, U.S. Federal Census, Southwest, Montgomery County, Illinois, page 147, dwelling 1042, family 1068, M. C. Wood, age 30, occupation farmer; Manerva Wood, age 27; William Wood, age 7; Deadenny Wood, age 5; George Wood, age 2; and Alaxand Wood, age 1.

23. May 1, 1885, Minnesota Territory Census, Manannah, Meeker County, page 513, line 38, Miller C. Wood, age 67.

24. 1870, U.S. Federal Census, Union Grove Township, Manannah Post Office, Meeker County, Minnesota, page 8, dwelling 5, Miller C. Wood, age 52, born in Kentucky, farmer; Lucinda S. Wood, age 33, born in Illinois; Alexander Wood, age 21, born in Illinois; Eugene Wood, age 10, born in Illinois; William W. Wood, age 8, born in Illinois; C. L. V. Wood, age 5, born in Minnesota; Martha M. Wood, age 3, born in Minnesota; Robert E. Lee Wood, age 11, born in Minnesota.

CHAPTER 11

THEOPHILUS MARION CAMPBELL

1.8 **Theophilus Marion Campbell** (abt. 1777–abt. 1855) was the eighth and last known child of **Adam Campbell** (1735–1779) and **Elizabeth (Morgan) Campbell** (1735–1798). He was born after his parents moved to Rowan County, North Carolina, in about 1775. This area became Iredell County in 1778. He and a possible sister, Malinda Mae (Campbell) Wood (Dec 1776–Sep 4, 1838), would have been the only children of Adam and Elizabeth born in North Carolina. A husband (**Donald Ray Raney**, 1933–2020) of a descendant of one of Theophilus Marion Campbell's children, **John Cook Campbell**, wrote a history of Theophilus Marion Campbell's family using genealogical sourcing.[1] Donald Raney was the first

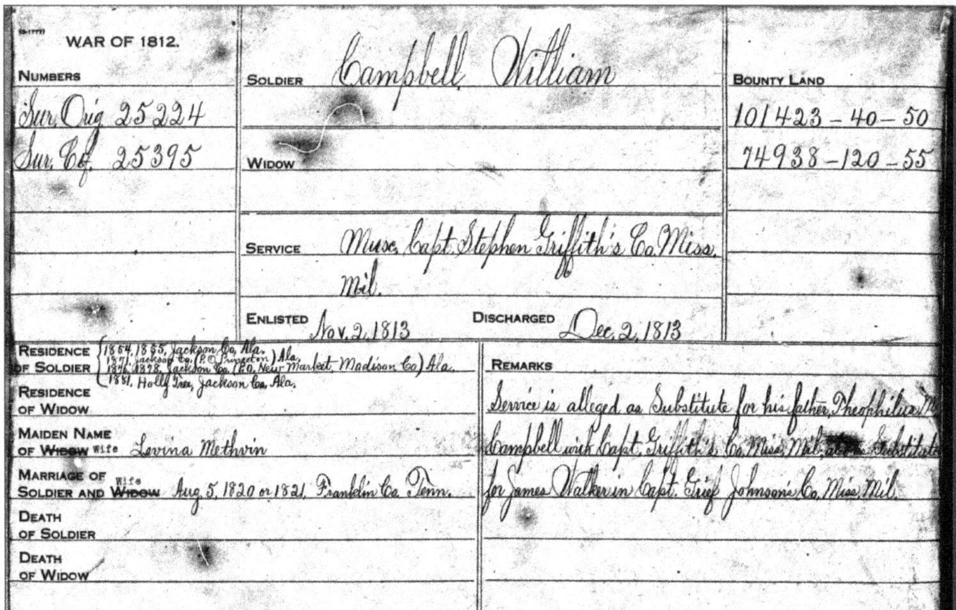
WAR OF 1812.

NUMBERS: Sur. Orig. 25224; Sur. Ctf. 25395

SOLDIER: Campbell, William

BOUNTY LAND: 101423 – 40 – 50; 74938 – 120 – 55

WIDOW:

SERVICE: Musc. Capt. Stephen Griffith's Co. Miss. Mil.

ENLISTED: Nov. 2, 1813 DISCHARGED: Dec. 2, 1813

RESIDENCE OF SOLDIER: 1854, 1855, Jackson Co. Ala. / 1871, Jackson Co. (P.O. Princeton) Ala. / 1876, 1878, Jackson Co. (P.O. New Market, Madison Co.) Ala. / 1881, Holly Tree, Jackson Co. Ala.

RESIDENCE OF WIDOW:

MAIDEN NAME OF ~~WIDOW~~ Wife: Levina Methvin

MARRIAGE OF SOLDIER AND ~~WIDOW~~ Wife: Aug. 5, 1820 or 1821, Franklin Co. Tenn.

DEATH OF SOLDIER:

DEATH OF WIDOW:

REMARKS: Service is alleged as Substitute for his father, Theophilus M. Campbell with Capt. Griffith's Co. Miss. Mil. [illegible] Substitute for James Walker in Capt. Grief Johnson's Co. Miss. Mil.

FIGURE 11.1
War of 1812 pension record for William Campbell, son of Theophilus Campbell. His wife, Levina Methvin, is also mentioned.[18]

to attempt to link Theophilus Campbell's family to Adam Campbell using Y-DNA testing. This effort became part of the Adam Campbell Y-DNA project on FamilyTreeDNA.com. The original research from Raney's book forms the basis for the history of this family with updated genealogical research and new Y-DNA evidence showing a linkage to Adam Campbell, as well as to an African American, Simon Campbell, who was a descendant of one of Theophilus's sons.

The record of a William Marion Campbell's War of 1812 pension application (Figure 11.1) shows his father was Theophilus Campbell and his wife was Levina Methvin and that they lived near Jackson, Alabama, and were married in Franklin County, Tennessee. In addition, the following affidavit was submitted in Jackson County, Alabama, on Sep 2, 1854, by Theophilus Campbell:[1, 18]

"On 2 Sep 1854* at Jackson County, Alabama, before James C. Scott, JP, appeared Theophilus Campbell, who stated that he is the identical person who appears on the original (War of 1812) muster rolls of Capt. (Stephen) Griffith's Company of Mississippi Territory Militia and further states that his son, William Campbell, took his place on the same day that the company was mustered into service (as a fifer about September/October 1813) and served the term of about three months (and was honorably discharged at New Market, Madison County, Alabama about November 1813) and received pay and a discharge in said deponent's name which (discharge) is lost or mislaid and further states that William Campbell done all the service and is entitled to receive all the credit and bounty and states further that he has not applied for nor received bounty land under this nor no other act, nor will he ever for bounty land for said service and waives the right to his son William."

Signed: Theophilus Campbell.

---

*In Raney's book (reference 1), the date is listed as Sep 2, 1854. In Valley Leaves (reference 18), the date is listed as Sep 2, 1852.

William Campbell's affidavit proves that William Campbell is the son of Theophilus Campbell. Raney's search of land records in Madison County, Alabama, revealed that John Cook Campbell, William Campbell, and George Washington Campbell all claimed land within one-half of a mile of each other. In addition, each of them named one of their sons Theophilus, and several of their children's names were repeated in each family. This circumstantial evidence is the basis for concluding that John Cook Campbell, William Campbell, and George Washington Campbell are all sons of Theophilus Campbell. Additional research supports the existence of two additional sons of Theophilus Marion Campbell, Adam Addison Campbell and James Campbell. The first son to be born in Alabama was William Marion Campbell, so it is thought that Theophilus Marion Campbell moved to Alabama before 1803, which would also be consistent with his service in the Mississippi Territory Militia during the War of 1812. While Theophilus Marion Campbell had five children, the name of his spouse is not known and does not appear in any records or family histories.

The sons raised their families in the area near Huntsville in what became Madison County, Alabama, which is in the northeast section of Alabama and borders on the Tennessee state line (Figure 11.2). Most of the settlers in this area followed the "Great South" Indian Trail from Virginia and North Carolina to settle in Madison County. This area was part of the Cherokee and Chickasaw Indian Nations until 1806, when the U.S. government purchased the land, signed the Cherokee and Chickasaw Indian Treaties, and opened a new Federal Land Office at Huntsville to distribute the land to settlers. The Mississippi Territory organized Madison County in 1808, and the move was on to settle the area. Prior to 1817, this portion of Alabama was in the Mississippi Territory. In 1817, Mississippi Territory was divided into Alabama Territory and Mississippi Territory. Alabama was admitted to the Union as the 22nd state in 1819.

Raney did not list a death date for Theophilus Campbell. There is a record showing a letter for "Theophulus Campbell" in the Huntsville Post Office on Jan 9, 1819.[2] Land ownership records show a T. M. Campbell in the northern part of Alabama in the Huntsville Meridian in 1823.[3] There are records of a T. Campbell in 1850 as a farmer and slave owner in Wilcox County, Alabama, in 1850.[4, 5, 6] Wilcox County is in the southern one-third of Alabama, so this may not be the same Theophilus Marion Campbell. He probably died in about 1855, after he signed his affidavit in Jackson County.[18] His burial location is not known.

The five sons of Theophilus Marion Campbell are described below, with names from Donald Raney's book appearing in bold.

ADAM ADDISON CAMPBELL

1.8.1 **Adam Addison Campbell** (1797–Sep 2, 1870) was born in North Carolina. He married **Elizabeth Ann Hambrick** (1817–Sep 2, 1870), daughter of **Greenberry Hambrick** and **Elizabeth Ann Dameron**, on May 23, 1839, in Madison County, Alabama. Adam was in

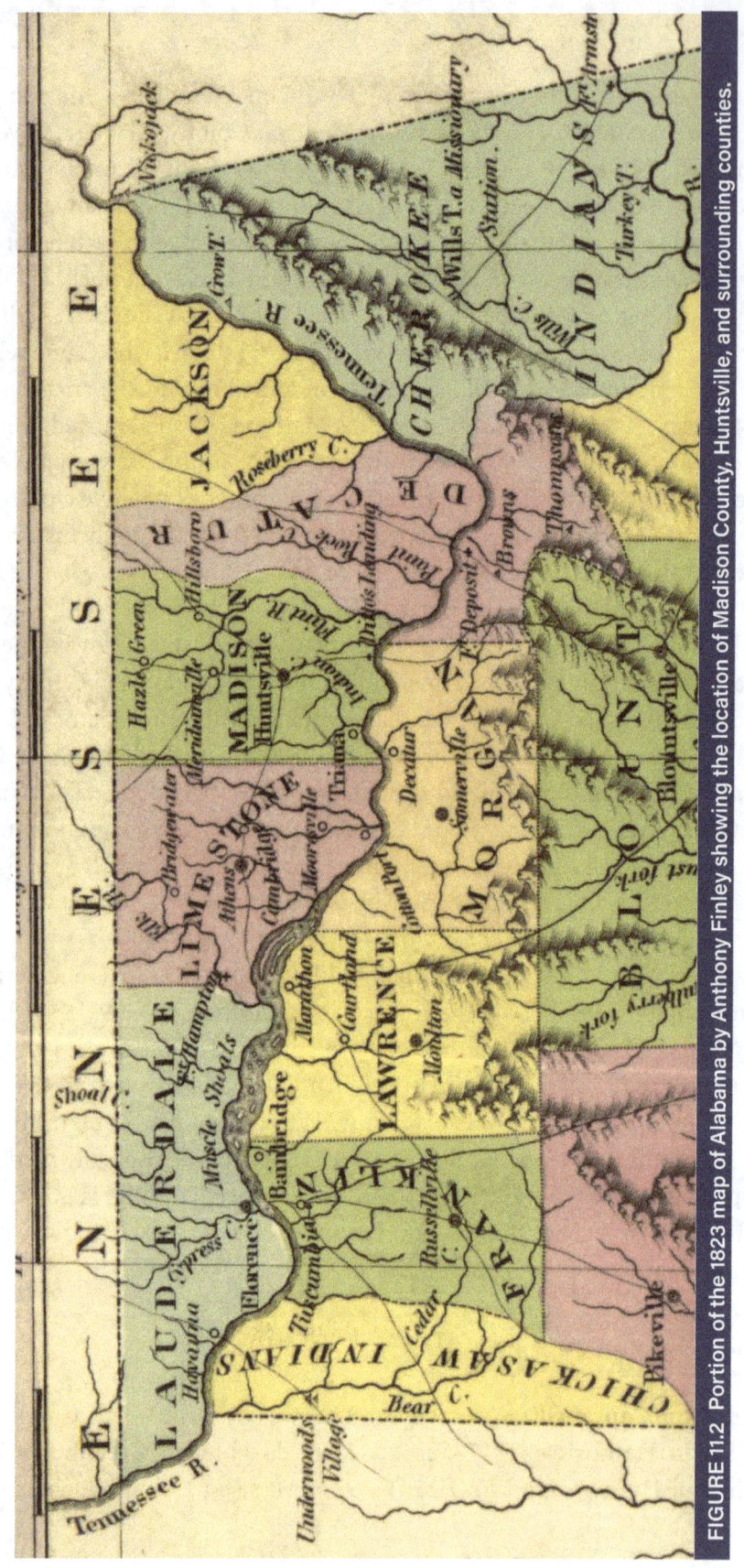

FIGURE 11.2 Portion of the 1823 map of Alabama by Anthony Finley showing the location of Madison County, Huntsville, and surrounding counties.

Left: FIGURE 11.3 Andrew Gipson Branum, abt. 1900, Madison County.

Middle: FIGURE 11.4 William Greenberry Campbell, abt. 1900, New Market.

Right: Figure 11.5 James Adam Campbell, abt. 1900, Madison County.

Alabama in the 1830 and 1850 censuses.[7, 8, 9, 10] Adam and Elizabeth had the following children:

1.8.1.1 Margaret Campbell (abt. 1833–abt. 1899) married Andrew Gipson Branum (Feb 1852–Dec 21, 1932) on Sep 23, 1868, in Madison County, Alabama. See Figure 11.3. Andrew was a farmer and blacksmith. He was buried at the Gurley Cemetery in Madison County.

1.8.1.2 William Green "Greenberry" Campbell (Sep 1833–Jul 10, 1917) married Lucindia Frances Crabb (Jul 2, 1843–Jul 17, 1907) in 1863 in Madison County. William was a sergeant with the 2nd Alabama Confederate Infantry, CSA, during the U.S. Civil War. See Figure 11.4. William and Lucinda were buried at the Cochran Cemetery in New Market, Madison County.

1.8.1.3 Alfred Campbell (abt. 1837–Aug 1, 1907) married Ellen Kirby (1839–aft. 1860) on Aug 20, 1860, in Madison County. Alfred was mortally shot in a fight in New Market.

1.8.1.4 Mary Ann Campbell (May 1, 1839–1905) married Samuel David Barley (Jan 1813–Mar 5, 1900) on Dec 11, 1856, in Madison County. Samuel had two previous wives before Mary. Samuel and Mary Ann lived on the Hayes Store Postal Route in Madison County. He was a farmer from Virginia and moved to Alabama before 1840. He owned a large plantation with 15 slaves in 1860. Mary and Samuel were buried at the Hambrick Cemetery in New Market, Madison County.

FIGURE 11.6 Sarah (Norris) Campbell, abt. 1900, Huntsville.

1.8.1.5 Sarah Jane "Sallie" Campbell (abt. 1841–aft 1872) married James T. Davis (abt. 1839–aft 1872) on Dec 22, 1871, in Madison County.

1.8.1.6 James Adam Campbell (Feb 1849–Nov 24, 1928) married Sarah "Sallie" Caroline Norris (Sep 1855–Dec 1, 1944) on Jul 26, 1872, in Lincoln County, Tennessee.

See Figures 11.5 and 11.6. James was a private in the 50th Alabama Infantry, CSA, during the U.S. Civil War. They lived in Huntsville and were buried at the Rice Cemetery in New Market, Madison County.

1.8.1.7 Albert Tone Campbell (Mar 10, 1851–Dec 28, 1899) married Charlotte Ragsdale (abt. 1854–Dec 7, 1917) on Dec 7, 1871, in Madison County.

JOHN COOK CAMPBELL

1.8.2 **John Cook Campbell** (1802–1881) was born in Iredell County, North Carolina. He married **Charity H. Bailey** (abt. 1803–abt. 1838), daughter of **Dr. Thomas Bailey** and **Elizabeth "Last Name Unknown,"** on Aug 14, 1819, in Madison County, Alabama. He later married **Delphia P. Bailey** (Feb 21, 1811–abt. 1881), daughter of **Rev. Hayman Bailey** and **Edith Stanphill**, on Oct 1, 1839, in Yalobusha County, Mississippi. He died after 1880 in Titus County, Texas, and was buried at the Union Hill Cemetery in Titus County, along with Delphia.[1]

The first record of John Cook Campbell was his marriage to Charity H. Bailey on Aug 14, 1819, as recorded in volume 1, page 325 of the *Madison County Marriage Records*. **Rev. Thomas Bailey** owned land joining John Cook Campbell on the northeast. According to Raney's book, "On Jul 1, 1830, John Cook Campbell purchased an 80.46-acre tract, number 2316, joining Thomas Bailey, described as 'East ½ of the Northwest ¼ of Section 11 in Township 2 South, Range 2 East in Madison County, Alabama.'"[1]

"On Jul 22, 1835, John purchased 40 acres listed as 'N1/2, W1/2, NE1/4 of Section 29, Townshp 22, Range 4E' in Yalobusha County, Mississippi,"[1] Yalobusha County was organized in 1834 on land previously owned by Native Americans.[11] See Figure 11.7. In its first census in 1840, Yalobusha County had a population of 12,248, with 56% of residents free and 44% enslaved. With 195 people working in industry, the new county had Mississippi's fifth-highest number of manufacturing employees. "On May 20, 1847, John purchased 161 acres listed as "SW1/4 of Section 21, Township 25, Range 7E, located about one-and-one-half miles northeast of Coffeeville, Mississippi. The Civil War Battle of Coffeeville was fought on Dec 5, 1862, near the Campbell farm."[1]

In about 1873, John Cook Campbell moved his family to Titus County, Texas, and settled on a farm near Union Hill. Local families formed Union Hill when the Union Hill church and cemetery were built on land donated by Alexander Tabb, who settled in the area in 1861. By 1984, only the church and cemetery remain where the town was located.

"Family tradition, as related by John Cook Campbell's granddaughter, Lula Jane Campbell, is that John Cook Campbell and Charity H. Bailey eloped on horseback to get married. Since they were only about 17 and 15 at the time of their marriage, this tradition is probably true. She also said that after Charity died that John Cook Campbell remained single for about a year and married Charity's first cousin, Delphia P. Bailey. Lula Jane Campbell said

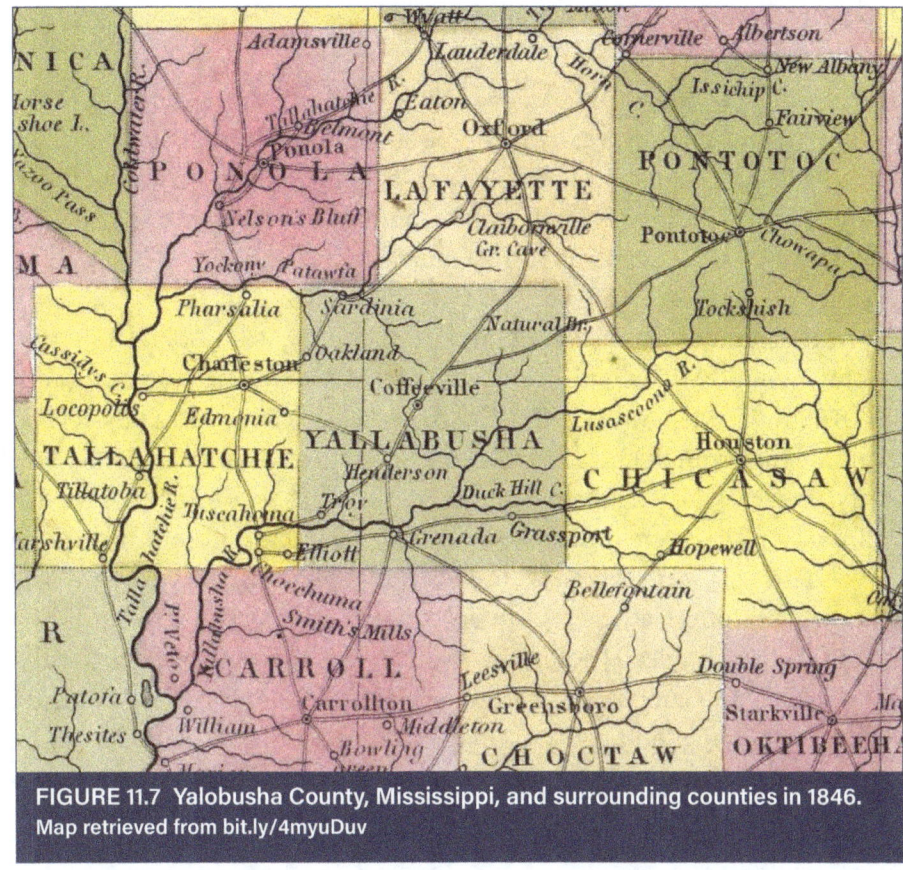

FIGURE 11.7 Yalobusha County, Mississippi, and surrounding counties in 1846. Map retrieved from bit.ly/4myuDuv

that John Cook Campbell was from North or South Carolina and that he was fair, blue eyed, and fat and merry. The best information from the census records indicates that North Carolina is his birthplace, although the 1880 Census records his birthplace as Kentucky."[1]

Children of John Cook Campbell and Charity H. Bailey

John Cook Campbell and Charity H. Bailey had six children. The first four were born in Madison County, Alabama, between 1840 and 1845. The next two were born in Yalobusha County, Mississippi, between 1847 and 1849.

1.8.2.1 Elizabeth Campbell (abt. 1823–bef. 1917) was born in Madison County. It is not known for sure if she married.

1.8.2.2 Albert Sylvester Campbell (Feb 6, 1825–Feb 22, 1877) was born in Madison County. He was a physician and a Mason. He married **Elizabeth Caroline Derden** (Jul 17, 1831–May 5, 1916) on Dec 6, 1848, in Yalobusha County. They lived in the Nebo section, Township 11, Oakland Post Office in Yalobusha County. Albert registered for a claim of 322 acres in Section 5, T24N, R7E in Yalobusha County. He was buried at the Derden Cemetery in

Yalobusha County. Elizabeth was buried at the Oak Hill Cemetery in Water Valley, Yalobusha County.

1.8.2.3 **William Marion Campbell** (Dec 31, 1826–Apr 5, 1899) was born in Madison County. He married **Amand Cassandra Houston** (May 9, 1839–Jun 20, 1908), probably in 1853 in Yalobusha County. He was a farmer and a schoolteacher in various counties in Mississippi, including Kemper, Holmes, and Leake Counties. They were both buried at the Oak Hill Cemetery in Water Valley, Yalobusha County.

1.8.2.4 **Pleasant Washington Campbell, MD** (Nov 20, 1829–Aug 25, 1877), was born in Madison County. He married **Linna Jane Harrelson** (Jun 20, 1841–Oct 1871) on Jul 11, 1855, in Calhoun County, Mississippi. He later married **Mary Jane Johnson** (abt. 1852–aft 1877) circa 1872 in Brinkley, Monroe County, Arkansas. Pleasant was a physician and obtained his medical degree from the Eclectic Medical Institute of Cincinnati, Ohio. He died in Monroe County, Arkansas, leaving three daughters as orphans. His brother, John Newton Campbell, heard that the girls were unhappy living with an uncle and sent his brother-in-law, Zachary Woodard Latson, to Arkansas to kidnap the girls. Zachary was arrested in Shreveport, Louisiana, and John Newton had to go by train to Shreveport to get him out of jail. After securing Zachary's release, John Newton brought the girls back to Titus County. Two of the girls, Lula Jan Campbell and Cora A. Campbell, appear to have been living with their grandparents, John Cook and Delphia P. Campbell, in the 1880 Census for Titus County. The children of Pleasant Washington Campbell were as follows:

1. Elizabeth Culverson Campbell (Jan 8, 1858–May 20, 1860) died as an infant.

2. **John Calhune Campbell** (Nov 8, 1858–Jun 24, 1878) died in Brinkley, Monroe County, Arkansas.

3. **Mary Pleasant Campbell** (Jan 7, 1862–Jan 2, 1863) died as an infant in Yalobusha County.

4. **Lula Jane Campbell** (Nov 15, 1863–Feb 10, 1959)was born in Arkansas and married **Zachariah "Zachary" Woodard Latson** (Mar 19, 1849–Jun 11, 1923) on Mar 17, 1881, in Titus County, Texas.

5. **Sarah Luella Campbell** (Jan 25, 1866–unknown) was born in Arkansas.

6. **Cora Elmira "Alma" Campbell** (Apr 30, 1869–Apr 28, 1908) was born in Arkansas and married **Jonathan Washington Rogers** (Feb 18, 1858–Oct 8, 1936) on Dec 21, 1887, in Randolph County, Missouri. They moved to Titus County, Texas, before 1900. They were buried at the East New Hope Cemetery in Titus County.

7. **Linna Campbell** (1871–Oct 1871) was born in Holly Grove, Monroe County, Arkansas, and died as an infant. Her mother probably died during her birth.

8. Pleasant Washington Campbell Jr. (Aug 27, 1877–Oct 1, 1919) was the only child of Pleasant Washington Campbell Sr. and Mary Jane Johnson. He married Henrietta

"Edna" Kate Powers (Sep 24, 1880–Apr 30, 1968) on Dec 8, 1901, in Franklin County, Alabama.

1.8.2.5 **Cora Elmira Campbell** (abt. 1834–aft. Sep 20, 1857) was born Yalobusha County. She married **E. G. Porter** (abt. 1832–bef. 1923) on Sep 20, 1857, in Yalobusha County. She died after Sep 20, 1857.

1.8.2.6 **Adam J. Campbell** (abt. 1835–aft. 1870) was born in Yalobusha County. He married **Laura Ann M. Seamons** (abt. 1838–aft. 1870) on Mar 17, 1855, in Yalobusha County.

Children of John Cook Campbell and Delphia P. Bailey

John Cook Campbell had an additional six children with his second wife, Delphia P. Bailey. All six children were born in Yalobusha County, Mississippi between 1840 and 1849.

1.8.2.7 **Andrew Jackson Campbell** (abt. 1840–Apr 6, 1862), who was a 2nd corporal in the 1st Infantry Regiment of the Georgia Regulars, CSA, during the U.S. Civil War. He died at the Battle of Shiloh in southwestern Tennessee.

1.8.2.8 **James C. "Jimmy" Campbell** (abt. 1842–1864), who was born in Mississippi and may have died fighting for the CSA during the U.S. Civil War.

1.8.2.9 **Mary Frances Campbell** (Oct 9, 1842–Mar 13, 1896), who was born in Yalobusha County. She married **James Alexander Tabb** (Jan 1, 1839–Nov 30, 1925) on Sep 29, 1860, in Yalobusha County (Figure 11.8). They moved to Texas in 1861. James was a 2nd lieutenant in the 18th Texas Infantry, CSA, during the U.S. Civil War. He enlisted in February 1862 and served until Jun 1865. After Mary died, James moved to Clarendon, Arkansas, in 1908. He may have taken another wife. He was farmer, a Mason for 63 years, and a Methodist for 63 years. James and Mary were buried at the Old Cookville Cemetery in Titus County, Texas.

FIGURE 11.8 James Alexander Tabb and Mary Frances Campbell, abt. 1900, Texas.

A rare glimpse into the conviction and motivations of family letters is contained in a letter James wrote to his sister, Elizabeth Jane (Tabb) Burgess, after he enlisted in the Confederacy. According to his scrapbook, which William Marion Tabb, son of James Alexander Tabb, inherited, he wrote the following:

Mt. Pleasant, Texas
April 27th, 1862 "Dear Sister: I seat myself for the purpose of dropping you a few lines. I wrote to you and the Doctor about two and a half months ago; haven't received any answer as yet. Where are you? Gone to the war? Surely not. What is the reason you don't write? Perhaps you have forgotten me! If so, hope when this reaches you that your memory will be sufficiently jogged to cause a reversion to that place."

"This leaves us all well. We have had a great deal of rain here this spring. Corn looks rather bad from the effect of frost of the 21st, though it did not do a great deal of damage. We have about 250 acres in corn, and it looks like making something."

"I am going to war. I belong to Capt. Wood's Company, now on its way to Jefferson Ochitree Regiment. Pa is gone down with them to haul their baggage, etc; consequently, I am compelled to stay home until he returns. I expect to start, in the course of 5 to 6 days, for three years, or duration of war!"

"Yes, I now belong to the Confederacy. Many of our kindred, friends and countrymen have already fallen; and if needs by my blood shall run as free as a mountain brook in our country's cause. I am going with the expectation of coming back, back to those that will miss me. But, if it is my lot to die, thank God I have one consolation: "Tis sweet to die in such a glorious cause." Our lot, in all probability, will be assigned to Mississippi, which is the land of my birth, and in its bosom lies the cold silent frame of my mother, brothers four and many kindred and friends. Not resist a foe that is trying to overrun such a country as that? Tis folly to think of staying at home when our lives, fortune and our sacred honor is at stake; when our peace and prosperity is about to be taken away from us; when our wives and children are menaced with insults; and any lady that falls into the hands of the invading foes basely insulted and cruelly used. I say it is folly to think of staying at home. I had rather died the death of a soldier a thousand times than to live to see my wife and baby, my sisters, and friends, of any portion of the Southern Confederacy thrown upon the equality with the thoughtless negroes, or to live under Lincoln's administration. Before I will submit to such a government, I will take my wife and babe—resort to the mountains in Brazil and endeavor to obtain sustenance by gathering roots, etc."

"Banishment of victory! Freedom or Death is the motto of"

"Your affectionate brother,"
Jim

1.8.2.10 **Sarah Margaret Campbell** (abt. 1845–bef. 1934), who was born in Yalobusha County.[1]

1.8.2.11 **John Newton Campbell** (Nov 23, 1847–Oct 17, 1927), who was born in Yalobusha County. John Newton was 16 in August 1864, when he volunteered for service in the CSA Army in Coffeeville, Yalobusha County, Mississippi, during the U.S. Civil War. He was a private in Company A, 1st Regiment of Mississippi Cavalry. D. T. Burns gave a deposition for Mary Elizabeth Campbell's Widow's Application for Confederate Pension number 51829 on Nov 9, 1927, in which he stated that he enlisted

FIGURE 11.9 John Newton Campbell and Mary Elizabeth Sealy, Titus County, abt. 1900.

with John Newton Campbell in the 1st Mississippi Battalion under Major Gorren. They served together for about three months until John Newton Campbell was transferred, and he did not see him again until after the surrender.[1]

John Newton married **Florence Josephine Latson** (Aug 19, 1856–Mar 8, 1886), daughter of **Simon Perkins Latson** and **Lennie Ann Phillips**, in 1876 in Titus County. Sometime in 1887, a Mr. McClintock told John Newton about two Sealy girls in Alabama. John Newton traveled to Clay County, Alabama, where he met and married **Mary Elizabeth Sealy** (Nov 11, 1857–Jan 16, 1940) on Aug 25, 1887, in Clay County, Alabama. See Figure 11.9. He brought her back to Titus County. John and both wives were buried at the Union Hill Cemetery in Titus County.[1]

The Confederacy assembled the 1st Regiment Mississippi Cavalry during the spring of 1862. The unit served in the Department of Mississippi and East Louisiana, then was assigned to W. H. Jackson's, Ross's, Cosby's and E. C. Armstong's Brigade, Department of Alabama, Mississippi, and East Louisiana. It contained 22 officers and 220 men in July 1862 and confronted the Union Army in various conflicts in Mississippi. Later, the regiment was involved in the operations in North Alabama and Middle Tennessee, where its casualties were 2 killed and 27 wounded. It went on to fight in North Georgia and Alabama, but only a few surrendered in May 1865.[1]

John Newton Campbell and Josephine Latson had three children (Figure 11.10):

1. **Olive F. (Campbell) Caldwell** (Sep 10, 1878–bef. 1910) died in Titus County. She may have married a Caldwell.

2. **Guy Newton Campbell** (Nov 16, 1882–Feb 28, 1916) married **Mattie Lelia Watkins** (Apr 15, 1885–Apr 2, 1937) on Dec 25, 1906, in Morris County, Texas. See Figure 11.11. They were buried at the Sardis Cemetery in Cass County, Texas. A great-grandson of

FIGURE 11.10 John Newton Campbell Family, Titus County, 1900; Front L to R: Olive Caldwell Campbell, Albert Paris Campbell, Theophilus Egbert Campbell, Mary Pauline Campbell, Zachary Campbell, Guy Newton Campbell; Back row L to R: Tommie Sealy Broadstreet, Mary Sealy Campbell, John Newton Campbell.

Guy Newton Campbell is a participant in the Adam Campbell Y-DNA Project that Don Raney (Figure 11.12) started.

3. **Zachary Alexander Campbell** (Feb 2, 1885–Jan 10, 1940) did not marry. He was buried at the Union Hill Cemetery in Titus County.

Left: FIGURE 11.11 Guy Newton Campbell's sons Rufus Edgar, Greeley Jenkins, Jonnie Nathaniel, and Preston Edbert Campbell; 1945, Morris County, Texas.

Right: FIGURE 11.12 Donald Raymond Raney, 2013, Dallas County, Texas.

John Newton Campbell and **Mary Elizabeth Sealy** (Nov 11, 1857–Jan 16, 1940) had three children:

4. **Mary Pauline Campbell** (Jul 11, 1888–Mar 10, 1922) married **James Emmett Ticer** (Feb 3, 1887–Nov 30, 1954) on Nov 24, 1908, in Titus County.

5. **Theophilus Egbert Campbell** (Dec 20, 1889–Jul 26, 1906) did not marry.

6. **Albert Paris Campbell** (Apr 12, 1891–Jul 27, 1983) married **Dovie Lee Wright** (Sep 9, 1894–Mar 15, 1969) on Jan 25, 1912, in Titus County.

1.8.2.12 **Theophilus Campbell** (abt. 1849–abt. 1865) was born and died in Yalobusha County. He did not marry.[1]

African American Descendants of John Cook Campbell

1.8.2.X Simon "John" Campbell (Apr 1841–Aug 8, 1918), according to DNA evidence (see Chapter 3 for details of Y-DNA analysis), was most likely the son of John Cook Campbell (1.8.2) with one of John Cook Campbell's female slaves. Simon and his descendants were African American. Simon married Elizabeth "Lizzie" Moore (Jan 1853–aft 1900) in Yalobusha County in 1860.[12,16] In 1870, Simon was living next to John Cook Campbell and his wife, Delphia, in Yalobusha County.[13] Simon's death certificate lists his father as John Campbell, who was born in Mississippi, and an unknown mother born in Virginia. In 1880 and 1900, Simon was living with Elizabeth and children in Pine Valley, Yalobusha County. Birth dates varied in different records. Simon died as a widower in Coffeeville and was buried at the Rocky Mound Cemetery on Aug 10, 1918. His age was estimated to be 82 on his death certificate, which would have his birth year in about 1836. In the 1900 Census, his birth was given as April 1841.[14, 16]

Their children, all born in Pine Valley, Yalobusha County, Mississippi, are:

1. Joseph "Joe" H. Campbell (Aug 1867–Feb 28, 1941), who married Philadelphia Buford (Oct 1873–aft 1910). The 1870 Census probably has an incorrect age and does not agree with the 1880 Census. [13, 15]

2. Louisa Campbell (1869–unknown), who was younger than Joseph and only appeared in the 1870 Census.

3. Sarah Francella Campbell (1871–aft. 1880). [15]

4. Lewis Campbell (1873–unknown).[15]

5. Cora Bell Campbell (Jan 4, 1875–Jan 28, 1940), who married Wallace Woodall (Jan 1874–bef. 1940) in 1895.[15]

6. Sylvester Campbell (Apr 23, 1879–Sep 3, 1947), who married Sophia "Last Name Unknown" (1883–aft 1950).[14, 15]

7. Wilbert Benjamin "Bernie" or "Ben" Campbell (Feb 11, 1880–Feb 15, 1967), who married Della Katherine Hall (Feb 1890–aft 1950).[16] See Figure 11.13.

8. Daisy "Disey" (Campbell) Carrol (Apr 1882–May 15, 1939).[12, 15, 16]

9. George Campbell (Dec 8, 1885–Aug 28, 1955), who married Excie Rey Clements (Oct 15, 1886–Nov 1986).[16, 17] See Figure 11.14.

10. John "Otis" Campbell (Oct 16, 1886–Mar 16, 1974), who married Hattie Pearlie Ezell (1891–1919) and later Effie Turner (Oct 28, 1900–Dec 4, 1991).[16] A great-grandson of John Otis Campbell is a participant in the Adam Campbell Y-DNA Project. See Figure 11.15.

FIGURE 11.13 Wilbert Benjamin Campbell, abt. 1960, Yalobusha County.

11. Tom Campbell (1888-unknown).[16]

12. Limett "Lem" or Preacher Campbell (Jan 8, 1890–Jan 13, 1923), who married Eliza Turner (abt. 1890–bef. 1930). Lem served in the U.S. Army during World War I and died because of cancer from exposure to chemical agents during the war.[16]

Simon's children were all born in Mississippi. The largest number lived and died in Yalobusha County (21), followed by Calhoun (13), Lafayette (2), and Bolivar (1) counties. Some family members (5) moved to Memphis, Tennessee, and there were two family members (Sylvester Campbell and his wife, Sophia) who moved to Detroit, Wayne County, Michigan, in the 1890s. By 1860, Yalobusha County's population had topped 16,000, and 56% of residents were enslaved. Yalobusha's farms and plantations practiced mixed agriculture,

Left:
FIGURE 11.14 George Campbell, abt. 1950, Shelby County.

Right:
FIGURE 11.15 John Otis Campbell, abt. 1970, Yalobusha County.

concentrating on corn, livestock, and cotton. The population remained steady in the early postbellum period, and in 1880, African Americans made up a small majority of Yalobusha's 15,649 people. About half of the county's farmers owned their land, and while manufacturing employed only 44 residents, the railroad became crucial to county life.

WILLIAM MARION CAMPBELL SR.

1.8.3   **William Marion Campbell Sr.** (1803–Aug 1883) was born in Iredell County, North Carolina. He married **Lovina Methvin** (abt. 1804–bef. 1880), daughter of **Levi Methvin Sr.** and **Anna "Last Name Unknown,"** on Aug 5, 1821, in Salem, Franklin County, Tennessee. He enlisted as a musician soldier under Capt. Stephen Griffith's Company, Mississippi Militia, from Nov 2 to Dec 2, 1813, during the War of 1812. William was living in Jackson County, Alabama, in 1854, 1855, 1871 (Princeton PO Box), 1876/1878 (New Market PO Box in Madison County), and 1881 (Holly Tree).[18] Raney's book does not list his children. The known children of William Marion and Lovina Methvin from other genealogical sources are:[1]

1.8.3.1   Theophilus Marion Campbell (Aug 12, 1823–Sep 11, 1899), who married Nancy Catherine Bradshaw (abt. 1824–aft. 1880) in about 1843 in Madison County, Alabama. They were buried at the Ragsdale Cemetery in Madison County. There are records of a son of Theophilus Campbell, William Campbell, marrying Margaret Griffin (abt. 1833–aft. 1881) on Aug 31, 1881, in Jackson County.[19]

1.8.3.2   John B. Campbell (abt. 1829–aft. 1865), who served in the 61st Alabama Infantry, CSA, during the U.S. Civil War. He mustered out of service during the surrender at Appomattox Court House, Virginia, on Apr 9, 1865.

1.8.3.3   George Washington Campbell (abt. 1833–aft. 1850), who was living in Jackson County in 1850 with his parents.

1.8.3.4   Margaret Campbell (abt. 1834–aft. 1850), who was living in Jackson County in 1850 with her parents.

1.8.3.5   William Marion Campbell Jr. (1838–Jul 10, 1918), who married Mary Anne McCrary (1839–Mar 1908) in Dale County, Alabama, in 1867. He died in Madison County.

1.8.3.6   Rhoda Catherine Campbell (1839–aft. 1880), who married Jerry Robinson (abt. 1840-aft 1880) on Mar 24, 1866, in Clarke County, Alabama.

1.8.3.7   Mary Polly Ann Campbell (1848–aft. 1860), who was living in Jackson County in 1860 with her parents.

GEORGE WASHINGTON CAMPBELL

1.8.4   **George Washington Campbell Sr.** (Apr 30, 1810–1856) was born in Madison County, Alabama. He married **Hariett S. Sloan** (abt. 1812–bef. May 1849) on Aug 3, 1832, in New

Market, Madison County, Alabama. He later married **Louisa Elizabeth Hambrick** (abt. 1829–Oct 18, 1917) on May 10, 1849, in Madison County, Alabama.[1] Their children are:

1.8.4.1 Sarah "Sally" Campbell (abt. 1835–aft. 1880), who married John Scott (1833–1880) on Aug 20, 1860, in Madison County.

1.8.4.2 Mary Campbell (abt. 1836–Dec 1879), who married Jason G. Hambrick (1833–1902) on Jan 23, 1854, in Madison County. Mary and her older sister Sarah, as well as her brother Morgan, were living with her grandmother Elizabeth Sloan in 1850 after her mother died.

1.8.4.3 Woods Campbell (abt. 1838– bef. 1871), who married Mary Narcissa Spence (Feb 1842–Sep 16, 1908) on Jan 6, 1858, in Madison County.

FIGURE 11.16 Rachel Norris and James Morgan Campbell, abt. 1900, Madison County.

1.8.4.4 James Morgan Campbell (Jan 1839–Jul 6, 1908), who married Rachell Mary Norris (1842–Feb 10, 1917) on Dec 17, 1873, in Madison County. See Figure 11.16.

1.8.4.5 Margaret Campbell (abt. 1841–Nov 15, 1884), who married William E. Norris (1838–Dec 20, 1920) in 1860 in Madison County.

1.8.4.6 Mary "Kizzy" Campbell (abt. 1842–Dec 1879), who died in Marshall County, Alabama.

FIGURE 11.17 Smith Alexander Campbell, abt. 1900, Madison County.

1.8.4.7 Susannah Carey Campbell (Apr 5, 1848–May 18, 1921), who married Paris A. Dameron (Aug 8, 1834–Nov 10, 1876).

1.8.4.8 Manerva Campbell (1851–aft. 1888), who married Andrew J. Robins (Dec 1841–aft. 1903) on Oct 18, 1888, in Madison County. Her mother was Louisa.

1.8.4.9 Smith Alexander Campbell (Oct 14, 1852–Jul 14, 1937), who married Martha Julia "Pinkie" Golden (Jan 1855–Jul 1, 1904) on Jan 25, 1880, in Madison County. He later married Mary Ann Elizabeth Martin/White (Aug 11, 1846–bef. 1930) on Dec 19, 1905, in Madison County. Mary Ann was the wife of Smith's cousin, Chess Campbell, who died in 1901. See Figure 11.17.

1.8.4.10 George Washington Campbell Jr. (1855–Sep 7, 1881), who married Sarah Ann Elmore (Nov 11, 1858–Jul 19, 1930) on Dec 16, 1877, in Madison County. George was killed by robbers who murdered him and stole his money. Sarah later married Henry Alexander Cagle (Jun 14, 1864–Aug 27, 1952) and moved to Live Oak County, Texas.

JAMES CAMPBELL

1.8.5 **James Campbell** (1815–May 11, 1894), who was born in New Market, Madison County, Alabama. He married **Hannah Minerva Hambrick** (1811–Jun 10, 1838), the daughter of Greenberry Hambrick and Elizabeth Ann Dameron, in 1832 in New Market, Madison County, Alabama. After Hannah's death, he married Mahala Haley (Hambrick) Gibbs (Mar 10, 1822–Nov 13, 1899) on Nov 21, 1838, in Lincoln County, Tennessee.[1] His children are:

1.8.5.1 Ruth Jane "Ruthie" Campbell (1835–1910), who married Thomas H. White (Sep 1835–1932) on Dec 1, 1856, in Franklin County, Tennessee.

1.8.5.2 Chesley "Chess" Campbell (Apr 13, 1837–1901), who married Mary Ann Elizabeth Martin/White (Aug 11, 1846–abt. 1930) on Oct 9, 1867, in Madison County, Alabama.

1.8.5.3 James Joseph Campbell (1839–1901), who married Anna Heard (1841–aft. 1860) on Feb 2, 1860, in Madison County. He was the first child with Mahala.

1.8.5.4 Margaret Polly Campbell (1841–bef. 1860), who was born in Madison County. She may have married Morgan Jones (abt. 1843–Sep 19, 1909) in Alabama.

1.8.5.5 Harriett Margaret Campbell (1843–aft. 1910), who was born in Madison County.

1.8.5.6 Adelia Mary Campbell (Sep 4, 1846–Feb 26, 1923), who married George Thomas Jones (Jun 9, 1844–Nov 24, 1906) on Apr 8, 1860, in Tallapoosa County, Alabama. They were buried at the Jones Cemetery in Madison County.

1.8.5.7 George Washington Campbell (Jan 25, 1848–Jan 7, 1914), who married Catherine "Katie" Lee Jones (Dec 25, 1847–Feb 9, 1909) on Sep 18, 1868, in Madison County. George was a 2nd lieutenant in the 5th Alabama Cavalry Regiment, CSA, during the U.S. Civil War. They were buried at the Jones Cemetery in Madison County. See Figure 11.18.

FIGURE 11.18 George Washington Campbell and Katie Jones, abt. 1900, Madison County.

1.8.5.8 Adam "Add" Campbell (Jan 1849–Oct 30, 1921), who married Sarah Ann Lewis (1852–1914) on Feb 24, 1876, in Madison County. They were buried at the Baker Cemetery in Madison County.

1.8.5.9 Eliza Jane Campbell (1851–aft 1880), who was born in Madison County.

1.8.5.10 Franklin "Frank" Jackson Campbell (Apr 8, 1852–Apr 2, 1937), who married Elizabeth R. "Betty" Giles (1852–Feb 6, 1883) on Dec 4, 1872, in Madison County. He later married Mary Susan Jones (Dec 1870–Feb 8, 1918) on Dec 17, 1882, in Madison County. He married Mary M. Gifford (1867–1918) on Jul 6, 1893, in Madison County. He married Sallie Johnnie

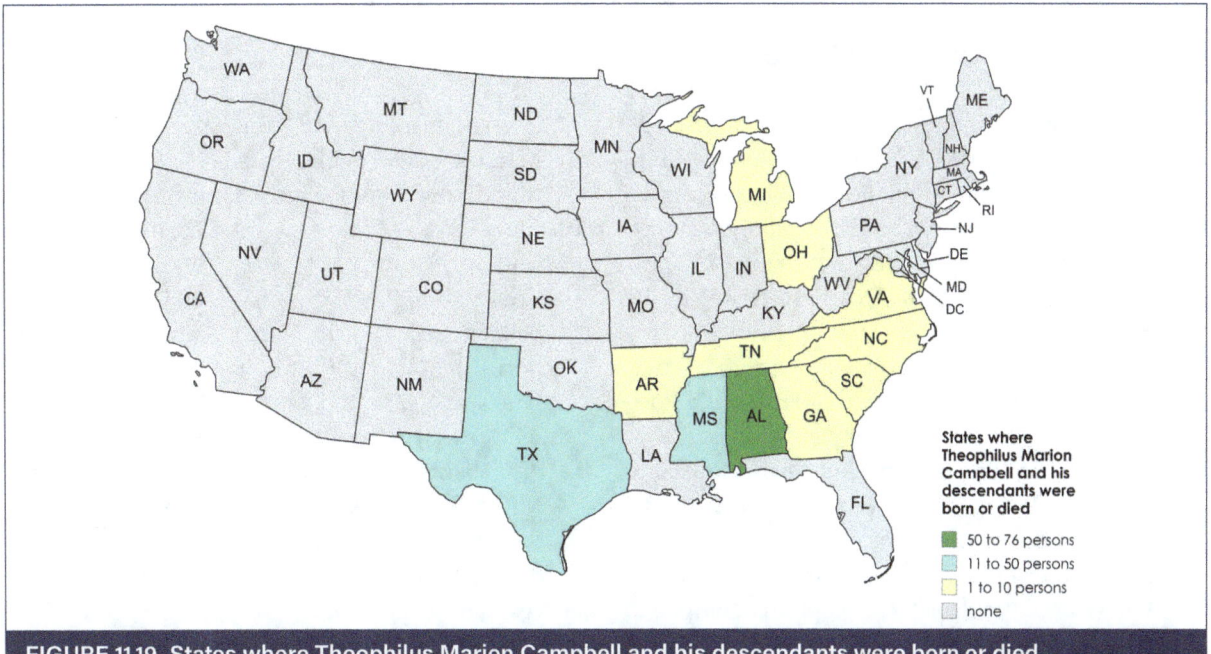

FIGURE 11.19 States where Theophilus Marion Campbell and his descendants were born or died. Created with mapchart.net.

Singletary (1879–1959) on Jul 7, 1919, in Texas. He died in Gilmer, Upshur County, Texas, and was buried at the Gilmer City Cemetery in Upshur County, along with Mary and Sally.

1.8.5.11 James Wesley Campbell (Jul 24, 1861–Sep 25, 1941), who married Amanda A. Nelson (1864–1890) on Sep 27, 1882, in Madison County. He married Magdaline Inez Barley (1872–1959) in 1900. He was buried, along with Magdaline, at the Courtland Cemetery in Cass County, Texas.

1.8.5.12 John Frank Campbell (1864–Apr 2, 1937), who married Diana "Vinie" Jones (1862–Jul 28, 1901) on Dec 17, 1882, in Madison County.

Figure 11.19 depicts the states where Theophilus Marion Campbell and his known descendants through the third generation lived and died. The largest number lived or died in Alabama (76 births and 71 deaths), Mississippi (37 births and 28 deaths), and Texas (10 births and 29 deaths). In Texas, the highest number of family members lived in Titus and Cass Counties. In Mississippi, most of his descendants lived in Yalobusha County. In Alabama, most of his descendants lived in Madison and Jackson Counties

CHAPTER 11 REFERENCES

1. 2013, *Raney Family History*, by Don Raney (1933–2020), Garland, Texas, Chapter 26, Theophilus Marion Campbell, available at Family Search, http://www.familysearch.org/library/books/idurl/1/55897, access date Feb 21, 2025, Public; and Campbell Y-DNA Project on Family TreeDNA.com.

2. Jan 9, 1819, Huntsville, Alabama Territory, letter left for Theophulus Campbell in Huntsville Post Office.

3. 1823, U.S. Indexed Early Land Ownership and Township Plats, T. M. Campbell, Huntsville Meridian, northern part of Alabama.

4. Oct 23, 1850, U.S. Federal Census Slave Schedule, Wilcox County, Alabama, Theophilus Campbell, slave owner, 14 slaves.

5. 1850, Alabama State Census, Wilcox County, T. Campbell, 1 white male under 21, 1 white male over 21, 1 white males between 18 and 45, 2 white females under 21, 1 white female over 21, 14 slaves, 19 total inhabitants.

6. Oct 19, 1850, U.S. Federal Census Non-Population Schedule, Wilcox County, T. Campbell, 200 acres of improved land, 600 acres of unimproved land, cash value of farm $2,800, value of farming implements and machinery $300, 4 horses, 2 asses and mules, 4 milch cows, 8 working oxen, 100 swine, value of livestock $700, Indian corn 600, ginned cotton bales 120, bushels of sweet potatoes 1,000, 20 pounds of butter, and value of animals slaughtered $400.

7. Aug 7, 1820, U.S. Federal Census for Iredell County, North Carolina, page 234, Sampson Ball; John Campbell; Purciphul Campbell, Esq; Adam Campbell; Perciphull Campbell Sr.; John Campbell; Reuben Fletcher; Mary Fletcher; James Fletcher, Reuben Morgan.

8. 1830, U.S. Federal Census for Ranges 1 and 2, Madison County, Alabama, George B. Campbell, John Campbell, Adam Campbell.

9. Nov 1, 1850, U.S. Federal Census, District 34, Madison County, Alabama, dwelling 148, family 148, Adam Campbell, age 46 (birthplace unknown, all others Alabama); Elizabeth, age 34; Margaret, age 16; Green, age 14; Alfred, age 13; Mary, age 11; Sarah, age 9; James, age 6/12.

10. Jun 11, 1860, U.S. Federal Census, District 1, Madison County, Alabama, Hayes Store Postal Route, dwelling 180, family 180, Adam Campbell, age 64, born in North Carolina (all others born in Alabama); Ann, age 35; Sallie, age 17; James, age 13; and Albert, age 11.

11. 1834, "Map of the States of Louisiana, Mississippi & Alabama/J.H. Young, sc.," by Samuel Augustus Mitchell, Mississippi Department of Archives & History, published in Philadelphia, https://da.mdah.ms.gov/series/maps/detail/191080, access date Mar 7, 2025.

12. Tennessee Death Record for Daisy Carroll, Certificate 11312; Memphis, Tennessee; parents Simon Campbell and Lizzie Moore, both born in Mississippi; born Aug 15, 1885; died May 15, 1939; burial: West Cannon Cemetery.

13. 1870, U.S. Federal Census, Township 25, Yalobusha, Mississippi, Dwelling 563, Delmon Campbell, age 23, farm laborer, birthplace Mississippi; Elizabeth Campbell, unknown age; Joseph H. Campbell, age 12; Louisa Campbell, age 10; Francella Campbell, age 8; Hary I. Sperry, age 48.

14. Mississippi Death Certificate 17776–18, Yalobusha County, Mississippi, informant: Sylvester Campbell of Coffeeville, Mississippi, filed on Aug 9, 1918, age 82, died Aug 8, 1918, widowed, occupation: farmer, burial: Rocky Mound on Aug 10, 1918, informant: Silvester Campbell of Coffeeville, Mississippi.

15. 1880, U.S. Federal Census for Calhoun, Mississippi, Simon Campbell, age 39, "mulatto," father born in Mississippi, mother born in Virginia, occupation: tenant; Lizzie Campbell, age 28; Joe H. Campbell, age 12; Sarah F. Campbell, age 9; Lewis Campbell, age 7; Cora Campbell, age 5; Sylvester Campbell, age 3.

16. 1900, U.S. Federal Census for Beat 2, Yalobusha, Mississippi, house 5, family 209, Simon Camel, age 60, Black, married 1860, father and mother

born in Mississippi, occupation farmer, rents home; Lizzie Camel, age 47; Disey Camel, age 18; Bernie Camel, age 17; George Camel, age 15; John Camel, age 13; Tom Camel, age 12; Lem Camel, age 10.

17. Tennessee U.S. Death Record no. 55–18852, George Campbell, place of death and residence Shelby County, Tennessee, occupation: laborer, father: Simon Campbell; mother, Lizzie Harrison; cemetery, Springdale (maybe Spring Hill) B.C.P. in Water Valley, Mississippi; informant, daughter.

18. U.S. War of 1812 Pension Application and Bounty Land Claims, Sur Orig 25224, 25395, 101423 40 50, 74938 120 55; soldier: William Campbell; wife: Levina Methvin; father: Theophilus Campbell; Raney quotes Theophilus Campbell's affidavit as Sep 2, 1854; also "Jackson County War of 1812 Pension Application, William Campbell" in *Valley Leaves, Tennessee Valley Genealogical Society, Inc. Quarterly*, vol. 45, issue no. 1, Sept 2010, pages 1–10, Theophilus Campbell's affidavit dated Sep 2, 1852.

19. Mar 31, 1881, "Alabama Marriage Records," Jackson Campbell, William Campbell and Margaret Griffin, consent of marriage by father, Theophilus Campbell, married at bride's residence.

INDEX OF PEOPLE

This index contains the names of people appearing in this book in alphabetical order. It includes Adam Campbell and Elizabeth Morgan (Chapter 1); Adam's neighbors (Chapter 2); Adam's possible ancestors (Chapter 3); and Adam's known descendants, slaves, and other family relations (Chapters 3 through 11). The d'Aboville Numbers are included for known descendants, slaves, and other family relations, so that they can be used to identify the chapter and order in which they appear in the chapters. Names that are in bold appeared in either the 1925 Campbell Family Reunion *History of the Campbell Family* handout or the 2013 *Raney Family History* book. People who appear in figures containing portraits, **P**; documents or maps, **D**; cemeteries or headstones, **C**; or houses, mills, stores, churches, or ships, **H**, are also indicated.

www.ingramcontent.com/pod-product-compliance
Lightning Source LLC
Chambersburg PA
CBHW080804120626
46556CB00009B/3218